India Studies in Business and Economics

The Indian economy is one of the fastest growing economies of the world with India being an important G-20 member. Ever since the Indian economy made its presence felt on the global platform, the research community is now even more interested in studying and analyzing what India has to offer. This series aims to bring forth the latest studies and research about India from the areas of economics, business, and management science, with strong social science linkages. The titles featured in this series present rigorous empirical research, often accompanied by policy recommendations, evoke and evaluate various aspects of the economy and the business and management landscape in India, with a special focus on India's relationship with the world in terms of business and trade. The series also tracks research on India's position on social issues, on health, on politics, on agriculture, on rights, and many such topics which directly or indirectly affect sustainable growth of the country.

**Review Process**

The proposal for each volume undergoes at least two double blind peer review where a detailed concept note along with extended chapter abstracts and a sample chapter is peer reviewed by experienced academics. The reviews can be more detailed if recommended by reviewers.

**Ethical Compliance**

The series follows the Ethics Statement found in the Springer standard guidelines here. https://www.springer.com/us/authors-editors/journal-author/journal-author-helpdesk/before-you-start/before-you-start/1330#c14214

Edakkandi Meethal Reji · Satyajit Majumdar
Editors

# Social Enterprise Values and Processes

## Entrepreneurship Studies from India

Springer

*Editors*
Edakkandi Meethal Reji
Centre for Social Entrepreneurship
Tata Institute of Social Sciences
Mumbai, Maharashtra, India

Satyajit Majumdar
School of Management and Labour Studies
Tata Institute of Social Sciences
Mumbai, Maharashtra, India

ISSN 2198-0012 ISSN 2198-0020 (electronic)
India Studies in Business and Economics
ISBN 978-981-97-3251-7 ISBN 978-981-97-3252-4 (eBook)
https://doi.org/10.1007/978-981-97-3252-4



This Springer imprint is published by the registered company Springer Nature Singapore Pte Ltd.
The registered company address is: 152 Beach Road, #21-01/04 Gateway East, Singapore 189721, Singapore

# Introduction: Social Enterprise Values and Processes

Social entrepreneurs bring possibilities of establishing sustainable society by creating economic and social value (Hlady-Rispal & Servantie, 2018; Ziegler et al., 2014). They establish social enterprises to realize social mission while operating with business-like approaches (Alvord et al., 2004; Hervieux & Voltan, 2018; Williams & Shepherd, 2016; Zahra & Wright, 2016). They are change-makers employing innovative practices to uplift marginalized communities by enhancing access to education, healthcare, natural resource conservation, waste management, renewable energy, and fostering individual and societal self-reliance. Social entrepreneurship has established credibility to transform lives of underserved and marginalized groups solving pressing their issues (Dees, 1998; Williams & Shepherd, 2016; Seelos & Mair, 2005). There has been a growing sense of optimism among policymakers, business leaders, and practitioners about the potential of social entrepreneurship to create social and economic value while delivering sustainable impacts (Bozhikin et al., 2019; Calo et al., 2018; Chandra, 2017; Cherrier et al., 2018).

## Research on Social Entrepreneurship

As a scholarly discipline, social entrepreneurship interests multiple disciplines such as social sciences, entrepreneurship, business management, economics, sociology, anthropology, public policy, and legal studies (Gupta et al., 2020; Dwivedi & Weerawardena, 2018; Hota et al., 2019 ; Mair & Marti, 2006). Scholars are advancing understanding of various facets of this field (Dwivedi & Weerawardena 2018; Mair et al., 2016; Maurer et al., 2011; Perrini et al., 2010; Seelos et al., 2011; Stephan et al., 2016); being a new field they mostly engage in establishing conceptual foundations, entrepreneurial characteristics, social innovation, outcomes, and impacts (Gupta et al., 2020). While experts engaged in practice are in agreement that social entrepreneurship holds tremendous potential to deal with diverse social problems and improving lives of marginalized groups of people we are yet to know as body knowledge of the enterprise dimensions and value creation processes (Bansal, 2003). We find that values and value creation processes are less researched areas in the scholarly literature on social entrepreneurship.

## Research on Social Enterprise

The social enterprise landscape is evolving in both developed and emerging markets (Lortie & Cox 2018; Mair & Schoen, 2007). Social enterprises design and offer innovative solutions to social and environmental challenges while bringing enduring social change (Ney et al., 2014; Zahra & Wright, 2016; Stephan et al., 2016). Role of social enterprises in driving social change is almost universally accepted (Hossain et al. 2017). Social enterprises drive mission of creating social value (Bedi & Yadav, 2019; Pless, 2012; Santos, 2012; Mair et al., 2012). They empower people and communities to participate in the market and market related activities by building their capacities, facilitating market connections, and providing timely credit, information, and other essential resources (Mair et al. 2012; Mair et al., 2016; Prahalad & Ramaswamy, 2004; Datta & Gailey, 2012).

## Social Enterprise and Values

Value creation as subject in research has been considered at society, organization, and individual levels (sources) for analysis with focus on value capture and slippage (Lepak, Smith & Taylor, 2007). However, the relationship between social change and value creation is intricate. Social values are deeply ingrained in society, evident in its institutions, symbols, and communication patterns. While social change involves large-scale transformation of social structures (Sheldon & Moore, 1968). Scholars agree that values serve as critical resources for social change to effect transformation (McMichael, 2016). Social entrepreneurs create systemic changes and tackle the underlying causes of societal problems (Dees, 1998). They effect positive change through innovative business models (Dacin et al., 2010; Mair & Martí, 2006).

On the other hand, values as results are also derived from the social mission of the social enterprises (Dorado, 2006). Societal trust also has positive impact on social enterprises (Pathak & Muralidharan, 2016). Mission forms the bedrock of 'why' they exist (Dwivedi & Weerawardena, 2018). Social enterprises pursue social mission, generate positive externalities for society through strategic orientation. Social enterprises consider creation of blended value by balancing the economic and social values (Emerson, 2003; Singh 2016). They own social and environmental responsibilities as guiding principles of their core value (George & Reed 2016; Torri, 2009). This materializes through a market-based approach and design of community engagement for social value creation (Wilson & Post 2013). Values guide the design and implementation of processes, while processes give life to these values.

## Social Enterprise, Values and Processes

Social entrepreneurs exhibit high levels of empathy in understanding the social needs (Shepherd et al., 2023; Kibler et al., 2018; Gawell, 2013). They are driven by the attributes such as altruism, integrity, and trust in others (Lortie & Cox, 2018). Inclusivity, diversity, and empowerment are values deeply ingrained in social enterprises (Chatterjee et al., 2022; Haugh & Talwar, 2016).

While values are the driving force behind social enterprises, they are intertwined with the processes that govern these organizations. A distinguishing feature of social entrepreneurship is that it creates social enterprises that apply business models that address social issues and make social impact (Mair & Marti 2006). They demonstrate openness on operations, finances, and impact while they holding themselves accountable to the communities and also to investors (Burga & Rezania, 2015). There is seamless interplay between values and processes to drive their transformative impact. Process design evolves as enterprises move forward (Hamel & Stanton, 1999) and creative use of resources to generate economic and social values is embedded in social entrepreneurship (Dees 1998).

Though scholars have established in literature that entrepreneurship has both 'generic' and 'distinct' natures (Moroz & Hindle, 2012) research in social entrepreneurship has yet not taken serious notice of the role and significance of value creation, handful of studies delved into the processes and organizational dimensions of value creation (Alvord et al., 2004; Amis et al., 2002; Kraatz et al., 2010; Gehman et al., 2013; Granados & Rivera, 2018). Negotiation of values in the change creation process remains underexplored. Though it is evident from the practice of social entrepreneurship, social change must be aligned with values with the social systems, scholarly research has yet not provided insights on this subject. We do not know about the engagement social enterprises practice in mobilizing resources for value creation and sustainability. As a result, our understanding of how social entrepreneurs introduce new practices and shape values remains limited. There is an evident urgency among researchers to address these research gaps. We submit, this is time to pursue these knowledge gaps and find answers on creation of sustainable economic, social, and environmental values.

## Chapters in This Volume

This edited volume offers an interdisciplinary view on theories, methodologies, and practices of social enterprise values and processes. It is an attempt on cross-pollination of ideas to foster collaboration among different knowledge areas and scholars. The Chapters in this Volume delve into the nuanced relationship between social enterprise values and processes, highlighting their interplay while emphasizing on the importance of holistic approach that fosters sustainable growth, innovation, and positive change. The chapters are organized into three parts: (i) Values, Sustainability, and Social Enterprise Models, (ii) Context, Innovation, and Technology, and (iii) Perspectives and Directions for Future Research. While each chapter focuses on a specific area, together they form a comprehensive account of knowledge pool of social entrepreneurship.

The first part on "Values, Sustainability and Models" consists of four chapters. In Chap. "Cooperative Model of Social Value Creation and Sustainable Development: A Case Study of Mann Deshi Mahila Sahakari (Women's Cooperative) Bank", Balram Bhushan examines the potential of cooperative organizations to facilitate Sustainable Development Goals (SDG) through social entrepreneurship. The study centers on Mann Desi Co-operative Bank, investigating its functioning over two decades. Notably, this research emphasizes the significance of a bottom-up approach, member-driven management, and collaboration with sister organizations as key factors in achieving SDGs through social entrepreneurship. Chapter "Social Entrepreneurship: Distinct Dimensions Leading to Inclusive Growth and Sustainable Development" underscores the transformative potential of social entrepreneurship in fostering inclusive and sustainable economic development. It recognizes that while traditional entrepreneurship has spurred innovation and productivity, it has often failed to address economic disparities. Social entrepreneurship, on the other hand, leverages social innovation and inclusion to create sustainable models that promote economic prosperity for all. In Chap. "Social Enterprise: Social Value and Process Challenges in Solid Waste Management During the COVID-19 Pandemic", Sumit Mitra and Aakriti Deepak delve into the realm of solid waste management during the Covid-19 pandemic, shedding light on the process challenges faced by social enterprises. In particular, they highlight the critical importance of resourcing, social networking, and empathy in waste management processes. These factors play a pivotal role in the mission of social enterprises during crises like the pandemic. Chapter "Exploring Social Finance as a Process for Value Creation in Social Entrepreneurship" by Purushottam Vishnu Bhandare and Samapti Guha engages with an emerging discipline of social finance and its role in value creation for social entrepreneurship. It traces the evolution of social finance and its relevance in addressing social challenges, with a specific focus on the Indian context. The chapter is instrumental in understanding the financial landscape of social entrepreneurship.

We present three chapters in the Part II of the Volume with focus on "Context, Innovation and Technology". Jackson Khumukcham, in Chap. "Exploring Value Proposition by Indigenous Entrepreneurs: Multiple Case Studies of Powerloom Enterprises of Manipur With Reference to Grassroots Innovation and Frugal Aspects" explores the value proposition crafted by indigenous entrepreneurs in Manipur, India. These entrepreneurs have earned recognition for their grassroots innovation and the incorporation of frugal practices into their ventures. The study delves into the strategies employed by these entrepreneurs and investigates the cultural dimensions intertwined with technological-based innovation. Anita R Singh and Uma Balakumar's field-based research in Chap. "Localisation of Social Entrepreneurship: Case Study of Women Entrepreneurs" utilizes the lens of positive social entrepreneurship and social capital to uncover the key characteristics of localization in social entrepreneurship. This chapter examines value creation in the context of women-owned micro social enterprises and offers insights with potential implications for policymakers and practitioners. Focusing on dementia care in India, Chap. "Service Design Through Continual Engagement: Case Study of a Dementia Care Home in India" authored by Gauri Tillu and Pramod Khambete presents a case study on service design engagement within a dementia care home setting. It elucidates the processes, methods, and benefits of service design, participatory design, and continual engagement within social organizations. This provides a comprehensive view of service design in a crucial healthcare context. While in Chapter "E-Commerce-Based Retailing and the Adoption of Information Technology by Small Shops to Manage Business Performance", Vicky Nandgaye's study explores the influence of e-commerce-based retailing (ECR) on small retail shops (SRS) and their business performance. The research investigates how SRS adapt to ECR and manage their business operations using information technology. It provides valuable insights into the transformation of the retail sector and the role of IT adoption.

Chapters in the Part III are on "Perspectives and Directions for Future Research". Chapter "Social Enterprise as Means to Solving Social and Environmental Problems: The Case of Four Indian Ecopreneurs" by Niraj U. Joshi offers an in-depth exploration of ecopreneurship as a form of social enterprise. Ecopreneurs focus on ecological preservation and sustainable development, and this research unveils how they create, deliver, and capture 'blended value' in their ventures. The study presents a range of strategies and business models employed by ecopreneurs, shedding light on this emerging field. In Chap. "Process of Talent Acquisition in Startups—Conceptualization and Implications on Future Research", Leena Barshikar and Satyajit Majumdar delve into the intricate process of talent acquisition in startups. This chapter dissects the causal factors, historical events, and patterns influencing talent acquisition, offering a conceptual framework for future research in this domain. The final chapter, authored by Kanchan Mukherjee and Satyajit Majumdar, introduces a framework for assessing the value of healthcare innovations in India within the context of Universal Health Coverage (UHC). This framework comprises dimensions such as relevance, effectiveness, frugality, and equity. The chapter also applies this framework to digital health innovations, offering practical insights into assessing their value for social enterprises and policymakers.

In conclusion, this collection of chapters paints a vivid picture of the intricate world of social entrepreneurship and its profound impact on value creation in diverse sectors. These chapters collectively offer a resource for researchers, practitioners, and policymakers in the realm of social entrepreneurship and its potential to drive sustainable development, inclusive growth, and innovative solutions to global challenges.

Edakkandi Meethal Reji
Assistant Professor
Centre for Social Entrepreneurship
School of Management and Labour Studies
Tata Institute of Social Sciences
Mumbai, Maharashtra, India
reji.edakkandi@tiss.edu

Satyajit Majumdar
Professor and Dean
School of Management and Labour Studies
Centre for Social Entrepreneurship
Tata Institute of Social Sciences
Mumbai, Maharashtra, India
satyajit@tiss.edu

## References

Alvord, S.H., Brown, L.D., & Letts, C.W. (2004). Social entrepreneurship and societal transformation: an exploratory study. *Journal of Applied Behavioural Science*, *40*(3), 260–282.

Amis, J., Slack, T., & Hinings, C.R. (2002). Values and organizational change. *Journal of Applied Behavioural Science*, *38*(4), 436–465.

Bansal, P. (2003). From issues to actions: the importance of individual concerns and organizational values in responding to natural environmental issues, *Organizational Science*, *14*(5), 510–527.

Bedi, H. S & Yadav, N. (2019). Social entrepreneurship: A conceptual clarity, *Our Heritage*, *67*(10), 1006–1016.

Bozhikin, I., Macke, J., & da Costa, L. F. (2019). The role of government and key non-state actors in social entrepreneurship: A systematic literature review. *Journal of Cleaner Production*,226, 730–747.

Burga, R., & Rezania, D. (2015). A scoping review of accountability in social entrepreneurship. Sage Open, *5*(4). https://doi.org/10.1177/2158244015614.

Calo, F., Teasdale, S., Donaldson, C., Roy, M. J., & Baglioni, S. (2018). Collaborator or competitor: Assessing the evidence supporting the role of social enterprise in health and social care. *Public Management Review*, *20*(12), 1790–1814.

Chandra, Y. (2017). Social entrepreneurship as emancipatory work. *Journal of Business Venturing*, *32*(6), 657–673.

Chatterjee, I., Shepherd, D.A., & Wincent, J. (2022). Women's entrepreneurship and well-being at the base of the pyramid. *Journal of Business Venturing*, *37*(4), https://doi.org/10.1016/j.jbusvent.2022.106222.

Cherrier, H., Goswami, P., & Ray, S. (2018). Social entrepreneurship: Creating Value in the Context of Institutional Complexity. *Journal of Business Research, 86*, 246–258.
Dacin, P.A., Dacin, M.T., Matear, M. (2010). Social entrepreneurship: why we don't need a new theory and how we move forward from here. *Academy of Management Perspective, 24*(3), 37–57.
Datta, P. B., & Gailey, R. (2012). Empowering women through social entrepreneurship: Case study of a women's cooperative in India. *Entrepreneurship Theory and Practice, 36*(3), 569–587.
Dees, G. (1998). The Meaning of 'Social Entrepreneurship'. Kauffman Centre for Entrepreneurial Leadership. https://centers.fuqua.duke.edu/case/wp-content/uploads/sites/7/2015/03/Article_Dees_MeaningofSocialEntrepreneurship_2001.pdf.
Dorado, S., (2006). Social entrepreneurial ventures: Different values so different process of creation, No? *Journal of Development Studies, 11*(4), 319–343.
Dwivedi, A., & Weerawardena, J. (2018). Conceptualizing and operationalizing the social entrepreneurship construct. *Journal of Business Research, 86*, 32–40.
Emerson, J. (2003). The blended value proposition: Integrating social and financial returnn, California, *Management Review, 45*(4): 35–51. https://doi.org/10.2307/41166187.
Gawell, M. (2013). Social entrepreneurship, action grounded in needs, opportunities and/or perceived necessities? Voluntas: *International Journal of Voluntary and Nonprofit Organizations, 24*(4), 1071–1090.
Gehman, J., Trevino, L.K., & Garud, R. (2013). Values work: a process study of the emergence and performance of organizational values practices. *Academy of Management Journal, 56*(1), 84–112.
George, C. & Reed, M. G. (2016). Building institutional capacity for environmental governance through social entrepreneurship: lessons from Canadian biosphere reserves, *Ecology and Society, 21*(1): 18. http://dx.doi.org/10.5751/ES-08229-210118
Granados, M. L., & Rivera, A. N. (2018). Assessing the value dimensions of social enterprise networks. *International Journal of Entrepreneurial Behavior & Research, 24*(3),734–754.
Gupta, P., Chauhan, S., Paul, J., & Jaiswal, M.P. (2020). Social entrepreneurship research: a review and future research agenda. *Journal of Business Research, 113*, 209–229.
Hamel G., & Stanton, S., (1999). How Process Enterprises Really Work. *Harvard Business Review*, November–December, 108-118
Haugh, H. M., & Talwar, A. (2016). Linking social entrepreneurship and social change: The mediating role of empowerment. *Journal of Business Ethics, 133*(4), 643–658.
Hervieux, C., & Voltan, A. (2018). Framing social problems in social entrepreneurship. *Journal of Business Ethics, 151*(2), 279–293.
Hlady-Rispal, M., & Servantie, V. (2018). Deconstructing the way in which value is created in the context of social entrepreneurship. *International Journal of Management Reviews, 20*(1), 62–80.
Hossain, S., Saleh, M. A., & Drennan, J. (2017). A critical appraisal of the social entrepreneurship paradigm in an international setting, a proposed conceptual framework. *International Entrepreneurship and Management Journal, 13*(2), 347–368.
Hota, P. K., Subramanian, B., & Narayanamurthy, G. (2019). Mapping the Intellectual Structure of Social Entrepreneurship Research: A Citation/Co-citation Analysis. *Journal of Business Ethics*. https://doi.org/10.1007/s10551-019-04129-4.
Kibler, E., Salmivaara, V., Stenholm, P., & Terjesen, S. (2018). The evaluative legitimacy of social entrepreneurship in capitalist welfare systems. *Journal of World Business, 53*(6), 944–957
Kraatz, M., Flores, R., & Chandler, D. (2020). The value of values for institutional analysis. *Academy of Management Annals, 14*, 474–512.
Lepak, D. P., Smith, K. G. & Taylor, M. S., (2007). Value creation and value capture: A multilevel perspective. *Academy of Management Review, 32*(1), 180-194.
Lortie, J., & Cox, K. C. (2018). Conceptualizing social entrepreneurship in the context of emerging economies: An integrative review of past research from BRIICS. *International Entrepreneurship and Management Journal, 14*(3), 639–648.

Mair, J., & Marti, I. (2006). Social entrepreneurship research: A source of explanation, prediction, and delight. *Journal of World Business*, *41*(1), 36–44.

Mair, J., & Schoen, O. (2007). Successful social entrepreneurial business models in the context of developing economies: An explorative study. *International Journal of Emerging Markets*, 2(1), 54–68.

Mair, J., Martí, I., & Ventresca, M.J. (2012). Building inclusive markets in rural Bangladesh: How intermediaries work institutional voids. *Academy of Management Journal*, *55*(4), 819–850.

Mair, J., Wolf, M., & Seelos, C. (2016). Scaffolding: a process of transforming patterns of inequality in small-scale societies. *Academy of Management Journal*, *59*, 2021–2044.

Maurer, C.C., Bansal, P., & Crossan, M.M. (2011). Creating economic value through social values: introducing a culturally informed resource-based view. *Organizational Science*, *22*(2), 432–448.

McMichael, P. (2016). *Development and Social Change: A Global Perspective*, New Delhi: Sage Publications.

Moroz, P. W. & Hidle K., (2012). Entrepreneurship as a Process: Towards Harmonizing Multiple Perspectives. *Entrepreneurship Theory and Practice*, July, 781-818.

Ney, S., Beckmann, M., Graebnitz, & D., Mirkovic, R. (2014). Social entrepreneurs and social change: tracing impacts of social entrepreneurship through ideas, structures and practices. *International Journal of Entrepreneurial Venturing*, *6*(1), 51–68.

Pathak, S., & Muralidharan, E. (2018). Economic inequality and social entrepreneurship. *Business & Society*, 57(6), 1150–1190.

Perrini, F., Vurro, C., & Costanzo, L.A. (2010). A process-based view of social entrepreneurship: from opportunity identification to scaling-up social change in the case of San Patrignano. *Entrepreneurship and Regional Development*, *22*(6), 515–534.

Pless, N. M. (2012). Social entrepreneurship in theory and practice- An introduction, *Journal of Business Ethics*, 111:317–330. https://doi.org//10.1007/s10551-012-1533-x

Prahalad, C.K., & Ramaswamy, V., (2004). Co-creation experiences: the next practice in value creation. *American Marketing Association*, *18*(3), 5–14.

Santos, F. M. (2012). A positive theory of social entrepreneurship, *Journal of Business Ethics, 111*(3):335–351. https://doi.org/10.1007/s10551-012-1413-4

Seelos, C., & Mair, J. (2005). Social entrepreneurship: Creating new business models to serve the poor. *Business Horizons*, *48*(3), 241–246.

Seelos, C., Mair, J., Battilana, J., & Dacin, M.T. (2011). The embeddedness of social entrepreneurship: understanding variation across local communities. *Research in the Sociology of Organizations*, 333–363. https://doi.org/10.1108/S0733-558X(2011)0000033013

Sheldon, E. B., & Moore, W. E. (1968). *Indicators of Social Change: Concepts and Measurements*, New York: Russel Sage Foundation.

Shepherd, D. A., Seyb, S., & Williams T. A. ( 2023). Empathy-driven entrepreneurship action: Well-being outcomes for entrepreneurs and target beneficiaries, *Journal of Business Venturing*, *38*(2), 1–20.

Singh, A. (2016). *The Process of Social Value Creation: A Multiple-Case Study on Social Entrepreneurship in India*, New Delhi: Springer

Stephan, U., Patterson, M., Kelly, C., & Mair, J. (2016). Organizations driving positive social change: a review and an integrative framework of change processes. *Journal of Management*, *42*(5), 1250–1281.

Torri, M. C. (2009). Community enterpreneurship among lower castes in India: A grassroots contributon towards poverty alleviation and rural development under conditions of adversity and environmnetal uncertainty, 14(4):413–432. https://doi.org/10.1142/S1084946709001338

Williams, T.A. & Shepherd, D.A. (2016). Victim entrepreneurs doing well by doing good: venture creation and well-being in the aftermath of a resource shock. *Journal of Business Venturing*, *31*(4), 365–387

Wilson, F., & Post, J. E. (2013). Business models for people, planet (& profits): Exploring the phenomena of social business, a market-based approach to social value creation. *Small Business Economics*, *40*(3), 715–737.

Zahra, S.A., Wright, M. (2016). Understanding the social role of entrepreneurship. *Journal of Management Studies*, *53*(4), 610–629.

Ziegler, R., Schulz, S., Richter, L., & Schreck, M. (2014). Following Gandhi: Social entrepreneurship as a non-violent way of communicating sustainability challenges. *Sustainability*, *6*(2), 1018–1036.

# Contents

# Editors and Contributors

## About the Editors

**Edakkandi Meethal Reji** is Assistant Professor at the Centre for Social Entrepreneurship, School of Management and Labour Studies, Tata Institute of Social Sciences, Mumbai (India). He completed his PhD from the School of Management and Labour Studies, Tata Institute of Social Sciences. He has more than 18 years of experience in teaching, research and consultancy in the areas of business and development management. His current teaching and research interests include public policy, inclusive value chains, small enterprise development, social innovation and sustainable development. He has published several research papers in international peer reviewed journals. He has also edited two books published by international publishers—'Methodological Issues in Social Entrepreneurship Knowledge and Practices' (2019), and 'Social Entrepreneurship and Sustainable Development' (2020).

**Satyajit Majumdar** is Professor at the Centre for Social Entrepreneurship and Dean of School of Management and Labour Studies of Tata Institute of Social Sciences, Mumbai (India). He has more than 42 years in teaching, research, mentoring, coaching and administrative areas related to enterprise creation, management and leadership. His research interest areas are entrepreneurship, social entrepreneurship, small business growth strategy and corporate social responsibility. He has several highly cited publications in these areas. With active engagement with the start-ups and other impact related organizations he actively engages in mentoring and guidance and policy decisions. He is recipient of Dr. V G Patel Memorial Award 2023 and Co-chair of the Steering Committee on Biotechnology Based Programme for Societal Development, Department of Biotechnology, Government of India.

## Contributors

**Uma Balakumar** BGS College of Engineering and Technology, Bengaluru, Karnataka, India

**Leena Barshikar** School of Management and Labour Studies, Tata Institute of Social Sciences, Mumbai, Maharashtra, India

**Purushottam Vishnu Bhandare** Centre for Social Entrepreneurship, Tata Institute of Social Sciences, Mumbai, Maharashtra, India

**Balram Bhushan** School of Rural Management, XIM University, Bhubaneswar, Odisha, India

**Aakriti Deepak** Indian Institute of Management, Kozhikode, Kerala, India

**Samapti Guha** Centre for Social Entrepreneurship, Tata Institute of Social Sciences, Mumbai, Maharashtra, India

**S. Jayadatta** KLE Society's IMSR, BVB CET Campus, Vidyanagar, Hubli, Karnataka, India

**Niraj U. Joshi** Global Economic Dynamics and the Biosphere Program, Royal Swedish Academy of Sciences, Stockholm, Sweden

**Pramod Khambete** Indian Institute of Technology Bombay, Powai, Maharashtra, India

**Jackson Khumukcham** Department of Social Work, Royal School of Humanities & Social Sciences, Royal Global University, Guwahati, Assam, India

**Kumar Mukul** CMS Business School, Faculty of Management Studies, Jain Deemed-To-Be University, Bengaluru, Karnataka, India

**Satyajit Majumdar** School of Management and Labour Studies, Tata Institute of Social Sciences, Mumbai, Maharashtra, India

**Sumit Mitra** Indian Institute of Management, Kozhikode, Kerala, India

**Kanchan Mukherjee** Centre for Health Policy, Planning and Management, School of Health Systems Studies, Tata Institute of Social Sciences, Mumbai, India

**Vicky J. Nandgaye** School of Management and Labour Studies, Tata Institute of Social Sciences, Mumbai, Maharashatra, India

**V. Padmaja** M. S. Ramaiah Institute of Management, Bengaluru, Karnataka, India

**Anita R Singh** M S Ramaiah Institute of Management, Bengaluru, Karnataka, India

**V. Srinija** Department of Management and Commerce, Sri Sathya Sai Institute of Higher Learning, Anantapur Campus, Anantapur District, Andhra Pradesh, India

**Gauri Tillu** Indian Institute of Technology Bombay, Powai, Maharashtra, India

# Abbreviations

| | |
|---|---|
| AI | Artificial Intelligence |
| AMUL | Anand Milk Union Limited |
| ANT | Actor-Network Theory |
| B2C | Business to Consumers |
| BC | Banking Correspondents |
| CAO | Chief Administrative Officer |
| CEO | Chief Executive Officer |
| COVID-19 | Corona Virus Disease-19 |
| CSR | Corporate Social Responsibility |
| DHEF | Digital Health Equity Framework |
| DIC | District Industrial Center |
| DRI | Differential Rate of Interest |
| ECHTA | Equity Checklist Health Technology Assessment |
| ECR | E-Commerce-based Retailing |
| FPC | Farmer Producer Company |
| GCMMF | Gujarat Co-operative Milk Marketing Federation Ltd. |
| GDP | Gross Domestic Product |
| GEM | Global Entrepreneurship Monitor |
| GOI | Government of India |
| GRDI | Global Retail Development Index |
| HDI | Human Development Index |
| HEMF | Health Equity Measurement Framework |
| HTA | Health Technology Assessment |
| HUL | Hindustan Unilever Limited |
| IBEF | India Brand Equity Foundation |
| ID | Identity Card |
| IPCC | Inter Governmental Panel on Climate Change |
| IPO | Initial Public Offering |
| IRDP | Integrated Rural Development Programme |
| IT | Information Technology |
| ITC | Indian Tobacco Company |

| | |
|---|---|
| KCC | Kisan Credit Card |
| MBA | Master of Business Administration |
| MDG | Millennium Development Goals |
| ML | Machine Learning |
| MMDG | Mann Deshi Mahila Group |
| MSE | Micro Social Enterprises |
| MSME | Micro, Small and Medium Enterprises |
| NABARD | National Bank for Agriculture and Rural Development |
| NBFC | Non-Banking Financial Company |
| NCC | National Cadet Corps |
| NGO | Non-Governmental Organisation |
| OECD | Organization for Economic Cooperation and Development |
| PHEIC | Public Health Emergency of International Concern |
| PLWD | Person Living with Dementia |
| PMEGP | Prime Minister's Employment Guarantee Program |
| PPE | Personal Protective Equipment |
| PRADAN | Professional Assistance for Development Action |
| QoL | Quality of Life |
| RBI | Reserve Bank of India |
| RCT | Randomised Clinical Trial |
| RIH | Responsible Innovation in Health |
| ROSCAs | Rotating Savings and Credit Associations |
| RRB | Regional Rural Banks |
| RWA | Resident Welfare Associations |
| SARS | Severe Acute Respiratory Syndrome |
| SBLP | SHG-Bank Linkage Program |
| SDGs | Sustainable Development Goals |
| SE | Social Entrepreneurship |
| SELCO | Selco Solar Private Limited |
| SFDA | Small Farmers Development Agency |
| SHG | Self Help Groups |
| SR | Systematic Review |
| SROI | Social Return on Investment |
| SRS | Small Retail Shops |
| SW | Solid Waste |
| SWM | Solid Waste Management |
| TN | Tamil Nadu |
| UHC | Universal Health Coverage |
| UK | United Kingdom |
| UN | United Nations |
| UNCTAD | United Nations Conference on Trade and Development |
| UNDP | United Nations Development Programme |
| USA | United States of America |

| | |
|---|---|
| USAID | United States Agency for International Development |
| WEAT | Women Entrepreneur Association of Tamil Nadu |
| WHO | World Health Organisation |

# List of Figures

**E-Commerce-Based Retailing and the Adoption of Information Technology by Small Shops to Manage Business Performance**



**Social Enterprise as Means to Solving Social and Environmental Problems: The Case of Four Indian Ecopreneurs**



**Framework for Assessing the Value of Healthcare Innovations in India for Universal Health Coverage**

# List of Tables

**Social Enterprise as Means to Solving Social and Environmental Problems: The Case of Four Indian Ecopreneurs**



**Process of Talent Acquisition in Startups—Conceptualization and Implications on Future Research**



**Framework for Assessing the Value of Healthcare Innovations in India for Universal Health Coverage**

# Values, Sustainability and Models

# Cooperative Model of Social Value Creation and Sustainable Development: A Case Study of Mann Deshi Mahila Sahakari (Women's Cooperative) Bank

**Balram Bhushan**

**Abstract** This chapter attempts to understand how a cooperative organisation can facilitate sustainable development goals (SDGs) through social entrepreneurship. This study identified a cooperative organisation practising social entrepreneurship and investigated its two decades of experience by interviewing key members, examining annual reports and web information. Interviews were conducted in two spells between 2015 and 2020. Analysis of narratives suggested that cooperative organisations with bottom-up approach, member-driven management, and nested with sister organisations are well-equipped to achieve SDGs. At the theoretical level, this research advances the debate on nurturing social value creation in social entrepreneurship and considers SDGs as an appropriate measure for the same.

**Keywords** Cooperatives · Social Entrepreneurship · Sustainable Development Goals · Social Value Creation · Empowerment · Case study

## 1 Introduction

Although labour is traditionally treated as one of the factors of production, technological innovations have amplified the rich and poor divide (Balleer, 2012). Similarly, efficiency-based management practices have restricted the ownership and control of the firm (D'Art & Turner, 2006). Cooperatives were evolved to address these anomalies inherent in the corporate settings (Birchall & Ketilson, 2009; Mori, 2014). However, cooperatives tend to focus on financial parameters and ignore social and environmental issues. For example, cooperative farming adds to social capital and economic prosperity but may negatively affect the environment (Mojo et al., 2015).

Social entrepreneurship (SE) responds to these limitations by serving basic human needs (Seelos & Mair, 2005). Although SE prefers a value-driven mission over financial performance parameters, (Parente et al., 2014), its business model

B. Bhushan (✉)
School of Rural Management, XIM University, Bhubaneswar, Odisha, India
e-mail: balram@xim.edu.in

 
E. M. Reji and S. Majumdar (eds.), *Social Enterprise Values and Processes*, India Studies in Business and Economics, https://doi.org/10.1007/978-981-97-3252-4_1

revolves around social and/or environmental issues rather than focusing on exclusive efficiency-based management practices (Dees, 2012). Social entrepreneurship considers profit as a by-product and embraces market-driven approaches (Bacq et al., 2013; Choi & Majumdar, 2014; Ormiston & Seymour, 2011).

The market-driven approaches enhance the efficiency, sustainability, and capacity of social enterprises (Bruneel et al., 2016). Hybrid organisations are perfect examples of such intermingling of purposes at the structural level, where one part of an organisation is a for-profit, and another is not-for-profit. The motive remains the same—social value creation (Lepoutre et al., 2013). Although integration of financial sustainability and social good is easy to appreciate, "praxis or wise action" is needed to achieve such integration (Zhu et al., 2016). One such approach is designing a hybrid organisation based on cooperative principles. The innovative social entrepreneurship approaches within the cooperative framework can create hope for present-day society to look for proper life instead of treating human money-making machines (Dey & Lehner, 2017).

The synergy between social entrepreneurship and cooperatives offers an opportunity to democratise social value creation. For example, following social entrepreneurship, credit cooperatives may foster financial empowerment among women and bring social change so that society can facilitate such empowering processes and negate the chances of domestic violence. This single intervention addresses multiple SDGs (Goal 1—no poverty; Goal 5—Gender equality; Goal 10—Reduce inequalities, etc.). Cooperatives following the path of social entrepreneurship are not rare but theoretical development on such organisations is limited. This research study attempts to fill this void by exploring how socially entrepreneurial process enables a cooperative organisation to achieve SDGs.

## 2 Literature Review

Cooperatives as an organisational form and social entrepreneurship as a process originated to challenge the inequality created by capitalism (Schneiberg, 2013). Recognising these inequalities, United Nations urges the member countries to set development priorities, aligned with SDGs. The idea is to go beyond the traditional development agendas and devise interventions that are changing people's lives (Coscieme et al., 2020). This requires multi-layered interventions and partnerships with wide array of institutions.

### *2.1 Cooperatives and SDGs*

Achieving SDGs requires holistic thinking, democratic participation, and integration of society (Raub & Martin-Rios, 2019). Different SDGs may not be compatible in given time and space. Hence a common understanding among various stakeholders facilitates their segregation (Castelló et al., 2016). Also, different SDGs may be conflicting with each other and need trade-off—for instance, innovation, and responsible consumption and production. When the present business world is looking for cut-throat competition through disruptive innovation, responsible production, and consumption is wishful thinking without changing the notion of disruption.

The seven cooperative principles (Concern for society, voluntary and open membership, democratic member control, economic participation of members, autonomy and independence, education, training and information, and cooperation among cooperatives) together can address such incompatibility and trade-offs among organisational goals (Novkovic, 2006), and help in mobilisation of resources (McLaughlin, 1996), and co-creation of values (Miedes-Ugarte et al., 2020). Yet, these principles limit the cooperation to like entities (cooperatives) and offer very little immunity to democratic governance under the influence of external factors (Hanisch, 2013). These two voids contribute to the failure of the cooperative movement and to regain the lost glory, and cooperatives need interventions countering them.

## *2.2 Cooperatives and Social Entrepreneurship*

Democratic participation and decentralised control in cooperatives offer a unique combination of disruptive innovation and sustainable consumption when the effort is to achieve Pareto efficiency (Cechin et al., 2013). Pareto efficiency ensures that the organisation uses the mobilised resources from the community for the betterment of the community and simultaneously achieves financial sustainability and social mission without negatively impacting any entity. This prioritises social innovation over technological and administrative innovation (Muñoz et al., 2020). Social entrepreneurship can integrate social innovation and financial sustainability through market orientation for social value creation (Choi & Majumdar, 2014).

As in the case of cooperatives, social entrepreneurship is also driven by the heroism of individuals and the strength of collectives (Harima & Freudenberg, 2020). Social entrepreneurship creates social value through co-creation, which requires a high level of community participation (Cornet & Barpanda, 2020). Furthermore, community-driven social entrepreneurship promotes decentralised control and shared ownership with the society (Montgomery et al., 2012). Also, the concept of empowerment is now gaining prominence in socially entrepreneurial initiatives aimed at social value creation and financial viability (Haugh & Talwar, 2016).

Cooperative principles offer reasonable avenues for social entrepreneurship to flourish and create value for society. They facilitate co-creation and social innovation. Additionally, they also shape opportunities for relevant actors (individuals or the community) to become a social entrepreneur. These opportunities created are people-centric rather than profit-centric and create social value along with financial success. Due to democratised participation and diversified ownership, the economic success of cooperatives gets reinvested in the next cycle of social value creation (Bauer et al.,

2012). Furthermore, cooperative principles integrate effectuation and causation logic to identify the cooperative goals and then relentlessly follow them (Leitch & Harrison, 2016). Yet, how a cooperative organisation espouses the social entrepreneurship process is not theorised yet.

### *2.3 Social Entrepreneurship and SDGs*

Although social entrepreneurship and development goals attempt to make the world a better place to live, they are contested concepts (Connelly, 2007). Both have different meanings for different people and are recognised as buzz words (Bleischwitz et al., 2018). A socially entrepreneurial organisation can consider time-bound SDGs to measure social value creation (Diaz-Sarachaga et al., 2018). The universal acceptance of SDGs may counter the pre-paradigmatic challenges of social entrepreneurship (Lehner & Kansikas, 2013).

Due to its dynamism and blurred boundaries, social entrepreneurship creates hope for achieving SDGs (Dees & Anderson, 2003). Social entrepreneurship provides an effective solution to social problems, but lack of efficiency, challenges the financial viability of the SE (Goyal et al., 2016). SDGs with its emphasis on efficiency beyond the financial parameters, may act as a yardstick to measure and compare the achievements of social entrepreneurship and social innovations.

It is imperative that, cooperative institutions can benefit from the innovative approaches of social entrepreneurship. Nevertheless, these innovations can fail to fulfil cooperative aspirations in the absence of acceptable efficiency parameters. Hence, there is a need to integrate SDGs within the cooperative structure and social entrepreneurship process. Although the literature indicates the complementarity of these concepts, achieving the same is not explored. Hence, this research raises two specific research questions. First, how to align the cooperative organisational structure with the process of social entrepreneurship? Second, how can social entrepreneurship helps to achieve SDGs?

## 3 Methodology

This research adopts a qualitative research approach and a case study method. The qualitative approach is preferred to address the literature void with research questions, starting with "how" (Atherton & Elsmore, 2007). A case study is recommended when literature is limited on the given concept (Eisenhardt, 1989). In-depth exploration of an ideal case helps the field understand the process of making that ideal (Gammelgaard, 2017). Hence, a single qualitative case study research methodology is used in this work.

## 3.1 *Identifying the Organisation*

To identify an ideal cooperative organisation following social entrepreneurship, I have followed a two-step process. I turned my attention to Ashoka Foundation which awards and facilitates social entrepreneurship and keeps track of the progress of respective organisations. As India provides a significantly high level of socially entrepreneurial opportunities, I limited my search to Ashoka India. Ashoka India enlists around 400 Ashoka Fellows recognised between 1982 and 2020. Looking at the vision and mission of these organisations, I found 81 social entrepreneurship organisations connected to cooperative principles.

The second step helped to identify the ideal cooperative organisation through the process of comparison. I removed all such cooperative organisations started recently and retained those operating for over 20 years and found 20 such organisations. I extensively analysed the information of these 20 organisations and found that three organisations have dominant cooperative organisational models. I listed all SGDs targeted by these organisations and selected Mann Deshi Mahila Group (MDMG) as it practises the most diverse efforts towards SDGs.

## 3.2 *Data Collection*

The data collection was collected in two stages: first in 2015 and then in 2020. A gap of 5 years has given significant time to observe the progress of SDGs parameters targeted by the organisation. During the first stage of data collection, the emphasis was to understand the working and ecosystem of the organisation. For this, I worked in the organisation for two months. I collected data through observation, semi-structured interviews, and informal conversations. I collected interview data in the form of narratives as they go beyond the clock-time. Initial informal interaction and theoretical underpinning helped to craft a semi-structured interview guide. I followed snowball and purposive sampling and interviewed people who have spent over three years in the organisation. I also interviewed different stakeholders. In the second stage of the data collection, I primarily collected data with the help of semi-structured interviews of five key members.

In the first stage, I have conducted 12 interviews. The average length of the interview was 62 min, with a minimum of 35 min and a maximum of 121 min. The complete transcript of these interviews runs for 120 pages. Similarly, I compiled the field notes in a notebook of 140 pages.

In the second stage, I have conducted five telephonic interviews. The duration of these interviews ranged between 20 to 45 min, with an average value of 33 min. The complete transcript of these interviews runs for 40 pages with 12 font size, times new roman, and single spacing.

# 4 Analysis, Findings, and Discussion

This section presents the analysis and findings of the data under different themes and sub-themes. These themes and sub-themes are developed through triangulation of data collected during the first and second stages and the verified information available in the public domain.

## *4.1 Organisational Structure and Evolution of MDMG*

The purpose of the MDMG is women empowerment, and for that, the organisation believes in "women empowering women"; hence women constitute the majority of the workforce. MDMG integrates Mann Deshi Mahila Bank, Mann Deshi Foundation, and Mann Deshi Tarang Vahini (the community radio). The Foundation and the community radio are sister organisations of the cooperative bank. The bank is a for-profit entity, and the Foundation is non-profit; hence, the aggregate structure of the MDMG is hybrid. The hybridity of the group is well reflected in their work because both the entities (bank and Foundation) play a supportive role (Fig. 1).

Although the workflow and designations are well defined, there is no separate office space for any person (including the founder, CEO, bank, and CAO) in the headquarters. However, separate spaces are maintained in branch offices of the bank. Similar to headquarters, there is no separate cabin for any person at different centres of the Foundation.

MDMG takes decisions through the active participation of all stakeholders, including beneficiaries, implementation staff, and senior management. The internal and external stakeholders are invited to headquarter and facilitate decision-making. To make the process more democratic, the organisation inducted one of its beneficiaries into the board.

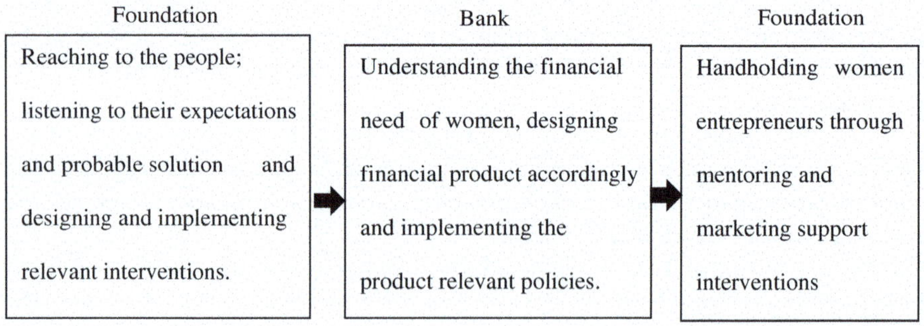


**Fig. 1** Working process in MDMG

### *4.2 Sustaining the Venture*

The bank maintains a 100% recovery rate to ensure profitability. The CEO says, "We do not get any subsidy. If someone is taking the loan, then must repay it. Otherwise, if our NPA (non-performing asset) goes up, then it will affect the profit." MDMG practises social innovation for reaching a 100% recovery. A senior recovery officer says, "If a woman is not paying the loan instalment, we revisit the woman. The idea is to give some time and help (through the Foundation) to address reasons for default. They can make clear backlogs later, and we can retain our customers."

The Foundation mobilise resources from national and international funding agencies and maintains a long-term association with them. It receives resources from Corporates under Corporate Social Responsibility. It also accepts funding from the government.

### *4.3 Structuring the Cooperation*

This theme captures the administrative innovations practised by the organisation and includes three sub-themes that emerged during the analysis.

#### 4.3.1 Generating Cooperation Within Conflict

Social entrepreneurship challenges the existing inefficient social order (Seelos & Mair, 2005), whereas a cooperative organisation uses unity of the same order as a strength (Gherardi & Masiero, 1990). Hence, cooperatives following the social entrepreneurship process face seemingly conflicting goals: exploiting unity of social order and annihilating the inefficient social order. Bringing these two together needs prioritising cooperation over annihilation first and then organically using this cooperation to bring social change (Kolk & Lenfant, 2016). It challenges the social order but not the immediate society itself. Instead, it separates its competing goals (SDGs) in time and space. Elaborating on this, Ms. Rekha Kulkarni, CEO of the Mann Deshi Mahila Bank, says

> When I joined, most of the employees in the bank were male. Think, a women cooperative bank with a majority of male employees! But now we have changed it. You can see women all around us, and that is why we call us- A bank for women and by women. But, in this process, we received much support from male members of our family and society. It is not like we are fighting against them.

As cooperatives are registered bodies there is a need to follow regulatory guidelines (Zhao & Gijselinckx, 2011). While addressing the regulatory requirements, the organisation may be forced to overlook one or many SDGs. To achieve them, cooperatives following SE processes develop a harmonious relationship with other institutions. Narrating the process through which MDMG achieves this harmony, the founder, Ms. Chetna Sinha, said

> I joined the social sector through JP Movement (a nationwide movement started by Jay Prakash Narayan), and it was just the beginning. After that, we were involved in many awareness initiatives where we challenged the inefficient functioning of government and even protested their decisions. Contrary to that, now we know how to work within the government system and change them.

Under normative and coercive isomorphic forces, cooperative social entrepreneurship organisations may face limits for selecting their entrepreneurial initiatives (Heugens & Lander, 2009). However, social entrepreneurship allows changes from outside (for example, through social activism) yet, within the cooperative structure, the organisation becomes part of the institutional framework to bring the change as summarised in Proposition 1.

**Proposition 1:** Cooperative social entrepreneurship organisation takes corrective measures to nullify the ill effect of institutional framework instead of challenging the institution.

### 4.3.2 Cooperating with Non-Cooperatives

Any organisation can opt SE process to serve their target group (Hulgård, 2010). When cooperatives practice SE, the legal framework governing the cooperatives may restrict them to certain issues or SDGs. Structural interventions, like spin-offs, help to focus such SDGs (Kannothra et al., 2018). For example, a non-profit arm of a cooperative bank can accept government grants and cooperate contributions.

As creating a hybrid organisational form or a spin-off may result in mission drift (Cornforth, 2014), governance mechanisms ensure that the mission, vision, and activities of hybrid organisations and/or constituents are consistent with the parent organisation (Ebrahim et al., 2014). As in the case of cooperatives and social entrepreneurship, if based on the same bottom-up approach, democratic participation remains the hallmark of structural interventions.

The constituents of MMDG (Mann Deshi Mahila Foundation, Mann Deshi Tarang Vahini, and Mann Deshi Mahila Bank) have overlapping board members to reduce conflict of interest and design the cooperative agenda. For instance, the Mann Deshi Mahila Foundation runs financial literacy programmes. Here, they train rural women about minute details of monetary transactions and how to maintain the balance sheet of their business. Aligned with that, it also runs formal training for rural women micro-entrepreneurs. This programme is called Deshi MBA (Indigenous Master of Business Administration). The bank provides financial support to these entrepreneurs. Working together, they ensure women empowerment. One of the senior members of the MDMG and the Chief Administrative Officer (CAO) of the Foundation, Ms. Vanita, elaborated on the collaborative effort of the Foundation as:

> There are a few initiatives that our bank cannot take. Look at this check-dam project. We are building several check dams to deal with water scarcity and also to protect the environment. The idea is not very different from our main motive. The logic is straightforward: if people survive well in the village, the bank can flourish well. For that we require water. However, building a check dam needs a collaborative approach of government, fund mobilisation from like-minded corporate and community participation. The Foundation provides a platform to integrate the efforts of all such institutions.

On a similar note, the CEO of the bank explained the role of farmer producer company (FPC) and said:

> We have established a for-profit women farmer producer company (FPC). For members, it conducts soil and water testing at no cost. We have also appointed consultants and experts, and they suggest to our farmers what they should grow in their field. We organise exhibitions at various locations to facilitate the selling of their field products. We also linked them to the market directly, and the FPC performs all these tasks.

### *4.4 Institutionalising the Cooperation*

The governance mechanism of sister organisations helps the cooperative to strengthen the cooperation among them. The CEO of the bank elaborated on the governance of the Foundation and explained her role:

> As a board member of the Foundation, I know the work of the Foundation well. I am directly involved in a project undertaken by the Foundation in collaboration with the Indian Institute of Technology, Bombay. And my participation in the work of the Foundation is not new. I started when I joined this bank and continue till today... We are for the same purpose and complement each other.

She further adds about the governing mechanism of another sister organisation, which is a farmer producer company (FPC). She said, "one of the board members of the bank leads this FPC." Here, sister organisations are vital in connecting MDMG to non-members (government, corporate, and others). In this sense, the boundary of sister organisations is more porous than cooperatives but less porous than the imaginary boundary of the group of organisations which separates it from the external world. The nested governance mechanism where cooperative members guide sister organisations to avoid mission drift and principal-agent problems by regulating the porosity of sister organisations (See Fig 2).

**Proposition 2:** Sister organisations of the cooperative have regulated porous boundaries than the cooperative organisation, and this regulation is achieved by nested governance mechanism to avoid the mission drift.

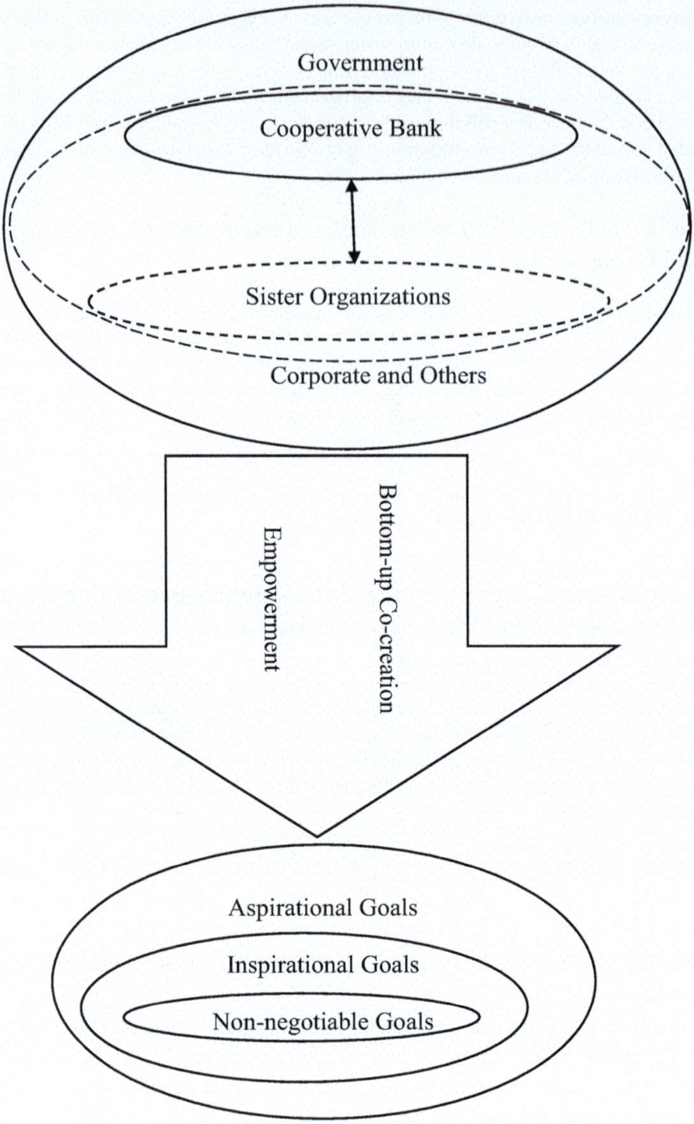


**Fig. 2** Enable cooperative model of social entrepreneurship for SDGs

## *4.5 Entrepreneuring Cooperation*

This theme captures the process innovations practised by the organisation and includes two sub-themes.

### 4.5.1 Bottom-up Co-creation

A developmental intervention is sustainable when accepted and espoused by the target group (Geller et al., 1982). The target group accepts the solution that addresses their problem without triggering another problem (Thabrew & Ries, 2009). Additionally, social entrepreneurship revolves around positive externalities (Santos, 2012). The decentralised decision-making with equal voting rights of cooperatives facilitates the acceptability of their intervention. Resonating with this understanding to go back to the community for addressing their needs, the founder said

> Just because they are poor, there is no need to offer a poor solution to their problems. They know how to solve those problems, and hence we should listen to them. They suggest simple solutions to complex problems, and then we work around those simple solutions.

Complementing her words, Ms. Mrunalini elaborated on designing interventions through close consultation. She said:

> We did a study on women entrepreneurs operating in informal markets of different villages. The informal market shifts its place every day, and hence they were working in different marketplaces on different days. They needed different amounts of money on different days. If they take a loan from JLG, even if they did not need the entire money, they still had to take the total loan amount of INR 10,000-15000. Additionally, coming to the bank wastes the entire day. If the loan processing takes 2-3 days, then they earn nothing on those days. Hence, they were taking loans from local moneylenders. That is why we have started door-step banking. (Fig. 2)

As the target group understands the holistic problem and is better equipped to evaluate positive and negative externalities, their involvement in designing interventions is the sine qua non. When they become a member of the cooperative bank, it removes the separation of ownership and control because of the monitoring mechanism through their voting rights.

Additionally, the deprived community may reject a genuine intervention because of socio-cultural constraints. Inviting suggestions and involving the community in designing interventions transfer the ownership of interventions to the community. Here, the organisation is not a driver of innovation but a facilitator of innovation. So, the community is more deeply engaged in this co-creation process and takes ownership. Bottom-up approach of co-creation empowers the community, and the organisation brings relevant technology to implement these solutions.

**Proposition 3:** Cooperative social entrepreneurial process involves members and larger sections of the community in the co-creation process where the organisation plays the role of facilitator rather than a driver of co-creation.

### 4.5.2 Empowerment

Education builds capacity and confidence to use opportunities (Sobels et al., 2001). It can negate the challenges of women empowerment rooted in the participants' socio-economic status (Cherayi & Jose, 2016). MDMG follows the cooperative principles of education training and education for women empowerment. Ms. Sinha narrated a story of women empowerment as:

> In a meeting with the top officials of the RBI, illiterate women of MDMG, whom I trained, challenged RBI officials and said, "Tell us to calculate the interest of any principal amount; if we fail, do not issue us the licence. Tell your officers to calculate the interest of the same principal amount without a calculator and then see who can calculate faster?" This courage is real women empowerment.

Apart from economic aspects, social aspects also hinder the progress of women. Following words of another senior member of MDMG elaborated on the same:

> Money does not ensure empowerment. Think about Indian women from the upper-middle class or upper class. They have money, but how many of them are empowered? Empowerment is imparting the know-how to use that money. It is about the decision-making ability to make better use of that money, which is the real meaning of empowerment.—This is what we do at our Deshi MBA program. We impart skills to run a successful business and how to make business decisions. In that sense, our program is the real MBA.

MDMG engages members in day-to-day business and provides appropriate training to understand its operations and start their own business. Additionally, it helps them effectively analyse the cooperative bank's performance to contribute beyond exercising their voting rights. Here, business-related training helps members to suggest strategic initiatives rather than communicating wishful thinking. This leads to Proposition 1.

**Proposition 4:** Sharing business know-how with members and the community members helps them contribute efficiently to bottom-up co-creation. Such members and the community feel empowered and evaluate interventions more effectively.

## *4.6 Integrating SDGs in Interventions*

Designing interventions to address nested social problems is challenging (Caulfield & Brenner, 2020) because problems exist at multiple levels, and interventions need multi-criteria decision-making (Pérez et al., 2015). Also, each intervention is placed and implemented synergistically with others to avoid systemic failure (Ramalingam et al., 2014). As social entrepreneurship challenges the existing order of society, hence a failure may lead to more damage than any good. Hence, every intervention is strictly scrutinised and analysed for its impact.

To keep the cooperative's mission intact while attempting to address deeper issues of society, the organisation needs to reinvent its goal and opt for core issues as a value-based selection criterion for all interventions (Ramus & Vaccaro, 2017). In other words, the core issue is an end and other issues surrounding it become a means to achieve that. Thus, repositioning SDGs to facilitate the holistic development of the community brings desired social change.

Ms. Sinha explained this through the story of the genesis of the cooperative bank as:

> One morning, a lady, her name is Kanta Bai, came to me and said, "I want to open a savings bank account. I went to all the banks, but none of them agreed to open my account." So, I accompanied her to one of the banks and asked the reason. The banker responded that Kanta Bai's savings are too small. Then the idea came to establish a cooperative bank for such women. So, we drafted a proposal and sent it to the Reserve Bank of India (RBI) for getting a banking licence. As most of the promoters of that proposal were rural non-literate women, they rejected the proposal. It was frustrating for me, but not for those women. They asked me to teach them reading and writing so that they could run a bank. After six months, we applied again …and got the approval.

This narrative explains how Mann Deshi Mahila (Cooperative) Bank was able to address SDG-4 (quality education) while focusing on SDG-1 (no poverty), SGD-16 (Peace, Justice and Strong Institutions), and SDG-5 (Gender Equality). Here, the cooperative started to address SDG-1 but keeping that at the core, it has used SDG-4 as a tool and finally achieved SDG-5.

As noted earlier, the Foundation is rooted in the JP movement; hence, social justice serves the organisation's criteria for selecting activities. The story of the establishment of cooperative banks is the testimony of this account. MDMG evaluates all interventions through the lens of justice and attempts to bring the prevailing concerns of society into the eyes of relevant actors. In this direction, the initiative of the cattle camp is noteworthy.

Recalling about the cattle camp initiative, the founder, Ms. Chetna Sinha, says:

> A lady came to our banks for a loan against her gold. I enquired about her needs and realised that her cattle were not getting enough fodder due to drought. So, she wanted money to purchase fodder for them. Then I realised that this was a prevailing situation around us and decided to organise a camp to care for these cattle. To our surprise, hundreds of households with thousands of cattle came to that cattle camp. Yes, we had resources, but not for so many cattle for over 18 months. However, we moved forward, and support poured in from all sides, including the government.

Linking this initiative with the environment and livelihood, Ms. Mrunalini said,

> Although it did not usually rain here, there has been good rainfall this year. All our check dams are full. So, older people are getting emotional and saying that this is our water, and we have made check dams to get this water for farming. Now they are thinking to cultivate new crops, for example, cultivating cash crops, not only sorghum or pearl millet. Now there is greenery all around.

CFO of the bank added that the women entrepreneurs supported by the Mann Deshi group are now selling their products through reputed online platforms. They are also reaching out to global customers.

These narratives explain that the cooperative bank, along with its sister organisations, focuses on issues of poverty (SDG-1), justice (SDG-16), gender equality (SDG-5), improving the contribution of women in economic growth (SDG-8), reducing inequality (SDG-10), and life on land (SDG-15). In order to achieve these goals, the organisation designs partnership (SDG-17), innovative products and services (SDG-9), takes care of the well-being of the community (SDG-3), and promotes production based on indigenous knowledge (SDG-12). Altogether, Mann Deshi Mahila Group can contribute to enhancing agricultural production to achieve SDG-2 (no hunger), share knowledge and equip rural women to run their own business (SDG-4), and improve the environment (SDG-13). I have not found any direct intervention for improving life below water (SDG-14), yet I hope their efforts of building multiple check dams will contribute to this. A detailed account of activities as per SDGs is presented in Table 1.

Cooperatives can classify these goals into three categories: non-negotiable, inspirational, and aspirational goals. There is zero tolerance for non-negotiable goals (For MDMG, SDGs 1, 5, 8, 10, 15, and 17). Inspirational goals facilitate their business to reach new heights (MDMG, SDGs 3, 9, 12, and 17). Finally, aspirational goals are those through which these organisations directly contribute to society (MDMG, SDGs 2, 4, 6, 13, and 14). The organisation is expected to inculcate a value system around non-negotiable goals, design interventions to achieve inspirational goals, and support aspirational goals wherever possible. Depending upon the business model, availability of resources at hand and the need of the community, the cooperatives can decide temporal and spatial segregation of these SDGs for successful implementation. However, the segregation should not result in any trade-off among non-negotiable goals or the primary intent of the social entrepreneurship process.

**Proposition 5:** Temporal and spatial segregation of intended and unintended goals integrates sustainable development goals. The segregation helps cooperatives design a holistic social entrepreneurial process without compromising the organisation's mission (Table 1).

## 5 Contributions

This research brings insights on the synergies between social entrepreneurship, cooperatives, and SDGs. As far as SDGs are concerned, there is a need to look at the efficient organisational machinery to achieve them. It is also important to evaluate the progress made in the last five years for designing strategies for the remaining ten years (Bidarbakhtnia, 2020). In this sense, the research community is encouraged to identify innovative administrative and structural changes needed for achieving SDGs. In this context, six transformations recommended by Sachs et al. (2019) may help. In addition to that, the business world is encouraged to redesign them and align their goals with SDGs (Tsalis et al., 2020). I suggest the separation of SDGs on time and space in terms of non-negotiable goals, aspirational goals, and inspirational goals.

For social entrepreneurship, this chapter contributes to the debate on social value creation. Although social value creation is considered a prime motive of social entrepreneurship, there is no consensus on measuring it (Austin et al., 2006). Zahra et al. (2009) suggested measuring the total wealth as a sum of economic wealth (economic value-economic cost/opportunity cost) and social wealth (social value—social cost). Here social wealth is measured at the societal level and economic wealth

**Table 1** Mapping activities of the Mann Deshi Mahila Group on different SDGs

| SDGs | Description | Primary data source | Secondary data source |
|---|---|---|---|
| GOAL 1: No Poverty | Business training and micro-lending to poor of the poorest | Interview data and field notes and observation | https://manndeshibank.com/ |
| GOAL 2: Zero Hunger | Support to agriculture by establishing Farmer Producer Company and its Farm to Market initiative | Interview data of CEO and CFO of the Bank | https://manndeshifoundation.org/community-empowerment/#farm-to-market |
| GOAL 3: Good Health and Well-being | Inviting prominent doctors to discuss health-related issues on Mann Deshi Radio | Interviews and Field notes, Observation a | https://onlineradiofm.in/maharashtra/satara/mann-deshi-tarang |
| GOAL 4: Quality Education | Digital Literacy, a Business school for rural women, distribution of bicycles for young girls so that they can reach school | Interview data and field notes and observation | https://manndeshibank.com/ |
| GOAL 5: Gender Equality | Sports intervention among school-going kids. Participation of both genders is equally encouraged | Interview data (employees and participants of these programmes), field notes, and observation | https://manndeshifoundation.org/community-empowerment/#mann-deshi-champions |
| GOAL 6: Clean Water and Sanitation | Enriching water table through its water conservation initiatives to build check dams | Interview data and field notes and observation | https://manndeshifoundation.org/community-empowerment/#water-conservation |
| GOAL 7: Affordable and Clean Energy | Mobilised people to raise the demand for electrification of the village | Interview data | |
| GOAL 8: Decent Work and Economic Growth | Promoting entrepreneurship among rural women through various support mechanisms, including the chamber of commerce of rural women | Interview data and field notes and observation | https://manndeshifoundation.org/women-empowerment/#chambers-of-commerce |
| GOAL 9: Industry, Innovation and Infrastructure | Building check dams and continuously innovating to improve cash flow for rural women entrepreneurs | Interview data | https://manndeshibank.com/about/our-approach/ |

(continued)

**Table 1** (continued)

| SDGs | Description | Primary data source | Secondary data source |
|---|---|---|---|
| GOAL 10: Reduced Inequality | The organisation is working to reducing inequality by promoting entrepreneurship among rural women | Interview data and field notes and observation | https://manndeshifoundation.org/women-empowerment/#business-schools |
| GOAL 11: Sustainable Cities and Communities | No direct intervention is found in this direction | | |
| GOAL 12: Responsible Consumption and Production | Promoting indigenous products and connecting producers to the world market | Interview data | https://manndeshifoundation.org/wp-content/uploads/2020/01/Mann-Deshi-CoC-Product-Directory.pdf |
| GOAL 13: Climate Action | Building check dams is improving green cover in the region | Interview data, field notes, and observation | |
| GOAL 14: Life Below Water | Although there is no direct evidence, building check dams improves life below water. A piece of indirect evidence is fisheries being opted as livelihood opportunity by many villagers (https://manndeshifoundation.org/community-empowerment/#water-conservation) | | |
| GOAL 15: Life on Land | Through cattle camp, it provides support to life on land. Also, improved facilities for agriculture and other businesses reduced out-migration | Interview data | https://thewire.in/rights/satara-cattle-camp-drought |
| GOAL 16: Promote just, peaceful and inclusive societies | The JP movement inspires the organisation; hence this goal is inherent in every action of the organisation | Interview data, field notes, and observation | https://www.asianage.com/life/more-features/050118/who-run-the-world-girls-1.html |
| GOAL 17: Partnerships to Achieve the Goal | The organisation partners with a sister organisation, government institutions, corporate, and various international organisations for achieving its goals | Interview data, field notes, and observation | https://manndeshifoundation.org/our-people/ |

*Note* All the weblinks were last accessed on October 31, 2020 at the organisation level (Santos, 2012). However, he positioned positive externalities at the centre but could not answer the limitation of the time dimension. Kroeger and Weber (2014) developed a time-bound mathematical formula of social value.

Nevertheless, this measure is based on a world value survey, and the feasibility of such a retrospective measure is not sure (Mair & Sharma, 2012). Further, stakeholders' perspective is needed to identify intended outcomes, positive externalities, and negative externalities. Here, SDGs can fill this void. SDGs are time bound. However, I believe that some of the issues of SDGs will remain relevant as long as humanity exists. For example, innovation, decent work, affordable energy, inequality, and sustainability are evolving concepts.

For cooperatives, this paper sets a high standard of functioning. Going back to the roots, I suggest cooperatives rethink their functioning to offer a viable alternative to crony capitalism. Cooperatives are also subjected to isomorphic pressures, directing them to behave like other organisations in their respective sectors (Mason, 2012). However, seven principles that build their foundation do not surrender to those norms (Zeuli et al., 2004). Hence, there is a need to strengthen evolutionary roots and improve community participation instead of blindly following the over-hyped scaling path (Alves et al., 2019). The idea is to grow organically instead of risking the mission. In this direction, this paper suggests two more cooperative principles, as noted below.

The first addition to the cooperative principle is related to ownership needed to ensure scale, scope, and viability (Monteiro & Stewart, 2015). Presently, ownership is exercised through memberships and votes. With most illiterate members, educated business graduates, who take decisions on behalf of cooperatives, are well skilled to manipulate the entire process. Hence, to avoid such manipulations, business training to cooperative members is required to prepare them to take decisive managerial roles and minimise principal-agent problems. The Deshi MBA programme of MDMG is one such initiative. So, the seventh cooperative principle proposed here is: Empowering members to evaluate managerial decisions.

The second addition to cooperative principles is exploring the possibility of scaling beyond survival (Tsoukas, 2011). Democratic participation is meaningless if voices are unheard. If there is an appreciation of voices, members open themselves and guide the organisation to prevailing issues. Suppose an organisation cannot address prevailing issues. In that case, there are chances that it may move away from its members, leading to an increasing proportion of inactive members, or members may leave the locality in search of better opportunities. Including this, I propose the eighth cooperative principle as Continuous evaluation of prevailing issues affecting the membership.

## 6 Limitations and Future Direction of Research

This study carries three limitations. The first limitation is related to the sample of the study. This single case study is designed to develop a theory on socially entrepreneurial cooperative organisations in the context of SDGs. Even if a single case study is an excellent approach to develop a theory, a comparative case study may bring more nuances. Apart from that, quantitative analysis may suggest a way forward towards the generalisation of the findings. Although these are significant limitations, yet the research question limited this study to a single ideal case. As significantly less is theorised about social entrepreneurship in general and cooperative social entrepreneurship organisations in particular, collecting quantitative data may be theoretically misleading. I invite research to use this work as a theoretical lens to develop hypotheses, collect data, and add or challenge it. This paper also sets the parameters which can be used to conduct a comparative case study to extend the theoretical contributions presented here.

The limited conceptualisation of social entrepreneurship in the context of cooperatives is the second limitation. Although social entrepreneurship is a multi-dimensional construct but this paper, social value creation is dominantly used. A better understanding needs the integration of all dimensions. In this study, I tried to respond to this limitation by bringing cooperative organisations with the market orientation, social innovation, and organisational form. Furthermore, the collective nature of social entrepreneurship is very similar to cooperatives. Here, other dimensions of social entrepreneurship are embedded in the context around social value creation. Future research may consider dimensions other than social value creation in the context of SDGs.

## 7 Conclusion

Cooperatives practising social entrepreneurship shed a ray of hope to the present world by challenging crony capitalism. It craves out ways of involvement from a larger section of society who can come forward and take ownership of societal development. There is a need to consider SDGs as performance parameters for these organisations and design their organisational structure and functioning to achieve them. Further, as nature and name suggest, cooperatives should look at cooperation at a more significant level and not limit cooperation within themselves. SDGs can help society envision a better future and keep track of societal development on the defined path through this process.

## References

Alves, W., Ferreira, P., & Araújo, M. (2019). Mining co-operatives: A model to establish a network for sustainability. *Journal of Co-Operative Organization and Management, 7*(1), 51–63.

Atherton, A., & Elsmore, P. (2007). Structuring qualitative enquiry in management and organization research: A dialogue on the merits of using software for qualitative data analysis. *Qualitative Research in Organizations and Management: An International Journal., 2*(1), 62–77.

Austin, J., Stevenson, H., & Wei-Skillern, J. (2006). Social and commercial entrepreneurship: Same, different, or both? *Entrepreneurship Theory and Practice, 30*(1), 1–22.

Bacq, S., Hartog, C., & Hoogendoorn, B. (2013). A quantitative comparison of social and commercial entrepreneurship: Toward a more nuanced understanding of social entrepreneurship organizations in context. *Journal of Social Entrepreneurship, 4*(1), 40–68.

Balleer, A. (2012). New evidence, old puzzles: Technology shocks and labor market dynamics. *Quantitative Economics, 3*(3), 363–392.

Bauer, C. M., Guzmán, C., & Santos, F. J. (2012). Social capital as a distinctive feature of Social Economy firms. *International Entrepreneurship and Management Journal, 8*(4), 437–448.

Bidarbakhtnia, A. (2020). Measuring Sustainable Development Goals (SDGs): An inclusive approach. *Global Policy, 11*(1), 56–67.

Birchall, J., & Ketilson, L. H. (2009). *Resilience of the cooperative business model in times of crisis*. International Labour Organisation.

Bleischwitz, R., Spataru, C., VanDeveer, S. D., Obersteiner, M., van der Voet, E., Johnson, C., Andrews-Speed, P., Boersma, T., Hoff, H., & Van Vuuren, D. P. (2018). Resource nexus perspectives towards the United Nations sustainable development goals. *Nature Sustainability, 1*(12), 737–743.

Bruneel, J., Moray, N., Stevens, R., & Fassin, Y. (2016). Balancing competing logics in for-profit social enterprises: A need for hybrid governance. *Journal of Social Entrepreneurship, 7*(3), 263–288.

Castelló, I., Etter, M., & Nielsen, F. Å. (2016). Strategies of legitimacy through social media: The networked strategy. *Journal of Management Studies, 53*(3), 402–432.

Caulfield, J. L., & Brenner, E. F. (2020). Resolving complex community problems: Applying collective leadership and Kotter's change model to wicked problems within social system networks. *Nonprofit Management and Leadership, 30*(3), 509–524.

Cechin, A., Bijman, J., Pascucci, S., Zylbersztajn, D., & Omta, O. (2013). Drivers of pro-active member participation in agricultural cooperatives: Evidence from Brazil. *Annals of Public and Cooperative Economics, 84*(4), 443–468.

Cherayi, S., & Jose, J. P. (2016). Empowerment and social inclusion of Muslim women: Towards a new conceptual model. *Journal of Rural Studies, 45*, 243–251.

Choi, N., & Majumdar, S. (2014). Social entrepreneurship as an essentially contested concept: Opening a new avenue for systematic future research. *Journal of Business Venturing, 29*(3), 363–376.

Connelly, S. (2007). Mapping sustainable development as a contested concept. *Local Environment, 12*(3), 259–278.

Cornet, S., & Barpanda, S. (2020). Exploring social innovation through co-creation in rural India using action research. *Social Enterprise Journal*. https://doi.org/10.1108/SEJ-12-2019-0099

Cornforth, C. (2014). Understanding and combating mission drift in social enterprises. *Social Enterprise Journal, 10*(1), 3–20.

Coscieme, L., Mortensen, L. F., Anderson, S., Ward, J., Donohue, I., & Sutton, P. C. (2020). Going beyond Gross Domestic Product as an indicator to bring coherence to the Sustainable Development Goals. *Journal of Cleaner Production, 248*, 119232.

D'Art, D., & Turner, T. (2006). New working arrangements: Changing the nature of the employment relationship? *The International Journal of Human Resource Management, 17*(3), 523–538.

Dees, J. G., & Anderson, B. B. (2003). Sector-bending: Blurring lines between nonprofit and for-profit. *Society, 40*(4), 16–27.

Dees, J. G. (2012). A tale of two cultures: Charity, problem solving, and the future of social entrepreneurship. *Journal of Business Ethics, 111*(3), 321–334.

Dey, P., & Lehner, O. (2017). Registering ideology in the creation of social entrepreneurs: Intermediary organizations, 'ideal subject' and the promise of enjoyment. *Journal of Business Ethics, 142*(4), 753–767.

Diaz-Sarachaga, J. M., Jato-Espino, D., & Castro-Fresno, D. (2018). Is the Sustainable Development Goals (SDG) index an adequate framework to measure the progress of the 2030 Agenda? *Sustainable Development, 26*(6), 663–671.

Ebrahim, A., Battilana, J., & Mair, J. (2014). The governance of social enterprises: Mission drift and accountability challenges in hybrid organizations. *Research in Organizational Behavior, 34*(1), 81–100.

Eisenhardt, K. M. (1989). Building theories from case study research. *Academy of Management Review, 14*(4), 532–550.

Gammelgaard, B. (2017). The qualitative case study. *The International Journal of Logistics Management, 28*(4), 910–913.

Geller, E. S., Johnson, R. P., & Pelton, S. L. (1982). Community-based interventions for encouraging safety belt use. *American Journal of Community Psychology, 10*, 183–195.

Gherardi, S., & Masiero, A. (1990). Solidarity as a networking skill and a trust relation: Its implications for cooperative development. *Economic and Industrial Democracy, 11*(4), 553–574.

Goyal, S., Sergi, B. S., & Jaiswal, M. P. (2016). Understanding the challenges and strategic actions of social entrepreneurship at base of the pyramid. *Management Decision, 54*(2), 418–440.

Hanisch, C. (2013). An autonomy-centered defense of democracy. *International Philosophical Quarterly, 53*(4), 371–384.

Harima, A., & Freudenberg, J. (2020). Co-creation of social entrepreneurial opportunities with refugees. *Journal of Social Entrepreneurship, 11*(1), 40–64.

Haugh, H. M., & Talwar, A. (2016). Linking social entrepreneurship and social change: The mediating role of empowerment. *Journal of Business Ethics, 133*(4), 643–658.

Heugens, P. P., & Lander, M. W. (2009). Structure! Agency!(and other quarrels): A meta-analysis of institutional theories of organization. *Academy of management journal, 52*(1), 61–85.

Hulgård, L. (2010). Discourses of social entrepreneurship—Variations of the same theme. *EMES European Research Network, 10*(1), 2–21.

Kannothra, C. G., Manning, S., & Haigh, N. (2018). How hybrids manage growth and social–business tensions in global supply chains: The case of impact sourcing. *Journal of Business Ethics, 148*(2), 271–290.

Kolk, A., & Lenfant, F. (2016). Hybrid business models for peace and reconciliation. *Business Horizons, 59*(5), 503–524.

Kroeger, A., & Weber, C. (2014). Developing a conceptual framework for comparing social value creation. *Academy of Management Review, 39*(4), 513–540.

Lehner, O. M., & Kansikas, J. (2013). Pre-paradigmatic status of social entrepreneurship research: A systematic literature review. *Journal of Social Entrepreneurship, 4*(2), 198–219.

Leitch, C. M., & Harrison, R. T. (2016). Identity, identity formation and identity work in entrepreneurship: Conceptual developments and empirical applications. *Entrepreneurship & Regional Development, 28*(3–4), 177–190.

Lepoutre, J., Justo, R., Terjesen, S., & Bosma, N. (2013). Designing a global standardized methodology for measuring social entrepreneurship activity: The Global Entrepreneurship Monitor social entrepreneurship study. *Small Business Economics, 40*(3), 693–714.

Mair, J., & Sharma, S. (2012). Performance measurement and social entrepreneurship. In *Social Entrepreneurship and Social Business* (pp. 175–189). Gabler Verlag.

Mason, C. (2012). Isomorphism, social enterprise and the pressure to maximise social benefit. *Journal of Social Entrepreneurship, 3*(1), 74–95.

McLaughlin, P. (1996). Resource mobilization and density dependence in cooperative purchasing associations in Saskatchewan, Canada 1. *Rural Sociology, 61*(2), 326–348.

Miedes-Ugarte, B., Flores-Ruiz, D., & Wanner, P. (2020). Managing tourist destinations according to the principles of the social economy: The case of the Les Oiseaux de Passage cooperative platform. *Sustainability, 12*(12), 4837.

Mojo, D., Fischer, C., & Degefa, T. (2015). Social and environmental impacts of agricultural cooperatives: Evidence from Ethiopia. *International Journal of Sustainable Development & World Ecology, 22*(5), 388–400.

Monteiro, N. P., & Stewart, G. (2015). Scale, scope and survival: A comparison of cooperative and capitalist modes of production. *Review of Industrial Organization, 47*(1), 91–118.

Montgomery, A. W., Dacin, P. A., & Dacin, M. T. (2012). Collective social entrepreneurship: Collaboratively shaping social good. *Journal of Business Ethics, 111*(3), 375–388.

Mori, P. A. (2014). Community and cooperation: The evolution of cooperatives towards new models of citizens' democratic participation in public service provision. *Annals of Public and Cooperative Economics, 85*(3), 327–352.

Muñoz, P., Kimmitt, J., & Dimov, D. (2020). Packs, troops and herds: Prosocial cooperatives and innovation in the new normal. *Journal of Management Studies, 57*(3), 470–504.

Novkovic, S. (2006). Co-operative business: The role of co-operative principles and values. *Journal of Co-operative Studies, 39*(1), 5–16.

Ormiston, J., & Seymour, R. (2011). Understanding value creation in social entrepreneurship: The importance of aligning mission, strategy and impact measurement. *Journal of Social Entrepreneurship, 2*(2), 125–150.

Parente, C., Lopes, A., & Marcos, V. (2014). Social entrepreneurship profiles: Lessons from organizational and management dynamics. *Journal of Social Entrepreneurship, 5*(1), 22–41.

Pérez, J. C., Carrillo, M. H., & Montoya-Torres, J. R. (2015). Multi-criteria approaches for urban passenger transport systems: A literature review. *Annals of Operations Research, 226*(1), 69–87.

Ramalingam, B., Laric, M., & Primrose, J. (2014). *From best practice to best fit: Understanding and navigating wicked problems in international development* (pp. 1–44). Overseas Development Institute.

Ramus, T., & Vaccaro, A. (2017). Stakeholders matter: How social enterprises address mission drift. *Journal of Business Ethics, 143*(2), 307–322.

Raub, S. P., & Martin-Rios, C. (2019). 'Think sustainable, act local'—a stakeholder-filter-model for translating SDGs into sustainability initiatives with local impact. *International Journal of Contemporary Hospitality Management, 31*(6), 2428–2447.

Sachs, J. D., Schmidt-Traub, G., Mazzucato, M., Messner, D., Nakicenovic, N., & Rockström, J. (2019). Six transformations to achieve the sustainable development goals. *Nature Sustainability, 2*(9), 805–814.

Santos, F. M. (2012). A positive theory of social entrepreneurship. *Journal of Business Ethics, 111*(3), 335–351.

Schneiberg, M. (2013). Movements as political conditions for diffusion: Anti-corporate movements and the spread of cooperative forms in American capitalism. *Organization Studies, 34*(5–6), 653–682.

Seelos, C., & Mair, J. (2005). Social entrepreneurship: Creating new business models to serve the poor. *Business Horizons, 48*(3), 241–246.

Sobels, J., Curtis, A., & Lockie, S. (2001). The role of Landcare group networks in rural Australia: Exploring the contribution of social capital. *Journal of Rural Studies, 17*(3), 265–276.

Thabrew, L., & Ries, R. (2009). Application of life cycle thinking in multidisciplinary multistakeholder contexts for cross-sectoral planning and implementation of sustainable development projects. *Integrated Environmental Assessment and Management: An International Journal, 5*(3), 445–460.

Tsalis, T. A., Malamateniou, K. E., Koulouriotis, D., & Nikolaou, I. E. (2020). New challenges for corporate sustainability reporting: United Nations' 2030 Agenda for sustainable development and the sustainable development goals. *Corporate Social Responsibility and Environmental Management, 27*(4), 1617–1629.

Tsoukas, S. (2011). Firm survival and financial development: Evidence from a panel of emerging Asian economies. *Journal of Banking & Finance, 35*(7), 1736–1752.

Zahra, S. A., Gedajlovic, E., Neubaum, D. O., & Shulman, J. M. (2009). A typology of social entrepreneurs: Motives, search processes and ethical challenges. *Journal of Business Venturing, 24*(5), 519–532.

Zeuli, K. A., Cropp, R. A., & Schaars, M. A. (2004). *Cooperatives: Principles and practices in the 21st century.* Cooperative Extension Publications.

Zhao, L., & Gijselinckx, C. (2011). Multi-stakeholder co-operatives in China: A resource mix structure approach. *Social Enterprise Journal, 7*(3), 259–279.

Zhu, Y., Rooney, D., & Phillips, N. (2016). Practice-based wisdom theory for integrating institutional logics: A new model for social entrepreneurship learning and education. *Academy of Management Learning & Education, 15*(3), 607–625.

# Social Entrepreneurship: Distinct Dimensions Leading to Inclusive Growth and Sustainable Development

**Kumar Mukul, V. Padmaja, S. Jayadatta, and V. Srinija**

**Abstract** This chapter explores the pivotal role played by social entrepreneurship in catalyzing more inclusive, comprehensive, and sustainable development. It also explores ways in which social entrepreneurs are creating a pathway leading to sustainable and inclusive growth of the economy, especially in a very challenging milieu of the COVID-19 pandemic. The present study, based on an extensive literature review and discussion on emergent themes from the previous studies, puts forth a conceptual framework incorporating the crucial dimensions of social entrepreneurship, alongside micro- and macro-level factors that contribute to fostering inclusive growth and sustainable development. It is argued that social entrepreneurs, armed with innovation, a resolute social mission, viable and scalable business models, and other distinctive attributes such as empathy and leadership, have the potential to introduce fresh solutions to enduring socio-economic challenges. They offer sustainable pathways to wealth generation, ultimately elevating overall living standards for all. This study underscores the transformative potential of social entrepreneurship, emphasizing its capacity to address deep-rooted disparities and facilitate a more equitable and prosperous society.

**Keywords** Social entrepreneurship · Inclusive growth · Social value creation · Sustainability · Sustainable development

---

Kumar Mukul (✉)
CMS Business School, Faculty of Management Studies, Jain Deemed-To-Be University, Bengaluru, Karnataka, India
e-mail: dr.kumar_mukul@cms.ac.in

V. Padmaja
M. S. Ramaiah Institute of Management, Bengaluru, Karnataka, India
e-mail: padmaja@msrim.org

S. Jayadatta
KLE Society's IMSR, BVB CET Campus, Vidyanagar, Hubli, Karnataka, India

V. Srinija
Department of Management and Commerce, Sri Sathya Sai Institute of Higher Learning, Anantapur Campus, Anantapur District, Andhra Pradesh, India



E. M. Reji and S. Majumdar (eds.), *Social Enterprise Values and Processes*, India Studies in Business and Economics, https://doi.org/10.1007/978-981-97-3252-4_2

## 1 Introduction

Social entrepreneurship is progressively drawing attention of practitioners, researchers, and policymakers owing to its potential to pave the way for the attainment of social and economic objectives through innovative, inclusive, and sustainable approaches (Defourny & Nyssens, 2013). Social entrepreneurship is seen as a viable solution for intractable social issues, inequality, poverty, and environmental degradation. It is being considered as a feasible answer for poverty alleviation and inclusive growth. Social enterprises, balancing between economic and social objectives are seen as catalysts of inclusive growth and sustainable development (UNCTAD, 2017). Its potential to address challenges of inequalities and ability to foster social cohesion as well as sustainable and egalitarian growth is helping it emerge as an effective catalyst in overall developmental efforts. Social entrepreneurship, as a concept and practice, integrates both the economic as well as social value creation. It is a key enabler in bringing the growth of socio-economically laggard sections of the society. These features make the concept and practice of social entrepreneurship a topic of critical significance, more so in an emerging economy like India where more innovative interventions are required to overcome its perennial problems of economic underachievement and socio-economic inequalities.

Social entrepreneurs function as agents of change by primarily applying their entrepreneurial skills and resources to provide systemic solutions to environmental and social problems (Partzsch & Ziegler, 2011). By doing so, they also ensure their own survival and sustainability (Mair & Martí, 2006). In many small and medium-sized businesses, lack of resources is the greatest impediment to responsible business practices; consequently, resource-constrained entrepreneurs seek out a variety of novel business models to ensure their survival (Halme & Korpela, 2014). Venture capitalists often come to the rescue of resource-starved enterprises acumen and innovative prowess which are critical for identifying opportunities for sustainable development (Hall et al., 2010). In the case of social enterprises, such funding options are not easily available (compared to for-profit enterprises), and hence the problem of resource constraints are more profound.

Social entrepreneurship is often recognized as a source of novel and innovative solutions which create conditions for sustainable economic and developmental activities (Rinkinen et al., 2016). The efforts through NGOs, government subsidies, grants, and charities have been major traditional approaches for addressing social inequalities. However, the efforts of these practices to support and raise the socio-economic levels of marginalized and weaker sections of people have yielded limited results. Social entrepreneurship is emerging as the most effective alternative to the delivery of goods, though it is still necessary to seek out other viable alternatives (Ghosh, 2009). One of the reasons for many of the persisting problems globally is the non-inclusive nature of developmental activities. The benefits of economic activities fail to reach out to marginal segments. Also, many 'inclusive' developmental efforts lack robust and effective business models to be self-sustainable for a long duration. Social entrepreneurship often comes up with ideas which result in outcomes which are inclusive and sustainable. They do not strive solely for business growth or profit maximization but for holistic development.

Inclusive and sustainable growth refers to development that incorporates under-represented groups in the social, political, and economic spheres, resulting in enhanced empowerment, well-being, and environmental and social sustainability (Gupta et al., 2015). Inclusive growth gives equal prominence to both the economic and social dimensions of development, alongside the equitable allocation of resources and growth avenues (Rauniyar & Kanbur, 2009). The realization of inclusive growth necessitates the provision of opportunities for all segments of society, despite their diverse backgrounds, to engage in and make contributions to the process (ibid.). Inclusive growth, according to research by Johnson and Andersen (2012), can foster innovation and more efficient problem-solving strategies. In order to increase the quantity of resources at the disposal of individuals who were previously excluded on the basis of their ethnicity, gender, or other characteristics, inclusive initiatives such as granting rights, a voice, capacity, and incentives will foster greater innovation and participation in development.

Sustainable development is achievable via two axes, inclusive growth and green growth, according to the UNDP (2012). Green growth expects the implementation of developmental policies that promote the significance of environmental friendly, sustainable, and low-carbon economic development in addition to inclusive social development, emphasizing both economic and environmental aspects (United Nations, 2009; UNDP, 2012).

Social entrepreneurship offers viable alternatives of growth which are considerate of human well-being, social progress, environmental sustainability, empowerment, and the inclusion of marginalized segments of society as outcomes of inclusive and sustainable initiatives (Gupta et al., 2015). In order to achieve sustainability, it is imperative to address three fundamental dimensions of development: economic, social, and environmental. While economic development is often the focus of business entrepreneurship, social entrepreneurship attempts to address all these aspects of development. Issues such as education, health, environment, and access to basic services are the life necessities which must be addressed in any approach toward sustainable and inclusive growth (Stoddart, 2011). Social entrepreneurship emerges as a viable option for such comprehensive development. The discussion on how entrepreneurs and social entrepreneurs will meet the unmet needs of the society is limited and not much work has been done in this area (Hall et al., 2010). Bansal et al. (2019) emphasize the presence of research deficiencies, specifically in relation to investigations that explore the causal relation of social entrepreneurship supporting sustainable development in underdeveloped and developing economies. Murthy et al. (2008) emphasized the significance of studying these concepts in developing nations due to the limited availability of data on social issues and the approaches employed to address them.

This chapter focuses on understanding the pivotal role which social entrepreneurship plays in contributing towards inclusive and sustainable growth, especially in a developing economy context of India. It also explores how social entrepreneurs are providing ample scope for creating a pathway leading to sustainable and inclusive growth of the economy, especially in a very challenging milieu of the COVID-19 pandemic.

The prime objective of the study is to comprehend the specific aspects of social entrepreneurship that encourage inclusive and sustainable growth. The study examines the significance of social entrepreneurship within the developing landscape of India. The attempt is to look at the growing relevance of social entrepreneurship given the challenges posed due to the COVID-19 pandemic. A conceptual framework has been created to illustrate the different aspects of social entrepreneurship and the interaction between social enterprises and their micro- and macro-level ecosystem components.

The subsequent sections of the paper are organized as follows. Section 2 presents a comprehensive literature review on various topics including social entrepreneurship, inclusive growth, sustainable growth, the role of social entrepreneurship in achieving inclusive and sustainable growth, and the significance of social entrepreneurship in the Indian context. Section 3 outlines our methodology, wherein we have listed the major research work reviewed related to the core themes of study in a tabular form. The methodology section is followed by a detailed presentation of our discussion and findings in Sect. 4. Afterwards, Sect. 5 provides a conceptual framework integrating the core themes of discussion. Implications and future possibilities of research are discussed in Sect. 6. Section 7 highlights major limitations of the study while Sect. 8 gives an overall conclusion for the study.

## 2 Literature Review

### *2.1 Social Entrepreneurship*

Social entrepreneurship has gained increasing scholarly attention in the past twenty years due to the perceived capacity of social entrepreneurs to address global problems using innovative methods and creative solutions (Dacin et al., 2010; Zahra et al., 2009). Social entrepreneurship involves the identification of viable market opportunities, allocation of resources, and the pursuit of creating social value (UNCTAD, 2017). Leadbetter (1997) proclaimed that social entrepreneurship uses entrepreneurial behavior for social motives instead of profit motives and the profit generated from economic activities is used for helping disadvantaged groups. Social entrepreneurship is not an easy idea to grasp. It is complicated, contentious, and can be thought of as a cluster of connected constructs, according to Choi and Majumdar (2014). Social entrepreneurship emphasizes two key components: a social mission and entrepreneurial activities (Corner & Ho, 2010). Hence, the entrepreneurs who think of both—creating a sustainable business based on innovative idea, with self-sustaining revenue generation capability as well as having a vision and commitment for creating some social value, can be categorized as social entrepreneurs. Social entrepreneurs are those who change the way we traditionally look at social problems, social upliftment, social value creation, profitability, distribution of wealth, and the newer (and better) ways of conducting business. According to Dees and Anderson (2006), social entrepreneurship is a process of change that is achieved through an entrepreneurial approach and aims to address social needs, solve social problems, and uphold social values.

Martin and Osberg (2007) describe social entrepreneurship as a process that can enhance people's social and economic well-being in three ways: (i) identifying the underlying causes of an unfair balance that is maintained through exclusion, marginalization, and human suffering due to limited access to financial and political power and resources, which must be utilized to advance the interests of these individuals; (ii) recognizing any opportunities that may exist within this unfair balance, developing programs based on social values, and promoting inspiration, creativity, direct action, and courage, which can contest the unjust societal equilibrium; and (iii) establishing a stable balance that can alleviate the suffering experienced by the less fortunate through formation of a stable ecosystem, thus enabling the formation of a new balance and offering the possibility of a healthier society in future.

Social entrepreneurs are individuals who recognize and seize opportunities, pool resources, and employ innovative strategies to achieve a social mission aimed at resolving social issues and generating social value. Social entrepreneurs willingly undertake risks in pursuit of social objectives or a social mission. Weerawardena and Mort (2006) have conceptualized social entrepreneurship as a multidimensional model that encompasses three dimensions: innovativeness, proactiveness, and risk management. Social entrepreneurship aims to create social value and necessitates the demonstration of three dimensions. Social entrepreneurship shares similarities with traditional entrepreneurship as it encompasses fundamental aspects such as identifying and capitalizing on opportunities, fostering innovation, and demonstrating resourcefulness. 'The social mission is clear and essential for social entrepreneurs' (Dees, 1998, p. 3). Nevertheless, it is the emphasis on social mission that sets it apart from commercial entrepreneurship.

Another distinct aspect of social enterprises, when compared to their larger counterparts (including government institutional bodies) is their simple organizational structures and smaller sizes. These features facilitate the maintenance of effective and productive relationships with communities, allowing for prompt response to local needs and the implementation of socially impactful initiatives. This, in turn, promotes and sustains their competitive advantage (Szczanowicz et al., 2016).

## *2.2 Social Entrepreneurship, Inclusive Growth, and Sustainable Development*

The economic development initiatives have failed to achieve inclusive growth, as a staggering 47 percent of the global population (equivalent to 2.56 billion people) continues to grapple with extreme poverty (World Bank, 2009). There is another segment of about 1.5 billion people apart from this group who are just managing with limited purchasing power. This large section of humanity is eternally struggling with problems related to proper food, housing, unemployment, education, health systems, skill deficits, environmental threats, indulging in anti-social activities, trust deficit toward existing institutions, etc. In developing economies, these challenges are far more serious and need prompt, pragmatic, and noble responses. Any sustainable development movement needs to keep this factor under consideration. This dire scenario has ample 'latent potential' for opportunity seeking and enterprising people. According to some estimates, the 4 billion people representing the poor section of the world offer a market worth US$ 4–5 trillion approximately. This situation of lop-sided growth provides good ground for social entrepreneurial initiatives to come up with innovative solutions and scale up to address the problems posed by 'non-inclusive' growth at the global level.

The growing emphasis on implementing inclusive growth strategies has arisen due to the fact that certain segments of society have not been able to engage in or reap the benefits of previous development initiatives (Johnson & Andersen, 2012). This leads us to an important element in any socio-economic discussion—the idea of inclusive growth. Scholars have interpreted the concept of inclusive growth in diverse manners, and there is no universally accepted definition for inclusive growth (Lee, 2019). According to Terry McKinley (2010), there are two elements to inclusive growth: (i) achieving long-term growth that generates and expands economic possibilities and (ii) ensuring that more people have access to these possibilities so that everyone may benefit from growth. The basic premise of inclusive growth is that such growth must ensure that equal opportunities are available to all segments of society to participate in developmental processes and have access to the fruits of development.

The central concept underlying inclusive growth is the provision of 'equal opportunities' (Rauniyar & Kanbur, 2009; Vujanovic, 2015). Johnson and Andersen (2012) highlighted the importance of involving the impoverished population in the development process, as it provides them with increased opportunities to actively participate in and reap the benefits of economic growth. Inclusive growth refers to a continuous economic growth that is accompanied by the fair and equitable distribution of opportunities for all sections of the population to take part in the economic progress. This distribution includes both monetary as well as non-monetary benefits (OECD/European Union, 2017). Subir Gokarn (2007) explains inclusive growth in terms of four characteristics: opportunity, capability, access, and security are the four pillars. So, a scenario where equal opportunity for growth is available to all, where everyone's capability is utilized and developed to full potential, where all segments have equal access to resources and outcomes of economic growth, and where all feel secure of their rights and future possibilities in the society. Inclusive growth empathizes non-income indicators of well-being and values human qualities such as health, literacy, employment, healthy environment, etc., as parameters to measure true developmental achievements. In general, inclusive growth guarantees social fairness and equality among individuals, in addition to economic progress.

Scholars suggest how social entrepreneurs act as potential innovators contributing to economically and socially sustainable development (Rinkinen et al., 2016). Sustainable development expresses a genuine commitment to social and environmentally friendly activities that is integrated into the business strategy (Smith & Sharicz, 2011). Survival of business, capability of business model to enable self-sustaining enterprises to make positive contribution to the needs of the community and environment over long periods of time to meet the essence of sustainability. To comprehend the connection between social entrepreneurship and sustained growth, it is imperative to undertake a social impact assessment process. This process involves the organization evaluating, analyzing, monitoring, and publicizing the changes that result from the planned operations of the social enterprise.

The role of social entrepreneurship to bring about strategic and long-term change depends on the involvement of all influential stakeholders associated, which together become the driving engine for entrepreneurial initiatives and overall growth agenda of socio-economic progress. In the field of research and practice, even after significant reflections, social entrepreneurship as such even today is still considered to be in a quiet nascent stage and doubts are raised by some stakeholders in its ability to produce results. Empirical evidence from India indicates that social entrepreneurship is experiencing growth. However, accurately measuring its impact has proven challenging due to its close association with social parameters of the social economy, the third world economic sector, and the non-profit sector. The challenge of objectively assessing the impact of social entrepreneurship arises from the presence of a diverse range of entities operating in this field. Furthermore, these entities exhibit differences based on geographical context and the varying perspectives of countries that have distinct interpretations of social entrepreneurship (OECD, 2010). Social entrepreneurship, despite these difficulties, has illustrated that it has unlimited potential to lead true development in developing countries like India, through investment in ingenious abilities of people and enabling them, often through technological support, to be catalysts of social innovation and change in more inclusive and justifiable ways.

## 2.3 *Social Entrepreneurship in Indian Context*

India accounts for approximately 17.5% of the global population and is ranked as the seventh-largest country in terms of land area. India is demographically recognized as the world's youngest country, with around two-thirds of its population being under the age of 35. India, although the second fastest growing economy after China, has a poverty rate of 30% among its population (Aggarwal, 2012). Also, in spite of an appreciable economic growth after independence, India still ranks 129 among 189 countries as per the Human Development Index (HDI) (Human Development Report, UNDP, 2019). India is facing widespread poverty and economic inequalities (Gore, 2003). It is home to widespread disparities in wealth and income. Around 370 million Indians account for facing some form of deprivation (Barowalia, 2010). The disparity has largely been because the economic growth has excluded the vast masses of Indian populace from the developmental benefits (Aggarwal, 2012). The disparity and lack of resources faced by marginalized populations must be tackled through equitable human development, which encompasses concerns such as healthcare, education, housing, infrastructure, access to clean water, and other related challenges (Barowalia, 2010). Such a scenario provides a rich field for the effective role of social entrepreneurs. There is great opportunity for social entrepreneurs to take a leadership role and help mitigate this situation. Social entrepreneurs are poised to emerge as victors in this situation due to their focus on comprehensive solutions to the existing societal issues. They generate social value and facilitate equitable social transformation (Nicholls, 2006).

## *2.4 Social Entrepreneurship and CSR*

Corporate houses in India have been involved in developmental initiative related to social cause since long time. Tata group, the Birla group, HUL, AMUL, ITC, and many other leading corporate houses have always been contributing in this regard through the 'Corporate Social Entrepreneurship' (CSR) means. According to Austin et al. (2005), numerous social initiatives are undergoing a process of reinvention and transitioning toward corporate social entrepreneurship. An exemplary instance in the Indian context is the e-Choupal initiative by the Indian Tobacco Company and the 'Project Shakti' by Hindustan Unilever Limited. ITC established e-Choupals, internet kiosks in rural areas, to provide farmers with easily accessible and current information on weather, prices, agricultural knowledge, and best practices. The kiosks are overseen by proficient local farmers who assist the nearby villagers and agricultural community in accessing crucial information in their native language. The farmers have successfully enhanced productivity, mitigated risk, enhanced quality, and attained improved prices. e-Choupal has expanded in recent years to encompass a range of services that cater to various rural requirements, including insurance and healthcare.

Hindustan Unilever Limited (HUL) implemented Project Shakti, a well-known initiative aimed at training and empowering impoverished and rural women from Self-Help Groups (known as Shakti Ammas) throughout India. The programme focused on cultivating an entrepreneurial mindset and achieving financial independence for these women. These women undergo training in the fundamental principles of distribution management and become acquainted with the company's products in order to sell them to small retail outlets in their local village, as well as directly to households within the community. Another instance is that of AMUL, overseen by the Gujarat Co-operative Milk Marketing Federation Ltd. (GCMMF). The AMUL Model, widely denoted as the 'White Revolution' in India, effectively bridged the divide between producers and consumers by establishing an organic network that directly connected dairy farmers to consumers. Dr. Verghese Kurien played a pivotal role in facilitating India's rise as the foremost milk producer globally. The dairy cooperatives have not only offered a reliable income stream to women, but have also contributed to their economic empowerment, given that they are the primary participants in dairy farming activities. These examples of corporate initiatives toward social entrepreneurship illustrate the significant contribution of corporate houses through their social entrepreneurship efforts to the development of the society by being inclusive in its approach and creating 'economic' and 'social value'.

## 2.5 *Social Entrepreneurship in Times of COVID-19 Crisis*

The COVID-19 pandemic, is unparalleled in terms of uncertainty and devastation in the history of our world. When the COVID-19 pandemic broke out, some social entrepreneurship researchers viewed it as a chance to uncover perennial societal concerns that may be addressed by social entrepreneurship. Ratten (2020) suggests that to effectively address the challenges caused by COVID-19, it is advisable to utilize social entrepreneurship and value co-creation strategies in order to facilitate positive transformation. This statement is derived from previous research indicating that social businesses, with their dual objective, are particularly advantageous during periods of economic instability. According to certain historians, the emergence of the social entrepreneurship movement in the United States can be attributed to reductions in federal funding for non-profit social service organizations (Kerlin, 2006). Non-profit organizations commenced engaging in commercial activities in response to a decline in federal assistance. Consequently, organizations were established with the explicit aim of attaining social and economic goals.

Bacq and Lumpkin. (2021) describe an event (called 'The COVID-19 Virtual Idea Blitz') hosted recently to brainstorm the challenges and solutions amidst the pandemic crisis, which drew over 200 people from five continents and ten nations. Attendees were seeking a productive channel to articulate their concerns regarding the virus, and the gathering seemingly yielded positive outcomes. One team, for example, enabled the distribution of almost 21,000 masks to those in need. This was a major societal worry during the early phases of the epidemic, when many towns were low on masks.

Financial capital is positively connected to innovativeness and effective outcomes thus social companies with sufficient financial capital are likely to do well (Meyskens et al., 2010). Nevertheless, before the pandemic, social enterprises that struggled with pricing and cash flow management might have faced the risk of bankruptcy. Consequently, socially responsible businesses that are financially secure are in a more advantageous position to capitalize on the COVID-19 pandemic as an opportunity to generate innovative solutions for persistent and escalating societal problems.

Social enterprises are a strategic approach to tackling social challenges that have emerged or been exacerbated by the COVID-19 pandemic. Currently, the industry, society, and social enterprises are still being speculated upon regarding the long-term consequences of the pandemic. Although empirical studies have made significant contributions to academic research in the field of social entrepreneurship, the literature has neglected the task of comprehending and quantifying social impact (Austin et al., 2006). There is an evident lack of research on the influence of contextual factors in the analysis of social enterprises and social value creation.

In order to identify essential issues for future research, policies, and practices in the social business sector, the present study takes a small step in exploring the distinct dimensions of social entrepreneurship and how it can be a major player in holistic and sustainable economic development and community development going ahead.

## 3 Methodology

The current study is grounded in a comprehensive examination of existing literature on the importance and function of social entrepreneurship in encouraging inclusive economic growth and fostering sustainable development. The literature review has focused on several significant search topics, such as social entrepreneurship, inclusive growth, social entrepreneurship and sustainable development, the role of social entrepreneurship in balanced growth, the role of social entrepreneurship in addressing social issues, social entrepreneurship in the Indian context, socio-economic inequalities and social entrepreneurship, social entrepreneurship during the COVID-19 pandemic, and related issues. The primary method used for conducting the article search involved utilizing databases such as Emerald, Proquest, Ebsco, JSTOR, Sage, SpringerLink, Science Direct, and Google Scholar. Through a thorough analysis of existing literature, an attempt has been made to simplify the discussion in order to effectively address the research objectives and generate a set of propositions that can serve as a groundwork for future research in the field.

The Table 1 depicts the major research papers referred to during the study to build the discussion around the 'distinct dimensions' of social entrepreneurship. These distinct dimensions later formed the base on which propositions were framed. The table systematically lists the themes of discussion, the authors whose works were referred to and cited, the year of those published works, and the essence of those papers.

## 4 Analysis and Discussion

### *4.1 Social Entrepreneurship as a Catalyst for Sustainable Development*

Social entrepreneurship aims to facilitate a lasting and strategic transformation by engaging all relevant stakeholders who are affected directly or indirectly by their work and operations, leading to an overall socio-economic progress. Social entrepreneurs make use of their vision, business ideas, skill-sets, and limited resources to identify unmet social needs and address them through innovative means. Their core emphasis

**Table 1** The 'distinct dimensions' of social entrepreneurship

| Sl. no | Themes | Authors and years | Essence |
|---|---|---|---|
| 1 | Innovation: Tool for social change and social value creation | National Innovation Council (2013), Singh (2016) | Innovations can help provide alternate ways of coming up with outputs in terms of products and services by applying new technology, more efficient means resulting in lower costs, and ultimately affordable prices for the target customers |
| | | Mulgan et al. (2007), Bognar (2005) | Social entrepreneurship is the practice of spreading innovation in order to improve the social abilities of a specific group of people |
| | | Hansson et al. (2014) | Social entrepreneurship, which involves the creation of social value through social innovation, is considered to have a significant impact on development |
| | | Bridgstock et al. (2010) | Social entrepreneurs through use of innovative tools bring creative ideas into existence |
| | | Austin et al. (2006) | In the realm of social entrepreneurship, innovation entails the development of novel ideas or solutions, rather than simply duplicating traditional approaches |
| | | Mazzucato and Wray, (2015), Schumpeter (1934) | The developments entail a dynamic process whereby innovative discoveries and new technologies render obsolete the old ones, resulting in transformative changes in society |
| | | Mair and Marti (2006), Porter and Kramer (2006) | Social enterprises innovate to amass, merge, and utilize resources in distinctive ways to generate social value. They generate social value by creating lucrative products or services that tackle social and environmental issues and promote fair market practices |
| | | Weerawardena and Mort (2006) | Innovativeness and proactiveness generate sustainable and unique solutions and are the core features propelling social entrepreneurship |
| | | Porter and Kramer (2006) | Social entrepreneurs generate social value through the creation of profitable products or services that tackle social and environmental issues while promoting fair market practices |

(continued)

**Table 1** (continued)

| Sl. no | Themes | Authors and years | Essence |
|---|---|---|---|
| 2 | Inclusive Growth and Sustainable Development | Rauniyar and Kanbur (2009), Kozuka (2014), Vujanovic (2015) | 'Inclusive growth' refers to a type of growth that is accompanied by equal opportunities. It is essential that this type of growth guarantees equal access to all segments of society<br>Inclusive development necessitates the provision of equitable opportunities for access to all segments of society |
| | | Smith and Sharicz (2011) | In developing countries, poverty, environmental threats, skill deficits, etc., need urgent responses. Sustainable development provides opportunities to enterprising people |
| 3 | Focus of Social Entrepreneurs | Corner and Ho (2010) | Achieving some social mission through entrepreneurial activities |
| | | Mulgan et al. (2007) | Focus of SE is on leveraging social innovation to meet certain social needs instead of profit maximization |
| | | Auerswald (2009) | Conventional entrepreneurs prioritize the creation of financial value, while social entrepreneurs prioritize the creation of social value and strive to enhance the overall quality of life in society |
| 4 | Acting as catalysts for social change | Alvord et al. (2004) | Social entrepreneurs often act as catalysts for social transformation through consistent, small, short-term changes that lead to large-scale changes over a period of time |
| | | Partzsch and Ziegler (2011) | Social entrepreneurs are now recognized as individuals who use entrepreneurial methods to develop comprehensive solutions to social and environmental issues, thus acting as catalysts for change |
| | | Dees (1998, p. 4) | Social entrepreneurship is seen as the most apt answer to the challenge of continuous change |
| 5 | Financial Self-Sufficiency and Scalability | Hebb et al. (2012) | Social entrepreneurs make sure that along with appropriate margins, the product or services they offer remain affordable for their customers |

(continued)

**Table 1** (continued)

| Sl. no | Themes | Authors and years | Essence |
|---|---|---|---|
| 6 | Leadership skills of social entrepreneurs | Kerlin (2006) | There may arise a conflict between the pursuit of financial gain and the attainment and progress of societal objectives. Therefore, leaders of social enterprises must demonstrate significant creativity and innovation |
| 7 | Accessibility and affordability for the customers | Van der Have and Rubalcaba (2016) | Social entrepreneurs face the task of ensuring that their innovative solutions enable the production of high-quality products at an affordable price |
| | | Islam et al. (2019) | Strategic use of social media is one way in which the social enterprises can address the issues of accessibility and reach |
| 8 | Driven by business ethics | Bull et al. (2010), Bornstein (2004), Drayton (2002). Smith et al. (2016), Spence (2014), Sijabat (2016), Zahra et al. (2009) | Adherence to business ethics is paramount in SE which facilitates building of trust-based relationships with business stakeholders and community members at large |
| 9 | Overcoming the challenges caused by market failures | Phillips et al. (2015) | Market-based demand and supply-driven economies lead to market failures and hindrances in achieving social needs of all |
| | | Rauniyar and Kanbur (2009) | Market failures hinder the participation and utilization of existing economic opportunities by specific social groups. SE helps in overcoming the lacunae left due to market systems and facilitate more equitable distribution economic growth outcomes |
| 10 | Alignment with universal goals | UN (2015) | SE helps achieve comprehensive development, integrating social, political, cultural, and environmental dimensions |
| 11 | Environmental concern and green business | UNCTAD (2017) | 'Green entrepreneurs' attempt to address environmental issues through and entrepreneurial solution<br>They are going to be pioneers in overcoming environmental challenges and pandemic situations (like the latest COVID-19 pandemic) |

(continued)

**Table 1** (continued)

| Sl. no | Themes | Authors and years | Essence |
|---|---|---|---|
| 12 | Responding to the left-out segments of society | Seelos and Mair (2005) | SE plays a critical role in putting forth the urgency of rural and community development |
| | | Cornwall (1998) | SE often plays a leading role in rural communities with more inclusive and egalitarian societal framework including underprivileged people |

*Source* Compiled by the authors

on social mission, their capacity to combine the available resources in innovative ways and reach out to the 'left-out' segments of society help them build a distinct set of 'social change' agents who are capable of involving the diverse set of people toward inclusive growth and sustainable development. It is evident from the extant literature in the domain that due to these reasons social entrepreneurship has received wide consideration recently and is professed to be a source of novel, innovative, and lasting solutions to persistent social problems.

There is an increased emphasis on inclusive development since not all segments of the society have been able to partake in or benefit from developmental initiatives (Johnson & Andersen, 2012). Inclusive growth proclaims equal opportunities for all and equal access to resources and growth outcomes are provided to all elements of society (Kozuka, 2014; Rauniyar & Kanbur, 2009; Vujanovic, 2015). The World Bank report published in 2009 suggests how nearly half of the world population is still struggling with extreme poverty and efforts are not sufficient in achieving inclusive growth. In developing countries, challenges pertaining to poverty, environmental threats, skill deficits, etc., are even more serious and need urgent responses. Development efforts need to consider this and thus provide opportunities to enterprising people. Smith and Sharicz (2011) opine that sustainable development includes a genuine commitment to social and environmentally friendly activities that are integrated into the business strategy. Scholars suggest how social entrepreneurs play an important role in this regard by acting as potential innovators (Rinkinen et al., 2016).

The extant literature on the topic suggests that there are certain distinct characteristics of social entrepreneurship which enable it to get such comprehensive developmental outcomes. In the following segment we discuss the major characteristics or 'dimensions' of social entrepreneurship which we found to be crucial in attaining inclusive growth and sustainable development.

### 4.1.1 The Importance of Social Entrepreneurs in the Contemporary Context

A meaningful and sustained program of social development is the pressing need of Indian society today. This program should identify and utilize a set of reliable social indicators to measure and determine the quality of life. The potential of social entrepreneurship becomes evident through the positive impact on the quality of life as measured by parameters similar to those used in the Human Development Index (HDI) and other social indicators employed by government agencies to track development progress. Such a strategic approach holds the promise of foreseeing impending challenges and effectively addressing crises, such as the ongoing pandemic situation. This can be achieved through the formulation and implementation of effective policies aimed at achieving sustainable social progress (Dube, 1988).

Amidst the significant impact of COVID-19 on disadvantaged and susceptible communities, social entrepreneurs and socially oriented companies are endeavoring to transform and adapt their enterprises. Despite the impact of revenue shortages on businesses, social entrepreneurs are demonstrating exceptional skill in innovating and identifying new avenues for survival and sustainability. Vincent Otieno Odhiambo, the regional director of Ashoka East Africa, a non-profit organization that collaborates with social enterprises, was cited in a November 2020 article published in Business Line. 'Social innovation is the DNA of social entrepreneurs', and that 'businesses aiming to do good while making a profit' has a lot to contribute to society, especially in crisis situations like the COVID-19 pandemic. These social entrepreneurs need to tackle perennial challenges along with the emergent ones, in the pandemic such as remote working, healthcare, and education. Crisis situations often provide new opportunities for business entrepreneurs as well as social entrepreneurs. A large number of emergent business opportunities during crisis situations paves the way for opportunities of developing them into social enterprises (Hibbert et al., 2002; Mair & Marti, 2006). This was highly apparent during the ongoing pandemic situation. Many social entrepreneurs have responded to the crisis by producing face shields and PPE kits for doctors and hospital staff. Additionally, they have facilitated job transitions for those who lost their jobs, connecting them with alternative careers to ensure their survival and sustainability.

Amidst the numerous difficulties posed by COVID-19, the crisis has provided an opportunity for social entrepreneurs to collaborate with multiple partners and create groundbreaking solutions. Social entrepreneurs have taken action to assist the individuals who are most susceptible to the health and economic consequences that have emerged from the crisis. An illustration of this is Goonj, a non-governmental organization located in New Delhi, which engaged in disaster relief, humanitarian assistance, and community development in various regions of 23 states throughout India. The organization regarded the waste in urban India as an abundant resource and an untapped wealth. A report published by the World Economic Forum in May 2021 highlighted that 'Goonj has distributed more than 8800 tons of rations and other essential items, provided more than 362,000 meals, sourced 2,25,000 kgs of vegetables from farmers, reached out to more than 380,000 families (about 1.5 million people) and produced more than 800,000 face masks and more than 12,00,000 cloth sanitary pads'. SEWA, an organization that assists self-employed women, has called on the government to provide income support to all families in the informal economy. Jan Sahas, a 20-year-old organization focused on community welfare, is another notable example of a social enterprise that responded actively during the COVID-19 pandemic. Amidst the lockdown, they garnered assistance from over 30 philanthropic and private sector benefactors to cater to the requirements of over 1,040,000 migrant families and individuals affected by sexual violence.

Social entrepreneurs, particularly those operating in emerging markets, have been significantly impacted due to their emphasis on serving low-income households, who are experiencing the crisis' effects more immediately and to a greater extent. The pandemic impedes the activities of social entrepreneurs due to factors such as mobility constraints, challenges in transitioning to virtual models, and a lack of strategic or transitional assistance. Their challenges encompass both financial and non-financial aspects, which vary at each stage of the crisis.

Entrepreneurs have been hampered in their efforts to ensure operational continuity in direct response to the crisis. Many are struggling to maintain their financial stability, market hold, and overall business impact during the pandemic. They are seeking new opportunities and strategies to regain growth in a changed market environment and rebuild their organizations.

Social entrepreneurs have eternal relevance given their consistent efforts to solve market generated disparities, bring vital resources to the fringes of society and being early responders during crisis situations. They exert great effort to generate employment opportunities and guarantee social welfare, particularly in light of the evident and severe consequences of income loss. Social entrepreneurs contribute value by employing unique and innovative approaches to tackle complex social and environmental issues in society. They consistently advocate for an inclusive and environmentally friendly economy, as well as a restructuring of markets, positioning themselves as proponents of the sustainable development agenda. Social entrepreneurs are effective agents of empowerment as they enhance the capabilities of communities so that they may generate their own solutions in future and advance their own growth trajectories.

Social entrepreneurs are in a unique position to represent a new generation of leaders in the twenty-first century. They play a crucial role in revitalizing the sustainable development agenda and constructing more inclusive, shock-proof, and resilient markets.

## *4.2 Distinct Dimensions of Social Entrepreneurship*

Approaches adopted by social entrepreneurs are closely associated with the results they aspire to achieve. Their vision, their way to recognize opportunities, their abilities to engage relevant technology in their practices, their interface with all stakeholders, and their ability to come up with deliverables in a sustained manner over a period of time and for most needy segments of society are remarkable and these distinguish them from any other business entrepreneur in general. Though at the core their vision, abilities, and approaches overlap with business entrepreneurs, there are obvious distinctions which are worth noting and analyzing in detail. In the segment below we try to point out the major '*distinguishing features*' in the practices and principles adopted by social entrepreneurs which make them a distinct breed of entrepreneurs and also make their enterprises potential catalysts of social change. These practices and principles, when implemented successfully, are the prime reasons behind their contributions toward sustainable and inclusive growth.

### 4.2.1 Focus of Social Entrepreneurs

The basic approach of entrepreneurs and social entrepreneurs differ and so do the outcomes attained by them. Achieving some social mission through entrepreneurial activities are defining features of social entrepreneurship (Corner & Ho, 2010). These enterprises are driven by some social mission and their offerings in terms of products or services address some critical problems facing specific social groups. Entrepreneurship typically focuses on creating new business ideas and maximizing profits. In contrast, social entrepreneurs use social innovation to address specific social needs (Mulgan et al., 2007). Warnock (2013) defines social entrepreneurs as individuals who actively bring about change by employing creative strategies to address society's most urgent social issues. While usual business entrepreneurs aim for profitability and business competitiveness, social entrepreneurs aim to address some social problems plaguing their societies and bringing social change for including the marginal and laggard segments into the mainstream of socio-economic development. Because of these divergent focuses business entrepreneurs and social entrepreneurs contribute differently to the development process. Business entrepreneurs speed up the economic development process whereas social entrepreneurs ensure equitable distribution of fruits of development and sustainability of the process. Consequently, social entrepreneurs are more likely to play the role of catalysts and change agents for sustainability. Social entrepreneurs need to balance their vision of creating social impact by investing and looking for the right opportunities keeping in mind the resource constraints of emerging economy and requirements of innovative solutions.

Social issues are defined as circumstances that hinder individuals from achieving their maximum capabilities. Some social issues that exist in society are poverty, unemployment, lack of equal opportunities, racism, malnutrition, inadequate housing, and workplace discrimination (Glicken, 2011). These issues are specially of high concern in countries which are lower in the HDI index (India ranks 129 in global HDI ranks as per UNDP, 2019 report). While conventional entrepreneurs prioritize the creation of financial value, social entrepreneurs prioritize the creation of social value and strive to enhance the overall quality of life in society (Auerswald, 2009).

### 4.2.2 Acting as Catalysts for Social Change

Social entrepreneurs are regarded as 'change agents' due to their objective of effecting social change while addressing social issues. The popularity of social entrepreneurship is driven by captivating anecdotes and inspiring narratives that explore the motivations and strategies behind effecting meaningful societal transformation. Social entrepreneurs often act as catalysts for social transformation through consistent, small, short-term changes that lead to large-scale changes over a period of time (Alvord et al., 2004).

There is an ever-increasing uncertainty operating in the economy, social and environmental domains which lead to greater variety of peoples' needs and demand frequent social changes (Seelos & Mair, 2005). There is a need for consistent and innovative approach toward social change which is inclusive and responsive to dynamic environmental requirements. Social entrepreneurs are now recognized as individuals who use entrepreneurial methods to develop comprehensive solutions to social and environmental issues (Partzsch & Ziegler, 2011). According to Dees (1998, p. 4), 'Social entrepreneurs play the role of change agents in the social sector, by: adopting a mission to create and sustain social value (not just private value), recognizing and relentlessly pursuing new opportunities to serve that mission, engaging in a process of continuous innovation, adaptation and learning, acting boldly without being limited by resources currently in hand, and exhibiting a heightened sense of accountability to the constituencies served and for the outcomes created'. Social entrepreneurship is seen as the most apt answer to the challenge of continuous change.

### 4.2.3 Leveraging Innovative Means

The poorer sections of society lack the purchasing power to buy products and services at competitive prices. Innovations can help provide alternate ways of coming up with outputs in terms of products and services by applying new technology, and more efficient means resulting in lower costs and ultimately affordable prices for the target customers. The National Innovation Council of India asserts that innovation has the potential to offer solutions to persistent problems that conventional methods have been unable to effectively address (National Innovation Council, 2013). Core to social entrepreneurship is innovation which is one of its distinguishing features and also holds the key to a more inclusive development-oriented approach. Social entrepreneurship also acts as a mode of innovation diffusion and adoption which ensures that capability enhancement of target groups is facilitated (Bognar, 2005; Mulgan et al., 2007). Such diffusion of innovation capabilities leads to an overall increase in capabilities across diverse segments, knowledge dispersion, and greater chances of participation in knowledge application for more affordable and viable growth options. Social entrepreneurs thus help create an enriched ecosystem wherein all social entities get enough opportunities to be part of the growth movement and reap the benefits of innovation and growth outcomes. Social enterprises through innovative means result in more effective, viable, and egalitarian ways of social value creation, which is ultimately manifested through betterment in the living conditions of the deprived sections of society.

Hansson et al. (2014), in their study noticed that the conventional methods, normally funded by public institutions and government institutions, were generally found to be inadequate to herald an egalitarian and inclusive model of development and social change. The ineffectiveness of these methods in bringing about desired changes in social life created a clear gap that needs to be addressed. Social entrepreneurship, through the means of social innovation and the creation of social value, is now considered to have a more significant role in the process of development than ever before.

Social entrepreneurs, through the use of innovative tools, bring creative ideas into existence (Bridgstock et al., 2010). Such innovative tools often help the conventional means to preserve resources and provide optimal solutions. Innovation in the context of social entrepreneurship involves creating something new rather than just replication of conventional ways (Austin et al., 2006). Innovation forms an integral part of the social entrepreneurial process and helps in achieving more than what is possible through the traditional means (Spear, 2006).

Seelos and Mair (2005) demonstrate the correlation between social entrepreneurship and social innovation in advancing inclusive and sustainable development. According to Phills Jr., et al. (2008), sustainable development can be achieved by following three approaches: firstly, meeting basic life needs; secondly, establishing communities that encourage collaborative norms, rights, and activities to foster active participation in social and economic development; and thirdly, taking into account the needs of future generations in all present-day social innovation endeavors, with a focus on novelty, improvement, and sustainability. Employing non-traditional approaches, such as engaging in collaborative and innovative work, can play a crucial role in attaining sustainability (Manzini, 2007). It is crucial to consult Joseph Schumpeter's 'Theory of Economic Development' for his introduction of the concept of innovation (Howaldt et al., 2015). As per Schumpeter, economic and technological advancements, referred to as 'creative destruction', have the potential to enhance the overall standard of living. The advancements entail a dynamic progression in which innovative breakthroughs and novel technologies render obsolete older ones, resulting in transformative changes within society (Mazzucato & Wray, 2015; Schumpeter, 1934).

### 4.2.4 Social Value Creation

Social entrepreneurs strive to set up societal transformations by employing inventive methodologies to address social issues and generate 'social value'. Social value creation in the context of social entrepreneurship is commonly regarded as the desirable social goals achieved as a result of the intentional endeavors of social entrepreneurs. Singh (2016) proclaims that social entrepreneurs through the process of social value creation can provide solutions to the major social problems troubling both developed as well as developed nations for ages. Social entrepreneurs spearhead the process of generating social value by virtue of their capacity to identify social problems, their proactive and prudent ways to create business models and enterprises to solve those issues, and their innovative and sustainable contributions leading to social change. Weerawardena and Mort (2006) consider innovativeness and proactiveness to generate sustainable and unique solutions, as core features propelling social entrepreneurship. The social impact which the beneficiaries experience, such as changes in the behaviors and attitudes impacting their lives and creating socio-economic benefits are loaded with potential for larger transformations and socio-economic upliftment of communities, if the innovations are scaled up and persisted with for a long duration. Social entrepreneurs have potential of being central actors leading to solution of perennial socio-economic issues (Auerswald, 2009; Townsend & Hart, 2008).

Emerging economies necessitate more robust mechanisms for creating shared social value due to their pressing socio-economic needs and limited resources. Social entrepreneurs find new ways to accumulate, combine, and use resources in order to explore unique possibilities to accelerate social change and create social value (Mair & Marti, 2006). They create social value by developing profitable products or services that address social and environmental concerns, and enable fair market (Porter & Kramer, 2006). Choi and Majumdar (2014) claim that there are four sub-concepts within social value creation: social innovation, social enterprise organization (managing the firm resources, processes, and practices), market orientation (being competitive in market despite being socially oriented), and the social entrepreneur as the leader at the helm managing everything.

Social entrepreneurs embrace the task of establishing a business based on an idea that is typically perceived as unprofitable and excessively risky by the majority of entrepreneurs and traditional businesses. The company establishes a commercial enterprise that addresses specific social issues while also being financially self-sufficient and profitable. This enables the company to expand its influence and achieve its primary social objectives, as stated by Humberg and Kleemann (2014). Social entrepreneurs leverage their social mission and entrepreneurial acumen to develop unique and inventive approaches, often leading to the creation of innovative models for generating social value.

Social entrepreneurs have a vision to see the alternate ways in which social values can be created within the restrains of limited opportunities and resources. Also, their understanding of 'social value' is holistic and inclusive of social entrepreneurs as well as beneficiaries, because they are both integral to the process of social value creation (Lepak et al., 2007). The distinct values systems and business abilities of social entrepreneurs enable them to envision and initiate the process of social value creation and achieve their social mission through their enterprises.

### 4.2.5 Financial Self-Sufficiency and Scalability

Though social entrepreneurs are driven by social missions, they do not compromise on the business model and self-sustaining revenue generation capabilities. Social enterprises have self-sustaining business models and they realize the importance of maintaining a healthy bottom line (Hebb et al., 2012). Unlike the normal business entrepreneurs, they don't allow the market forces to solely determine their pricing strategies. They make sure that along with appropriate margins, the product or services they offer remain affordable for their customers. Social entrepreneurship doesn't depend on subsidies, grants, or charities for their business and prefer to generate revenue consistently through their business operations.

As the segment of population at the lowest rung of social hierarchy is quite huge in number and cuts across geographical and political boundaries, the social enterprises working to address their problems through their products and services have huge opportunities to scale up. Being socially conscientious in approach and environmentally friendly in operation, they are likely to get a lot of support from the communities they support as well as other pragmatic citizens of the world. Social enterprises have great chances of scaling up their enterprises to reach out to vast masses in need of their offerings. The ability to innovate and leverage the latest technology makes the task of scaling much easier for social entrepreneurs (Westley & Antadze, 2010). The ability to scale up the grassroot innovations is likely to determine the power of social enterprises to cause transformational changes (Hermans et al, 2016; Perrini et al., 2010).

### 4.2.6 Leadership Skills of Social Entrepreneurs

Social entrepreneurship is not only about the person or a leader called as a social entrepreneur; it is about the zeal and passion with which the social entrepreneur works to ensure sustainable development. Social entrepreneurs are often seen as 'transformational leaders', transforming the lives of marginalized and laggard sections by providing them access to resources and avenues for better lives (Alvord et al., 2004; Renko, 2012), Most successful social enterprises are led by dynamic and visionary leaders who make the organization cause-centric or issue-based apart from maintaining business robustness and adhering to most effective management practices. A strong and charismatic leader who is committed to the job sets up the value systems and cultural edifice and efficiently manages people contributing to the firm's vision. A business minded leader, lacking genuine passion and commitment toward social mission will be hesitant to give priority to social objectives often compromising these for profit maximization.

Battilana (2018) discusses the unique pressures that leaders face in social enterprises. Further, he also discusses about how four major functions and areas can help to overcome these challenges. These encompass the alignment of business objectives with social objectives, the organization and arrangement of initiatives that advance these objectives, the facilitation of socialization processes for newly hired employees through training, compensation, and the establishment of informal interactions. Given the potential conflict between financial gain and the pursuit of social objectives, leaders of social enterprises must demonstrate significant creativity and innovation (Kerlin, 2006).

### 4.2.7 Accessibility and Affordability for the Customers

Just coming up with innovative solutions is not enough for social enterprises to address many persisting social problems, they also need to ensure that the offerings are accessible to the right sections of customers, these offerings must be easily usable and also affordable, given their low purchasing powers. Expensive goods and services are rarely available to the impoverished. Low prices, on the other hand, do not imply a lack of quality. Since, there is typically a skill shortage among the poor, social entrepreneurs need to make their products or services simple to use and easy to get in terms of technology, market access, and pricing. Because they care about doing business ethically, social entrepreneurs are unlikely to compromise or cut corners on any of these accounts. They have a challenge of making high-quality products affordable through innovations (Van der Have & Rubalcaba, 2016). Strategic use of social media is one way in which the social enterprises can address the issues of accessibility and reach (Islam et al., 2019).

### 4.2.8 Driven by Business Ethics

Ethics play a very important role in any business environment. Social entrepreneurs' endeavor to include an ethical code of conduct in their agendas of their social enterprise, thus highlighting the presence of ethics and good conduct. The relevance and creation of ethical capital in social enterprises through a mix of economic capital and social capital allow social entrepreneurs to mobilize their resources morally and ethically (Bull et al., 2010). Social entrepreneurs are consciously driven by a moral and an ethical obligation and a deep desire to work toward the improvement of societies (Zahra et al., 2009).

It is worth identifying the key ethical frameworks that have been employed in social entrepreneurship research. Spence (2014) highlights these key ethical frameworks explicitly in her work on small and medium enterprises which include research from the works of Kant, theories and concepts based on utilitarianism, egoism, social contract theory, virtue ethics, and other contemporary theories of ethics.

While the concept of a social enterprise is not just to 'do good', but also examine how the outcomes are achieved with the right intentions. The representation of social entrepreneurs as 'embodiments of ethical virtuousness that enables them to pursue social mission' (Bornstein, 2004; Drayton, 2002), clearly emphasizes on the importance of virtues while doing business.

While discussing about ethics, we also need the understand the role of 'moral intensity'. High levels of 'perceived moral intensity' may have a positive influence of scaling up in order to achieve greater accuracy, speed, and an increase in the scope of social impact (Smith et al., 2016).

Social entrepreneurs are driven by social motive which is often termed the 'humanity factor'. In terms of money, the value achieved through social entrepreneurship is not as high as that produced by business firms and large corporates. But the non-economic value is of high significance as a motivating factor for the social entrepreneurs. Social entrepreneurs aim to create value for all the stakeholders (individual/organization/society), including owners/capital providers/investors, workforce/employees, suppliers, consumers, community, society, and environment. The advancements in social entrepreneurship research need a support through proper ethical analysis (Cornelius et al., 2008). Since social enterprises are socially motivated, they need to be ethically sound, principled, morally justified, and ethically acceptable.

Business ethics coupled with being honest and accountable to the partners and stakeholders are of utmost importance in social entrepreneurship (Sijabat, 2016). These high moral standards and ethical codes drive the social enterprises to ensure fairness in the distribution of outcomes pertaining to growth thus resulting in overall growth and inclusion and inclusion of all in the growth process. Social entrepreneurship needs to overcome a variety of challenges as it has to pass through the prism of disciplinary perspective (Perrini, 2006). Economic, social, and ethical capital are all equally critical in case of social enterprises (Ridley-Duff & Bull, 2011). Application of business ethics allows the social enterprises to build trust–based relationships with community members at large. These relationships are driven by values of mutual accountability, collaboration, openness, and honesty.

### 4.2.9 Overcoming the Challenges of Market Failures

Market failures are normal outcomes of market-based and demand and supply-driven economies which cause various social needs to go unfulfilled (Phillips et al., 2015). The major issue with market-driven system is that people with purchasing power get access to the outcomes of market economy while the underprivileged often remain ignored. Market failures foil the aspirations of the marginalized and resource-starved sections of society from contributing and taking advantage of economic activities (Rauniyar & Kanbur, 2009). Market systems are driven by profit maximization goals and hence have little concerns for the anomalies in distribution of their growth outcomes. Social entrepreneurship strives to fill in the gaps left by market-oriented approach by coming up with inclusive models of economic development which has an egalitarian approach in including marginalized sections in mainstream developmental processes. These socially oriented approaches meet the unfulfilled demands of the fringe elements of society, while at the same time ensure economic viability by being innovative, competitive in market through their innovative practices and approaches. They are able to generate ample goodwill, networks, and social capital in the communities they operate and are able to draw support from them to overcome the tough times during market down-turns.

### 4.2.10 Alignment with Universal Goals

Doukas, et al. (2014) proclaimed that the firms with goals limited to meet the organization's goals as per the established norms often achieve inferior results as compared to the ones aligning their firm objectives social development-related issues, striving to meet the highest standards of environmental practices and making sincere efforts toward fulfillment of corporate social responsibility (CSR) expectations. The goals set by a company, the goals of government of a country, and the goals of global-level bodies like the United Nations often converge more harmoniously in the case of social enterprises when compared to business ventures. *S*ocial entrepreneurship helps achieve all-inclusive development, taking care of social, political, cultural, and/or environmental dimensions of development aligning the holistic list of goals identified by the UN (as Sustainable Development Goals [SDGs]) for sustainable development (UN, 2015). These goals are often holistic, futuristic, and aim at sustainable development supporting social, economic, and environmental aspects (Lourenço, 2013).

### 4.2.11 Environmental Concern and Green Business

There is urgent need of balancing the usage of resources to fulfill the current generation's economic needs and ensuring sufficient availability of natural resources for future generations. Social entrepreneurs' contribution in this balancing act is of paramount significance. Recent surge in environmental disturbances and consequent problems like pandemics, extreme pollution, new diseases, heightened stress, etc., are only going to be more pronounced in the coming days. In such a scenario the role of 'green entrepreneurs' who balance productivity with optimal and balanced extraction of resources from environment are going to be all the more important. Those social entrepreneurs who attempt to address environmental issues through an entrepreneurial solution are termed as 'green entrepreneurs' (UNCTAD, 2017). Such entrepreneurs are going to be pioneers in overcoming environmental challenges and pandemic situations (like the latest COVID-19 pandemic).

Green entrepreneurial techniques have been crucial in tackling resource shortages and growing environmental restrictions by improving economic gains, empowering social welfare, and preventing environmental degradation (Jiang et al., 2018). This system, also known as green entrepreneurship, reorganized the use of scarce resources to boost productivity while also promoting environmental protection (Chuang & Yang, 2014). As a result, these methods enhance the potential for business growth and market value (Jiang et al., 2018). The natural resource-based perspective suggests that, in order to sustain and safeguard the survival of businesses, especially in light of the growing number of environmental concerns, businesses should incorporate external environmental factors into their strategies and practices (Hart, 1995; Yunus & Michalisin, 2016).

### 4.2.12 Responding to the Left-Out Segments of Society

Social entrepreneurs are equipped with the capacity to identify the unfulfilled socio-economic requirements of society, their social aim, and their aptitude for problem-solving, hence they are unique and highly regarded. By giving the disadvantaged groups in society better, non-discriminatory access to electricity, health care, education, and sanitation, social entrepreneurs have increased value, wealth, and dignity. Numerous examples can be found which demonstrate the tremendous efforts that different social entrepreneurs have made to support the oppressed by being incredibly inclusive. According to the Schwab Foundation (2020) report, by safeguarding livelihoods, promoting social inclusion movements, and promoting environmental sustainability, its network of approximately 400 preeminent social innovators and entrepreneurs has significantly improved the lives of over 622 million people in over 190 countries.

There are numerous instances of social entrepreneurs reaching out to 'left-out' segments of society in Indian context as well. For instance, Dr. Armida Fernandez, founder trustee at SNEHA, an NGO that has been working on lack of health amenities, undernourishment, and violence issues in Mumbai's urban slums. Dr. Fernandez (in 1989) set up Asia's first milk bank at Sion Hospital and later launched SNEHA in the early 1990s with the goals of controlling maternal and neonatal mortality and gender-based violence. She found that people in slums were not taking proper preventive and post hospitalization care. It was evident that women were not empowered enough to look at their own and their family's health. She realized that hospitals and existing institutions were not able to solve these issues. Dr. Armida Fernandez decided to work in the slums herself and made substantial difference in the living standards of people in those areas. Similarly, Geeta Ramanujam, Executive Director at Kathalayas International Academy of Storytelling India, made sincere efforts to bring social change through storytelling. She tried to transform the behavior of children and other underprivileged through storytelling. She believes that storytelling is a powerful tool with the potential to play a transformative role in society through influencing the thought process, and creative ways of connecting with humane touch. There are various other studies and research which show how the lives of the beneficiaries have changed due to the efforts of the social entrepreneurs in creating social value.

Rural development and involvement of rural community in the mainstream of socio-economic growth march is sine qua non for the holistic and sustainable development of any society, more so in developing economies where agrarian contribution is high (a notable example being India). Unfortunately, conventional developmental efforts have often failed this critical segment of society. Social entrepreneurs play a vital role in putting forth the urgency of rural and community development. Studies of social entrepreneurship have demonstrated (see Seelos & Mair, 2005) that social entrepreneurs help communities with basic life necessities, enhance their capabilities, and give them tools to be economically more productive. Rural communities (including aspiring entrepreneurs in those communities) face many challenges and resistances in implementing innovative approaches for inclusive growth (Yang & Li, 2008). Social entrepreneurs often play a leading role in rural communities toward evolving a new social vision with a more inclusive and egalitarian societal framework which doesn't exclude underprivileged people (Cornwall, 1998).

There are perennial problems facing rural communities. For instance, farmers do not receive decent prices for their produce, the market reach is immensely limited for them, there are continuous technology lags with regard to new agricultural devices and farming practices. There is ever-increasing need for green and organic approach to agriculture for sustainability and farmers constantly need expert inputs and guidance in that. Similarly, capacity to support international sales, finding an international market, obtaining certification for their organic products, awareness of organic agriculture techniques, etc., all require expert inputs from time to time (Sijabat, 2016). Social entrepreneurs help them 'bridge' these gaps and help them realize their deserved potentials. The ability of social entrepreneurship to develop capacity, market access, and information flow helps farmers to produce and sell their products in the most profitable ways.

Reaching the population at the bottom rung of the social hierarchy is the prime principle of social entrepreneurs and they keep striving to ensure that there is an equitable dispersal of 'the overall fruits of development'. They illustrate alternative development models to achieve socio-economic prosperity of all.

## 5 Discussion

### *5.1 Social Entrepreneurship, Inclusive Growth, and Sustainable Development*

Based on a comprehensive consideration of the various facets of social entrepreneurship, the authors have crafted a conceptual framework (Fig. 1) that delineates the distinct dimensions, and their role in sustainable growth in specific environmental contexts. Social entrepreneurship is seen as a phenomenon with distinct features which enable to operate in given environment and make the best use of available resources to come out with economically viable and socially relevant solutions. The interplay of social enterprises with the context (comprising both micro- and macro-level factors) has been discussed in detail in the earlier sections of the chapter. The interface between social enterprise and the macro and micro factors influences the effectiveness and outcomes of social enterprises contributing to inclusive growth and sustainable development. The distinctive dimensions empower social entrepreneurs to optimize available resources and navigate the macro-environmental factors that influence the business landscape. Social entrepreneurs exhibit a remarkable ability to adapt and respond to macro-level environmental uncertainties while efficiently utilizing micro-level resources. These distinctive features set social entrepreneurs apart from conventional entrepreneurs, thereby fostering inclusive growth and sustainability.

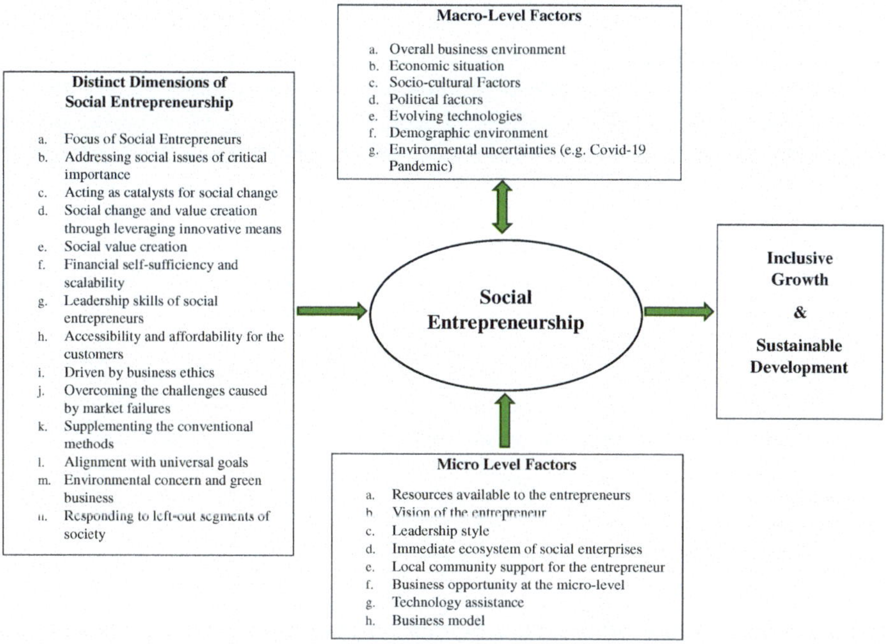


**Fig. 1** The conceptual framework: Social entrepreneurship, inclusive growth, and sustainable development (*Source* Developed by the authors)

The conceptual framework highlights the key dimensions of social entrepreneurship along with micro- and macro-level factors that impact social entrepreneurship thus contributing to inclusive and sustainable development. The distinct dimensions of SE such as addressing social issues, leadership skills of social entrepreneurs, and alignment with universal goals have been highlighted in the left side column. It is contended that social enterprises, driven by technology and innovation, controlled through viable and scalable business models, working toward social value creation, and led by empathetic leadership create possibilities of noble and viable solutions to persistent socio-economic challenges. They provide creative and sustainable solutions for more inclusive and equitable wealth generation. The distinct dimensions depicted in the framework demonstrate the key aspects which also differentiate social enterprises from other business enterprises and have been discussed elaborately in earlier sections of the paper. There is a constant exchange between the social enterprises and their ecosystems—at immediate or micro-level environment as well as overall context or macro-level factors operating in a community or nation. The framework focuses on the macro factors that include the overall business environment, economic situation socio-cultural factors, political factors, evolving technologies, demographic situation, and the environmental uncertainties such as the COVID-19 pandemic which impact social entrepreneurship. Social entrepreneurship helps achieve comprehensive development, aligning the micro factors (firm-level factors and immediate environmental factors of the enterprise) with the macro-level factors (social, political, cultural, and other macro-environmental dimensions) of development which is in tune with the holistic developmental goals identified universally by global agencies like UN. The macro-level ecosystem factors have an impact on the functioning, strategizing, survival, and success of social enterprises. Also, in the long run, the outcomes of social enterprises will have positive influence in shaping the macro environment. Also, the micro-level factors influence the functioning of social enterprises. The micro factors impacting SE include firm-level resource availability, vision of the entrepreneurship, leadership style, opportunity sensing and strategies for social value creation, immediate ecosystem of the social enterprise, technology adoption, and business model.

Overall, a combination of micro and macro factors and the distinct dimensions impact the environment and ecosystem in which social enterprises operate, leading to more inclusive and sustainable development.

## 5.2 *Implications and Future Research*

The research study will have significant implications for policy makers as it delves into issues pertaining to inclusion and balanced development. Social entrepreneurs create a vision and through innovative means, they make efforts to identify the unmet social needs and address them. Social entrepreneurs have been illustrated as change catalysts who use entrepreneurial ways for coming up with systemic solutions to social, economic, and environmental problems. These will be found useful by policy makers and development planners. The study highlights how social entrepreneurship helps fill in the gaps left by market-oriented approach by opting for more inclusive models of economic development with egalitarian philosophy drawing the marginalized sections into the mainstream of developmental processes. These findings help government and non-government agencies, NGOs, and other change champions in framing policies for more balanced socio-economic development. They will gain new perspectives and useful insights on making their enterprises self-sustainable and independent of charity, philanthropic initiatives, and government subsidies or support. Various NGOs and self-help groups involved in crisis management will have useful takeaways from the study.

The study found social entrepreneurship to be critical contributors in responding to the unique challenges of the COVID-19 pandemic. The values of empathy, creative problem-solving abilities, and crisis management were visible during the COVID-19 pandemic when many social entrepreneurs came forward to help the urgent needs of the society in various ways such as arranging for medicines, food, blood, ambulances, etc. Their core emphasis on achieving social mission and their capacity to combine the available resources in novel ways helps them to reach out to the 'left-out' segments of society. It enables them to bring about 'social change' toward inclusive growth and sustainable development. This aspect can have implications in case of disaster management plans for similar future disasters offering alternate pathways to overcome such crisis situations.

The research has implications for social entrepreneurs themselves who can gain insights and further their cause of contributing meaningfully toward the society. This can lead to further research pertaining to inclusion of social enterprises in mainstream of economic growth plans. Apart from this, this research also has a significant contribution toward social entrepreneurship teaching, training, and educational initiatives. The study offers a useful framework to students and educators for structured interaction on SE topics. The various concepts discussed in the paper are aligned with the sustainability goals of UNDP framework and can be useful reading for courses on SE. The research has abundant potential to act as the groundwork for future research in the domain. The findings provide a platform for framing hypotheses to be used by researchers in their future research.

## 6 Limitations of the Study

The given research is an exploratory study trying to identify the role of social entrepreneurship in helping holistic, sustainable, and all-inclusive growth and is restricted to deliberations of ideas at a conceptual level. Hence it lacks the support of empirical data. The findings of the study could have been theoretically more credible if tested through empirical surveys or cases of extensive interviews and data-based analysis. The study could have highlighted the core themes of discussion in more emphatic ways if some pertinent, topical case studies on social entrepreneurship could have been included. The researchers aim to take the study ahead and address these issues in their future work.

## 7 Conclusion

In conclusion, this study underscores the transformative potential of social entrepreneurship, emphasizing its capacity to address deep-rooted disparities and facilitate a more equitable, inclusive, and prosperous society. It offers innovative, technology-driven solutions that are accessible in more equitable ways and emphasizes sustainable and replicable approaches. As Christie and Honig (2006) aptly emphasized, social entrepreneurship is expected to become even more relevant in the future. This is because all stakeholders, including governments, public agencies, non-profit organizations, and entrepreneurial firms, recognize its significant contribution to holistic and sustainable development. The heightened uncertainties in business, social, and environmental realms following the COVID-19 pandemic only serve to underscore the prominent role of social entrepreneurship in the development process.

The unforeseen challenges posed by the COVID-19 pandemic are forcing business enterprises—whether profit-oriented or non-profit-oriented to redefine their purposes and perspectives. It has forced all to come up with more novel solutions. Contributing toward social causes and being responsive to environmental concerns along with the usual focus on financial performances is going to be the new norm henceforth. A recent study conducted by Deloitte suggests that nearly 86% of millennial respondents who were surveyed said that the success of a business is more than just generating profits and that employer should be contributing toward doing 'right' things for the benefit of the society. While COVID-19 is threatening progress and advancement of the economy, social entrepreneurs are trying to improve the lives of people by providing better access to employment, education, energy, sanitation, and health. The emerging opportunities of providing effective solutions to problems and social concerns are providing ample scope for social enterprises to explore new avenues. New technologies and innovations in the digital space are also encouraging social enterprises to contribute toward the social impact of the society.

When compared to business entrepreneurs, there is a greater likelihood of social entrepreneurs to play the role of change agents and catalysts for inclusive growth and sustainable development. Social entrepreneurs contribute toward comprehensive development, integrating social, political, cultural, and/or environmental dimensions of development. Social entrepreneurs emphasize on meeting the needs (both economic and social) and aspirations of marginalized segments of the population through creative business ideas and sustainable strategies.

Furthermore, it is evident that social entrepreneurship is creating significant opportunities for the youth in our country, enabling them to be innovative and creative in devising sustainable solutions to long-standing issues. Today, the youth view social entrepreneurship as a viable career alternative, thereby making a valuable contribution to sustainability. Young social entrepreneurs no longer perceive this path as a short-term endeavor but pursue it with great enthusiasm, channeling their creativity into this domain. The innovations driven by social entrepreneurship can prove highly influential, particularly during turbulent times, as they explore alternative avenues for social change and strive to make a positive and meaningful impact.

## References

Aggarwal, A. (2012). India's services sector: Gateway to development? *Economic & Political Weekly, XLVII* (26 & 27), 119–123.

Alvord, S. H., Brown, L. D., & Letts, C. W. (2004). Social entrepreneurship and societal transformation: An exploratory study. *The Journal of Applied Behavioral Science, 40*(3), 260–282.

Auerswald, P. (2009, Spring). Creating social value. *Stanford Social Innovation Review*, 49–55.

Austin, J., Leonard, H., Reficco, E., & Wei-Skillern, J. (2005). Corporate Social Entrepreneurship: The new frontier. In M. Epstien & K. Kanson (Eds.), *The Accountable Corporation*. Praeger.

Austin, J., Stevenson, H., & Wei-Skillern, J. (2006). Social and commercial entrepreneurship: Same, different, or both? *Entrepreneurship Theory and Practice, 47*, 370–384.

Bacq, S., & Lumpkin, G. T. (2021). Social Entrepreneurship and COVID-19. *Journal of Management Studies, 58*, 285–288. https://doi.org/10.1111/joms.12641

Bansal, S., Garg, I., & Sharma, G. D. (2019). Social entrepreneurship as a path for social change and driver of Sustainable Development: A systematic review and research agenda. *Sustainability, 11*, 1091. https://doi.org/10.3390/su11041091

Barowalia, A. (2010). Public private partnership in social sectors for harmonised development in India. *OIDA International Journal of Sustainable Development, 1*(4), 29–37.

Battilana, J. (2018). Cracking the organizational challenge of pursuing joint social and financial goals: Social enterprise as a laboratory to understand hybrid organizing. *Management, 21*(4), 1278–1305.

Bognar, G. (2005). The Concept of Quality of Life. *Social Theory and Practice, 31*(4), 561–580.

Bornstein, D. (2004). *How to change the world: Social entrepreneurs and the power of new ideas.* Oxford University Press.

Bridgstock, R., Lettice, F., Özbilgin, M. F., & Tatli, A. (2010). Diversity management for innovation in social enterprises in the UK. *Entrepreneurship and Regional Development, 22*, 557–574.

Bull, M., Ridley-Duff, R., Foster, D., & Seanor, P. (2010). Conceptualising ethical capital in social enterprise. *Social Enterprise Journal, 6*(3), 250–264. https://doi.org/10.1108/17508611011088832

Choi, N., & Majumdar, S. (2014). Social entrepreneurship as an essentially contested concept: Opening a new avenue for systematic future research. *Journal of Business Venturing, 29*(3), 363–376.

Christie, M. J., & Honig, B. (2006). Social entrepreneurship: New research findings. *Journal of World Business, 41*, 1–5.

Chuang, S. P., & Yang, C. L. (2014). Key success factors when implementing a green-manufacturing system. *Production Planning Control, 2014*(25), 923–937.

Corner, P. D., & Ho, M. (2010). How opportunities develop in social entrepreneurship. *Entrepreneurship Theory and Practice, 34*, 635–659.

Cornelius, N., Todres, M., Janjuha-Jivraj, S., Woods, A., & Wallace, J. (2008). Corporate social responsibility and the social enterprise. *Journal of Business Ethics, 81*(2), 355–370.

Cornwall, J. R. (1998). The entrepreneur as a building block for community. *Journal of Developmental Entrepreneurship, 3*, 141–148.

Dacin, P. A., Dacin, M. T., & Matear, M. (2010). Social entrepreneurship: Why we don't need a new theory and how we move forward from here. *The Academy of Management Perspectives, 24*(3), 37–57.

Dees, J. G. (1998). The meaning of social entrepreneurship. Accessed on May 20, 2020 from http://www.fntc.info/files/documents/The%20meaning%20of%20Social%20Entreneurship.pdf

Dees, J. G., & Battle Anderson, B. (2006). Framing a theory of social entrepreneurship: Building on two schools of practice and thought. In R. Mosher-Williams (Ed.), *Research on social entrepreneurship: Understanding and contributing to an emerging field* (pp. 39–66). Aspen Institute.

Defourny, J., & Nyssens, M. (2013). Social innovation, social economy and social enterprise: What can the European debate tell us? In F. Moulaert, D. MacCallum, A. Mehmood, & A. Hamdouch (Eds.), *International handbook on social innovation. Social innovation, collective action and transdisciplinary research* (pp. 40–52). Edward Elgar.

Doukas, H., Tsiousi, A., Marinakis, V., & Psarras, J. (2014). Linguistic multi-criteria decision making for energy and environmental corporate policy. *Information Sciences, 258*, 328–338.

Dube, S. C. (1988). *Modernization and development the search for alternative development.* The United Nations University.

Drayton, W. (2002). The citizen sector: Becoming as entrepreneurial and competitive as business. *California Management Review, 44*(3), 120–132. https://doi.org/10.2307/41166136

Hansson, F., Norn, M. T., & Vad, T. B. (2014). Modernize the public sector through innovation? A challenge for the role of applied social science and evaluation. *Evaluation, 20*(2), 244–260.

Ghosh, B. (2009). NGOs, civil society and social reconstruction in contemporary India. *Journal of Developing Societies, 25*(2), 229–252.

Glicken, M. D. (2011). *Social work in the 21st century: An introduction to social welfare, social issues, and the profession.* SAGE Publications Inc.

Gokarn, S. (2007). Dimensions of Inclusiveness—I, Business Standard, 31 December 2007, http://www.igidr.ac.in/pdf/drSubirMedia/2007_Dec_31_Dimensions_of_Inclusiveness-I.pdf

Gore, M. S. (2003). *Social development: Challenges faced in an unequal and plural society.* Rawat Publications.

Gupta, J., Pouw, N., & Ros-Tonen, M. (2015). Towards an elaborated theory of inclusive development. *European Journal of Development Research, 27*(4), 541–559.

Halme, M., & Korpela, M. (2014). Responsible innovation toward sustainable development in small and medium-sized enterprises: A resource perspective. *Business Strategy and the Environment, 23*, 547–566.

Hall, J. K., Daneke, G. A., & Lenox, M. J. (2010). Sustainable development and entrepreneurship: Past contributions and future directions. *Journal of Business Venturing, 25*, 439–448.

Hart, S. L. (1995). A natural-resource-based view of the firm. *Academy of Management Review, 1995*(20), 986–1014.

Hebb, T., Madill, J., & Brouard, F. (2012). Exploring social transformation, financial self-sufficiency, and innovation in Canadian social enterprises. https://doi.org/10.3138/9781442694477-012

Hermans, F., Roep, D., & Klerkx, L. (2016). Scale dynamics of grassroots innovations through parallel pathways of transformative change. *Ecological Economics, 130*, 285–295.

Hibbert, S. A., Hogg, G., & Quinn, T. (2002). Consumer response to social entrepreneurship: The case of the Big Issue in Scotland. *International Journal of Nonprofit and Voluntary Sector Marketing, 7*, 288–301.

Howaldt, J., Kopp, R. & Schwarz, M. (2015). Social innovations as drivers of social change—Exploring Tarde's contribution to social innovation theory building. https://doi.org/10.17877/DE290R-16448; http://hdl.handle.net/2003/34374

Humberg, K., & Kleemann, L. (2014). *Enhancing the contribution of social business to sustainable development*. OECD.

Islam, M. and Ozuem, W. (2019, June). *The impact of social media on social entrepreneurship in a developing country.* Conference, Oxford, United Kingdom. https://www.researchgate.net/publication/333677213_The_impact_of_social_media_on_social_entrepreneurship_in_a_developing_country

Jiang, W., Chai, H., Shao, J., & Feng, T. (2018). Green entrepreneurial orientation for enhancing firm performance: A dynamic capability perspective. *Journal of Cleaner Production, 198*, 1311–1323.

Johnson, B., & Andersen, A. D. (2012). *Learning, innovation and inclusive development: New perspectives on economic development strategy and development aid*. Aalborg University Press.

Kerlin, J. (2006). Social enterprise in the United States and Europe: Understanding and learning from differences. *VOLUNTAS: International Journal of Voluntary and Nonprofit Organizations, 17*(3), 246–263.

Kozuka, E. (2014). Inclusive development: Definition and principles for the post-2015 development agenda. In JICA Research Institute (Ed.), *Perspective on the post-2015 development agenda* (pp. 109–122). JICA-RI.

Leadbetter, C. (1997). *The rise of social entrepreneurship.* Demos.

Lee, N. (2019). Inclusive growth in cities: A sympathetic critique. Regional Studies. *Taylor & Francis Journals, 53*(3), 424–434.

Lepak, D. P., Smith, K. G., & Taylor, M. S. (2007). Value creation and value capture: A multilevel perspective. *Academy of Management Review, 32*, 180–194.

Lourenço, F. (2013). To challenge the world view or to flow with it? Teaching sustainable development in business schools. *Business Ethics: A European Review, 22*, 292–307.

Mair, J., & Marti, I. (2006). Social entrepreneurship research: A source of explanation, prediction, and delight. *Journal of World Business, 41*, 36–44.

Manzini, E. (2007). Design, social innovation and sustainable ways of living: Creative communities and diffused social enterprise in the transition towards a sustainable network society, Draft. https://www.scribd.com/document/122762793/Ezio-Manzini-Design-Social-Innovation-and-Sustainable

Martin, R. L., & Osberg, S. (2007). Social entrepreneurship: The case for definition. *Stanford Innovation Review*, 28–39.

Mazzucato, M., & Wray, L. R. (2015). *Financing the capital development of the economy: A Keynes-Schumpeter-Minsky. Levy Economics Institute*. Levy Economics Institute of Bard College.

McKinley, T. (2010). Inclusive Growth Criteria and Indicators: An Inclusive Growth Index for Diagnosis of Country Progress, ADB Sustainable Development Working Paper Series, Asian Development Bank, June 2010. https://www.adb.org/sites/default/files/publication/28493/adb-wp14-inclusive-growth-criteria.pdf

Meyskens, M., Robb-Post, C., Stamp, J., Carsrud, A., & Reynolds, P. (2010). Social ventures from a resource-based perspective: An exploratory study assessing global Ashoka Fellows. *Entrepreneurship Theory & Practice, 34*(4), 661–668.

Mulgan, G., Tucker, S., Ali, R., & Sanders, B. (2007). *Social innovation: What it is, why it matters and how it can be accelerated*. The Young Foundation.

Murthy, R. K., Sagayam, J., Rengalakshmi, & Nair, S. (2008). Gender, efficiency, poverty reduction, and empowerment: Reflections from an agriculture and credit programme in Tamil Nadu, India. *Gender and Development, 16*, 101–116.

National Innovation Council. (2013, November). *Report to the people: Third year*. National Innovation Council Government of India. https://static1.squarespace.com/static/5356af05e4b095ff0fea9e11/t/5398b142e4b02d32b20de300/1402515778055/Report+to+the+People+2013+-+National+Innovation+Council+%28English%29.pdf

Nicholls, A. (2006). Introduction. In A. Nicholls (Ed.), *Social entrepreneurship: New models of sustainable change* (pp. 1–35). OXFORD University Press.

OECD. (2010). Social entrepreneurship and social innovation. *SMEs, entrepreneurship and innovation*. OECD Publishing. https://doi.org/10.1787/9789264080355-50-en

OECD/European Union. (2017). *Boosting social enterprise development: Good practice compendium*. Local Economic and Employment Development (LEED), OECD Publishing. https://doi.org/10.1787/9789264268500-en

Partzsch, L., & Ziegler, R. (2011). Social entrepreneurs as change agents: A case study on power and authority in the water sector. *International Environment Agreements: Politics, Law and Economics, 11*, 63–83.

Perrini, F. (2006). *The new social entrepreneurship: What awaits social entrepreneurship ventures?* Edward Elgar.

Perrini, F., Vurro, C., & Costanzo, L. A. (2010). A process-based view of social entrepreneurship: From opportunity identification to scaling-up social change in the case of San Patrignano. *Entrepreneurship and Regional Development, 22*, 515–534.

Phillips, W., Lee, H., James, P., Ghobadian, A., & O'Regan, N. (2015). Social innovation and social entrepreneurship: A systematic review. *Group & Organization Management, 40*(3), 428–461.

Phills Jr, J. A., Miller., D. T., & Deiglmeier, K. (Fall 2008). Rediscovering social innovation. *Stanford Social Innovation Review*, 34–43.

Ratten, V. (2020). Coronavirus (Covid-19) and entrepreneurship: Changing life and work landscape. *Journal of Small Business & Entrepreneurship, 32*(5), 503–516.

Rauniyar, G., & Kanbur, R. (2009). *Inclusive growth and inclusive development: A review and synthesis of Asian Development Bank literature*. Independent Evaluation Department, Asian Development Bank.

Renko, M. (2012). Early challenges of nascent social entrepreneurs. *Entrepreneurship Theory and Practice, 37*. https://doi.org/10.1111/j.1540-6520.2012.00522.x

Ridley-Duff, R., & Bull, M. (2011). *Understanding social enterprise: Theory and practice*. Sage.

Rinkinen, S., Oikarinen, T., & Melkas, H. (2016). Social enterprises in regional innovation systems: A review of Finnish regional strategies. *European Planning Studies, 24*, 723–741.

Porter, M. E., & Kramer, M. R. (2006). Strategy and society: The link between competitive advantage and corporate social responsibility. *Harvard Business Review, 84*(12), 76–92.

Schumpeter, J. (1934). *The theory of economic development (originally published in 1911)*. Harvard University Press.

Seelos, C., & Mair, J. (2005). Social entrepreneurship: Creating new business models to serve the poor. *Business Horizons, 48*, 241–246.

Singh, A. (2016). *The process of social value creation: A Multiple-case study on social entrepreneurship in India*. Springer Publications.

Sijabat, R (2016, July–September). Promoting inclusive and sustainable development through social innovation and social entrepreneurship. *TECH MONITOR*.

Smith, B. R., Kistruck, G. M., & Cannatelli, B. (2016). The impact of moral intensity and desire for control on scaling decisions in social entrepreneurship. *Journal of Business Ethics, 133*(4), 677–689. https://doi.org/10.1007/s10551-014-2447-6

Smith, P. A. C., & Sharicz, C. (2011). The shift needed for sustainability. *The Learning Organization, 18*(1), 73–86. https://doi.org/10.1108/09696471111096019

Spear, R. (2006). Social entrepreneurship: A different model? *International Journal of Social Economics, 33*, 399–410.

Spence, L. J. (2014). *Business ethics and social responsibility in small firms*. In E. Chell & M. Karatas¸-özkan (Eds.), *Handbook of research on small business and entrepreneurship*. Edward Elgar.

Stoddart, H. (2011). *A pocket guide to sustainable development governance*. Retrieved May 10, 2016, from http://www.uncsd2012.org/content/documents/A%20Pocket%20Guide%20to%20Sustainable%20Development%20Governance.pdf

Szczanowicz, J., & Saniuk, S. (2016). Evaluation and reporting of CSR in SME sector. *Management, 20*, 96–110.

Townsend, D., & Hart, T. (2008). Perceived institutional ambiguity and the choice of organizational form in social entrepreneurial ventures. *Entrepreneurship Theory and Practice, 32*, 685–700.

UN. (2009). *Green growth and sustainable development*. Retrieved May 15, 2016, from http://www.un.org/en/ga/second/64/greengrowth.pdf

UN. (2015) *Transforming our world: The 2030 Agenda for Sustainable Development*. Seventieth session.

UNCTAD. (2017). *Promoting entrepreneurship for sustainable development: A selection of business cases from the empretec network*.

UNDP (2012). *Case studies on sustainable development practice: Triple wins for sustainable development*. Retrieved April 9, 2016, from http://www.undp.org/content/dam/undp/library/Cross-Practice%20generic%20theme/Triple-Wins-for-Sustainable-Development-web.pdf

UNDP. (2019). *Human Development Report 2019*. UNDP.

Van der Have, R. P., & Rubalcaba, L. (2016). Social innovation research: An emerging area of innovation studies? *Research Policy, 45*(9), 1923–1935.

Vujanovic, P. (2015). *Policies for inclusive and sustainable growth in Indonesia*. OECD Publishing.

Warnock, R. (2013). *Using social innovation to drive entrepreneurship among young unemployed people*. Winston Churchill Memorial Trust.

Weerawardena, J., & Mort, G. (2006). Investigating social entrepreneurship: A multi-dimensional model. *Journal of World Business, 41*, 21–35.

Westley, F., & Antadze, N. (2010). Making a difference: Strategies for scaling innovation for greater impact. *The Innovation Journal: The Public Innovation Journal, 15*(2).

World Bank Report. (2009). *The World Bank Annual Report 2009*. https://doi.org/10.1596/978-0-8213-7946-2

Yang, J. Y., & Li, J. (2008). The development of entrepreneurship in China. *Asia Pacific Journal of Management, 25*, 335–359.

Yunus, E. N., & Michalisin, M. D. (2016). Sustained competitive advantage through green supply chain management practices: A natural-resource-based view approach. *International Journal of Services and Operations Management, 2016*(25), 135–154.

Zahra, S. A., Gedajlovic, E., Neubaum, D. O., & Shulman, J. M. (2009). A typology of social entrepreneurs: Motives, search processes and ethical challenges. *Journal of Business Venturing, 24*(5), 519–532. https://doi.org/10.1016/j.jbusvent.2008.04.007

## *Web References*

https://timesofindia.indiatimes.com/spotlight/why-social-entrepreneurship-is-the-need-of-the-hour-during-covid-19/articleshow/76281889.cms?fbclid=IwAR1rNkEkEQ0ltybcIhAzOCPU-32f8cGbI_j0rFLVhPNIq8BxbYuEwPVQavc

https://www.weforum.org/agenda/2020/05/schwab-foundation-covid-response-alliance-social-entrepreneurs-coronavirus-recovery-response/

http://okapia.co/uploads/projects/attachment/257049627260814%20Health%20Report.pdf

https://www.weforum.org/agenda/2021/05/6-ways-social-entrepreneurs-are-saving-lives-in-india/

https://www.thehindubusinessline.com/news/world/social-entrepreneurs-turn-creative-in-this-pandemic-time/article33130118.ece

https://openknowledge.worldbank.org/bitstream/handle/10986/35701/Social-Entrepreneurship-for-Inclusive-Growth-in-the-Democratic-Republic of Congo.pdf?sequence=1&isAllowed=y

Outlook. (2020, June). The world economy on a tightrope. http://www.oecd.org/Economic-outlook/june-2020/#

World Bank. (2020, June 8). Projected poverty impacts ofCOVID-19 (coronavirus). https://www.worldbank.org/en/topic/poverty/brief/projected-poverty-impacts-of-COVID-19. According to a COVID Response Alliance for Social Entrepreneurs 2020 analysis.

# Social Enterprise: Social Value and Process Challenges in Solid Waste Management During the COVID-19 Pandemic

**Sumit Mitra and Aakriti Deepak**

**Abstract** This chapter focuses on understanding of solid waste management, highlighting the changes being attempted and the challenges being faced at the interphase of waste generation and collection in the context of the COVID-19 pandemic. One of the challenges in waste management is the absence of a culture of segregation of waste at the generation points. An additional dimension to segregation of solid waste is the health hazard due to the infectious nature of the waste, particularly mixing with the general non-infectious waste making the entire mass potentially infectious. Using a qualitative case method, this research examined the process challenges of social enterprises engaged in solid waste management when facing external emergencies like the COVID-19 pandemic. Data was gathered by interviewing project coordinators and founder-operations heads of social enterprises involved in solid waste management in urban and rural areas. The findings suggest that, in emergencies like the pandemic, social enterprises highlight the criticality of resourcing, social networking, and empathy in waste management. They do this through processes adopted for addressing the problems of fear of contact, spread of infection through handling of waste, and easing the reluctance to participate in segregation, collection, and disposal of waste.

**Keywords** Waste management · Social enterprise values · Processes change · Resourcing · Networking · Empathy

## 1 Introduction

Banga (2011) provides a classification of solid waste. According to her, solid waste is the byproduct of human and animal activities. These can be classed based on their original use (such as packaging waste), material (glass, paper, or plastics), physical features (combustible or biodegradable), origin (household, commercial, industrial,

---

S. Mitra (✉) · A. Deepak
Indian Institute of Management, Kozhikode, Kerala, India
e-mail: smitra@iimk.ac.in



E. M. Reji and S. Majumdar (eds.), *Social Enterprise Values and Processes*, India Studies in Business and Economics, https://doi.org/10.1007/978-981-97-3252-4_3

or agricultural), and safety factors (hazardous or radioactive). Banga (2011) provides evidence that multiple studies recommend the reuse and recycling of solid waste (SW) (Banga, 2008; Ekere & Drake, 2009).

However, Banga (2011) highlights that before any recycling activity can take place, the garbage must be segregated. Here, according to her, one of the issues with trash management is the lack of a culture of classifying waste by kind at the production sites. This leads to the mingling of various types of garbage. Recycling may necessitate further solutions, but the separation of solid waste at the source is the first step. Ehrampoush and Moghadam (2005) propose that effective recycling campaigns should be designed to enhance public knowledge of environmental issues, as well as attitudes and behaviors connected to recycling.

An additional dimension to the segregation of solid waste is the health hazard due to the infectious nature of the waste. A special category of solid waste that includes sharps, human tissues or body parts, and other infectious materials (Baveja et al., 2000), is referred to as "Hospital Solid Waste" and "Biomedical Solid Waste" (Manohar et al., 1998). If the infectious component gets mixed with the general non-infectious waste, the entire mass becomes potentially infectious. In late December 2019, the world woke to the truth of a pandemic of Coronavirus Disease (COVID-19), with the possibility of causing dangerous respiratory difficulties and quick transmission putting COVID-19 in the rundown of the Public Health Emergency of International Concern (PHEIC). During this pandemic condition, the expulsion of biomedical waste created from crisis facilities treating COVID-19 patients demanded unprecedented thought as they were potential bearers of the disease SARS-CoV-2 (Ramteke & Sahu, 2020).

A number of social enterprises (SE) like Saahas and Swachha Eco Solutions work closely with urban municipal corporations and village local self-governments (panchayats) in solid waste management. Such social enterprises directly involve themselves in one or more aspects of solid waste collection and disposal and support local government in an advisory capacity, thus helping link CSR projects of corporations to solid waste management by local self-government. Therefore, the activities of such social enterprises are challenged by recent health hazards associated with solid waste management in the wake of the spread of the COVID-19 pandemic. It is important to understand how such challenges to solid waste management have impacted the values of social enterprises as enshrined in their mission and manifested in the processes adopted by them. This chapter's objective is to fill this gap by having a better understanding of the challenges to the mission of social enterprises in the field of solid waste management when facing external emergencies like the COVID-19 pandemic, which severely test their work processes.

## 2 Background

COVID-19 pandemic conditions increase manifold biomedical waste management's special case, wherein hazards and risks exist not just for the generators and operators but also for the general community (Sandhu & Singh, 2003). Therefore, in the solid waste management process, there are a number of critical break points that impact the success or failure of the process, beginning with the segregation of waste at the point of generation. At the bulk solid waste generation level, the onus lies on hospitals and other health care institutions to ensure that there are no adverse health and environmental consequences as a result of their waste handling, treatment, and disposal activities (Abor, 2013; Patil & Pokhrel, 2005; Pokhrel & Viraraghavan, 2005). Beyond hospital waste in the case of COVID-19, sanitation laborers and cloth pickers are in danger of dealing with plain clinical waste rising out of homes where COVID-19 patients are isolated. Disposed-off covers, gloves, and tissues could be potential hotspots for the spread of this profoundly infectious disease. Additionally, it is essential to guarantee that this waste doesn't arrive at regular dumping grounds (Ramteke & Sahu, 2020).

As per Banga (2011), in the extraordinary condition of solid waste management during the COVID-19 epidemic, the design process should begin by assessing the public's prior understanding of recycling activities. This should include the amount of knowledge, its sources, and practical application also corroborated by other authors like Palmer (1995) and Tucker et al. (1998). Banga (2011) continues that other authors like Ballantyne and Packer (1996) and Ballantyne (1998) highlighted the importance of the public's attitudes and present practices in the context of waste disposal in the times of the COVID-19 pandemic.

When asked if they had ever heard of recycling, many households in Kampala, Uganda said they had not, but practiced it by selling scrap metal, plastics, paper, polythene, and glass so scrap dealers made them conscious of recycling (Banga, 2011). As a result, the majority of homes separated waste because they earned money from it or used it to make compost and manure from vegetable and other decomposable waste, which they deposited in a pit. However, the same homes demonstrate a lack of awareness and ignorance by being careless in disposing of other objects, such as broken bottles and tin, as well as other scrap items with no commercial sale value. As reported by Banga (2011), in a survey conducted in Kawempe Division of Kampala, Uganda, even those who are separating are only partially aware of the toxicity, pollution, and destruction of garbage when they state

> I always remove anything plastic from the waste because the plastics do not rot and thus, they spoil our land. I remove them and burn them. I know it is not right to burn the plastics but it is better than leaving them to spoil the land.

Krishna of The Independent Media Centre India (2004) noted there was a prevalence of reuse/recycling of biomedical waste due to: (i) lucrative monetary returns and (ii) a lack of awareness about the problems associated with biomedical waste. Importantly, in many situations, it indicated lackadaisical implementation of rules, which again is a case of ignorance.

One approach to ensuring better solid waste management (SWM), particularly of the infectious type, was to have Biomedical Solid Waste (Management and Handling) Rules 1998 that make it mandatory for hospitals, clinics, other medical institutions, and veterinary institutions to dispose of biomedical solid waste as per the law. As per regulation, non-infectious and domestic waste was collected in black polyethylene bags and placed in bins, while infectious waste was collected in red, yellow, and blue color-coded polyethylene bags placed within blue high-density polyethylene bags labeled with a biohazardous infectious materials symbol in specific bins. Such infectious waste was packaged to: (i) protect waste handlers and the public from possible injury and disease that could result from exposure to the waste and (ii) avoid attracting rodents and vermin and be disposed of in an incinerator. Fresh and stringent guidelines for handling COVID-19 waste were put out by the GOI's Central Pollution Control Board as late as March 18, 2020. The guidelines suggest that handlers of such wastes need to be provided with adequate training and PPE, including three-layered masks, splash-proof aprons, gloves, gumboots, and safety goggles (Kulkarni & Anantharama, 2020). In view of the urgency of the situation and precaution from fear of catching the infection, it needs to be seen how it impacts the historical attitude toward segregation of waste as discussed before, particularly in terms of the expected change in attitude at the transaction point between the generator of waste and its handling and disposal.

For successful enforcement of regulation, cooperation to inform and educate waste generators and collectors, as well as to alter attitudes toward waste management in light of the society-wide adverse impact of the pandemic nature of COVID-19 becomes necessary. This needs to be accompanied by training, and financial and physical resources like PPE uniform, gloves, masks, anti-splash aprons, etc. Some prominent ideas generated globally included decentralized waste management, reduction in curb side mixed waste collection and recycling, due to reluctance of citizens to use recycled material for fear of infection (Kahlert & Bening, 2020).

While most discussions center around safety guidelines and capacity issues in COVID-19 waste management, little is known about the process challenges these create for social enterprises operating with a social mission, limited resources, the need to work in cooperation with different stakeholders and stringent regulation.[1]

## 3 Social Enterprise: Value Creation and Its Process

The social mission is clear and important to social entrepreneurs. It goes without saying that this influences how social entrepreneurs view and evaluate possibilities. Instead of wealth creation, mission-related effects become the primary criterion.

[1] Parts of the literature on solid waste management during COVID-19 have been taken from the authors earlier publication referenced as Mitra, S., & Deepak, A. (2024). Role of Technology in Solid Waste Management: Social Enterprise in a Pandemic. *Journal of Entrepreneurship and Innovation in Emerging Economies, 10*(1).

Because social entrepreneurs act as change agents in the social sector and have as their goal the development and sustainability of social value (rather than just private wealth), it is therefore intrinsically difficult to quantify the creation of social value (Dees, 1998). More so as social value creation is done by engaging in a process of continuous innovation, adaptation, and learning (Austin et al., 2006; Mair & Marti, 2006; Perrini, 2006). This helps to formalize the project's underlying social aim and core values by highlighting the roles that people, context, and organizational arrangements play as the process progresses (Perrini et al., 2010). Social entrepreneurs therefore look for an opportunity for value creation without regard to the potential for value capture (or profits) (Santos, 2010). This is manifest in the use of any combination of available institutions and resources as also empowerment not control of beneficiaries and partners in achieving value creation.

Multiple authors have referred to the criticality of resources for the success of SE. These include financial resources, human resource skills in terms of marketing, planning, bookkeeping, stakeholder interaction, and risk mitigation (Sharir & Lerner, 2006; Wronka, 2013). While SEs require the same set of resources as any other enterprise (Meyskens et al., 2010), they have to deal with the trade-off between achievement of social mission and efficiency of resource utilization. Moreover, the predominant focus on social value creation and the inability to provide market rates of return on investment make SEs less attractive for traditional profit seeking investors (Lumpkin et al., 2013; Peredo & McLean, 2006). Consequently, SEs end up operating under resource constrained conditions, having to rely on obtaining resources below the market rate or use non-economic exchange through sponsorship, volunteers, and grants to obtain them (Haugh, 2007). The maintenance of relationships, networks, and political skills was critical because trust and reciprocity, rather than pure market transactions, dominated access to such embedded resources (Austin et al., 2006). Consequently, securing sufficient funding has always depended on how SEs convey their capacity to create social impact through value creation and how they interact with pertinent stakeholders (Mish & Scammon, 2010; Peñaloza & Mish, 2011). This shows that the effectiveness of SEs' social networking efforts and their resource allocation are closely related.

Nonetheless, there is still a lack of understanding of the broader systemic, cultural, socio-economic, political, and historical elements that influence the kinds of social enterprises that arise in a particular setting (Hazenberg et al., 2016). Specifically, socio-economic and cultural settings found in various parts of the world might contribute to geographical disparities between regions (Doherty et al., 2009). One variable identified as a success factor for SE is social networks (Sharir & Lerner, 2006). This includes partnership, or the ability to negotiate and sustain a core set of relationships for the benefit of the SE, including the involvement of local stakeholders and beneficiaries for the long term (Boyer et al., 2008). Others, like Wronka (2013), have focused on social capital and local community involvement. An essential component of social network theory that pertains to comprehending how individuals, groups, actors, and organizations interact with one another inside networks is provided by Granovetter's (1985) groundbreaking work on embeddedness. According to Brass (1984), Mehra et al. (2001), and Qureshi et al. (2016), social network theory explains how an actor's or organization's positionality within a network or ecosystem acts as both an enabler and a constraint on their behavior, mediating their development and the successful pursuit of their goals. The ties among actors and organizations also operate as mediators in the flow of resources, knowledge, and information (Uzzi, 1996), including financial and emotional resources (Jack, 2005). The nature of "strong ties" and "weak ties" in the relationship with stakeholders (Granovetter, 1973) should influence the nature and amount of resources. Weak ties are crucial because they represent bridges to access networks or groups of people (Soetanto, 2017). Yet, in comparison with strong ties, the amount of information, support, or empathy to be evoked through weak ties is uncertain (Cruz & Fromm, 2018).

It is seen that the social network of individuals and organizations or institutions not only links to tangible resources like physical and financial but also intangible resources like knowledge and emotions like empathy. In discussing empathy in the context of public administration, Edlins (2021) observed the capacity for empathy, or the capacity to identify, comprehend, and react to the sentiments of another, provides a means of genuinely transforming public service, mainly through involving the "Other" and strengthening the bond between the people and their government. But according to Zanetti (2011), the industry seldom considers empathy as a core working value. According to Brewer et al. (2000), empathy is understood as pro-social qualities such as altruism, moral conviction, and impartiality. It is also associated with concepts like open-minded reasoning, impartiality, accountability, fairness, and empathy (Guy et al., 2008). Additionally, empathy is linked to ideas of love, caring, empathy, and devotion (Perry et al., 2008). Edlins (2021) has pointed out that empathy is often linked to other positive attributes, such as compassion (Brewer et al., 2000; Guy et al., 2008; Horton, 2008), respect (Lewis & Gilman, 2012; Paarlberg et al., 2008), and inclusion (Lewis & Gilman, 2012). However, in all of these cases, empathy is portrayed in an obscure and inadequate manner, and vaguely defined.

We adopt the definition of empathy provided by Guy et al. (2008) which states that empathy is "the capacity to comprehend and value the circumstances of the citizen and react appropriately." We also agree with their assertion that empathy is commonly linked to "the deliberate inhibition of one's own emotions while simultaneously displaying a different emotion" (2008, p. 66). As stated by Anderson and Konrath (2011), individuals vary in their ability to empathize, which is an inherent skill. They assert that while some individuals possess a natural aptitude for it, others must actively cultivate and refine it as a learned ability.

We experience a certain portion of the empathy process. But there are other dimensions to empathy as well, such as the fact that we often act in ways that other people could perceive or feel. The majority of these are to making decisions, responding appropriately, and demonstrating empathy for others' emotions (Gerdes & Segal, 2009; Hojat, 2007; Wiseman, 1996). As a result, empathy is not only an emotion but also a behavior. Practicing empathy can change the behavior of the person who is giving empathy, since it enables them to establish connections with others that encourage collaboration and togetherness instead of conflict and isolation (Konrath et al., 2011).

Empathy-givers may behave differently as a result, possibly in ways that change the course of events. As Zanetti and King put it, empathy "epitomes the existential human dilemma of how people come to grips with the inevitable conflicts between their egoistic needs and their social obligations." This is precisely the significance of empathy in public service (Hoffman, as referenced in Zanetti & King, 2013). In an empathetic connection, this allows the empathy-giver to "feel satisfied because he/she senses they have been of help and fulfilled the need to be useful to others" (Wiseman, 1996). Furthermore, empathy-receivers "feel valued and more ready to understand themselves and change" because they satisfy their fundamental desire to be understood (Wiseman, 1996).

Consequently, empathy makes it possible for people to put aside their judgments, which fosters more collaborative and interactive environments. This suggests that empathy for the social enterprise's beneficiaries promotes human flourishing, which in turn helps social businesses grow (Pavlovich & Krahnke, 2012). This claim implies a close relationship between the social enterprise mission and empathy as motivation. Through expanding upon and utilizing empathy, social entrepreneurs can cultivate fruitful relationships with legislators, recipients, and employees. Empathy can support the accomplishment of a social objective and have an impact on organizational behavior and job satisfaction. Empathy, in turn, encourages transparent and genuine leadership in a new way. According to Gerdes et al. (2010), conducting more studies on empathy enhances knowledge of social entrepreneurship, which aids in the creation of social structures that are both environmentally and morally sound.

## 4 Research Method

An extensive literature review was done to understand the issues and challenges faced by social enterprises in solid waste management during the COVID-19 pandemic. It was evident from the literature review that social enterprises working in the area of waste management had faced changes in values and processes in an attempt to keep their mission alive when it was severely put to the test due to the change in composition and quantity of waste generated due to emergencies like that faced during the current pandemic.

This research focuses on an understanding of solid waste management, highlighting the changes being attempted and the challenges being faced at the interphase of waste generation and collection in the context of the COVID-19 pandemic. In the lockdown and social distancing context, data was gathered by extensively interviewing project coordinators and founder-operations heads of two social enterprises involved in solid waste management, from bulk waste generators to households.

Given the exploratory nature of the study, an inductive multiple case-study approach (Eisenhardt, 1989) was adopted. As the research explores a "how" question investigating a process, a case-study approach was adopted (Eisenhardt & Graebner, 2007; Yin, 2003). Compared to a single case study, the multiple case-study research design offers a more grounded, robust, generalizable, and testable framework (Eisenhardt & Graebner, 2007). The way to prove something is real is to replicate it using several case studies (Mir & Watson, 2001). The deliberate selection of case studies assures valuable information on the phenomenon being studied (Eisenhardt, 1989) that suitably recognizes the unique context of the COVID-19 pandemic situation. To select cases that help maximize what we learn (Stake, 1995), the primary concern was in the selection of social enterprises (SE) involved in solid waste management. To understand the process completely, it was necessary to ensure that the SE worked in both urban local body areas and rural panchayat areas.

To "tease out and disentangle a complex set of factors and relationships in one or a small number of instances" (Easton, 2010, p. 119), a mix of purposive and snowballing techniques for selection was used based on prior information. Information on one of the samples "Saahas" from a case study on the company[2] analyzed as part of coursework on social innovation by the second author helped choose "Saahas" as a sample. The other case "Swachha Eco Solutions" was identified by its association with "Saahas" as also recommended by an expert in solid waste management when the subject of research was being discussed with her as part of Delphi or expert input. When approached with the objective of the research, the social enterprises agreed to participate in the research. The data was collected through semi-structured interviews conducted over Zoom, Google Meet, and/ or WhatsApp video in adherence to pandemic protocols. Data was also collected through secondary sources like websites and online articles for triangulation.

An interview protocol, including a semi-structured questionnaire covering the key areas on which data was to be collected, was developed after going back and forth between the authors and another expert working in the field of solid waste management (Yin, 2003). The expert had extensive experience working with different solid waste constituencies, having organized hackathons in the area involving diverse stakeholders to find solutions to solid waste management problems. This helped clearly identify the critical set of stakeholders in solid waste management, both on the governance side and on the field application side, allowing to closely identify the type of issues arising from the pandemic.

The semi-structured questionnaires were mailed to the interviewees in advance, which served as a background for the discussion. Subsequently, with interview protocol serving as a conversational guide to direct conversation, interviews broadly followed this semi-structured questionnaire but delved deep into a subject with a trail of follow-up questions building on one another (Rubin & Rubin, 2005). The interviews were recorded, duly transcribed, and sent back to the interviewee for comments and clarifications as part of the reliability and validity of information provided, forming the basis for a follow-up interview or clarification over email. This process of back and forth was continued till saturation was reached in line

---

[2] *Saahas Zero Waste Solutions; Getting to a Product Market Fit While Cleaning Up India* by Suresh Bhagavatula, Deepa Iyer, Menaka Rao, Indian Institute of Management Bangalore case number IMB 775.

with the primary area of investigation of the research so as to develop linkages and frameworks in a pre-paradigmatic stage (Eisenhardt, 1989; Miles et al., 2014).

# 5 Case Background

## *5.1 Saahas*[3]

Saahas is a hybrid organization with a non-profit wing working in the field of waste management. Saahas is into urban and rural waste management, consultancy, research, and working for the welfare of waste workers and the informal sector. At Saahas, they believe that *waste segregated at the source is a resource.* By recycling a large part of the waste after segregation, they want to reduce the burden on landfills. By engaging the informal sector in this chain of waste management, they not only acknowledge their efforts but also hope to economically uplift the informal sector. Saahas has been working actively to ensure compliance with Municipal Solid Waste Management Rules (2016) by targeting a change in behavior by creating awareness through its programs like "Stump the Right Bin" during cricket's IPL event, attempting to implement source segregation. Community waste processing centers, built under public–private partnerships, were set up by Saahas. Segregated waste from the community was brought here and processed. Saahas had a cohesive team to execute these diverse projects. The company follows a vision of India to become a leading "Circular Economy" where "Nothing is Waste." For this, it pursues a mission to pilot innovative resource management programs; collaborate closely with communities, administrators, businesses, and law makers; and evolve next practices for adoption of Circular Economy. Two senior project managers (henceforth PM1-Saahas and PM2-Saahas) were extensively interviewed for about 120 min each in different sittings.

## *5.2 Swachha Eco Solutions*[4]

Swachha is a one stop solution for waste management consulting services and recycling of waste streams for all the sectors. Their goal is to gift the coming generations a zero-waste future with the slogan …towards a greener future…. Swachha provides waste management services for various businesses, commercial and residential settlements, and municipalities. Besides solid waste, the services include wet waste management, landscape collection, recycling, and waste audits. They

[3] Website: https://saahas.org/.

[4] Website: http://www.swachhaecosolutions.com/.

wanted to make a difference in the field of waste management through their professional services by providing the best support with high standard of service. With the changing nature of rules and regulations, Swachha Eco Solutions aims to make waste management a relaxed process for their clients by understanding their unique waste management requirements. Besides inputs from the expert mentioned before, who worked closely with Swachha, and helped develop the questionnaire, one of the founder-directors of Swachha was interviewed for about 90 min separately (henceforth FD-Swachha) to capture the broad perspective emerging from solid waste management in pandemic times and steps taken by Swachha in response.

## 6 Findings

As both SEs Saahas and Swachha identified, solid waste management was challenging, given the lack of segregation. This resulted in inefficient incineration and material recovery resulting in a lot of banned material finding its way into landfills and remaining there polluting soil, water table, etc. To this were added the health hazards of the infectious pandemic COVID-19. As a result, in the immediate vicinity of the waste generator and waste collector, there prevailed a fear of spread of the infection from handling waste, particularly where COVID-19 patients were known to reside. This put the SE mission targeting zero waste in a circular economy to severe test. As identified by one of the interviewees:

> Besides the existing shortcomings in segregation waste there was reluctance on part of both waste generators and collectors to improve the existing processes to meet SE mission in times of pandemic. There is a tremendous increase in the number of employees and the number of projects in the field of waste management. With Swach Bharat Abhiyaan more corporates are venturing into the field of waste and there has been a 200% increase in the projects. [PM2-Saahas]

### *6.1 Resourcing*

In its resource provision role to SWM, SEs like Saahas secure private corporate CSR project funding for which it guides and facilitates funded waste management projects. These projects require networking with different levels of the government right up to the village level under the Panchayat to have their SWM projects qualify for funding. Accordingly, Saahas helps set up community waste processing centers built under public–private partnerships where segregated waste from the community is brought for processing to avoid carrying waste over long distances to landfills [PM1-Saahas]. Valuable human resources needed for these activities and provided by SEs, involve recruitment and training of staff in the mission and values of SE pivotal on “nature knows no waste” to fulfill SE mission while working on SWM projects of partners—corporate and government. This highlights the adoption of a process that is effective only when financial and human resource generation work in tandem with efficient management of networking across different stakeholders including corporate and government bodies contributing to SWM. As highlighted by an interviewee during discussions:

> On the ground implementations of a SWM project revolves around primary protocols of awareness building among waste generators and collectors through education on waste. For this mobilization of another set of resources to break economic and caste barriers where required, involving ASHA workers, school and college students to enact street plays in public premises and schools is necessary. This requires SEs to network with government bodies and educational institutions to access the ASHA workers and school students. [PM1-Saahas]

Another process challenge faced during COVID-19 solid waste management operations as highlighted in an interview:

> Collection of dry SW became irregular from two days a week in many areas of Bangalore City. With longer accumulation of waste in households' tendency was to mix dry waste with Covid waste in the same bin. Not just this put the waste collectors at a risk of catching infection from waste, at times, the collection vehicle was so small that all dry waste landed up being tossed up together in a small auto rickshaw. [PM2-Saahas]

To remedy this, SEs like Swachha entered into networking with a different set of stakeholders to create resources. They manage to create self-help groups out of ragpickers with government issued identity cards (ID). To become vehicle suppliers to contractors removing SW in specific areas, such self-help group members were trained as drivers and their helpers and were assisted by Swachha to either buy vehicles or rent them. [FD-Swachha]. According to FD-Swachha, "This way they are thus encouraged to become micro entrepreneurs."

SEs like Swachha create more resources for consumption of non-recyclable plastics by sending for co-processing in the cement factories or for shredding to make tiles. This required tying up with cement kilns like Ultratech Bharti for providing this waste plastic feed in return for money. This segregation and subsequent aggregation of waste from authorized recycling centers by SEs before selling to Swaacha, needed documentation to ultimately obtain a certificate of the amount of waste destroyed/reused. Such accounts were audited [FD-Swachha].

These programs of physical contact were however seriously challenged in times of COVID-19 demanding alternative contactless programs and processes. A complete shift to technology is needed, for example, use of recorded programs over loudspeakers attached to garbage collection vehicles and mobile apps and camera-based recording of segregation of waste [PM1-Saahas]. This required a new set of networks to be developed by SEs including their acceptance and use by both waste generators and collectors to achieve goals of awareness on segregation of SW. Simultaneously, the risk was of losing the personal level trust-based relationships in SWM developed so far together with the resources discussed.

All the above networking challenges of SE mostly in the domain of "weak ties" outside of family and close acquaintances (entirely professional and hence transactional), not only affected the effectiveness of the changes envisaged but also raised questions on the strength of the emotional bonding of different stakeholders to the message communicated, particularly "empathy" that may be central to segregation in SWM but dependent on delivering promises. In this connection, in one of the interviews, the project manager from Saahas expressed that

> As a result sustainability of SWM projects undertaken by such SEs, beyond the CSR funding of corporates, with self-financing using waste generators payment for the removal of waste remains uncertain. Generators of waste had to see effective results in terms of improved SWM before they agreed to pay, particularly in the context of handling pandemic waste. Measures of effectiveness of the project shifted to effectiveness in handling of Covid-19 waste. [PM1-Saahas]

With the onset of the COVID-19 pandemic, the use of disposable PPE, masks, and gloves by waste collectors increased the cost of CSR projects, impacting their viability. Together with renewed interactions with the government to understand and implement their stricter COVID-19 protocols, this added a cost burden for segregation of COVID waste that was infectious [PM2-Saahas].

According to Saahas interviewees [PM1 & PM2], Saahas nevertheless distributed all kinds of protective gear to its employees/waste workers to be able to be on duty and handle increased SWM challenges. They made it mandatory to use face masks, face shields, and gloves while dealing with COVID waste. Saahas project managers also regularly monitored waste worker health. The protocol also required a reduction of waste by replacing plastic masks and other non-recyclable items with reusable items like cloth masks and their scientific disinfection.

The challenges of SWM in the midst of the pandemic, the mission of SEs involved in it, not only included identifying new resources to be mobilized but simultaneously involved redesigned networks in terms of partners as well as renewed relationships with existing partners as the above discussion indicates. However, actively discharging duty by accepting to handle COVID waste and also adhere to protocols while on duty required empathy from all stakeholders to the heightened risk in SWM due to the pandemic.

## 6.2 *Social Networking*

Communication designed by SEs like Saahas, in line with Municipal Solid Waste Management Rules (2016), targeted capacity building for executing agencies and education of stakeholders, through face-to-face contact based "Stump the Right Bin" during an IPL event, "Alag Karo" in Gurugram, and "Be Responsible" Bengaluru.[5] Similarly, Swachha partnered with various municipalities, residential complexes, and commercial settlements to help them manage waste effectively by providing solutions [FD-Swachha]. All such SWM suddenly came to an abrupt end given the changed COVID protocols of distancing and use of protective gear. As a result, Saahas found that not only did the existing networking with different stakeholders in generation, collection, and disposal of SW collapse, but even frequent real-time interaction between corporate CSR personnel and SE for planning of such projects in the

[5] Website of Saahas.

pandemic, shifted to remote updating over social media like WhatsApp, and frequent virtual meetings. From physical verification on site, virtual estimation required a more structured approach and relied on more nuanced experience of all stakeholders of such SWM projects [PM1-Saahas]. In greater emergency and crisis situations of the pandemic, the networks demanded more family-type "strong ties" relying on trust and transparency in a more professional "weak ties" setting. Process challenges for SEs arising out of this included scaling up of resources, faster capacity building for executing agencies, education of stakeholders, and ensuring adherence to government regulations.

But in highlighting contrast in challenges faced by SEs to bring about required process changes in Bengaluru urban and rural SWM, Swachha identified

> The fact that the response of different stakeholders as members of a social network addressing SWM problem varied is highlighted by SE observation that some residential areas in Bengaluru needed an active intervention by SE volunteers and Urban Local Bodies (ULB) needed to recruit few Waste Marshalls (ex-army, NCC cadets) to ensure segregation of waste, wearing of masks, and no open dumping of the waste to put the waste segregation process in place during the pandemic. [FD-Swachha]

In contrast, smaller Panchayats[6] in the outskirts of the city exhibited greater enthusiasm in educating their members regarding waste segregation and participating to set up an effective process for it. Such village projects received strong support from the panchayat who provided space to store dry waste. On the other hand, urban SWM problems were on a larger scale, multi-layered with many different contractors, municipalities, and other authorities (multiple stakeholders) involved in the chain of waste management [PM2-Saahas].

Not only did these different social networks mobilize resources at different paces but may have been assisted in doing so by the extent of empathy created through the process as adopted by SEs. This may have depended on the depth and complexity of the network, which was simpler in a village setting with the SE project manager and awareness team members interacting with Panchayat (local administration) members and other officials.

Bringing so many diverse groups together not only reflected different priorities when it came to resource generation and utilization but captured different degrees of empathy for the pandemic-related problem at hand, as captured through the effectiveness of the process put in place in SWM.

Given segregation at source was more voluntary than mandatory, different stakeholders including generators, felt that once the waste somehow left their household and was with the waste collector, it was the collector's responsibility to dispose of it somewhere far away, preferably outside city limits in large landfills. The only solution was appealing to the clients continuously to segregate waste as they are generated which was mostly ineffective as the predominant waste disposal followed the age-old NIMBY (Not In My Back Yard). Accordingly, the areas with a high number of COVID-19 cases stopped segregating waste.

[6] Rural elected self government.

## *6.3 Empathy*

As an expression of empathy toward the SWM stakeholders at field level, SEs like Swaacha helped rag pickers and other scavengers of the informal sector open bank accounts and maintain direct links with the government. It gives them job-training sessions like driving lessons, assistance with loans for vehicles, and the ability to chalk out operating processes and routes for them. Hand holding them for the first three years until they become independent. By empowering this vital stakeholder group, Swachha facilitates in resourcing the value chain of waste. This was challenged by expressing lack of empathy, as captured here:

> However, with the onset of the pandemic, like earlier times, they are not offered any water to drink by the households. The garbage vehicles are also stopped outside the society gate and all the collected garbage is also put outside the gate. On the brighter side it has made the work of the waste picker easier but as far as segregation of the same waste is concerned the percentage has certainly gone down. [FD-Swachha]

Therefore, for the effectiveness of the SWM process put in place by SE, empathy in understanding the mindset of government bodies, waste managers, private corporates as CSR partners, NGOs, and most importantly, the stakeholders generating and disposing waste, particularly in the emergency of the pandemic, hoped to bring about change.

As an example, SEs found that for sheer want of space, low-income households do not have a place to keep two dustbins at home for appropriate segregation of waste. SE experience also found that due to their daily survival struggle and low levels of education, they also did not have the required knowledge of segregation and its benefits. Under the circumstances, because of the nature of general household waste changing into an infectious one during the pandemic, the residents stopped segregating waste because of the fear of catching infection from handling waste. With the pandemic posing so many other problems, including livelihood loss, these households did not have segregation of waste on their priority list. It may therefore be expected that, under the circumstances, the empathy of low-income households toward other stakeholders driving segregation of waste may be a far-fetched idea, rendering processes adopted by SE ineffective.

As SE experience showed, on the other hand, high-income households behaved differently, as explained by one interviewee

> High income households are generally scared to even touch waste, they have no direct contact with the waste picker as well and do not prefer to come close to the collection staff for the fear of catching the virus. [PM2-Saahas]

In contrast, explaining behavior of middle-income households

> The middle-income household in contrast started segregating SW even more carefully with the outbreak of the pandemic. Acknowledging their membership to a larger social network that included waste workers, they identified the critical role of these workers in maintaining community health. In empathizing with the role of these waste collectors such middle-income households through their Resident Welfare Associations (RWA) collected money to distribute PPEs and sanitizers to the waste workers. [PM2-Saahas]

Given their deliberate avoidance of entering into social networks and keeping the social interactions transactional, high-income households tend to show characteristics of low empathy associated with "weak ties" again rendering processes adopted by SE in times of COVID ineffective, but for reasons that may be quite different from those of low-income households. In contrast, the behavior of middle-income households was symbolic of strengthening and supporting the processes adopted by SEs to fulfill their mission.

As a safety net for the work they do, if a waste worker with the Municipal Corporation catches the virus, the state government and the government of India have schemes in which the hospital expenses are taken care of. But only approximately half of all the sanitation workers were eligible. The rest all work on contractual basis and therefore in times of COVID are dependent on the contractor's empathy in the face of the perils of their job [PM2-Saahas]. Then the availability of such human resources to SE is uncertain unless these SEs exhibit empathy in providing protective gear and treatment expenses for such contract workers under corporate CSR or other donor funded schemes. In providing such treatment, SEs need to also be empathetic to the fact that about 10% of waste collectors are not strictly following rules as they find it very cumbersome to wear masks, PPE sets, and shields all day long while working in the heat and dust outdoors [PM2-Saahas].

In bringing into discussion a very different issue, Saahas SE observed,

> When a particular household is doing a good job in segregating waste or composting it, Saahas used to give a token of appreciation. But it ended up creating differences between the households. So, we have started to appreciate personally but not give token of appreciation when we see someone leading by exemplary work. [PM2-Saahas]

There are only certain expressions of empathy with SWM work as incorporated in the processes of SE that are valued, while others have the risk of creating biases among stakeholders adversely affecting the community level network of SE.

To continue to have scrap dealers as critical resources in SWM, helping them become small time entrepreneurs through material sourcing is needed to include training on safety issues related to COVID-19 infection when collecting scrap from dump yards. In spite of this, when sorting and recycling of waste had gone down, adversely affecting the "Kabadiwalas" or scrap dealers' regular income, as an expression of empathy, SEs like Saahas raised donations to support about 2000 such families by distributing food and ration kits.

## 7 Discussion

From SWM practice, we understand that recycling and reuse of waste are critical for its management. However, for any recycling activity to take place, the waste has to be segregated. One of the problems in waste management is the absence of a culture of segregating waste by type at the generation points. For this to occur researchers and experts have mandatorily called for an increase in society's environmental knowledge, its attitudes as well as its behavior toward recycling. With the spread of COVID-19, if the infectious component of SW gets mixed with the general non-infectious waste, the entire mass becomes potentially infectious for the society at large (Baveja et al., 2000; Ramteke & Sahu, 2020).

A number of SEs like Saahas and Swachha Eco Solutions, working closely with urban municipal corporations and village local self-governments (panchayats) in SWM, faced these hazards from COVID-19 spread. During these times, the values of these SEs as enshrined in their mission and their manifestation in the processes came under test. More than the safety guidelines and capacity issues, how pandemic-related challenges to SWM tested the values of social enterprises and the processes adopted by them was critical to be understood.

From the findings as identified in this paper, the SEs highlight the criticality of processes that help SWM in times of fear of contact, spread of infection through handling of waste, and hence of reluctance to participate in segregation, collection, and disposal of SW in the middle of the pandemic. Such processes stress on their effectiveness in resourcing efforts of SWM, identifying the impact of social networking across diverse stakeholders in the effectiveness of SWM and empathy in binding together the different stakeholders in the process. Therefore, resourcing, social network, and empathy form the apexes of a triangle that represents an effective process of SWM in times of crises like the pandemic for SEs that continue serving such missions as "zero waste" as in Fig. 1.

Resourcing in terms of providing for financial and human resources to manage SW during the COVID-19 pandemic, needs building and leveraging linkages across stakeholders, whether they be corporates with CSR projects or government bodies employing manpower who need to be reskilled, educated, and provided with protective gear. Such processes would lie along the continuum between resourcing and social networks. Disposal of the non-recyclable waste material needed access to cement kilns and tile making facilities. This process was organized such that different SEs like Saahas could use a single conduit of another SE like Swachha to access these consumers of non-recyclable material leveraging their social network.

Strong networking across different stakeholders in the chain of SWM at the time of the pandemic saw replacement of repeated personal contact and trust building similar to "strong ties" with faceless, technology-driven processes, supposed to create low

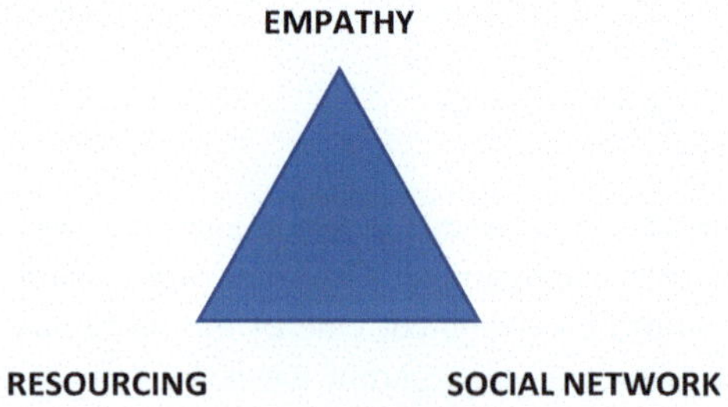


**Fig. 1** Conceptual framework (*Source* Developed by authors)

levels of empathy in professional "weak ties." However, these weaknesses were overcome by reinforcing "empathy" in different transactions by SEs whether it be in organizing scavengers into self-help groups to be trained in driving, support in getting loans to buy vehicles for SW transportation, or SE providing PPE and other gears for safety of waste handlers, organizing their health check and treatment. This was particularly effective for the large number of unorganized labor in the SWM business. Much of these processes are to be found on the continuum between empathy and social networks. Nature and extent of empathy created could however depend on the complexity and layered nature of networks. Greater empathy for the effectiveness of SWM, even in a pandemic, was created in simpler and wider rural networks involving SE, local government or panchayat, and other rural bodies. More complex networks in urban SWM did not evoke the required empathy and hence rendered SE processes ineffective in meeting their mission during crises like pandemic and/or inordinately expensive.

In understanding the diverse responses of different economic strata of society toward SW removal during the pandemic, SE exhibited empathy in adopting processes to solve the problems as in the case of assisting Kabadiwalas. This highlighted the role of SE processes in addressing issues lying on the continuum between empathy and social network. Essentially, empathy in its role as facilitating both resourcing and networking, highlighted how nuanced processes could be adopted for complex multi-layered networks in times of resource scarcity arising out of COVID-19 pandemic emergencies.

SE processes that show empathy toward waste collectors by providing protective gear and/or insurance and medical attention for COVID-19 cases, helped in keeping so many more such workers on the job of managing SW even in the midst of the pandemic. In that sense such processes clearly lie on the continuum between empathy and resourcing. So also when SE adopted processes to financially support scrap dealers as entrepreneurs and their families when their scrap collection business dropped during the pandemic. This way so many SWM resources were retained and helped to tide over the crisis.

## 8 Conclusion

Having SE mission-focused processes that built around the SE necessities of resourcing, social networking, and empathy in SWM during the crises of a pandemic, highlights how some combination of available institutions and resources, as also empowerment not control of beneficiaries and partners helped achieve value creation. The framework with the three apex objectives and processes along the continuum highlights how trust and reciprocity help access embedded resources in lieu of pure market transactions, manage relationships, network, and political skills through an understanding of the role of empathy.

The framework helps understand how individuals, groups, institutions, and organizations interact with each other within networks to explain the positionality of actors within a network or ecosystem that acts as both an enabler and a constraint on their behavior, thus mediating their development in the successful pursuit of SE mission and hence values. (Brass, 1984; Mehra et al., 2001; Qureshi et al., 2016). The relationships between actors also mediate the flow of resources, including financial and emotional (Jack, 2005), indicating a link of networks with resourcing and empathy as in the framework in Fig. 1. Since, in comparison with strong ties the amount of information, support, or empathy to be procured through weak ties is uncertain (Cruz & Fromm, 2018), this framework includes a reinforcing empathy in professional weak ties across stakeholders to compensate.

The framework in this paper seems to have heard what Zanetti (2011) argues, "we seldom," perhaps never, "see outright calls for empathy as a working value" in highlighting empathy in the framework. As claimed in literature, empathy here is not that is just felt but something that is done and therefore visible for others to appreciate and value, in turn helping SEs achieve their mission through the processes they adopt.

Therefore, empathy enables SEs and their stakeholders to suspend judgment (as in the case of attitude toward SWM of different socio-economic groups) to create more interactive and cooperative environments, suggesting empathy with the beneficiaries of social enterprise.

The importance of empathy in public service was recognized by social entrepreneurs engaged in SWM during the epidemic, as emphasized by Zanetti and King (2013). According to the same authors, this was the existential crisis that people faced: balancing their own selfish desires with their societal responsibilities. By doing so, SEs help both the people receiving empathy (such as SWM personnel) and the people giving it (the waste generators) to "feel valued and more ready to understand themselves and change" (Wiseman, 1996). However, for a complete understanding of SE values and processes in times of crisis, more studies in diverse contexts and natures of crisis need to be undertaken.

## References

Abor, P. A. (2013). Managing healthcare waste in Ghana: A comparative study of public and private hospitals. *International Journal of Healthcare Quality Assurance, 26*(4), 375–386.

Anderson, P., & Konrath, S. (2011, July 31). 'Why Should We Care?'—What to do about declining student empathy. *The Chronicle of Higher Education.* https://www.chronicle.com/article/Why-Should-We-Care-What/128420

Austin, J., Stevenson, H., & Weiskillern, J. (2006). Social and commercial entrepreneurship: Same, different, or both? *Entrepreneurship Theory and Practice, 30*(1), 1–22.

Ballantyne, R. (1998). Interpreting "Visions": Addressing environmental education goals through interpretation. In R. Ballantyne & D. Uzzell (Eds.), *Contemporary issues in heritage and environmental interpretation.* The Stationery Office.

Ballantyne, R., & Packer, J. (1996). Teaching and learning in environmental education: Developing environmental conceptions. *The Journal of Environmental Education, 27*(2), 25–32.

Banga, M. (2011, May). Household knowledge, attitudes and practices in solid waste segregation and recycling: The case of urban Kampala. *Zambia Social Science Journal, 2*(1), 4.

Banga, M. (2008). *The economics of solid waste management: The case of Kampala City, Uganda* [PhD Thesis]. Dar-es-Salaam University.
Baveja, G., Muralidhar, S., & Aggarwal, P. (2000). Hospital waste management—An overview. *Hospital Today, 5*(9), 485–486.
Brass, D. J. (1984). Being in the right place: A structural analysis of individual influence in an organization. *Administrative Science Quarterly, 29*, 518–539.
Brewer, G. A., Selden, S. C., & Facer, R. L. I. (2000). Individual conceptions of public service motivation. *Public Administration Review, 60*(3), 254–264.
Boyer, D., Creech, H., & Paas, L. (2008). Critical success factors and performance measures for start-up social and environmental enterprises. *Report for SEED Initiative Research Programme*, 115–139.
Cruz, A. D., & Fromm, I. (2018). Understanding the emergence of a social enterprise by highly skilled migrants: The case of Honduras Global Europa. *International Journal of Entrepreneurial Research and Behaviour, 25*(5), 801–818.
Dees, J. G. (1998). *Enterprising non-profits*. Harvard Business Review.
Doherty, B., Foster, G., Mason, C., Meehan, J., Meehan, K., Rotheroe, N., & Royce, M. (2009). *Management for social enterprise*. Sage.
Easton, G. (2010). Critical realism in case study research. *Industrial Marketing Management, 39*(1), 118–128.
Edlins, M. (2021). Developing a model of empathy for public administration. *Administrative Theory and Praxis, 43*(1), 22–41.
Ehrampoush, M. H., & Moghadam, B. (2005). Survey of knowledge, attitude and practice of Yazd University of Medical Sciences students about solid waste disposal and recycling. *Iranian Journal of Health Science and Engineering, 2*(2), 26–30.
Eisenhardt, K. M., & Graebner, M. E. (2007). Theory building from cases: Opportunities and challenges. *The Academy of Management Journal, 50*(1), 25–32.
Eisenhardt, K. M. (1989). Building theories from case study research. *Academy of Management Review, 14*(4), 532–550.
Ekere, W. J. M., & Drake, L. (2009). Factors influencing waste separation and utilization among households in the Lake Victoria Crescent, Uganda. *Waste Management, 29*, 3047–3051.
Gerdes, K., Segal, A., & Lietz, C. (2010). Conceptualising and measuring empathy. *British Journal of Social Work, 40*, 2326–2343.
Gerdes, K. E., & Segal, E. A. (2009). A social work model of empathy. *Advances in Social Work, 10*(2), 114–127.
Granovetter, M. (1985). Economic action and social structure: The problem of embeddedness. *American Journal of Sociology, 91*(3), 481–510.
Granovetter, M. (1973). The strength of weak ties. *American Journal of Sociology, 78*(6), 1360–1380.
Guy, M. E., Newman, M. A., & Mastracci, S. H. (2008). *Emotional labor: Putting the service in public service*. M.E. Sharpe.
Haugh, H. (2007). Community-led social venture creation. *Entrepreneurship, Theory & Practice, 31*(2), 161–182.
Hazenberg, R., Bajwa-Patel, M., Roy, M. J., Mazzei, M., & Baglioni, S. (2016). A comparative overview of social enterprise 'ecosystems' in Scotland and England: An evolutionary perspective. *International Review of Sociology, 26*(2), 205–222.
Hojat, M. (2007). *Empathy in patient care: Antecedents, development, measurement, and outcomes*. Springer Science & Business Media.
Horton, S. (2008). History and persistence of an idea and an ideal. In J. L. Perry & A. Hondeghem (Eds.), *Motivation in public management: The call of public service*. Administrative Theory & Praxis and Oxford University Press.
Jack, S. L. (2005). The role, use and activation of strong and weak network ties: A qualitative analysis. *Journal of Management Studies, 42*(6), 1233–1259.

Kahlert, S., & Bening, C. R. (2020). Plastic recycling after the global pandemic: Resurgence or regression? *Resource Conserve Recycle.* https://doi.org/10.1016/j.resconrec.2020.104948. Accessed 5 January 2021.

Konrath, S. H., O'Brien, E. H., & Hsing, C. (2011). Changes in dispositional empathy in American college students over time: A meta-analysis. *Personality and Social Psychology Review, 15*(2), 180–198.

Krishna, G. (2004). *Health care workers—Victims of occupational hazards.* IMC India, Independent Media Center. http://www.in-dia.indymedia.org/ downloaded on 27 January 2019.

Kulkarni, B. N., & Anantharama, V. (2020, November). Repercussions of COVID-19 pandemic on municipal solid waste management: Challenges and opportunities. *Science of the Total Environment, 743*, 140693.

Lewis, C. W., & Gilman, S. C. (2012). *The ethics challenge in public service: A problem-solving guide.* Wiley.

Lumpkin, G. T., Moss, T. W., Gras, D. M., Kato, S., & Amezcua, A. S. (2013). Entrepreneurial processes in social contexts: How are they different, if at all? *Small Business Economics, 40*, 761–783.

Manohar, D., Reddy, P. R., & Kotaih, B. (1998). Characterization of solid waste of a super specialty hospital: A case study. *Indian Journal of Environmental Health, 40*(4), 319–326.

Mair, J., & Marti, I. (2006). Social entrepreneurship research: A source of explanation, prediction, and delight. *Journal of World Business, 41*(1), 36–44.

Mehra, A., Kilduff, M., & Brass, D. J. (2001). The social networks of high and low self-monitors: Implications for workplace performance. *Administrative Science Quarterly, 46*, 121–146.

Miles, M. B., Huberman, A. M., & Saldana, J. (2014). *Qualitative data analysis.* Sage.

Mir, R., & Watson, A. (2001). Critical realism and constructivism in strategy research: Towards a synthesis. *Strategic Management Journal, 22*(12), 1169–1173.

Mish, J., & Scammon, D. L. (2010, Spring). Principle-based stakeholder marketing: Insights from private triple-bottom-line firms. *Journal of Public Policy and Marketing, 29*(1), 12–26.

Meyskens, M., Robb-Post, C., Stamp, J. A., Carsrud, A. L., & Reynolds, P. D. (2010). Social ventures from a resource-based perspective: An exploratory study assessing global Ashoka fellows. *Entrepreneurship Theory and Practice, 34*(4), 661–680.

Patil, G. V., & Pokhrel, K. (2005). Biomedical solid waste management in an Indian hospital: A case study. *Waste Management, 25*, 592–599.

Paarlberg, L., Perry, J., & Hondeghem, A. (2008). From theory to practice: Strategies for applying public service motivation. In J. L. Perry & A. Hondeghem (Eds.), *Motivation in public management: The call of public service.* Oxford University Press.

Palmer, J. A. (1995). Environmental thinking in the early years: Understanding and misunderstanding concepts related to waste management. *Journal of Environmental Education Research, 1*(1), 35–45.

Pavlovich, K., & Krahnke, K. (2012). Empathy, connectedness and organization. *Business Ethics, 105*, 131–137.

Perry, J. L., Brudney, J. L., Coursey, D., & Littlepage, L. (2008). What drives morally committed citizens? A study of the antecedents of public service motivation. *Public Administration Review, 68*(3), 445–458.

Peñeloza, L., & Mish, J. (2011). The nature and processes of market co-creation in triple bottom line firms: Leveraging insights from consumer culture theory and service dominant logic. *Marketing Theory, 11*(1), 9–34.

Peredo, A. M., & McLean, M. (2006). Social entrepreneurship: A critical review of the concept. *Journal of World Business, 41*, 56–65.

Perrini, F., Vurro, C., & Costanzo, L. A. (2010). A process-based view of social entrepreneurship: From opportunity identification to scaling-up social change in the case of San Patrignano. *Entrepreneurship & Regional Development, 22*(6), 515–534.

Perrini, F. (2006). *The new social entrepreneurship: What awaits social entrepreneurial ventures?* Edward Elgar.

Pokhrel, D., & Viraraghavan, T. (2005). Municipal solid waste management in Nepal: Practices and challenges. *Waste Management, 25*, 555–562.

Qureshi, I., Kistruck, G. M., & Bhatt, B. (2016). The enabling and constraining effects of social ties in the process of institutional entrepreneurship. *Organization Studies, 37*(3), 425–447.

Ramteke, S., & Sahu, B. L. (2020, September). Novel coronavirus disease 2019 (COVID-19) pandemic: Considerations for the biomedical waste sector in India. *Case Studies in Chemical and Environmental Engineering, 2*, 100029.

Rubin, H. J., & Rubin, I. S. (2005). *Qualitative interviewing: The art of hearing data* (2nd ed.). Sage Publications Inc. https://doi.org/10.4135/9781452226651

Sandhu, T. S., & Singh, N. (2003, June 30). *A hazard going unnoticed—Biological waste is a threat to the community at large*. The Tribune, online edition, Chandigarh, India, Monday.

Santos, F. M. (2010). *A theory of social entrepreneurship* [Working Paper, INSEAD, Fontainebleau].

Sharir, M., & Lerner, M. (2006). Gauging the success of social ventures initiated by individual social entrepreneurs. *Journal of World Business, 41*(1), 6–20.

Soetanto, D. (2017). Networks and entrepreneurial learning: Coping with difficulties. *International Journal of Entrepreneurial Behavior & Research, 23*(3), 547–565.

Stake, R. E. (1995). *The art of case study research*. Sage.

Tucker, P., Murney, G., & Lamont, J. (1998). Predicting recycling scheme performance: A process simulation approach. *Journal of Environmental Management, 52*(1), 31–48.

Uzzi, B. (1996). The sources and consequences of embeddedness for the economic performance of organizations: The network effect. *American Sociological Review, 6*, 674–698.

Wiseman, T. (1996). A concept analysis of empathy. *Journal of Advanced Nursing, 23*(6), 1162–1167.

Wronka, M. (2013, June 19–21). *Analyzing the success of social enterprises—Critical success factors perspective*. Conference Paper, Zadar, Croatia.

Yin, R. K. (2003). *Case study research design and methods* (3rd ed., Applied Social Research Methods Series, Vol. 5).

Zanetti, L. A., & King, C. S. (2013). Reflections on theory in action transformational public service revisited possibilities for changing the discipline. *Administrative Theory & Praxis, 35*(1), 128–143.

Zanetti, L. A. (2011). Cultivating and sustaining empathy as a normative value in public administration. In C. S. King (Ed.), *Government is us 2.0*. M.E. Sharpe.

# Exploring Social Finance as a Process for Value Creation in Social Entrepreneurship

**Purushottam Vishnu Bhandare and Samapti Guha**

**Abstract** This chapter aims to comprehend the ongoing developments within the emerging discipline of social finance and its role in value creation in social entrepreneurship. The discourse surrounding social finance is still in its infancy, yet it has attracted scholarly interest, prompting further exploration across various geographical contexts and dimensions. Social finance, now more commonly referred to as impact investment, has transformed over the past decade, driven by several factors. Among these factors is the increasing commitment of individual and institutional investors to address social issues on local, national, and global scales. The rise of social enterprises in recent years has been instrumental in driving the development of social finance. This study engages in literature-based discussions revolving around the theme of social finance. It conducts a critical assessment of research in this field, contrasting it with developments specific to India. The chapter commences by providing a brief overview of social finance and its relevance within the specific context of India. Subsequently, it delves into the various delivery systems and institutions operating within India's social finance realm. In conclusion, it offers insights and recommendations to enhance the impact of social finance further.

**Keywords** Social finance · Social value · Social entrepreneurship · Impact investing

P. V. Bhandare (✉) · S. Guha
Centre for Social Entrepreneurship, Tata Institute of Social Sciences, V N Purav Marg, Deonar P O, Mumbai, Maharashtra, India
e-mail: puru@uchicago.edu

S. Guha
e-mail: samapti@tiss.edu

 
E. M. Reji and S. Majumdar (eds.), *Social Enterprise Values and Processes*, India Studies in Business and Economics, https://doi.org/10.1007/978-981-97-3252-4_4

## 1 Introduction

The social finance initiatives were introduced long back in India with the nationalization of banks and the establishment of cooperative banks (Burgess & Pande, 2005). Social finance offers a distinctive chance to establish a robust and supportive financial system, ultimately fostering broader economic prosperity for the population. It is equally essential to recognize the social sector's positive contributions in many developing countries. The social banking system's inclusiveness and social orientation is the critical pillar of grassroots development. The banking business needs to be aligned with the developmental needs of the society it operates in. Social finance should be in sync with societal priorities, whereas our financial system is losing its social orientation and growing into an exclusive universe, disconnected from the social sector. Despite several social banking initiatives, penetration of social finance has not been seen as expected to be realized in terms of social and rural development.

Social finance juxtaposes social banking, which focuses on social capital needs. It provides the support needed to address societal priorities and intends to achieve financial returns and significant social and environmental impact. Typically, social finance involves activities such as socially responsible investing, environmental finance, development finance, and impact investing. Its aim is to enhance people's well-being by generating income and economic activity, creating employment opportunities, improving access to social services, and providing protection against unexpected risks (Burgess & Pande, 2005).

Social finance involves many stakeholders, including investors, policymakers, intermediaries, and service providers. In the Indian scenario, they are regulators, bankers, financial institutions, non-banking financial institutions (NBFCs), non-governmental organizations (NGOs), Self-help groups (SHGs), Banking correspondents (BCs), Bank Mitra, etc. They work in collaboration, fostering successful social finance. Having access to financial services plays a pivotal role in reducing income inequality and facilitating economic growth. Financial systems with a social focus enable individuals facing financial constraints to stabilize their expenses and safeguard themselves against economic uncertainties. Financial access encourages poor people to adopt banking practices such as savings and borrowing. This facilitates the building assets, investment in education, and pursuit of livelihood opportunities, ultimately leading to an enhancement in their quality of life (Agarwal & Mazumder, 2013).

The need for social and inclusive finance arises with evolving societal development or social problems. One of them is the inversion of social values. Social banking and social finance are centered around unleashing creative potentials, often referred to as Liberation Finance (Benedikter, 2011). Philosophically, it aligns with economic and ethical endeavors to work effectively under challenging situations and achieve overall growth.

Amartya Sen's capability approach (Sen, 1999) is a theory of human development that focuses on the freedom that people have to live the lives they value. Sen argues that development should be measured by expanding people's capabilities rather than by income or gross domestic product (GDP) growth. Amartya Sen's freedom approach has more relevance to social banking. In a broad sense, social banking encompasses the promotion of freedom and its facilitation, allowing individuals the liberty to choose specific values, opinions, and beliefs within their financial activities and decisions. He has argued that freedom is a multidimensional concept, including political and economic freedom and social freedom, such as freedom from hunger and poverty (Sen, 1999). The constitution serves political freedom, whereas economic and social freedom come together. Therefore, social banking is an attempt to provide economic freedom so that the nation will have social freedom. However, the social banking system does not provide any belief or ideology. In need of changing situations, social finance plays a crucial role in allocating financial resources to urgent needs, which may lead toward the integrated general economic equilibrium.

Given the background, this study addresses two main research questions: (i) what is social finance in India? (ii) How does social finance contribute as a process in value creation by social entrepreneurs? A review of policies and literature is conducted, and an analytical discussion is presented to answer these questions.

The chapter is structured as follows: the first section provides the background and introduction, followed by a brief review of the evolution of social finance in India. In the third section, a review of the literature is presented. The fourth section analyzes the relationship between social entrepreneurship, social finance, and social value creation. The fifth section discusses effectiveness and regulatory aspects, followed by a critical analysis of social finance in India. The chapter concludes with a discussion of key inferences and recommendations.

## 2 The Evolution of Social Finance in India

Social finance came into existence with specific goals. The historical evolution explains the relevance of the banking of social nature. The first-generation social banking activity is of moneylenders who lend to the socially deprived people in the society. However, the lending practices turned exploitative, leading to the borrowers' burdensome interest and repayment obligations.

The second-generation social banking is associated with directed lending to socially relevant sectors, popularly known as priority sector lending approaches. Eventually, the focus got diverted toward profit maximization, with which the social aspect remained ignored. Lastly is the third generation of the financial system, in which the banks attend to social problems by providing financial access to the deprived. These banks aimed to create social and environmental values together with economic value. Such characterization distinguishes social banks from traditional banks.

Though the banks are socially concerned, they have challenges too. Some banks faced problems raising capital for them as the investor expects them to maximize their profit. At the same time, there needs to have support from the government, which should be actively involved in the social priorities such as capacity building, poverty alleviation, and providing health, education, and essential services to the people. The main focus has always been on reducing poverty and inequality.

Social finance institutions engage in grassroots operations to build long-term customer relationships. We have a successful example of the Grameen Bank model of Bangladesh based on the same grassroots-level operation. This gives more insight into the social problems and requirements of credit. Grassroots entrepreneurs need credit for investment, working capital, and consumption requirements such as marriage or a sudden dip in production activities. Even these depend on the climatic conditions as they cause the loss in the farm harvest (Ray, 1998).

Two sets of institutions were seen operating in the social finance arena. An unorganized sector, commonly referred to as the informal sector, comprises local money lenders, landlords, traders, merchants, and similar entities that operate without direct regulation or oversight by the government. The organized sector has a set of two distinct models engaged in social finance activities: the organizational model and the institutional model. If we trace back to the banking activities in Indian history, we see a wide range of institutions existed for banking services.

Organized institutes include the State Bank of India (then Imperial Bank), descended from Presidency Bank and other regional state banks. In 1969, fourteen larger banks were nationalized with the motive of social control over bank credit. This event was regarded as a milestone in the history of Indian banking, perceived as a significant opportunity to extensively involve these banks in agricultural finance, thereby establishing a robust foundation for overall economic development. Subsequently, RBI introduced the "Lead Bank Scheme" in 1969 as an initiative for social banking to reach the banking services in rural areas. With the failure of the Lead Bank Scheme, RBI introduced the "Service Area Approach" in 1989; with this approach, banks were allotted fixed areas around their locations to provide facilities such as credit to agriculture and allied activities, small-scale industries, cottage industries and mostly self-employable schemes. It tried to enhance the developmental activities in the rural sector. Though the commercial banks were restructured with nationalization developmental schemes, a large segment of the rural economy was still beyond the reach of these banks.

To solve these problems, RBI has created "Regional Rural Banks (RRBs)" by special Act. RRBs came into existence in 1975 to facilitate banking services to the rural economy and provide various financial assistance to the weaker and poorer sections of the rural community. Even with these efforts, the model didn't work out well as it faced many problems due to the operational cost involved and poor recovery of advances.

NABARD has been established to encourage commercial banks and other eligible financial institutions to be more active in social banking programs (Joshi, 2006). Here, NGOs, Banks, and SHGs partnerships play a very prominent role as NGOs are aware of local settings and environment and banks with credit schemes provide direction and support to the SHGs for income-generating projects. It is effective for poverty alleviation.

Likewise, the Kisan Credit Card (KCC) stands as an innovative and pivotal product crafted and launched by NABARD to streamline and broaden the credit disbursal mechanism of banks. As a pioneering innovation in credit delivery, the KCC scheme's primary objective is to offer timely and sufficient credit assistance from the banking sector to farmers, catering to their diverse cultivation requirements. Originally introduced in 1998, the scheme underwent revisions in October 2004 to encompass term loans for agricultural and allied activities, further enhancing its scope and impact within the agricultural community.

Microfinance is the most recent and successful form of social banking, representing a significant advancement in banking activities. Microfinance is descended from the Rotating Savings and Credit Associations (ROSCAs) and European credit cooperatives, involving groups for lending activities. ROSCAs were called poor man's banks. To combat rural poverty, European credit cooperatives established novel financial institutions targeting low-income families lacking collateral. These cooperatives exemplify how formalized group-based mechanisms have effectively addressed the challenges traditional banks face when extending loans to impoverished borrowers. Notably, cooperatives foster beneficial "peer monitoring" among members, contributing to their success in supporting individuals with limited financial resources (Armendáriz & Morduch, 2010).

Microfinance institutions usually acquire funds from sources outside the local area, often from international sources, to fulfill the financial requirements of borrowers. Conversely, both Rotating Savings and Credit Associations (ROSCAs) and credit unions primarily rely on local savings to sustain their operations and cater to the financial needs of their members. On these lines, microfinance activities started with Grameen Bank in Bangladesh, which made small loans to the villagers. Grameen operates with the mechanism of group lending. Group lending entails arrangements where individuals lacking collateral come together and form groups to access loans from a lender. A distinctive aspect of this setup is that the loans are extended individually to each group member. However, all members collectively bear responsibility if any individual encounters significant repayment challenges. This shared accountability encourages peer support and mutual responsibility within the group to ensure timely repayments and reduce default risks.

The *Integrated Rural Development Programme* (IRDP) was a significant social finance initiative launched in India in 1980. Its primary aim was to enhance production and productivity not only in agriculture but also in various other sectors within rural areas. The overarching goal was to enable rural families to become economically viable and self-sufficient. Under the IRDP, the government offered subsidies ranging from 25 to 50 percent of the total capital investment, depending on the classification of beneficiaries. These subsidies were intended to support and incentivize rural families in their efforts to invest in income-generating activities and improve their overall economic conditions (Joshi, 2006).

*The Differential Interest Rate (DIR)* scheme, introduced in 1972, aimed to offer bank credit at concessional rates to the disadvantaged sections of society through the public sector. Banks identified eligible beneficiaries and determined loan conditions. Commercial banks applied different interest rates based on borrowers' income and repayment capabilities, fostering financial inclusivity for economically vulnerable group.

To cater to the financial requirements of small-scale farmers, the establishment of the *Small Farmers Development Agency* (SFDA) aimed to support cultivators with small yet potentially profitable land holdings. Traditionally, both the organized and unorganized banking sectors had overlooked the needs of small farmers. So, SFDA initiative marked a crucial milestone in rural finance. Serving as a vital link within the network of organized financial institutions, SFDA facilitated the inflow of funds into the rural economy, emphasizing the importance of uplifting this sector.

In India, the evolution of social banking can be delineated into three distinct phases. The initial phase (1960–1990) commenced after bank nationalization, focusing primarily on directing credit toward marginalized sectors, particularly the weaker sections of society. This phase primarily relied on "branch multiplication" and the implementation of Priority Sector Lending as key strategies. Priority sector lending encompassed extending loans specifically to support the financial needs of the disadvantaged segments of society. Since the nationalization of banks, an important objective of government policy has been to broaden and enhance credit access. This policy aimed not only to support sectors significantly contributing to national income and employment but also to rectify the historical neglect of certain segments in terms of institutional credit accessibility. Initially, agriculture, small industry, and self-employment were identified as key sectors in dire need of financial support. As a result, these sectors were given priority status in credit allocation by banks. This strategic decision laid the foundation for directed credit programs implemented by banks in the post-nationalization era (Shajahan, 1998).

In the second Phase (1990–2005), social banking initiatives were primarily executed through programs like the SHG-Bank Linkage Programme launched in 1992 by NABARD with RBI support, the program aimed to facilitate cohesive group activities among the impoverished, ensuring their seamless access to banking services. This period witnessed a concerted effort to leverage these initiatives to foster financial inclusion and support economic empowerment at the grassroots level.

In the third phase, from 2005 onwards, financial inclusion was extensively exercised on the national level with a primary emphasis on providing basic banking facilities through no-frill accounts (Shobana & Aparna, 2013). All these efforts focused on poverty alleviation and capability building in the rural areas. SHGs were encouraged for entrepreneurial activities for the sustainable livelihood option generation, leading to personal well-being.

## 3 Review of Literature

### *3.1 Social Finance*

The term social finance encompasses various aspects and dimensions in the literature. Nicholls and Pharoah (2008, p. 11) opine that social finance is more than just the flow of money into social or environmental projects; it represents an ethos about money usage. Benedikter (2011) perceives this as a relatively recent advancement in the banking and finance sector. Lehner and Nicholls (2014) and Belleflamme et al. (2014) describe social finance as a narrative involving diverse instruments such as community investing, microfinance, social impact bonds, and crowdfunding. It primarily focuses on distributing finance for social and environmental returns, sometimes with a financial return. Moore et al. (2012) argue that social financing can be an innovation in itself or as a means to finance social innovation. A precise and unified definition for these finance types is elusive and might even be unattainable due to the distinct traditions from which ethical finance actors have emerged (De Clercq & Dakhli, 2009).

Kramer and Cooch (2007, p. 43) highlight the opportunity for social finance to address market failures and alleviate social problems. Burgess and Pande (2005) emphasize the social elements in banking programs aimed at poverty reduction. Y. V Reddy (1999)[1] notes the challenges in catering to the changing demands of the social and rural sectors, given the integration of rural and urban areas and people experiencing poverty continued to access services from non-institutional sources to meet their financial exigencies (Parekh, 2015). Parekh has revisited the traditional model of financing the poor and questioned its success. Tyler et al. (2012) advocate for a significant change in mindset, urging the sector to prioritize a deeper comprehension of the value essential in providing banking services for individuals living in poverty.

Studies also discuss the role of self-help groups (SHGs) and NGOs in microfinance in India (Baland et al., 2019; Natu et al., 2008). Hans and Seibel (2002) explore the viability of SHG linkage programs for banks, while Patel (2006) emphasizes the need for banks to expand their roles beyond credit provision. Shylendra and Bhirdikar (1999) discuss the Public Sector Bank's (PSB) contribution to India's SHG-Bank Linkage Program (SBLP). Kabeer and Noponen (2005) highlight the positive impacts of PRADAN's SHG-Bank Linkage model on livelihoods in India. Badatya and Puhazhendi (2002) discuss the social empowerment of SHG members through different savings products. Self-Help Groups (SHGs) have transformed into influential political and social entities within society, exerting an impact that extends beyond their role as mere financial intermediaries (Reddy & Manak, 2005). Garg and Pandey (2006) propose collaboration between moneylenders and formal institutions to address the inefficacy of the formal financial system. They suggest innovative redesign based on bank-moneylender linkages.

The varied literature comes up with the considerable gaps associated with social finance.

[1] Ram Reddy Memorial Trust invited lecture by V Y Reddy at Potti Sreeramulu Telugu University Auditorium Public Gardens, Hyderabad on December 4, 1999.

## *3.2 Social Entrepreneurship*

Social Entrepreneurship aims to solve social problems and create social value (Alvord et al., 2004; Dees, 1998). It involves innovative solutions to social problems and mobilizes resources for sustainable social change. Stevens et al. (2015) and Sharir and Lerner (2006) characterize social entrepreneurs as change agents to create and sustain social value.

Social entrepreneurship is multidimensional and involves behaviors such as recognizing social value opportunities, innovativeness, proactiveness, and risk-taking (Mort et al., 2003). It centers on creating social value, social return on investment (SROI), social impact, and social enterprise. Social value is the broader impact on individuals, communities, and the environment, while SROI measures the outcomes of an activity or organization. Social impact considers the effect on the social fabric and well-being of communities. Social enterprises trade for a social purpose to address social problems.

Social value in developing economies represents benefits or cost reductions for society beyond individual gains and general market activity (Phills et al., 2008). These authors have defined social value in the context of the market process. But contrary to this, the individuals doing something to address the problems they see in society don't even know about social value and have significance in their activities.

Social Entrepreneurship has indeed become a global phenomenon, evolving within the context of societal and environmental advancements worldwide. It serves as a catalyst for effecting social change and has swiftly developed into a distinct field of both research and practical implementation. It can be presented in different modes: first, the social enterprise that is similar to any entrepreneurial initiative and second, Social innovation as introduced by (Schumpeter, 1947). Primarily, we need to look for the three levels of analysis, *individuals* leveraging entrepreneurial spirit for social change, *enterprises* utilizing business tools for social goals, and *social impact investors* providing resources to such enterprises.

## *3.3 Social Entrepreneurship and Social Finance*

Social Entrepreneurship has evolved in many countries with different contexts and needs. Chell et al. (2010) have pictured the positioning of social entrepreneurship in a global context. In Europe, social enterprises were recognized in the early 1990s, which are referred to as third-sector organizations. France and Belgium have a social economy with public and private enterprises as major entities. The United States also recognized social entrepreneurship in the early 90s when Harvard established the Social Enterprise Initiative.

Schools of thought have been the deciding factor for the positioning of social entrepreneurship. The first and still dominant school of thought on social entrepreneurship revolves around non-profit organizations utilizing commercial activities to further their mission (Defourny & Nyssens, 2010). The second prominent school of thought was heavily influenced by B. Drayton and his organization, Ashoka, established in 1980. It emphasized identifying and empowering exceptional individuals with transformative ideas for driving social change. Only these assumptions are not enough for generalizations.

Social enterprises are seen as engaged in activities that promote social value or change, with less or no emphasis on the business-like profit-making nature.

## 4 Social Entrepreneurship and Social Finance:

Moore et al. (2012) have shed light on the historical journey of social entrepreneurship. Social entrepreneurs historically depended on grants and contracts from government agencies or foundations as their primary financial support. However, during periods of fiscal constraint, these sources may become more limited. Additionally, the rise in complex societal challenges has led to a greater number of social entrepreneurs competing for the same funding sources, a trend likely to persist. In their report on Social Investments, Cheng et al. (2010) formulated a spectrum of organizational models which is quite explanative of what type of enterprises are on to the creation of social impact (Fig. 1).

The economic advantages of social investments manifest in various ways. They include minimized production costs, higher productivity, reduced expenses, a growing pool of skilled workers, and punitive payments stemming from environmental impacts, among others.

Kramer and Cooch (2007) summarize the challenge as foundations typically aim to address significant social issues like poverty, homelessness, global warming, and inadequate healthcare by providing grants to non-profit organizations. However, these social problems are not typically caused by the absence of grant funding. Instead, they often stem from market failures, wherein a disconnect between social objectives and economic incentives contributes to these societal issues.

Social entrepreneurship finance is important for at least two reasons. Firstly, social finance has the potential to spur social innovation by diverging from conventional investor rationalities, as noted by Nicholls (2010); Such investments often challenge established institutional logic, fostering an environment for experiments that challenge prevailing resource allocation patterns associated with dominant social

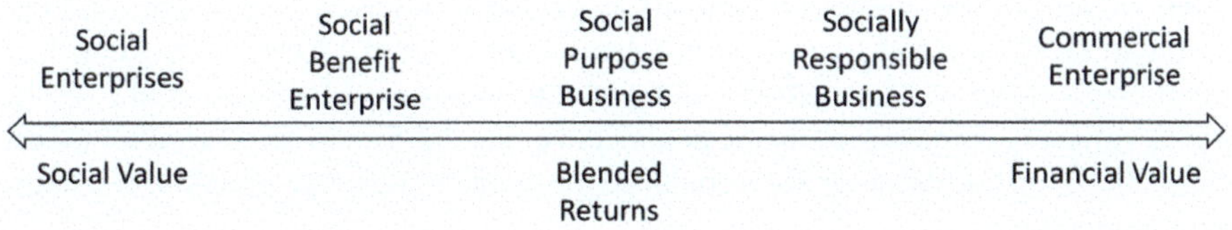


**Fig. 1** Spectrum of organizational models (*Source* Adapted from Cheng et al. [2010])

structures. Secondly, it can directly support social entrepreneurship and innovation in their various stages—from development and adoption to implementation.

In this regard, we look at social entrepreneurship as a process with which the utilization of social finance services can be maximized to the marginal level. Entrepreneurs with social vision are called social entrepreneurs. These entrepreneurs create both social and economic value. And the organizations are social enterprises when they don't have profit as a primary objective, but the main motto is to bring positive social change (Singh, 2016). Such social enterprises can build social capital. Here, social capital is the creation of community-based assets which also create social and economic value. So, with that regard, there is a need for social finance for building social capital.

## *4.1 Social Value Creation*

Can profit be a motive in social entrepreneurship? As it is an intervention purposefully focused on social value creation, one cannot think about the profit-making out of the social enterprise. Value is a notion of significance that is intricately tied to the utility and perception of a product or service by customers, rather than being objectively determined, as highlighted by (Dumond, 2000). Lepak et al. (2007) suggest that "value creation depends on the subjective value realization of a user—whether individual, organization, or society— and translates into the user's willingness to exchange a monetary amount for the value received". This value creation process happens at different levels. Intentionally or unintentionally members in societies create value for society and for themselves. This process may encompass innovation and entrepreneurship at the firm level. Value creation at the individual level is associated with traits such as creativity and job performance, while at the organizational level, it often pertains to fostering innovation and the generation of knowledge.

The value that is created out of an entrepreneurial intervention has no comparison with the economically transacted value. Economists arguably relate value creation with the utility theory and exchange value the consumer pays for the product. This is correct in the case of commercial entrepreneurship, but the utility theory doesn't seem to fit in social entrepreneurship. For example, Aravind Eye Care hospitals, with their innovativeness, proved that conventional utility theory might not always effectively measure the extent of value creation achieved through innovation.

It is supposedly a prerequisite for social entrepreneurship that it should create social value. So, social entrepreneurship is primarily focused on a social mission, aiming to tackle societal issues and problems (Alvord et al., 2004), address critical social needs (Mair & Marti, 2006), and generate social wealth (Zahra et al., 2009). Social Value encompasses altruistic goals (Tan et al., 2005), virtuous behavior (Mort et al., 2003), and advocating for a social purpose and values like equality, freedom, and tolerance.

Shri Mahila Grih Udyog Lijjat Papad, a social enterprise in Mumbai, Maharashtra, was founded in 1959 by seven Gujarati women who made papad (a thin, crispy flatbread) at home (Ramanathan, 2004). Eventually, the intervention received a great response to their homely produced papad. The Gruh Udyog group expanded its papad production business across different branches, primarily aiming to create social value. This initiative not only helped alleviate some debt but also empowered women by providing them with educational and skill-building opportunities, including typing, cooking, sewing, and more. It also contributed to community development, such as building the first tarred road in a rural village in Gujarat.

Tsai and Ghoshal (1998) proposed a value creation model based on three dimensions of social capital. First, the structural dimension includes social interaction involving the interaction of entrepreneurs that provides certain advantages in value creation. Second, the relational dimension in social contexts involves assets formed within relationships, like trustworthiness. Trust pertains to the relationship itself, whereas trustworthiness is an attribute of an individual participant in that relationship (Barney & Hansen, 1994). Meanwhile, third, the cognitive dimension encompasses attributes like a shared code or paradigm, facilitating a common understanding of collective goals and appropriate conduct within a social system. All of these dimensions get interlinkage to create value as resource exchange and combination between these three social capital dimensions leads to Value creation.

Singh (2016) presented comprehensive contextual case studies to understand the process of value creation. A social value can be presented in the context of beneficiaries and entrepreneurs. The Social value creation process involves three dimensions: opportunity recognition, resource mobilization (resourcefulness), and the entrepreneur's capabilities.

There are contrasting views on social value creation. Sinkovics et al. (2015) emphasize its importance as a common denominator and reframe it as social constraint alleviation. Social entrepreneurship has evolved significantly in the last decade, with traditional funding sources falling behind the innovations these entrepreneurs offer. To bridge this gap, social investment or impact investment has emerged, providing financial and social returns. Despite the potential, the disconnect between social investors and enterprises often arises due to a lack of understanding and skills.

Along with increased scale and credibility, new funding avenues are emerging aiming to yield both financial and social returns for investors. This form of financing is often referred to as social investments or impact investing and is supplemental to the grants and government subsidies. Social investors usually support organizations deeply committed to driving social change and income generation but may not yet be commercially appealing. Ironically, despite successful social entrepreneurs demonstrating their efficacy, they encounter a shortage of capital, while social investors express limitations in finding viable investment opportunities.

Achleitner et al. (2011) argue that improved information and mutual metrics can address this challenge, ensuring timely social investments to support the growth of social entrepreneurship. Major research articles focus on easing the struggling phase of social entrepreneurship by providing social investments at the right time to their enterprise evolution.

### 4.2 Social Investment Process

Achleitner et al. (2011) formulated the process of Social Investment, which entails the following steps.

1. Finding the most appropriate financing instrument
2. Finding the right social investor
3. Approaching the social investor
4. Passing initial screening and participating in the due diligence process
5. Negotiating the financing terms
6. Working with the investor, including performance measurement
7. Exiting the investment.

The most important step is to identify the best-suited finance instrument for the enterprise. Schwab Foundation (2011) has listed out possible finance instruments for social entrepreneurs as listed in the Table 1.

*Grants* are a traditional financing method in social sector and serves as a crucial funding source for social enterprises. Typically, grants are allocated for specific projects, often excluding overhead costs and expenses related to the development of the social enterprise. They are usually short-term, unpredictable, and impose high fundraising costs on these enterprises. *Equity capital* poses the highest risk for the investor. In exchange for a percentage share of the company (e.g. 7% of total shareholdings) an investor invests a certain amount. Unlike regular annual payouts, the social investor receives a portion of the profits generated by the social enterprise. Additionally, the investor may hold certain control and voting rights, depending on the enterprise's legal structure and are typically outlined in the contract between the two. *Debt capital* is usually a long-term project financing affirming constant cash flows over the next years. Annual interest payment is provided to the debt capital provider. These are typical term loans for a period of five to seven years. *Mezzanine capital* is a combination of equity and debt capital offering an alternative when pure equity or debt capital isn't feasible. Often interest is linked to company profits and the entire amount is repaid within the decided period or converted to equity. The adaptable structure of mezzanine capital makes it an appealing choice for both social entrepreneurs and investors. *Hybrid capital* features grants, equity, and debt capital. Its grant-like nature is evident from the absence of interest costs, and under specific pre-arranged circumstances, the financing instrument can transform into a grant.

## 5 Effectiveness and Regulation of Social Finance

The effectiveness of social finance can be measured with the four key indicators (Lavrov & Krichevsky, 2006). *The Social impact*—measures improvement in the quality of people's lives as a result of the social investment activities. *Social efficiency*—gives an idea of the quantitative aspect of social progress objectives, changes

**Table 1** Financing instruments and their implications for social enterprises

| Financing instrument | Term sheet | | Implications for social enterprise |
|---|---|---|---|
| Grants | Duration:<br>Annual Payments:<br>Repayment: | Short-term<br>None<br>None | • Usually restricted use for predefined projects<br>• High fundraising costs<br>• Low entrepreneurial flexibility |
| Debt Capital | Duration:<br>Annual Payments:<br>Repayment: | Long-term (3–7 years)<br>Interest payment (variable)<br>Yes | • Annual interest payments require low-risk business model<br>• No dilution of ownership<br>• Far-reaching rights of capital providers in case of default<br>• High entrepreneurial flexibility in the use of capital |
| **Equity Capital** | Duration:<br>Annual Payments:<br>Repayment: | Unlimited<br>Dividend payments (variable)<br>None | • Dilution of ownership<br>• Social investor receives control and voting rights<br>• Profit participation for social investor<br>• Potential impact on corporate culture |
| Mezzanine Capital | Duration:<br>Annual Payments:<br>Repayment: | Long-term (3–7 years)<br>Interest payment (variable)<br>Yes | • Annual interest payments require predictable cash flows<br>• Dilution of ownership only if converted into equity<br>• Mandatory repayment<br>• Profit participation for social investor |
| **Hybrid Capital** | Duration:<br>Annual Payments:<br>Repayment: | Long-term (3–7 years)<br>None<br>Depends upon structure | • Inexpensive financing instrument<br>• No dilution of ownership<br>• Risk sharing with the social investor<br>• Great structuring flexibility |

*Source* Schwab Foundation (2011)

in the consumer price index, housing, reducing unemployment, increasing fertility, and reducing mortality. *Socio-economic efficiency*—Socio-economic efficiency is determined after the social effects through the spectrum of positive indicators such as reduction in transaction costs, unemployment, etc. *Cost-effectiveness* is based on the minimization of costs for development and implementation.

Hemerijck (2018) suggests two basic principles for the regulation of social investment: the principle of social justice and the principle of social and economic efficiency. The main motive for the encouragement of the regulation of social investments is to perform four basic functions toward the social sector: the production and redistribution of essential social goods and services, social finance, stimulate social investment process. The purpose of regulation of social investment should be focused to achieve the optimal variant of interaction between government, investors, and consumers in the process of improving the level and quality of life in the country.

Production and redistribution of social goods and services for a long time and with varying degrees of effectiveness is expected to be observed. Similar evaluation can be assigned to the execution of the functions to stimulate social investment process. Information support of social investment function has no system to implement, often supply information relevant materials in the media, especially in controlled regional governments or large corporate entities, is engaged character.

Special attention should be given to the process of financing social investment. Public funding of social investments should be carried out in the social sphere, where state presence is necessary in education, health, physical education and sport, culture, and art, in the field of social services and employment. The main thing in the public financing of social investment is to follow the selected performance indicators, such as reduction morbidity, increase employment, decrease in payments from insurance and other social funds. The regulation of the social sphere, especially those of its branches, which are financed by the state, is a delegation of authority from the individual citizen to public institutions created including the execution of such functions. Inefficient and unjustified budget spending will lead to a reduction in tax collection.

## 6 Social Finance: A Critical Analysis

In this fast-paced world, social finance has got critical attention as it grows older with increasing popularity. The issue related to the definition of social finance persists as it is subjectively understood all over the world. There can be only one bottom line about social finance, which is social impact leads to creating a social value. The definition includes everything all, from small donations to investments that provide a market rate of return or above, which sounds a lot like a plain vanilla investment. Social investing is the practice of putting money, loans, or equity into socially missioned organizations which expect less returns than what the market offers. Investments with big financial returns may not always be considered as social finance. On the other side of social finance, social investments appear as a great deal as organizations get easy funds and investors get real impact out of their investment as and when the government/agency is promoting the program. This further led us to the confusion about when social finance works and when it doesn't.

The existence of non-governmental organizations (NGOs) itself shows the lack of efficient government. What for these NGOs are set up? There is a need for assessment for non-profit organizations. Many not-for-profit organizations take loans for sustainability, and some have even lost donors due to intermittent economic slowdowns. Both philanthropy and social investing are valid ways of doing better, but sometimes, they are being applied in the wrong way, and either can do harm. A perfect funding structure is one that provides maximum impact or change in the social sector. For the poor in the country, one needs to go to work daily to meet their basic needs. Most philanthropic investments are procured for the following reasons:

1. Solutions that address the fundamental needs of the poor and will get investors' money back. But are we able to generate money from scalable rural livelihoods, health care, education solutions, and clean water? No, but with very few exceptions. Certain projects are long-term projects that give investors a regular small return. Investors are looking for such opportunities and deals because there are very few deals like this out there! Basic services to the large number of farmers are also an area for social investment, but the problem is just about the investments. Do such projects give investors a return overnight? It's clear that it won't make any money. However, there exist multiple levels of uncertainty. This is an explanatory example of market and government failure.
2. Here comes the other way to save from the above failure. It is a subsidy which supposedly required to overcome market failure. The point we want to make here is that social investment should aim for a positive long-term impact, which may not be visible immediately after investment is made. It is not realistic to expect a quick return from the social investment in terms of impact. At times, even microfinance initiatives must rely on the huge government subsidies.
3. In the case of social investments, the actual returns will not match the profit. There are few organizations that work under the pressure of the social investors and are already making good impact as in sense of social change as well as economic return, such organizations should be targeted for investments.
4. Socially focused investments sometimes can drive the organizations off the social mission as they are under pressure to give return to the investors. Here, nothing comes into the picture when we demarcate the bottom line for social finance as social impact where there is no way to think about the profit. It comes with the motive that someone puts efforts into the social change or social upliftment of the marginalized people in the region but at the same time they must figure out what is the impact that should come out because of the efforts that are going to put for such social change.

It is clearer that social finance plays a larger role for social entrepreneurs, which is a favorable thing. The question arises whether the social finance investors are motivated by private equity benefits or by the social impact they want to achieve through their investments. In the section on social investment, we have seen various types of instruments that are available for social investment. With this regard, the skeptical views about the investor's intention are not mutually exclusive. Sustainable finance is the key for surviving of the social enterprises, but it depends on how entrepreneurs do it with the finance available rather than focusing on the various approaches. Here, social bricolage (Domenico et al., 2010) will fit as far as the financial resources are concerned. Whatever is available is not sufficient but still the mission that has been adopted toward social impact needs to look from the outcome perspective. It's all about what is taken out of the investment for the targeted societal priority. In short, social entrepreneurs need to have clarity about the mission of an enterprise. This perspective finds very few social ventures that could reach the targeted people for the social upliftment program along with the minimum expected profit so that they can become the viable business enterprise with social mission.

This makes us think that market finance doesn't contribute to a social impact, but emerging economies are the best examples to prove it wrong. Social investments are also becoming more likely in places like Mexico, Ghana, and even India. Now that the grants are irrelevant, the social enterprises are moving on to more sustainable ways to get money. Many social entrepreneurs prefer to have revenue models which impose unrealistic economic expectations rather than the motive of social value creation. In fact, nobody wants to be dependent on donations and subsidies. Social entrepreneurs need to think wisely while choosing finance options as it is equally important to be cautious about the capital needs, social mission, growth stage of an enterprise and the problems that they face at every stage of the social mission.

For Social Entrepreneurship, can profit be a motive? This question attracts the attention of several entities involved in the process of social change. Few things we need to look at very keenly. There is a major problem of sustainability for social enterprise if it doesn't have profit as motive. Every social enterprise needs to earn revenue to bring sustainability of their enterprises. Further, the employees working at the social enterprise should get the same benefits as those of any commercial enterprise. Whether these things are surely provided by what we call social impact investing then it could be phenomenal to see real social change.

As social enterprises are not specially treated organizations it's not that there won't be any competition in the market. It should put on test for the risk bearing ability of social enterprises. We know every market participant in the economy has to go through increasing volatility, Uncertainty, Complexity and Ambiguity (VUCA) conditions. Even social ventures also go through these conditions. So, do we have any structure that can ease these conditions at least for socially motivated enterprises?

The operating environment of the public enterprises and social enterprises is different with priorities as social enterprises are missioned with the welfare of society. At the same time, various problems that social enterprises try to address should cover all the needed sectors in society. There shouldn't be any tradeoff in serving the needful. So there exist conflicting views in social entrepreneurship. Entire society in developing countries needs to be attended for the betterment of the lives. We have children, women, adults, health, education, and many more things to address. Overall, every section of society wants upliftment from their current state. Organized and planned setup is helpful in case of such scenario as it can seamlessly handle the social issues better. But mere social investments will not get the expected change suddenly. If all the social enterprises are willing to address the same issue, then it will result in the tradeoff. So, it would be advisable to target different issues by different social enterprises.

## 7 Conclusion and Recommendations:

The realm of social finance and social entrepreneurship is multifaceted, encompassing various funding mechanisms and approaches to create positive social change. As explored in the literature, social finance takes different forms, each with its advantages and limitations. The effectiveness of social finance is measured through indicators like social impact, social efficiency, socio-economic efficiency, and cost-effectiveness. However, navigating the complexities of social finance can be challenging, with debates surrounding its definition, purpose, and impact.

Social Value has been considered the prerequisite for social entrepreneurship, as any organization can be called a social enterprise only if it creates value as an outcome of its activity. There has been a misconception about what social value is in the arena of social entrepreneurship. The concept of social value has been debated due to its contextual and subjective understanding. One of the central discussions in the realm of social finance is the tension between social impact and financial returns. While social entrepreneurs aim to address pressing societal issues, they also need sustainable financial models to ensure long-term impact. Striking a balance between generating profits and achieving social value is a critical challenge for social enterprises. This challenge is particularly pronounced in emerging economies, where social enterprises must often rely on innovative financial strategies to secure funding. Moreover, the effectiveness of social finance hinges on clarity of mission and outcome orientation. Social entrepreneurs must have a clear understanding of their social mission and the intended impact of their initiatives. This clarity is essential for selecting appropriate financing options and navigating the financial landscape effectively. Without a well-defined mission and outcome perspective, social enterprises risk becoming overly focused on revenue generation at the expense of their social goals.

Another key discussion revolves around the role of regulation in social finance. Regulation should align with the principles of social justice and economic efficiency to optimize the interaction between government, investors, and consumers in the pursuit of improved quality of life. Efficient regulation can foster a supportive environment for social investments and ensure that resources are directed toward impactful initiatives. However, the effectiveness of regulation depends on its ability to balance social objectives with economic viability.

While it is crucial for social enterprises to create social value with their enterprise, they may prioritize clarity of mission and outcome orientation. This involves defining their social goals, understanding the expected impact, and aligning their financial strategies with these objectives. Social enterprises could explore a mix of financing options that align with their mission and stage of development. While grants are essential for certain projects, other financial instruments like equity, debt, and mezzanine capital can provide sustainable funding. Striking a balance between these options can enhance financial stability.

On regulatory fronts, governments and regulatory bodies should develop a conducive regulatory framework for social finance. This framework should promote transparency, accountability, and the efficient allocation of resources. It should also encourage social impact measurement and reporting to ensure that social enterprises stay true to their mission.

Creating a collaborative ecosystem that brings together social entrepreneurs, investors, government agencies, and civil society organizations can facilitate knowledge sharing and capacity building. Such collaboration can help address the multifaceted challenges of social finance more effectively. Robust impact measurement and evaluation practices are crucial. Social enterprises should adopt standardized metrics to assess their social impact, allowing for comparisons and benchmarking. This will enhance transparency and accountability.

In conclusion, social finance and social entrepreneurship hold immense potential for addressing pressing societal challenges and creating social value. However, to unlock this potential, social enterprises must navigate the complexities of finance, maintain a strong commitment to their social mission, and collaborate effectively with stakeholders. With the right strategies and regulatory support, social finance can become a powerful force for positive social change in emerging economies and beyond.

## References

Achleitner, A.-K., Spiess-Knafl, W., Heinecke, A., Schöning, M., & Noble, A. (2011). Unlocking the mystery: An introduction to social investment. *Innovations: Technology, Governance, Globalization, 6*(3), 145–154. https://doi.org/10.1162/INOV_a_00090

Agarwal, S., & Mazumder, B. (2013). Cognitive abilities and household financial decision making. *American Economic Journal: Applied Economics, 5*(1), 193–207.

Alvord, S. H., Brown, D. L., & Letts, C. W. (2004). Social entrepreneurship and societal transformation: An exploratory study. *Journal of Applied Behavioral Science, 40*(3), 260–282. https://doi.org/10.1177/0021886304266847

Armendáriz, B., & Morduch, J. (2010). *Economics of microfinance* (2nd ed.). The MIT Press.

Badatya, K. C., & Puhazhendi, V. (2002, November). *SHG-Bank linkage programme for rural poor—An National Bank for agriculture.* In Seminar on SHG-Bank Linkage Programme at New Delhi.

Baland, J., Somanathan, R., & Vandewalle, L. (2019). Socially disadvantaged groups and microfinance in India. *Economic Development and Cultural Change, 67*(3), 537–569. https://doi.org/10.1086/698310

Barney, J. A. Y., & Hansen, M. H. (1994). Trustworthiness as a source of competitive advantage. *Strategic Management Journal, 15*(1994), 175–190. https://doi.org/10.2307/2486817

Belleflamme, P., Lambert, T., & Schwienbacher, A. (2014). Crowdfunding: Tapping the right crowd. *Journal of Business Venturing, 29*(5), 585–609. https://doi.org/10.1016/j.jbusvent.2013.07.003

Benedikter, R. (2011). Social banking and social finance. *Social Banking and Social Finance.* https://doi.org/10.1007/978-1-4419-7774-8_1

Burgess, R., & Pande, R. (2005). Do rural banks matter? Evidence from the Indian social banking experiment. *American Economic Review, 95*(3), 780–795. https://doi.org/10.1257/0002828054201242

Chell, E., Nicolopoulou, K., & Karataş-Özkan, M. (2010). Social entrepreneurship and enterprise: International and innovation perspectives. *Entrepreneurship & Regional Development, 22*(6), 485–493. https://doi.org/10.1080/08985626.2010.488396

Cheng, P., Goodall, E., Hodgkinson, R., & Kingston, J. (2010, September). Financing the big society: Why social investment matters. *CAF Venturesome*, 1–16.

De Clercq, D., & Dakhli, M. (2009). Personal strain and ethical standards of the self-employed. *Journal of Business Venturing, 24*(5), 477–490. https://doi.org/10.1016/j.jbusvent.2008.04.008

Dees, J. G. (1998). The meaning of "social entrepreneurship." In F. Allhoff, A. Sager, & A. J. Vaidya (Eds.), *Business in ethical focus: An anthology* (2nd ed., pp. 1–6). https://doi.org/10.2307/2261721

Defourny, J., & Nyssens, M. (2010). Conceptions of social enterprise and social entrepreneurship in Europe and the United States: Convergences and divergences. *Journal of Social Entrepreneurship, 1*(1), 32–53. https://doi.org/10.1080/19420670903442053

Di Domenico, M., Haugh, H., & Tracey, P. (2010). Social bricolage: Theorizing social value creation in social enterprises. *Entrepreneurship: Theory and Practice, 34*(4), 681–703. https://doi.org/10.1111/j.1540-6520.2010.00370.x

Dumond, E. J. (2000). Value management: An underlying framework. *International Journal of Operations & Production Management, 20*(9), 1062–1077. https://doi.org/10.1108/01443570010339154

Garg, A. K., & Pandey, N. (2006). *Making money work for the poor in India: Inclusive finance through bank-moneylender linkages* (Working Paper [2224]).

Hans, B., & Seibel, D. (2002, November). *Commercial aspects of self-help group banking in India: A study of bank transaction costs.*

Hemerijck, A. (2018). Social investment as a policy paradigm. *Journal of European Public Policy, 25*(6), 810–827.

Joshi, D. P. (2006). *Social banking: Promise, performamce, and potential.* Foundation books.

Kabeer, N., & Noponen, H. (2005). *Social and economic impacts of PRADAN's self help group microfinance and livelihoods promotion program analysis from Jharkhand, India* (No. 23755, Working Papers from University of Sussex, Imp-Act: Improving the Impact of Microfinance on Poverty: Action Research Program).

Kramer, M. R., & Cooch, S. E. (2007). The power of strategic mission Investing. *Stanford Social Innovation Review, 5*(4), 43–51. http://proquest.umi.com/pqdweb/?did=1424245511&Fmt=7&clientId=27520&RQT=309&VName=PQD

Lavrov, V., & Krichevsky, N. (2006). *What is "social investment"?* ANH. http://www.apn.ru/publications/article1776.htm

Lehner, O. M., & Nicholls, A. (2014). Social finance and crowdfunding for social enterprises: A public-private case study providing legitimacy and leverage. In *Venture capital* (Vol. 16, Issue 3, pp. 271–286). Taylor & Francis. https://doi.org/10.1080/13691066.2014.925305

Lepak, D. P., Smith, K. G., & Taylor, M. S. (2007). Value creation and value capture: A multilevel perspective. *Academy of Management Review, 32*(1), 180–194. https://doi.org/10.5465/AMR.2007.23464011

Mair, J., & Marti, I. (2006). Social entrepreneurship research: A source of explanation, prediction, and delight. *Journal of World Business, 41*(1), 36–44. https://doi.org/10.1016/j.jwb.2005.09.002

Moore, M.-L., Westley, F. R., & Nicholls, A. (2012). The social finance and social innovation Nexus. *Journal of Social Entrepreneurship, 3*(2), 115–132. https://doi.org/10.1080/19420676.2012.725824

Mort, G. S., Weerawardena, J., & Carnegie, K. (2003). Social entrepreneurship: Towards conceptualisation. *International Journal of Non-Profit and Voluntary Sector Marketing, 8*(1), 76–88. https://doi.org/10.1002/nvsm.202

Natu, A. J., Bansal, A., Kurian, A., Khurana, G. P. S., & Bhushan, T. (2008). Linking financial inclusion with social security schemes. *Institute for financial management and research centre for microfinance* (No. 22, Working Paper Series).

Nicholls, A. (2010). The institutionalization of social investment: The interplay of investment logics and investor rationalities. *Journal of Social Entrepreneurship, 1*, 1. https://doi.org/10.1080/19420671003701257

Nicholls, A., & Pharoah, C. (2008, March). *The landscape of social investment: A holistic topology of opportunities and challenges.*

Parekh, N. (2015). From the canvas of Indian inclusive finance models: Problems of hybridisation without regulation microfinance models in India. *ACRN Oxford Journal of Finance and Risk Perspectives, 4*(4), 63–77.

Patel, A. (2006). Linking self-help-groups with banks in India: "Need for expanding banks" role. https://www.Findevgateway.Org/Case-Study/2005/01/Linking-Self-Help-Groups-Banks-India-Need-Expanding-Banks-Role

Phills, J., Deiglmeier, K., & Miller, D. (2008). Rediscovering social innovation. *Stanford Social Innovation Review, Fall*, 34–43. https://doi.org/10.1111/j.1369-7625.2010.00656.x

Ramanathan, M. (2004). Women and empowerment: Shri Mahila Griha Udyog Lijjat Papad. *Economic and Political Weekly, 39*(17), 1689–1697. http://www.jstor.org/stable/4414928

Ray, D. (1998). *Development economics.* Princeton University Press.

Reddy, C., & Manak, S. (2005). *Self-help groups: A keystone of microfinance in India—Women empowerment & social security* (p. 20).

Reddy, Y. V. (1999). *Future of rural banking.* In Ram Reddy Memorial Trust Invited Lecture by V Y Reddy at Potti Sreeramulu Telugu University Auditorium Public Gardens, Hyderabad on December 4, 1999.

Schumpeter, J. (1947). The creative response in economic history. *The Journal of Economic History, 7*(2), 149–159. https://doi.org/10.1017/S0022050700054279

Sen, A. (1999). *Development as freedom.* Oxford University Press.

Shajahan, K. M. (1998). Priority sector bank lending: Some important issues. *Economic and Political Weekly, 33*(42–43), 2749–2756.

Sharir, M., & Lerner, M. (2006). Gauging the success of social ventures initiated by individual social entrepreneurs. *Journal of World Business, 41*(1), 6–20. https://doi.org/10.1016/j.jwb.2005.09.004

Shylendra, H. S., & Bhirdikar, K. (1999). *Microfinance by a mainstream bank: The case of a leading public sector bank (PSB)* (pp. 17–35). Institute of Rural Management Anand.

Singh, A. (2016). *The process of social value creation.* Springer. https://doi.org/10.1007/978-81-322-2827-1

Sinkovics, N., Sinkovics, R. R., Hoque, S. F., & Czaban, L. (2015). A reconceptualisation of social value creation as social constraint alleviation. *Critical Perspectives on International Business, 11*(3/4), 340–363. https://doi.org/10.1108/cpoib-06-2014-0036

Stevens, R., Moray, N., & Bruneel, J. (2015). The social and economic mission of social enterprises: Dimensions, measurement, validation, and relation. *Entrepreneurship: Theory and Practice, 39*(5), 1051–1082. https://doi.org/10.1111/etap.12091

Tan, W. L., Williams, J., & Tan, T. M. (2005). Defining the 'social' in 'social entrepreneurship': Altruism and entrepreneurship. *International Entrepreneurship and Management Journal, 1*(3), 353–365. https://doi.org/10.1007/s11365-005-2600-x

Tsai, W., & Ghoshal, S. (1998). Social capital and value creation: The role of interfirm networks. *Academy of Management Journal, 41*(4), 464–476. https://doi.org/10.2307/257085

Tyler, E., Ravi, A., Bhat, S., Ramji, M., & Ballem, A. (2012). *From social banking to financial inclusion: Understanding the potential for financial services innovation in India* (Issue October). http://www.newamerica.net/sites/newamerica.net/files/policydocs/From_Social_Banking_to_Financial_Inclusion_2012.pdf

Zahra, S. A., Gedajlovic, E., Neubaum, D. O., & Shulman, J. M. (2009). A typology of social entrepreneurs: Motives, search processes and ethical challenges. *Journal of Business Venturing, 24*(5), 519–532. https://doi.org/10.1016/j.jbusvent.2008.04.007

# Context, Innovation and Technology

# Exploring Value Proposition by Indigenous Entrepreneurs: Multiple Case Studies of Powerloom Enterprises of Manipur With Reference to Grassroots Innovation and Frugal Aspects

**Jackson Khumukcham**

**Abstract** This chapter deals with the technology-based innovation initiated by indigenous entrepreneurs at the grassroots level. It explores their value propositions and the strategies employed to bridge the gaps in the grassroots community market of Manipur, a northeastern state in India. This study also examines the cultural aspects interwoven with technological-based innovation. The findings of this research suggest that while it is imperative to demonstrate the value of a product through a structured methodology known as a value proposition, understanding the strategic approach to target customers or the community within the value proposition is equally crucial. This study uncovers that over time, as contemporary challenges have surfaced in the informal market, the indigenous entrepreneurs have adapted to the new realities and they have earned recognition for their grassroots innovation and the incorporation of frugal practices into their ventures.

**Keywords** Indigenous entrepreneur · Grassroots innovation · Frugal innovation · Value proposition · Indigenous knowledge · Technology · Powerloom

## 1 Introduction

Indigenous entrepreneurship, an exclusive field of study for entrepreneurial activities of indigenous people, has emerged as a field of research in the recent decade. The majority of scholars are considering this field as an explicit and globally relevant research (Dana & Anderson, 2007; Hindle & Moroz, 2010; Peredo & Anderson, 2006). In academic discourses, the prevalence of role and importance of culture in building indigenous entrepreneurial ecosystem and the cultural aspects on opportunity identification and entrepreneurship are recorded (Dana, 2007; Lindsay,

J. Khumukcham (✉)
Department of Social Work, Royal School of Humanities & Social Sciences, Royal Global University, Guwahati, Assam, India
e-mail: jacksonkhumukcham@gmail.com

 
E. M. Reji and S. Majumdar (eds.), *Social Enterprise Values and Processes*, India Studies in Business and Economics, https://doi.org/10.1007/978-981-97-3252-4_5

2005; Peredo & Anderson, 2006). Similarly, the social and community perspectives that are embedded with community-based entrepreneurial activities are highlighted (Anderson et al., 2007; Farrelly, 2012). Moreover, due to its nature of functioning in a very unique way, many of the authors and scholars are sparingly projecting the image of indigenous entrepreneurship research as different from mainstream entrepreneurship theory (Lindsay, 2005) because some of the cultural values of indigenous people are often incompatible with the basic assumptions of mainstream theories (Dana, 2007) and even the wisdom of mainstream entrepreneurship is inapplicable in indigenous circumstances (Hindle & Moroz, 2010). To make a clear stand on such context, Dana and Anderson (2007) asserted that 'Western-style, mainstream entrepreneurship is not for everybody, and should not be forced upon people with incompatible values (like Indigenous).' In this milieu, in developing the boundary of indigenous entrepreneurship as a field of research, this study raised the question of whether to contribute to indigenous entrepreneurship by sticking with the available domain of studies or to explore some other aspects of indigenous entrepreneurship that is needed to bring attention to the academics and practitioners, like—to explore the innovative activities initiated by indigenous entrepreneurs at the grassroots level by incorporating technology. So, this study, rather than dragging in the debate of who are indigenous people, indigenous entrepreneur, what is indigenous entrepreneurship and their relationships, will visualise the suitable context that fits to the objectives of this study.

Generally, indigenous entrepreneurs have indigenous knowledge which is unique to a given culture and society (Ohmagari & Berkes, 1997) and has proven to be useful in solving many problems faced in modern society (Onwuegbuzie, 2017). One of the important aspects of indigenous knowledge is that it comprises of skills and experiences that are involved in maintaining and improving livelihood (Capel, 2014; Onwuegbuzie, 2017). Indigenous entrepreneurs are well known for having a deep (indigenous) knowledge of how to use available resources to create valuable solutions and can change current production methods and influence a new generation of solutions for the future (Agwu & Me, 2018). So, they apply indigenous knowledge in their entrepreneurial process (Agwu & Me, 2018; Onwuegbuzie, 2017) and act as a rich source of entrepreneurial solutions by providing alternative solutions in the society (Agwu & Me, 2018). The knowledge they possess is made up of the culture, skills, experiences (originates from trial and error) and insights (Subba, 2006), generally, used to craft grassroots innovations (Agwu & Me, 2018; Capel, 2014; Onwuegbuzie, 2011). That is why, many scholars referred to indigenous entrepreneurs as grassroots innovators (e.g. Gupta et al., 2003; Srinivas & Sutz, 2008). Grassroots innovations applied by indigenous entrepreneurs hold great potential for solving contemporary problems faced in their community (Gupta et al., 2003; Onwuegbuzie, 2009). Such grassroots innovations are defined as need-based, simple and cost-effective (Gupta, 2001; Onwuegbuzie, 2009, 2011). Most of the time, in the beginning, such innovations are generated under the conditions of scarcity which generally aspire to address problems that are essential to them (Pansera & Sarkar, 2016) or to address the problems faced by indigenous communities (Onwuegbuzie, 2011). Having this background knowledge in mind, the provocative feature that ignites to carry out this study is that—indigenous knowledge has the flexibility to go through the process of modification through outside influences and acculturation (Capel, 2014). In this context, many authors are found to favour the potential and possibilities of integrating grassroots innovation with technology blending (Onwuegbuzie, 2009). In a similar line, Ganguli (2000) valued the innovation generated by combining indigenous knowledge applied by indigenous entrepreneurs with modern technology. Such emerging trends in grassroots innovation especially when it is blended with technological aspects are popularly referred to as 'frugal innovation.' According to Angelica Gustilo Ong and Eduardo Gustale (2020), 'grassroots innovations usually emerge in resource constraint environments; these innovations tend to be frugal, using local materials, and designed by and for the community.' Frugal innovations that originate at the grassroots level serve underserved customers and promote sustainability (Sarkar, 2018). So, for this study, frugal innovation is considered as one aspect of grassroots innovation that is carried by the indigenous entrepreneurs at their community level by incorporating technology-based innovation. Furthermore, frugal innovations are understood as products, services, technologies (Tiwari et al., 2014) and is possible for indigenous communities to adjust technology to their uses for production purposes that incorporate cultural value (Jokhu & Kutay, 2020). At this juncture, this study is articulated to understand how indigenous entrepreneurs engage in grassroots innovation and grasp value proposition aspects through technology-based innovations.

The next section will follow by highlighting literature review that connects various aspects of diverse domains of grassroots innovation and frugal innovation by integrating with the aspects of value proposition. Then a conceptual understanding is developed for integrating indigenous entrepreneurs, grassroots innovation and technology. This will be followed by the contextualisation of frugal innovation and value proposition. By citing methodology that includes the information of participants as well as the data collection and analysis procedure, the chapter is followed by the findings section. The chapter ends with a discussion and concluding remarks with a blend of implication at policy level and contribution to the literature and theoretical level.

## 2 Literature Review

Literature review for this chapter is conducted from a diverse domain that is relevant for this study i.e. grassroots innovation and frugal innovation by integrating with the aspects of value proposition. But the quest for literature review is to search for a relevant study that conducted at the grassroots level in the context of indigenous entrepreneur. There are few literature found to fall in the domain of grassroots innovation and value proposition. For instance: Parwez and Chandra Shekar (2019) attempt to understand grassroots innovation based on available knowledge from India. They focus on various forms of value generated by grassroots innovations in the form of economic values, socio-psychological values, and known values. Also, extend to explore frugal innovation and confirmed that the central tenet behind frugal innovation is maximising the value for the customer. Gupta (2001) in proposing a comprehensive framework to describe factors contributing to the feasibility and value of grassroots innovation categorised the outcome on the basis of the sustained value, i.e., commercial and non-commercial value. The commercial value is characterised in economic terms, i.e., profitability, sales, revenue, etc., while the non-commercial value involved social and environmental benefits—such as social inclusion, community empowerment, enhanced productivity, better health and hygiene, and waste reduction. Sheikh and Bhaduri (2020) highlighted innovations in the informal economy that are often undermined due to their inability to generate exchange values. They mentioned that grassroots innovations generate a diverse set of values, ranging from use value to socially embedded reciprocal exchange value to different forms of relational and non-relational intrinsic values. Martin and Upham (2016) posited that despite the growing interest in the potential of grassroots innovations to play a role in the transition to sustainable production and consumption systems, the role of values has been little considered in relation to the development and diffusion of grassroots innovations. They develop a conceptual model of how citizens' values are mobilised by grassroots innovations and explore how participants' values are mobilised and expressed. Smith (2016) provides a brief personal reflection on developments in the research fields of socio-technical transitions theory and grassroots innovation. The study propagated that grassroots innovation plays a vital role to create changes that promote innovation and simultaneously create values that are more human-centred. Besides, in the domain of frugal innovation and value proposition, a handful number of authors is found to engage (e.g. Farooq, 2017; Hossain, 2021; Santos et al., 2020; Tiwari & Herstatt, 2012; Winterhalter et al., 2017). Winterhalter et al. (2017) investigate how firms can set up value creation and value capturing mechanisms to reach new customer segments in remote rural areas with unprecedented value propositions. By advancing the detail of value proposition for frugal innovation, they argue that frugal innovation creates new markets. Santos et al. (2020) addressed frugal innovation as a kind of innovation strategy that helps companies to innovate in resource-constrained environments. They asserted that frugal innovation strategy is beyond cost innovation and has an economic, social, and environmental value proposition. Hossain (2021) explores how frugal innovations emerge at the grassroots level of developing countries through visualising various elements of business model elements—value proposition, value creation, and value capture. This study highlighted that the main value propositions comprise of affordable products, natural products, electricity-free operation, focus on niche markets, female empowerment, and easy access to cheap and sustainable products. Farooq (2017) attempts to propose a conceptual model of frugal innovation and examine how it is linked to value creation. He propagates that frugal innovation is a multi-dimensional construct and acts as an important predictor of value creation. Tiwari and Herstatt (2012) using multiple case studies of affordability-driven innovations from India investigate how firms can effectively reduce market and technology. They mentioned that the inherent characteristic of frugal innovations lies in their value proposition. However, none of the studies are found to incorporate the aspect of grassroots innovation that incorporates frugal innovation and value proposition with reference to indigenous entrepreneur/indigenous entrepreneurial activities/indigenous entrepreneurship. Therefore, this study is to fill this gap.

## *2.1 Indigenous Entrepreneur, Grassroot Innovation and Technology*

Indigenous entrepreneur represents a unique breed that acquires knowledge capital (See: Capel, 2014), when it applies, has the potential to transform the market. On the other hand, it is said that indigenous people who are the original inhabitants of a particular geographical area act as the custodians of indigenous technology (Gumbo, 2014). As a grassroots innovator, they consciously or unconsciously, internalised, observed and come up with new forms of innovations that address the gaps in excising market. Kumar and Bhaduri (2014) provide a relevant aspect of grassroots innovator that suits this research context. They mentioned that grassroots innovators who have low or no formal education generally do not understand the science behind the technologies. However, their technical training comes through learning by doing that categorises their knowledge as tacit or experiential knowledge; and their learning methods are often informal and based on trial and error experiments. They select raw materials for experimentation from their immediate environment. Besides, the grassroots innovation which is carried out at the informal sector are according to Bhaduri and Kumar (2009: 4–5), mostly represent minor or incremental changes in existing technological artefacts where: on one hand, some grassroots innovations are based on locally available traditional knowledge; while on the other hand, grassroots innovations also represent modifications of mainstream modern technologies. Furthermore, according to Jokhu and Kutay (2020), indigenous knowledge can be considered as the product of cultural and technological products from a society or culture interaction and engagement with daily living. They asserted that technology innovation creates several possibilities for the future of indigenous communities. Indigenous technology maybe refer to the technological knowledge and skills that constitute an important part of its cultural heritage. In the same line, Seyfang and Smith (2007) mentioned that community-based innovations are usually social as well as technology-related. In general understanding, technology is regarded as human knowledge applied to the solution of existing practical problems (Waks, 1995). Technology may refer to the totality of the means employed to provide objects necessary for human sustenance and comfort (Arnoldi & Hardin, 1996). It includes the application of scientific and other organised knowledge to practical tasks by hierarchically ordered systems that involve people and machines (Naughton, 1981). Technology can therefore be defined as a disciplined process where human knowledge, skills, and resources are used to construct tools in order to find a solution to existing practical problems (Gumbo, 2014). Such context may be aligned with Lindtner et al. (2012) propagation about cultural appropriation approach the ways in which people take up technologies into the social, economic, and political spheres of their lives through processes of imagination. This approach stresses that appropriation is not only a matter of unexpected reuse or instrumental transformation but is also a matter of re-encountering technologies that is, of finding them meaningful in new ways. The appropriation may lie in how technology is framed and articulated, that is, transformed not as a technical artefact but as a cultural object. Above all, indigenous knowledge acts as a rich source of entrepreneurial solutions that can transform society by providing effective alternative solutions (Agwu & Me, 2018). In fact, an indigenous entrepreneur possesses indigenous knowledge that has the potential to understand the situations and use imagination and intuition in addressing the problem they come across.

## 2.2 *Frugal Innovation and Value Proposition*

It is found that frugal innovation presents a promising way to tackle societal problems with new business models (Hossain et al., 2021). There is no obsolete or unified single definition of frugal innovation. However, it can be understood from context-sensitive approaches where innovations are emerging at the grassroots level (Nair et al., 2015).

In developing countries like India, where a lack of technology based on innovation is prevalent, customers at the grassroots level sought for localised, functional, and affordable solutions in addressing their needs (Prahalad, 2004). As an answer to it, the innovators at the grassroots level gained in-depth knowledge about the low-income customers and provided affordable solutions with a precious value proposition (Hossain, 2021). Such phenomena are applicable to indigenous entrepreneurs too. Moreover, it produces affordable products or services to serve customers who cannot afford conventional equivalents (Zeschky et al., 2011) making it a promising option in resource-scarce environments. In point of fact, it is informed that grassroots innovators use traditional knowledge, skills and materials to adapt to scarcity (Bhatti et al., 2018; Gupta et al., 2003). In other words, the frugal innovation at grassroots context aims at the development of basic solutions that are affordable for price-sensitive customer groups. Such innovations might have tremendous long-term impacts through enhanced productivity, sustainability, poverty reduction and inclusion promotion (Pansera & Sarkar, 2016). Furthermore, frugal innovation involved economical use of resources to provide products affordable to those on a lower income. It can perhaps help to create a bridge between traditional and alternative practices that incorporate manufacturing and service delivery processes (Bhatti et al., 2018) with the potential of export to other developing countries or even the developed world. Wooldridge (2010) asserts that frugal innovation radically redesigns products and services to make them much cheaper for the emerging middle-class customers.

It is understood that frugal innovation takes the specific needs of base-of-the-pyramid markets as a starting point (Silicon India, 2010 as in Bhatti et al., 2018). Wooldridge (2010) points out that frugal innovation is not just about redesigning products but also involves rethinking entire production processes and business models by taking consumers as the starting point. In this line, Tiwari (2016) asserted that frugal innovations seek to create attractive value propositions for their targeted customer groups. Using frugal innovation, one can translate business models with multi-dimensional value propositions that create value by solving the problems of people (Hossain, 2021). So, to attract and retain a large portion of the customer base, there is the prime need for innovation relating to value proposition (e.g. Al-Debei & Avison, 2010). Massa and Tucci (2013) mentioned about the need for offering the right value to customers for making the offering to be attractive—by allowing entrepreneurs to connect with innovative products and technologies. Advancing to it, Hossain (2021) suggests a condition that to develop frugal innovation at the grassroots level, there is need for long-term dedication and technological support. In a similar line, Onwuegbuzie (2009) mentioned about value proposition advantages that can be derived from collaborations between indigenous knowledge and mainstream innovations that can involve technology orientation. As customer is the core of the value proposition, the entrepreneur must have a thorough understanding of the target customer and spell out the business value based on an intimate knowledge of the customer situation (Camlek, 2010) with the objective to make the customer's life easier (Osterwalder & Pigneur, 2010). So, the enterprise concerned must be based on innovation relating to the value proposition in order to attract and retain a large portion of their customer base (Al-Debei & Avison, 2010). While doing this, the entrepreneur must keep in mind that value proposition should encompass solving target customers' problems by being distinctive, measurable and sustainable (Lindič & Da Silva, 2011). Value is created when product attributes (e.g. design, service or support) match specific customer needs (Lindič & Da Silva, 2011). Osterwalder and Pigneurs (2010) propagate value proposition as the bundle of products and services that create value for a specific customer segment. It focuses on solving a customer's problem or satisfies a customer's need. In a similar line, Sommerrock (2010) mentioned that value proposition is central to customer need and satisfaction.

## 3 Methodology

To fulfil the objective of this study, the qualitative methodology is found appropriate as it allows to study small sample with expected common themes as a result from exploring the data to address the research question (Denzin & Lincoln, 2011) and is convinced to study case study of small business owners and entrepreneurs within this methodology. As the case study can be either a single case or multiple cases, for this study, a multiple case study is adopted. Instead of giving focus on contrasting results for expected reasons, differences and similarities between the cases, the study chose to augur similar results in the studies so that to analyse the data within each situation and across situations (Yin, 2003). Multiple case study is convinced to obtaining information from more than a single participant and gain additional insights (Denzin & Lincoln, 2011). Above that, it allows conducting an empirical study where there is poor availability of literature or existing knowledge, and either offering no clues for notable propositions or conceptual framework (Bickman & Rog, 2008).

*Selection of Participants*: In addressing the research question, the effort was made to identify suitable indigenous entrepreneurs who have their own powerloom enterprises. Through this approach, an attempt is made to understand the context of the powerloom, the innovation involved and the value proposition. Four indigenous entrepreneurs who have powerloom enterprises in Manipur are selected on the basis of—respondent's availability and agreement to participate in the interview regarding the study. This was done by employing purposive sampling that include connecting through personal contacts as well as browsing the contacts through social media. Other criteria are to have a manufacturing unit of their own and have a registered powerloom enterprise within the state. All the four entrepreneurs are from Manipur and have their own enterprises namely: Biren Innovative Powerloom Pvt. Ltd. (Bishnupur, Ward No. 7, Manipur); Leimaren powerloom industries, Pvt. Ltd. (Heirangoithong, Imphal Manipur); Magha Powerloom Manufacturing Private Limited (Thoubal, Manipur): Smart powerloom Pvt. Ltd. (Thoubal Haokha, Manipur).

*Data collection and analysis*: Data was collected through visiting the production unit of one of the entrepreneurs, Biren Powerloom, but due to the Covid19 situation, the other three entrepreneurs are connected through telephonic interviews. Other sources of data collection include secondary data (mostly available literature, videos and online news), and observation (only got the opportunity to visit Biren Powerloom). Conducted in-depth interviews using the semi-structured interview guide so that the participants could express themselves freely which align with the purpose of the interview guide. The interview question was assisted by the knowledge gained from news blogs and YouTube videos of the respective enterprises. The interviews lasted for 2 h per entrepreneur. The recorded interview files were transcribed manually from Manipuri language to the English language by listening to the recorded Mp3 files (twice a time). Then, the transcripts were read and re-read to get emergent themes through manually coding using Microsoft Excel. From the emerging themes, those themes that match and are suitable for grasping value proposition and innovation aspects are given preference to use for this chapter. For this purpose, open coding is adopted by reading the data rigorously and identifying codes—mainly done according to the key elements of value proposition and innovation aspects.

## 4 Data and Findings

Since time immemorial, Manipur is known for producing hand-woven traditional fabrics in both valley and hilly regions. Large numbers of indigenous artisans from rural and semi-urban areas who belong to economically disadvantaged groups have been engaging in economic activities through producing fabric by using traditional looms. However, with the time changes, many grassroots innovators have come up that focus on increasing the production level of traditional fabric by situating an effort to preserve the cultural importance of traditional fabric. While doing this, the indigenous entrepreneurs come up with modern powerloom machine that propagates value in various aspects. In the following sections, some of the aspects of the value proposition through the modern powerloom that incorporate technology innovation will be discussed:

### 4.1 Inception Frugal Idea for Creating Value

The story of the inception of the innovative idea based on locally available resources for making powerloom is ignited from the entrepreneurs on personal experience. For instance: One of the entrepreneurs, in one evening, an incident encounters at one late evening when the entrepreneur with his friend was returning from visiting a traditional ritual place. On Thursday evening, 5 of them after returning from Mondum Mahadev, cycle chain of one of his friends was cut off and another has tire puncture. It was near Moirang Khunou. This place is far from his house. As it was late evening, they couldn't return home during that time. They decided to enter a nearby house. The condition of living in that house was found extremely poor. Even the thatch roof of the house was so old that small grass was growing on it. In the house, an old grandma, her daughter-in-law and a grandson were there. There was nothing to eat also and the time was too late. The entrepreneur with his friend requested to allow for staying that night. The grandma provides them with a place in the courtyard of their house. After that, the entrepreneur was surprised by the act that till midnight the old grandma was making traditional Meitei towels by using traditional wooden loom which is locally known as Yongkham. During that time with curiosity, the entrepreneur asked the grandma:

*Entrepreneur: Ema (mother), why this late midnight you are still making clothes?*

*The grandmother replied: Ebungo (young child), what I am making is due to compulsion. If I do not finish it by today, then tomorrow there will be nothing to eat. There is no rice for tomorrow. That is why I am making it.*

According to the entrepreneur, from that very reply, he was not able to sleep the whole night by thinking about that answer. That incident makes him think in such a way that the problem was converted to opportunity and he started to look for a solution to it. He said:

*I started to think that: can it be possible to put the machine to the traditional loom and convert it into machine-oriented loom. From that incident, I keep on thinking to make machine where fabrics can be produced by using powerloom.*

Another Entrepreneur of this study also found to get motivation to make powerloom from his personal experiences.

*In 2016-17, I bought a wooden loom to make traditional fabric. However, it was not functioning well. I took it from, Toubal, Sabal. It was an old model powerloom where wood was used as a frame and a motor is put to move the shuttle. When I called the manufacturer to check the problem which was rising, they came to see but they do not have proper knowledge on how to properly fix the issue. Whenever they fixed, on the next day, the same problem will start. Due to calling them frequently, they were feeling reluctant to come to my place. So, I was thinking to see by myself to fix the problem. Then I started to disassemble part by part.*

In the beginning, the entrepreneur doesn't know anything about how to make the powerloom and how it functions. As the entrepreneur started to dig into the problem and keep understanding the issue part by part, he was able to understand and detect the issue. In this regard, he said:

*When I was fixing a part. It was not working. Then I look for another part. It also does not happen. It took me around 2 years to understand the working system of each part. Now, the system of earlier of functioning loom and present one which is ensemble by me is completely different. Now, the product which I have is an updated one is easier to use and comfort.*

Not only this, all the entrepreneurs who involve in initiating the frugal activities of making powerloom are found to aim knowledge from the process but not having prior knowledge on it. Most of them during the course of making the product are engaged in iron soldering, carpentry, electrical activities, etc.

## 4.2 Improvising the Prototype With Customer as a Central Concern

The prototype of powerloom which they are having now is found not up to the limit of satisfaction to the entrepreneurs. They are fund to come up with a new improvised model and they are doing too. If one observed their work, the model which they are making now is far different from what was there in the beginning. One of the respondents started to observe traditional loom and its functioning and started to think for improvising machine-oriented powerloom by using available resources in the form of cycle parts, scooter parts, motorcycle parts. It is found that most of the entrepreneur, family members, apart from the mental support, contributed to improving the idea of the product. In this regard one of the entrepreneurs narrated about the role of his wife and contribution:

*This innovation of powerloom might not succeed to such level if my wife was not skilfull in weaving clothes. A she is an expert in this field, from her, the input, suggestions and experience she provided are very useful. I incorporate it and make the powerloom by advancing to another level. She always suggested that if you do like this way then it will be more better. I collaborate her input with my idea together and make the machine more advance. It can be said that from her suggestion and knowledge only, the variation in making of different fabric is possible. Otherwise, there will be only one fabric design machine.*

The entrepreneurs by themselves also possess the zeal to keep improvising the powerloom through engaging in powerloom making. From starting the powerloom making, their improvisation is always found at making easiness of the machine and developing it in such a way where users can make the fabric without any complication. In this regard, one of the entrepreneurs said that:

*From 2018-19, I started to update the machine by making both underpick and overpick. Underpick is more suitable for the customer. As the flying shuttle which is used in the machine is 1500 RPM, the speed cannot be made high for shuttle for every kind of fabric. I put the speed suitable to the breath of the fabric and also maintain the time of kicking the shuttle. Otherwise, the weft will be cut off. Then, while I was working on making more effective powerloom, I came to know that for each fabric, there is a need for controlling the speed of shuttle as per the fabric. If not, then the customer who made the fabric will face many challenges during production. So, there is a need for adjustment of speed.*

Besides, entrepreneurs hinted about relying on social media like YouTube for improvising their prototypes. However, it is not that they take the whole concept from YouTube, somehow they tried to gain knowledge about how other people are doing. Ultimately, their intuition and imagination are the biggest factors that make the prototype possible. One of the entrepreneurs mentioned that:

*I keep improvising the powerloom by looking at YouTube. Any knowledge on machine is available on YouTube and I take guidance by watching relevant videos from it. At first, I assemble the powerloom, then part by part I will observe that area where it is not working. Then, if there is any problem arises, I will refer to the video.*

Furthermore, it is the feedback of the customer that adds in advancing the idea and contributes to the articulation and improvising of the model of the machine. In this regard, one of the entrepreneurs added that:

*With the passage of time, I received a lot of feedback and suggestion from various customers in a various ways: like - if I put the design they suggested then it will be better. For example: if the shuttle that carries thread is made more flexible then the fabric will be better. After receiving such feedback, I make the design more comfortable to use. The present machine is developed in this way.*

More or less, such activities of improvising are keep on doing till the powerloom meets the satisfactory level. Even today, they are looking forward to making an advanced machine where human intervention will be very less and soundless one. So that the powerloom, at night also people can make fabric without any disturbance to the neighbour.

## *4.3 Valuing Customers Through Frugal Mindset*

Concern for the customer and meeting their expectation is one of the objectives of all the respondents of this study. In order to meet customer needs, they have been giving effort for making advanced level of powerloom by producing newer model. For them, addressing the complaint which comes from the customer is of serious concern. In the beginning, whenever the complaint comes on the machine, they used to rush to the place and correct the problem. There are also cases where they send employees to the customer's place. With the changing time, they are using social media for video calling and corrects the problem. In this regard one of the entrepreneurs said:

*At present, there is minor complaint arises. There are complaints about the timing problem of the machine and the gear. There is one thing called alignment of the weft for making the fabric. Whenever there is a complication in weft and shuttle alignment, they (customer) called through the phone and I directed them the way to fix it. I advise them like put this gear for the big weft and another gear for the thin weft. Like that I direct them.*

Not only this, in satisfying the customer and adding value to the powerloom, they act as per the frugal mindset. As Manipur, as a state lacks of technological infrastructure, they are found to manage in assembling various parts from various sources to build the powerloom. One of the entrepreneurs, in the context of prioritizing customer comfort, mentioned that:

*Whenever we make a new powerloom as per the customer customisation, we will ask for the type of fabric to make. As per the fabric they wanted, we will install the machine and give a demo of starting the machine. For this purpose, I will call them and teach of how to make the fabric. I will adjust the shuttle speed as per the fabric. For this, I give them instructions and teach them how to use the machine for 3-4 days. But they have to come to my place. After that, when any problem comes up, I go and fix the problem. But, if there is any minor problem, as the machine is using local products which are locally available, I told them to buy the parts and replace them. In this way, I make extra effort to make the customer understand the functioning of the machine so that they can easily handle it. Above that, I also make them understand: if such cases arise in the machine, then that is the warning signal of cut out of weft or fabric. Then in such a case check that particular part that is giving disturbance. In such a way, I teach them in detail. Even I teach them the uses of thick and thin yarn. I am doing this because I faced many challenges when I bought a new powerloom. During those days, when some problem come up, I was helpless. So, I don't want to make my customer suffer the same.*

In the same context, another entrepreneur also found to give their own signature effort which is unique to their machine. Such unique features are made to make customers use the machine with comfort. However, according to them, to give a comfortable powerloom to the customer is not a cup of tea. In this regard, one of the entrepreneurs said that:

*What customers want is when they make very thin fabric or very thick or medium one, they are looking for the easiest way to adjust the connecting link. My whole contribution to this machine is to work on this connecting link only. This is what I told you that it took me 2 and a half years to work on the link. There were many nights which I was not able to sleep due to failure. And even I lost my money which I feel shy to share with my family. Till today, I never tell them about this. There are days where I face a huge demotivation. But after a long time of effort, it gave me the result.*

Besides, entrepreneurs are found to concern about the consumption of electricity. For that, the powerloom which is made by them (frugal innovators who are working at the grassroot level) is consuming only 370 watts which is around a half horsepower. Any inverter can be used for running this power loom. The inverter must be 1200 or 1400 V which can easily run the machine with two batteries of 150–150 amp. Even in extreme cases where electric connectivity is not there, this machine can be used by relying on solar energy. Even if the customer doesn't want to use electricity, can use solar panels of 400 watts by putting together two 200 W panel. Such feature of this powerloom become one of the attractive products for many locals and increasing in demand.

## 4.4 A Doorway for Livelihood and Cultural Preservation

In Manipur, powerloom is not used for industrial purposes where the fabric is produced in high number but, people of this state are using powerloom for producing cultural or traditional fabric for the product like wrap-around of Meitei women/girl, traditional dhoti of Meitei boys/male and also for traditional attire of hilly tribe of Manipur. So, most of them use this machine at the locality level. So in this context, entrepreneurs informed that with the introduction of powerloom, local people are able to produce more ethnic fabric that after selling, customers are earning their livelihood. One of the entrepreneurs said that:

> *With the successful introduction of powerloom in our community, the production of fabric is increased by 10 times as compared to that of the traditional handloom. It means that when a weaver produces one piece of fabric in a day, the powerloom will produce 10 pieces of fabric in a day. However, as per the fabric quality which is using, there might be some differences in the number of production. By learning this fact, those weavers who are doing full-time weaving business came to see the powerloom. Now the model I have is the 7th model. It is now made compatible with those machines of outside Manipur. This 7th model is able to perform weaving of varieties of yarn and produce better fabric very quickly. Most of the machines from outside which I come to know are found to make a particular type of fabric. For my powerloom, it can make varieties of fabric using varieties of raw materials. Even the yarn is weak also, you can put it in our machine. That is why local weavers and from outside the Manipur want our machine.*

Now, by producing the traditional fabric, local weavers are earning more than the traditional one. The earnings made by local weavers are also contributing to preserving the traditional culture of Manipur by keeping on the wrap-around and traditional dhoti alive. Also, the powerloom itself should get credit for it. In this regard, one of the entrepreneurs said that:

> *For the customer, we mainly put original parts so that there is no problem arises while they are using the machine. If we put many accessories, then the customer has to have technical knowledge. So we do not put technology like a sensor. That weaver who take powerloom with high automated one, after some days, informed us to convert it into a normal one. So, we focus more on making easy and friendly machines. Customers do not want very complicated machines. Now, from this powerloom, in an hour, 40-45 metres of fabric is produced. In one month, 15-20 K can earn very easily. Even, I make powerloom to meet the order by agencies like CELCOM and SELCO. They keep ordering to make powerloom for encouraging loom and livelihoods. Whenever the demand they made, are fulfilled.*

With it, the powerloom also provides a better quality of fabric as compared to the traditional handmade one. For instance: the working and functioning are now different, like—the beater which is used to press by hand in the traditional handloom cannot guarantee about pressing in a uniform way. Due to the fluctuation of energy of the weaver, the intensity of pressing the beater reduces. But for powerloom, the beater will keep on beating the fabric in the same intensity of energy. However, as the Manipur state is a concern, the affordable level of common people is still a big issue. For making the availability of powerloom to the common people government's role is important to either subsidise the product or through liaisoning with the available loan. Most of the machine from the outside the state is based on three-phase of electricity. The powerloom which is developed in Manipur can be executed by using a single-phase only. Above that, most of the outside machine has the capacity of consuming 1 horsepower. That is around 750 watts. For this power loom, 375 watts will be consumed. The power loom of the outside is better for use in industrial areas, but for this machine, it can be used in houses and localities without any disturbances to the neighbourhood. Due to its embedded value and production level, at present, order comes not only from within the state but also from the state like Punjab, Gujarat, Rajasthan, Odessa and even from Nepal and Bangladesh. One of the reasons is the consumption of less electricity and the parts of the machine like motor and gear are easily available in their market. For many, if the machine is complicated, they have to call an engineer from the company, but by using the powerloom from Manipur, they do not have to call the engineer again and again. According to the entrepreneurs, by understanding the affordable level of the local weaver, they put those parts in powerloom that are of both high and average quality of parts where anyone can buy from the nearby mechanic store. Furthermore, there is a consideration in the pricing of the machine. It is found that in most of the cases, they look for reducing the cost of the machine to marginal profit. And if there are cases where the place of order is far off, the transportation charge is exempted. When the person who wants to buy is very passionate to use powerloom, then there is a consideration that if they are not able to make full payment, they can take the product and the remaining amount can be paid after they sell the fabrics.

## 5 Discussion and Conclusion

The research demonstrates that grassroots level innovation that is carried out by indigenous entrepreneurs by incorporating technology-based innovation converts into value propositions that are compelling to customers' needs and satisfaction of the community. Above that, this study extends the horizon of looking at frugal innovation and value propagation at the grassroots level by exploring cultural dimension of the grassroots innovation as well as of the technology-based product. In this regard, the restudy claimed that the studies made by various authors in the domain of frugal innovation and value proposition (e.g. Farooq, 2017; Gupta, 2014; Hossain, 2021; Santos et al., 2020; Tiwari & Herstatt, 2012; Winterhalter et al., 2017) lack to tap such perspectives. On the other hand, the finding agrees with Al-Debei and Avison (2010) that modern organisations are highly concerned with innovation relating to the value proposition in order to attract and retain a large portion of their customer base. Furthermore, the value which is created through powerloom is congruent with Osterwalder and Pigneur (2002) that value is created by making the customers' life easier through the reduction of their efforts. The overall finding is consistent with Butler and Szromek (2019) that value captured by an enterprise is not only about making a profit or increasing the scope of the targeted market but also about other benefits resulting from the business activity being carried out as well as contributing to the economic development of the local community and supporting its cultural heritage. Furthermore, the research is congruent with Capel (2014) that indigenous knowledge can go through the process of modification through outside influences and acculturation as well as can gain market acceptance due to its potential to add value.

This research showed that indigenous entrepreneurs do not necessarily have to stick to traditional knowledge but the background knowledge possessed is enough to combine with modern technology. The indigenous knowledge shared by the indigenous entrepreneur has proven to be potential for understanding the context of the product. As a manufacturer, the entrepreneur not only thought of incorporating indigenous knowledge with the machine but also the products (fabric) which are going to be relevant to the present trend. The research showed that indigenous knowledge, even if it is contextual and evolved from particular culture and society, when combined with modern knowledge and technology, has the potential to impact on the community as well as outside the community. An indigenous entrepreneur not necessarily keep on grounding to indigenous knowledge for doing innovation but can use the indigenous element for doing innovation by connecting to the existing knowledge or technology. E.g. indigenous entrepreneur sees opportunity in indigenous technology and think about combining it with modern technology. Such initiative needs proper nurturing and support from the government side. It may act as a role model to many and also if such initiative is scale-up, the impact will be wider. For future research, there is scope for looking at the possible market of indigenous technology that is relevant to present needs. There is the possibility of connecting such technology-based innovations/initiatives with schemes of entrepreneurship development and startup funding.

## 6 Research Implication

To begin with, this study opens a pointer from where numerous lines of research and intervention can be drawn that encourages grassroots innovation as well as developing socio-economic scenarios of the grassroots community (Bottom of the pyramid). At the ***policy and practitioner level:*** The innovation initiated by indigenous entrepreneurs at grasroots level has the potential to catch the informal market and has the potential for export with low cost and affordable product. Understanding the importance and significance of this domain by policymakers and practitioners may provide a wider level of impact to the grassroots innovations as well as impacting the grassroots community. For this, consideration must be made to ensure the support production unit of their frugal innovation workshop. There is a need to polish and channel the skill they have by combining both the existing traditional knowledge with modern technical knowledge. With that, capital to start with and to look for (experiment for) advanced level of technology is still a hurdle for almost all the indigenous entrepreneurs. So, the question comes that, if they are encouraged in doing grassroots innovation, then what type of intervention from the government or policy level can be done. Insight drawn from this study visualised that integrated ways of approaches are needed where the existing schemes of the government sector, banks and other related NGOs can come up together to link indigenous as beneficiaries with their support. Even, practitioners without any hesitation can join this league for accelerating the process.

*At the literature and theoretical level*: This study opens a doorway where researchers who are interested in the fields like—grassroots innovation, frugal innovations and indigenous entrepreneurship can either take part in this journey of advancing the indigenous entrepreneurship research domain or start reflecting with the existing one. One thing which is prominent in doing such type of research is opening the Pandora box of cultural perspectives. Almost all the literature which is available in this domain lacks positioning culture as one of the prime components which give acceptance to the community level. In such parlance, this research is considered to be the first step towards building a theory of indigenous entrepreneurship, frugal innovation and grassroots innovation (and their interlinked perspectives) where a contextual model can be developed by centring around cultural aspects. Having said that, this study gives a hint to pursue and the possibility of future research building a fresh research domain of entrepreneurship where indigenous people and their way of doing entrepreneurship will be explored by incorporating with grassroots innovations. Furthermore, this study contributes to a certain extent by connecting different perspectives to bring gather which is an enriching act toward the literature of management and entrepreneurship field.

## References

Agwu, E., & Me, A. (2018). Changing the present and creating the future through indigenous knowledge and entrepreneurship. *Academy of Entrepreneurship Journal, 24*(1), 1–15.

Al-Debei, M. M., & Avison, D. (2010). Developing a unified framework of the business model concept. *European Journal of Information Systems, 19*(3), 359–376.

Anderson, R. B., McGillivray, S., & Giberson, R. J. (2007). The Nk'Mip cellars: Wine and tourism with an Aboriginal flavour. In L. P. Dana & R. B. Anderson (Eds.), *International handbook of research on indigenous entrepreneurship* (pp. 336–351). Edward Elgar Publishing.

Arnoldi, M. J., & Hardin, K. L. (Eds.). (1996). *African material culture*. Indiana University Press.

Bhaduri, S., & Kumar, H. (2009). *Tracing the motivation to innovate: A study of grassroot innovators in India* (No. 0912). Papers on Economics and Evolution.

Bhatti, Y., Basu, R. R., Barron, D., & Ventresca, M. J. (2018). *Frugal innovation: Models, means, methods*. Cambridge University Press.

Bickman, L., & Rog, D. J. (Eds.). (2008). *The Sage handbook of applied social research methods*. Sage Publications.

Butler, R. W., & Szromek, A. R. (2019). Incorporating the value proposition for society with business models of health tourism enterprises. *Sustainability, 11*(23), 6711.

Camlek, V. (2010). How to spot a real value proposition. *Information Services & Use, 30*(3–4), 119–123.

Capel, C. (2014). Mindfulness, indigenous knowledge, indigenous innovations and entrepreneurship. *Journal of Research in Marketing and Entrepreneurship, 16*(1), 63–83.

Dana, L. P. (2007). Towards a multidisciplinary definition of indigenous entrepreneurship. In L. P. Dana & R. B. Anderson (Eds.), *International handbook of research on indigenous entrepreneurship* (pp. 3–7). Edward Elgar Publishing.

Dana L. P. & Anderson, R. B. (Eds.). (2007). *International handbook of research on indigenous entrepreneurship* (pp. 3–7). Edward Elgar Publishing.

Denzin, N. K., & Lincoln, Y. S. (Eds.). (2011). *The Sage handbook of qualitative research.* Sage Publications.

Farooq, R. (2017). A conceptual model of frugal innovation: Is environmental munificence a missing link? *International Journal of Innovation Science, 9*, 320–334.

Farrelly, T. (2012). Community-based ecotourism as indigenous social entrepreneurship. In A. Holden & D. A. Fennell (Eds.), *The Routledge handbook of tourism and the environment* (pp. 447–459). Routledge.

Ganguli, P. (2000). Intellectual property rights: Mothering innovations to markets. *World Patent Information, 22*(1–2), 43–52.

Gumbo, M. (2014). Indigenous technology. *Encyclopedia of Science Education* (pp. 1–2).

Gupta, A. K. (2001). *Framework for rewarding indigenous knowledge in developing countries: Value chain for grassroots innovations.* WTO Expert Committee (pp. 1–5).

Gupta, A. K. (2014). Frugal innovation is not just about affordability.

Gupta, A. K., Sinha, R., Koradia, D., Patel, R., Parmar, M., Rohit, P., ... & Vivekanandan, P. (2003). Mobilizing grassroots' technological innovations and traditional knowledge, values and institutions: Articulating social and ethical capital. *Futures, 35*(9), 975–987.

Hindle, K., & Moroz, P. (2010). Indigenous entrepreneurship as a research field: Developing a definitional framework from the emerging canon. *International Entrepreneurship and Management Journal, 6*, 357–385.

Hossain, M. (2021). Frugal innovation and sustainable business models. *Technology in Society, 64*, 1–7.

Hossain, M., Levänen, J., & Wierenga, M. (2021). Pursuing frugal innovation for sustainability at the grassroots level. *Management and Organization Review, 17*(2), 374–381.

Jokhu, P. D., & Kutay, C. (2020). Observations on appropriate technology application in indigenous community using system dynamics modelling. *Sustainability, 12*(6), 1–12.

Kumar, H., & Bhaduri, S. (2014). Jugaad to grassroot innovations: Understanding the landscape of the informal sector innovations in India. *African Journal of Science, Technology, Innovation and Development, 6*(1), 13–22.

Lindič, J., & Da Silva, C. M. (2011). Value proposition as a catalyst for a customer focused innovation. *Management Decision, 49*(10), 1694–1708.

Lindsay, N. J. (2005). Toward a cultural model of Indigenous entrepreneurial attitude. *Academy of Marketing Science Review*, 1–18.

Lindtner, S., Anderson, K., & Dourish, P. (2012). Cultural appropriation: Information technologies as sites of transnational imagination. In *Proceedings of the ACM 2012 conference on computer supported cooperative work* (pp. 77–86).

Martin, C. J., & Upham, P. (2016). Grassroots social innovation and the mobilisation of values in collaborative consumption: A conceptual model. *Journal of Cleaner Production, 134*, 204–213.

Massa, L., & Tucci, C. L. (2013). Business model innovation. *The Oxford Handbook of Innovation Management, 20*(18), 420–441.

Nair, A., Guldiken, O., Fainshmidt, S., & Pezeshkan, A. (2015). Innovation in India: A review of past research and future directions. *Asia Pacific Journal of Management, 32*, 925–958.

Naughton, J. (1981). What is 'technology' anyway? In A. Cross & B. McCormick (Eds.), *Technology in Schools* (pp. 2–10). Open University Press.

Ohmagari, K., & Berkes, F. (1997). Transmission of indigenous knowledge and bush skills among the Western James Bay Cree women of subarctic Canada. *Human Ecology, 25*, 197–222.

Ong, A. G., & Gustale, E. (2020). Frugal innovations to accelerate sustainable development. Accelerator labs UNDP, United Nations Development Programme. https://www.undp.org/acceleratorlabs/blog/frugal-innovations-accelerate-sustainable-development

Onwuegbuzie, H. (2017). The role of diaspora in disseminating indigenous knowledge entrepreneurship. *Marketing, 2*(4), 20–24.

Onwuegbuzie, H. N. (2009). *Integrating mainstream knowledge with indigenous knowledge: Towards a conceptual framework of the innovation process of indigenous entrepreneurs* (pp. 1–9). SSRN.

Onwuegbuzie, H. N. (2011). *Changing the present and creating the future through indigenous knowledge and entrepreneurship* (pp. 1–24). SSRN.

Osterwalder, A., & Pigneur, Y. (2002). An eBusiness model ontology for modeling eBusiness. *15th Bled electronic commerce conference e-reality: Constructing the e-economy.*

Osterwalder, A., & Pigneur, Y. (2010). *Business model generation: A handbook for visionaries, game changers and challengers.* Wiley.

Pansera, M., & Sarkar, S. (2016). Crafting sustainable development solutions: Frugal innovations of grassroots entrepreneurs. *Sustainability, 8*(1), 1–25.

Parwez, S., & Chandra Shekar, K. (2019). Understanding of grassroots innovations in India: Evidence from the countryside. *Society and Business Review, 14*(4), 273–299.

Peredo, M. A., & Anderson, R. B. (2006). Indigenous entrepreneurship research: Themes and variations. In C. S. Galbraith & C. H. Stiles (Eds.), *Developmental entrepreneurship: Adversity, risk, and isolation* (pp. 253–273). Emerald Group Publishing.

Prahalad, C. K. (2004). *The fortune at the bottom of the pyramid: Eradicating poverty through profits.* Wharton School Publishing.

Santos, L. L., Borini, F. M., & Oliveira Júnior, M. D. M. O. (2020). In search of the frugal innovation strategy. *Review of International Business and Strategy, 30*(2), 245–263.

Sarkar, S. (2018). Grassroots entrepreneurs and social change at the bottom of the pyramid: The role of bricolage. In Sarkar, S. (Eds.), *Social entrepreneurship and bricolage* (pp. 160–188). Routledge Publication.

Seyfang, G., & Smith, A. (2007). Grassroots innovations for sustainable development: Towards a new research and policy agenda. *Environmental Politics, 16*(4), 584–603.

Sheikh, F. A., & Bhaduri, S. (2020). Grassroots innovations in the informal economy: Insights from value theory. *Oxford Development Studies, 48*(1), 85–99.

Silicon India. (2010). Frugal innovation to accelerate financial growth in India. https://www.siliconindia.com/shownews/Frugal_innovation_to_accelerate_financial_growth_in_India-nid-68373-cid-3.html

Smith, A. (2016). Alternative technology niches and sustainable development: 12 years on. *Innovation, 18*(4), 485–488.

Sommerrock, K. (2010). *Social entrepreneurship business models: Incentive strategies to catalyze public goods provision.* Springer Publication.

Srinivas, S., & Sutz, J. (2008). Developing countries and innovation: Searching for a new analytical approach. *Technology in Society, 30*(2), 129–140.

Subba, D. (2019). Antecedent and consequences of organizational identification: A study in the tourism sector of Sikkim. *Future Business Journal, 5*(1), 1–9.

Tiwari, R. (2016). *India's potential as a lead market for frugal innovation and the role of socio-cultural context factors* (Working Paper, 94). Hamburg University of Technology, Technology and Innovation Management.

Tiwari, R., & Herstatt, C. (2012). *Open global innovation networks as enablers of frugal innovation: Propositions based on evidence from India* (Working Paper, 72). Hamburg University of Technology, Technology and Innovation Management.

Tiwari, R., Kalogerakis, K., & Herstatt, C. (2014). *Frugal innovation and analogies: Some propositions for product development in emerging economies* (Working Paper, 84). Hamburg University of Technology, Technology and Innovation Management.

Waks, S. (1995, August 10 and 11). A systematic approach to curriculum design and implementation in Technology Education (Discussion forum to accelerate the development of technology education). University of Pretoria.

Winterhalter, S., Zeschky, M. B., Neumann, L., & Gassmann, O. (2017). Business models for frugal innovation in emerging markets: The case of the medical device and laboratory equipment industry. *Technovation, 66*, 3–13.

Wooldridge, A. (2010). First break all the rules: The charms of frugal innovation. *The Economist*. https://www.economist.com/special-report/2010/04/17/first-break-all-the-rules

Yin, R. K. (2003). *Case study research: Design and methods*. Sage Publications.

Zeschky, M., Widenmayer, B., & Gassmann, O. (2011). Frugal innovation in emerging markets. *Research Technology Management, 54*(4), 38–45.

# Localisation of Social Entrepreneurship: Case Study of Women Entrepreneurs

**Anita R Singh and Uma Balakumar**

**Abstract** Using the theoretical lens of positive social entrepreneurship and social capital, this field-based research aims to identify the key characteristics of localisation and understand value creation by social entrepreneurship. In this multiple-case study research, rich qualitative data is collected from by using open-ended semi-structured interviews with twenty-six women-owned micro social enterprises. Based on the findings, the study has formulated propositions and a conceptual framework of localisation of social entrepreneurship which may serve as guidelines for future empirical research using larger samples. The research contributes at the intersection of literatures on social entrepreneurship, women entrepreneurship, and social enterprises. The findings of the study have implications for policy makers and practitioners advancing social entrepreneurship.

**Keywords** Social entrepreneurship · Women entrepreneurs · Localisation · Social capital · Micro-enterprises · Multiple-case study · India

## 1 Introduction

In the past three decades, social entrepreneurship (SE) as a global phenomenon has drawn the attention of researchers, practitioners, and policy makers. While researchers have highlighted the importance of localisation efforts by social entrepreneurs (Guo & Bielefeld, 2014), this study has made an attempt to examine the localisation of social entrepreneurship by investigating women-owned micro social enterprises (MSEs). With the aim to understand how entrepreneurs identify the neglected problems of the society and address them. In order to delve deeper into

A. R. Singh (✉)
M S Ramaiah Institute of Management, Bengaluru, Karnataka 560 054, India
e-mail: anitarsingh@gmail.com

U. Balakumar
BGS College of Engineering and Technology, Bengaluru, Karnataka 560 086, India



E. M. Reji and S. Majumdar (eds.), *Social Enterprise Values and Processes*, India Studies in Business and Economics, https://doi.org/10.1007/978-981-97-3252-4_6

this complex phenomenon, it also explores the role of social capital in value creation for intended beneficiaries and local community.

This enthusiasm is evident globally from non-governmental organisations (NGOs) and foundations such as Ashoka, Avina and Skoll (Fridhi, 2021), to corporates, youth social entrepreneurship report,[1] institution of social entrepreneur awards, and the rise in social enterprises since COVID-19.

Researchers have highlighted that societal needs are met in different ways as developing economies (Goyal & Sergi, 2015), have an uncertain, informal, rural and heterogeneous ecosystem with a large population of poorer people (Esposito et al., 2012). Such conditions have led to the emergence of social enterprises, which are distinct from traditional forms of entrepreneurship in developed economies (Nidumolu et al., 2009). Several scholars have studied large successful social enterprises, such as Grameen Bank (Seelos & Mair, 2005), Self-Employed Women's Association (Guha & Majumdar, 2021), and Aravind Eye Hospital (Huybrechts & Nicholls, 2012) and underlined their solutions to societal problems in developing countries.

Studies have also highlighted the importance of social capital for social entrepreneurs (Basu, 2012; Estrin et al., 2013; Humbert, 2012; Light & Dana, 2013; Pillai et al., 2021), including women entrepreneurs (Datta & Gailey, 2012; Haugh & Talwar, 2016; Neumeyer et al., 2019; Setini et al., 2020). The extant literature, however, highlights the need to study social entrepreneurship from multiple theoretical perspectives for deeper understanding of the local context. This study is thus intended to fill this gap.

From the theoretical lens of positive theory of SE (Santos, 2012) and social capital (Coleman, 1994), our study on SE is significant for many reasons. First, it delineates the "social" aspect of social enterprises and focuses on women-owned micro-enterprises, which have not received as much academic attention as large well-established social enterprises. Second, to understand SE in the context of developing economies, it defines localisation as the embeddedness of entrepreneurs and their enterprise in the local context. The main contribution of our study is the formulation of propositions and conceptualisation of a framework for localisation of SE. This multiple-case study thus hopes to contribute to the theory and practice of SE and women entrepreneurship and have implications for practitioners and policy makers advancing SE.

[1] https://www.un.org/development/desa/youth/wp-content/uploads/sites/21/2020/07/2020-World-Youth-Report-FULL-FINAL.pdf.

## 2 Theoretical Background/Literature Review

This section reviews the literature on SE, women SE and social capital.

### *2.1 Social Entrepreneurship*

SE has a social mission and involves entrepreneurial activities in the pursuit of economic, social, and environmental goals (Austin et al., 2006; Mair & Marti, 2006; Santos, 2012). While different researchers have offered rich and diverse definitions of SE, it primarily aimes at finding solutions to social problems (Chowdhury & Santos, 2018; Elkington & Hartigan, 2008; Guha & Majumdar, 2021; Santos, 2012; Seelos & Mair, 2005) while generating income to sustain itself financially (Boschee, 2001). Although SE remains a complex and an ambiguous concept (Hoogendoorn, 2011; McKay et al., 2010), the social impact dimension makes it distinct from entrepreneurship.

Social entrepreneurs have created social enterprises of varied organisational forms—from social business, charity, to non-profit, and cooperatives. These organisations may span from the social and private (Gomez & Helmsing, 2020; McKay et al., 2010; Morales et al., 2021), to the public sectors (Leyden, 2016; Morris et al., 2020), and could vary from small and medium (Kandaiya, 2020) to informal MSEs (Anderson et al., 2019).

The positive theory of SE (Santos, 2012) considers the social aspect as the default option and positive externalities and value creation as unique characteristics of SE. Santos highlights that while ensuring financial sustainability, social entrepreneurs must create value not just for the beneficiaries of their products or services, but also for the larger society and stakeholders.

Entrepreneurship researchers are thus trying to understand 'localisation' from varied perspectives—from knowledge, to industrial district, and a dynamic process in time (Becattini, 1990; Figurska, 2014; Lecoq, 2002). In the context of SE, studies have highlighted localisation of legislation and policy, resources and business, and efforts by social entrepreneurs (Goyal & Sergi, 2015; Guo & Bielefeld, 2014; Lee et al., 2021; Zang, 2016).

### *2.2 Social Capital and Social Entrepreneurship*

Traditionally, it has been believed that any economic development requires investment of natural capital, physical capital and human capital (Grootaert, 1998). Hasan (2005) however, has Examining the link between social capital and social entrepreneurship, Studies have revealed the positive impact of social capital on outcomes as actors interact and facilitate actions within the social structure (Coleman, 1994; Grootaert & Bastelaer, 2001). Since social enterprises face complex and uncertain environments, social capital is considered critical and developing diverse networks, with strong- and loose-ties, not just becomes essential for those in early growth (Hasan, 2005; Humbert, 2012; Myers & Nelson, 2010) but also in matured stages (Stam et al., 2014). In entrepreneurship research, the ecosystem in which entrepreneurs, especially women, carry out their activities has thus, gained importance (Neck et al., 2004; Spigel, 2017), and the (ecosystem) concept is loosely defined as a social network where diverse stakeholders, such as individuals, institutions, organisations and regulatory agencies have reciprocal ties (Isenberg, 2010; Neumeyer et al., 2019).

### *2.3 Women Social Entrepreneurship*

While SE as an emerging research field has received much global attention in entrepreneurship literature, scholars have highlighted the role of gender (apart from education and culture) in examining social entrepreneurial intention (Bastida et al., 2020; Cardelle et al., 2021; Chipeta et al., 2020). Among factors that motivate women to choose a social entrepreneurial career, Notais and Tixier (2017) reveal that economic returns and social role attraction were the most important, as they naturally lend themselves to the creation of social value (Lortie et al., 2017).

Scholars have also examined varied aspects of women social entrepreneurs as change agents, including their success (Agarwal et al., 2020; Rosca et al., 2020) and focused on women-owned micro-enterprises, especially in developing economies (Datta & Gailey, 2012; Mayoux, 1995).

Literature on women in SE has also examined how gender plays a significant role in leveraging social capital to engage in collective entrepreneurship (Datta & Gailey, 2012) and act as a governance mechanism to increase loan repayment rates (Bhatt & Altinay, 2013).

## 3 Research Gap

Social enterprises, whether owned by men or women, have been found to pursue activities, often with a particular focus on services (Huysentruyt, 2014). This research is thus undertaken to fill this gap and study formal enterprises involved in making products, though on a small scale. Besides, there are many women-owned micro-enterprises which remain conspicuously hidden, this research aims to bring deeper understanding of how they address unmet societal needs in developing economies. While there are well-known examples of social enterprises, with a few exceptions (Caldwell & Akintunde, 2020; Cherrier et al., 2018; Surie, 2017), research on societal problems of health and hygiene, waste management and environmental concerns remain scant. In the last decade, studies have asserted that social capital is becoming an integral part of entrepreneurship, including SE (Basu, 2012; Estrin et al., 2013; Light & Dana, 2013; Naranjo-Valencia et al., 2020; Pillai et al., 2021), involving women entrepreneurs (Humbert, 2012; Setini et al., 2020). While studies have addressed issues related to women SE in cooperatives and in developing countries (Agarwal et al., 2020; Bastida et al., 2020; Datta & Gailey, 2012; Haugh & Talwar, 2016; Rosca et al., 2020; Sahrakorpi & Bandi, 2021), including social capital (Osei & Zhuang, 2020; Sengupta et al., 2018), except for a few exceptions (Asfiah et al., 2018; Mayoux, 1995), research on women entrepreneurs of MSEs remains scarce. It is also unclear as to how women entrepreneurs navigate (Jeong & Yoo, 2022). This research on women entrepreneurs thus aims to fill this gap by examining how women entrepreneurs leverage social capital to create value in the *local* context of the Southern Indian State of Tamil Nadu. It thus responds to calls to undertake research in value creation by social enterprises (Gupta et al., 2020).

## 4 Scope of the Study

Public policies, government actions and investment improve the generic environment for entrepreneurship and business growth (Bennett, 2014; Minniti, 2008) hence, it is important to understand the context of the study. This research is carried out in the rural and semi-urban regions of Tiruchirappalli, in the State of Tamil Nadu (TN) in India. The choice of Tiruchirappalli is driven by the fact that it is an agrarian economy as well as a significant manufacturing hub with many Micro, Small and Medium Enterprises (MSMEs) in the private sector.[2] The Government has also undertaken initiatives to promote entrepreneurship in India through various programs. As a result, in Global Innovation Index 2019, India is ranked at 63 for Ease of Doing Businesses globally and the World Bank 2020 report too states country's notable improvement in doing business.[3] In 2020, the government issued a notification for a new criteria for classifying MSMEs and introduced Udyam Registration. Furthermore, the new MSME Policy 2021 and the central and TN governments have taken several initiatives to make the state the most vibrant ecosystem for enterprises to launch, scale up and attract new investments.[4] Hence, it may be important to conduct an in-depth study of micro-enterprises in the specific context of Tiruchirappalli.

---

[2] http://www.msmedi-chennai.gov.in/GARMS_Admin/basictools/images/DIPSReport/Trichy.pdf.

[3] https://www.babson.edu/media/babson/assets/global-entrepreneurship-monitor/2019-2020-GEM-Global-Report.pdf.

[4] https://cms.tn.gov.in/sites/default/files/go/msme_e_11_2021.pdf.

## 5 Methodology

This multiple-case study (Eisenhardt, 1989) was conducted for an in-depth analysis of four cases comprising 26 women-owned MSEs, engaged in making different products in the district of Tiruchirappalli. A qualitative research design is particularly appropriate for this research given the paucity of extant theory to explain the relationship between women entrepreneurs and localisation of SE and the focus on "how" and "why" questions rather than "what" or "how many" questions (Yin, 1994). Moreover, multiple-case study is suitable for two reasons: first, it can reveal common features of the localisation of SE phenomenon across different contexts (Taylor, 2013), second, it facilitates generalisation (Yin, 2009). For this, data was collected through open-ended structured interviews with the owner-entrepreneurs of these MSEs. The list of women-owned enterprises from the district was obtained from Women Entrepreneur Association of Tamil Nadu (WEAT), an NGO which fosters women entrepreneurship through skills training. From the list, first, micro-enterprises—defined as those with investment in plant and machinery not exceeding Rs 10 million and turnover not exceeding Rs 50 million[5]—were identified, then only those in the manufacturing sector were selected. Finally, social enterprises were screened from this list. Despite increasing interest in social enterprises, reliable data is hard to obtain, especially for MSEs, as they essentially constitute what sociologists refer to them as the hidden population (Huysentruyt, 2014). The difficulty of distinguishing social from commercial enterprises makes it challenging to readily retrieve data on social enterprises from databases.

"Social enterprises" in this paper are defined as organisations which are involved in activities that address the neglected problems of the society. This screening criteria generated 26 MSEs and this was considered an appropriate sample size (Creswell, 2007; Marshall et al., 2013). All the MSEs in the sample were single owners and were registered under the District Industrial Center (DIC). Eleven enterprises were involved in making sanitary napkins (SN) addressing inadequate health and hygiene measures among girls and women, 13 making products from jute (JP) and areca nut leaves (ANLP) addressing environmental concerns, and two in extracting banana fibre (BF) thus addressing ineffective waste management practices.

For this research using non-probability purposive sampling (WEAT proposed owner-entrepreneur who could articulate and interact with the researcher), women-owned MSEs were interviewed. Thus, 26 interviews, each of 45 minutes duration were conducted by the second author in Tamil (the language spoken in TN) on the business premises. The open-ended structured interview enabled the researcher to collect qualitative data on the entrepreneurs, their backgrounds, and the operational, manufacturing and marketing aspects. Interview data was supplemented by observations which were made during visits, two discussions in person with the President of WETA, and an interview over telephone with Muruganantham (from Coimbatore), the social innovator of the low-cost SN machine. These multiple data sources were recorded, transcribed and analysed to reveal the findings.

---

[5] https://cms.tn.gov.in/sites/default/files/go/msme_e_11_2021.pdf.

The MSEs were grouped product-wise into four categories or "cases"—six making JP, eleven producing SN, two extracting BF and seven making ANLP. Table 1 describes the demographic profile of the four cases. The cases differed in terms of technology harnessed, initial investment, products manufactured, landownership, annual profits, workers employed, and finally, the demographic profile of the owner (e.g., age, education, marital status and family background).

Moreover, tables were used to compare cases, as this can generate new understanding and reveal unexpected patterns (Alvord et al., 2004; Yin, 1984), as shown in Tables 2 and 3.

## 6 Case Analysis and Findings

The interview data revealed that the local entrepreneurs were taking the opportunity of the agrarian belt and using locally grown natural raw materials, such as areca nut leaves, banana stem, jute, and wood pulp, to make eco-friendly products. They were thus protecting the environment and addressing the health and hygiene needs. Moreover, the success of early entrepreneurs encouraged other local women to set up micro-enterprises requiring low investment.

Table 2 presents across cases, three levels of harnessing technology and social capital, and Table 3 similarly describes the levels of value creation. A closer look at the tables shows that the cases centred on different products, harnessed varied levels of technology and created social capital and value in different ways. Their entrepreneurial activities were, however, aimed at addressing unmet social needs.

### *6.1 Harnessing Technology*

The first column of Table 2 rates harnessing locally available technology as high, medium and low. The ANLP making machine was developed in Southern India, where areca nut is cultivated widely. Among the seven enterprises in the ANLP case, for working on areca nut leaves only four were harnessing fully automatic machines (FAMs) and three using machines operated manually (MMs). Men workers were preferred for using MMs because it required more physical strength. In the BF, SN and JP cases, women entrepreneurs used semi-automatic machines (SAM), which were developed locally.

For making SNs, while multinationals invest approximately Rs. 7.5 to 25 million,[6] employ a relatively complex technology, which increases the price of their product, Muruganantham, however, explained that women entrepreneurs were using SAM (for an investment of approximately Rs. 5,50,000), though for small batch production.

[6] https://msmehyd.ap.nic.in/Documents/Left%20Panel/COVID%20Project%20profiles/SANITARY%20NAPKIN.pdf.

**Table 1** Demographic profile of entrepreneur and their enterprise

| Case (Product Category) | Entrepreneur | Enterprise |
|---|---|---|
| Areca Nut Leaf Products Case (7 MSEs) | *Age*: 4 are in the age group 25–34, and rest in 35–44 age group<br>Education: 3 are graduates, 1 Post graduate, 1 diploma holder and 2 have completed higher secondary education<br>Marital Status, Family background: 6 are married and 1 is a widow. All are from nuclear family. 4 have one child each; others have 2–3 children. 4 from lower-middle class, others from middle class Section 4 from business, and others from non-business background | *Product*: Making Plates, cups from areca nut leaves<br>Workers: Most of them employing average 3–6 local workers and others employing 2 workers<br>Land ownership: Most on own land, others in a rented place<br>Investment in technology: Is less than Rs. 5,00,000 in plant and machinery<br>Annual Profit: 4 entrepreneurs <Rs. 1,00,000 and others >Rs. 3,00,000 |
| Sanitary Napkin Case (11 MSEs) | Age: 7 from 35–44 age group, 3 from 25–34, and one from 45–54 age groups<br>Education: 2 have completed senior and 5 higher secondary education, 2 are diploma holders, and 2 graduates. 9 are from lower-middle class, and 2 middle class sections<br>Marital Status, Family background: All are married. 8 from nuclear family and rest from joint family. All have 1–3 children. 9 from non-business and 2 from business background | Product: Producing sanitary napkins<br>Workers: Employ on an average 5 women as local workers<br>Land ownership: Few on own land, most in a rented place<br>Investment in technology: Is <Rs. 5,00,000 in plant and machinery<br>Annual Profit: Most earning >Rs. 1,00,000 |

(continued)

**Table 1** (continued)

| Case (Product Category) | Entrepreneur | Enterprise |
|---|---|---|
| Jute Products Case (6 MSEs) | Age: 3 from 35–44 age group, 3 from 45–54<br>Education: 4 are graduates, 1 completed higher secondary education, and 1 diploma<br>Marital status & Family background: All married, from nuclear family, have 2–3 children. 5 are from lower- middle class, 1 from middle class section. All from non-business background | Product: Make bags, purse, folders, and wallets from jute<br>Workers: Employ 2–12 local workers, average of 4<br>Land ownership: All have own place<br>Investment in technology: Is <Rs. 5,00,000 in plant and machinery<br>Annual Profit: Most earning <Rs. 1,00,000 |
| Banana Fibre Case (2 MSEs) | Age: Both of them are >25 and <44 years of age<br>Education: Both are post-graduates and from middle-class family<br>Marital status & Family background: They are married, from nuclear family, and have 2 children each. Both from business background | Product: Silk fibre extraction from banana pseudo stem<br>Workers: 3–10 local workers<br>Land ownership: They operate from a rented place<br>Investment in technology: 1 invested Rs 10,00,000 and other <Rs. 5,00,000 in plant and machinery<br>Annual Profit: earning >Rs. 1,00,000 |

Harnessing locally available technology thus enabled women entrepreneurs to make low-cost SN available in the market for adolescent girls and women from lower-income families. Similarly, the machine used to extract banana fibres, invented by Murugan from Tiruchirappalli, was simple to use and relatively low priced.

Moreover, for harnessing technology, it was critical that entrepreneurs provided technical and process skills, and instructions on the safety precautions to the workers. The FAMs for making ANLPs were more complex involving training over two days, SAMs involving hydraulic stamping press required training for six hours, and finally, one-hour training was sufficient to teach pedal-operated MMs. While those making JPs were provided training to operate the sewing machine, and processes such as cutting, designing and printing on jute material. The BF case workers were given training to identify and extract silk quality fibre from banana stem. Imparting skills

**Table 2** Rating for harness technology and social capital

| Case (Product Category) | **Harness Technology**<br>*High*: harnessing fully-automatic machine not involving much manual work<br>*Medium*: semi-automatic machine involving some manual work<br>*Low*: manual machine involving more labour intensive work | **Social Capital**<br>*High*: systematic effort towards creating social capital through bonding and bridging<br>*Medium*: effort towards bonding or bridging<br>*Low*: some effort towards bonding and no bridging |
|---|---|---|
| Areca Nut Leaf Products Case (7 MSEs) | 1 High, 3 Medium, 3 Low MSEs | 7 High MSEs |
| Sanitary Napkin Case (11 MSEs) | 11 Medium MSEs | 11 High MSEs |
| Jute Products Case (6 MSEs) | 6 Medium MSEs | 6 Low MSEs |
| Banana Fibre Case (2 MSEs) | 2 Medium MSEs | 2 Medium MSEs |

was done using different training methods—from trial and error, observation, job instruction, to on-the-job training. The complexity of technology and processes, however, determined the duration and the training method. Developing the capacity of the local workers, thus, enabled women entrepreneurs to embed the activities of their enterprises in the local community.

## 6.2 *Social Capital*

Women entrepreneurs of established enterprises, mainly from ANLP and SN cases, helped the newcomers with information to navigate the overwhelming launching phase. They shared information on technology, procurement of raw materials, wastage minimisation, quality control and marketing. Moreover, close interaction and bonding in strong-tie networks among entrepreneurs of the same product category lead to building trust, creating shared business knowledge, and better understanding of individual behaviour. An SN entrepreneur pointed out that she shared information with new entrepreneurs which helped them launch their enterprise and promote their products. She also provided training and sometimes outsourced the manufacturing to the trained entrepreneurs. She then marketed the products as she was well-established and networked.

Women entrepreneurs were also creating weak linkages externally, partnering with institutions. In Table 2, the second column rates high, medium and low, the initiatives by women entrepreneurs to create both strong ties through bonding and weak linkages through bridging social capital. ANLP and SN cases were rated as "high", JP case as "low" and BF case as "medium" in creating social capital.

**Table 3** Ratings for value creation with externalities

| **Description of Ratings for Value Creation with Externalities** | | |
|---|---|---|
| ***Low*** | ***Medium*** | ***High*** |
| | Jute Case | Sanitary Napkin, Areca nut, Banana Fibre Cases |
| *Empowerment of women*: mostly spouse make decisions in business-related aspects such as procurement of raw materials, sales, marketing of products; and in family-matters such as children's education *Financial Independence*: spouse mostly take decisions regarding expenses towards household, healthcare, education, handle debt, and business loans and repayment *Socio-cultural status*: women's confidence relatively low, earn some respect in family and community, spouse sometimes shares responsibilities in household tasks, leading to lower enhancing women's status in family and community *Economic growth:* Employment generation as workers from other areas are engaged. Does not lead to emergence of other enterprises locally | *Empowerment of women*: mostly women make decisions and spouse may be consulted on business-related aspects such as procurement of raw materials, sales, marketing of products; and women and spouse together take decision in family-related aspects such as children's education *Financial Independence*: spouse consults them in decisions regarding household expenses, debt handling, better healthcare, education, and business loans and repayment *Socio-cultural status*: more women's confidence, other women in the community look up to them for advice, earn greater respect in family and community, spouse more often shares responsibilities in household tasks, leading to moderate enhancement of women's status in family and community Economic growth: Employment generation as local workers are engaged. Leads to emergence of few enterprises locally | *Empowerment of women*: solely women take decisions in business-related aspects such as procurement of raw materials, sales, marketing of products; and women and spouse together take decision in family-related aspects such as children's education *Financial independence*: women participate in decisions regarding household expenses, debt handling, better healthcare, education, and business loans and repayment *Socio-cultural status*: Empowerment and financial independence has greatly enhanced women's confidence, they have become role models for other women in the community, earn lot of respect in family and community, spouse routinely share responsibilities in household tasks, leading to greater enhancement of women's status in family and community. Creating higher health and hygiene awareness *Economic growth:* Employment generation as local workers are engaged. Leads to emergence of more enterprises locally |

Most of the entrepreneurs of the SN case explained that they partnered with their largest client, the government, who deliver the procured product to women having a ration card (issued to people below the poverty line). Others partnered with academic institutions to bring awareness about health and hygiene and build market for SNs. Women entrepreneurs of BF, ANLP and JP cases recognised that their bridging skills helped them partner with various government divisions (for registering as an enterprise, availing subsidies, setting up stalls in expositions and exporting), NGOs, banks, hospitals and suppliers. This complex interdependence and interaction among entrepreneurs and institutions helped the enterprises reinforce their activities in the local ecosystem.

### 6.3 Value Creation with Externalities

Table 3 rates value creation with externalities (i.e., for the local community, beyond the intended customers of the products) as high, medium and low. Analysis of cases revealed four types of value—women's empowerment, financial independence, socio-cultural status and economic growth. The JP case is rated medium, the SN, ANLP and BF cases are high, while none is low. A closer examination, thus, established that in all the cases, value was created with positive externalities.

Many women entrepreneurs shared that since they do not qualify for formal employment, they have started their enterprises. Launching their ventures, helped them engage fruitfully, generate income for the family and create employment opportunities for local workers—both men (JP, ANLP and BF cases) and women (especially in the SN case as shown in Table 1). The enhanced purchasing power and capacity building of workers through technical training created value for the local community. Furthermore, entrepreneurs of the BF and the ANLP, and particularly of the SN case, stood out as role models, which encouraged other local women to launch their enterprises.

Data from the cases also points out that managing enterprises empowered women entrepreneurs resulting in enhanced financial position, purchasing power positively contributing to the local region's economic growth, confidence, assertiveness, status in the family and society, and independence to break free from being a full-time homemaker and venture into public space. Furthermore, this was changing the attitude of their male spouse. They became more accepting and encouraging of the women-owned enterprises. The improved social status of women workers made their family proud, which in turn, encouraged other women to gain employment in these enterprises. Finally, more adolescent girls and women were using SNs, thus changing their hygiene habits.

## 7 Discussion

The four cases of SN, BF, ANLP and JP then highlight that local women entrepreneurs are identifying local societal problems and providing solutions originating from the local context, for instance, inadequate personal hygiene by making sanitary napkins, environmental damage by using environment-friendly raw material such as areca nut leaf and jute to make products, and ineffective waste management practices by extraction of fibre from bio-degradable banana stems. These solutions are not adequately addressed by the state (Hoogendoorn et al., 2012), especially in developing economies. The findings reveal that women entrepreneurs address these local problems by harnessing local technology, to make their products, such as SN available at an affordable price to the bottom of the pyramid (Chesbrough, 2010; Prahalad & Hart, 2002). Furthermore, the solutions developed locally have global relevance (Santos, 2012), noteworthy is the success of low-cost SN machines, which is being replicated in other developing countries (House et al., 2013; Zahra et al., 2008).

**Proposition 1:** Women entrepreneurs of MSEs are likely to harness *local* technology in order to address neglected problems of society, by developing solutions, which originate from the local context, and yet they have global relevance.

Social entrepreneurs must also develop effective strategies to overcome resource challenges to financially sustain their enterprises (Dees, 2001; Guclu et al., 2002). The study reveals that to solve this problem, women entrepreneurs tap into other capitals, such as their networks, to gain access to information and learn from others (OECD, 2010). The findings also highlight the emergence of a "*symbiotic bond*" of knowledge sharing among the well-established and new-entrants. Studies have shown that such sharing of knowledge can minimise market failures due to insufficient information, opportunism and free riding, and instead bring them to act collectively (Collier, 1998; Dasgupta & Serageldin, 2000; Serageldin & Grootaert, 2017), thus positively impacting entrepreneurship (Anderson & Jack, 2002).

**Proposition 2a:** Women entrepreneurs of MSEs will likely develop a "*symbiotic bond*" with other entrepreneurs in strong-tie networks to share knowledge and information.

Critical studies, however, show that overreliance on strong-tie networks can have negative impact on enterprises, making them less effective and creating roadblocks for women entrepreneurs (Light & Dana, 2013; Locke et al., 1999). Our study however indicates that besides bonding, women entrepreneurs are bridging, to develop weak-ties by partnering with other stakeholders in the ecosystem. Social entrepreneurs build social capital to survive and financially sustain their enterprises.

**Proposition 2b:** Women entrepreneurs of MSEs are likely to develop strong ties with homogeneous group members and weak-ties with heterogeneous partners in the *local* ecosystem.

Furthermore, our findings highlight that women entrepreneurs create value for the local community beyond the intended beneficiaries of their products. Other studies corroborating these findings (Sarin & Chand, 2019; Singh et al., 2011) highlight the pivotal role played by women entrepreneurship (Bastian et al., 2019; Nawaz, 2019).

**Proposition 3:** Women entrepreneurs of MSEs are likely to create value with positive externalities in the *local* community.

Based on the analysis and findings, our study presents a conceptual framework on localisation of SE, as seen in Fig. 1.

The framework presents how local societal problems can be addressed by local entrepreneurs by harnessing local technology. Moreover, to overcome resource

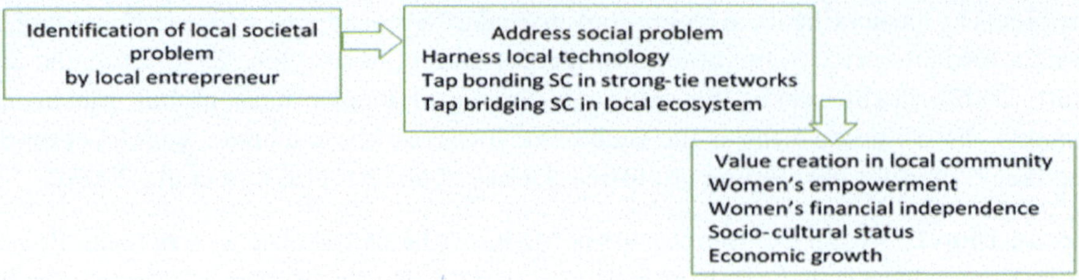


**Fig. 1** Localisation of social entrepreneurship. *Source* Authors

scarcity, social entrepreneurs create strong- and weak-ties in the local ecosystem. The objective of networks is to make and sell products or services to customers, and create value for the local community.

## 8 Conclusions, Implications and Future Research Directions

Via multiple-case study design, this paper answered the research questions on how women entrepreneurs identify neglected problems of the society, address them and create value for the community. Moreover, examining the "lesser known" micro-enterprises, it examined the role of social capital. Finally, the study proposes four propositions and a conceptual framework for localisation of SE, thus contributing to the discipline of women SE.

Our study also extends the positive theory of SE to women entrepreneurship. Moreover, through its focus on localisation, it underpins that an understanding of the local context in which local women entrepreneurs carry out the activities of their enterprises can significantly enrich the literature on social entrepreneurship. Examining the pattern of relationships and linkages emerging from the interactions of women entrepreneurs can advance the theory of social capital and deepen our understanding of the relationship between women entrepreneurs and social entrepreneurship.

Though the results of this research studying only women-owned MSEs in Southern India cannot be generalised, our study lays a foundation for future research on social entrepreneurship. A cross-national study could be conducted to understand if there were substantial differences in localisation and value creation. Further, based on our propositions, future empirical research may be conducted using larger samples. Finally, a longitudinal study can be conducted to better understand the degree of localisation across enterprise life cycle, since women entrepreneurs may face different stage-specific challenges.

The findings of our study have implications for the government, policy makers, educational institutions and practitioners. Implementing the localisation of SE framework, however, requires bringing about significant changes in policies at local level, such as greater access to finance. However, the RBI report 2021 highlights the limited spread of Small Finance Banks (SFBs) in rural (18%) and smaller semi-urban centres. Unfortunately, the SFBs show a branch distribution pattern similar to Private Sector Banks (PVBs).[7] Such imbalanced distribution of banks calls for an increased concentration of SBFs in rural and semi-urban areas. Moreover, policy makers could encourage innovation activities where heterogeneous stakeholders can team up to develop new or adapt technology originating from the local context to address societal problems. While a network of local support organisations will help women entrepreneurs, especially in times of crisis, such support from regional, national and even international levels will give them exposure to best practices and benchmarks. This can be achieved with a dedicated entrepreneurship policy, tweaked to support local social entrepreneurship among women.

COVID and the subsequent lockdowns, made vulnerable, enterprises which were lagging in adoption of digital technologies (Weaver, 2020). This phenomenon was further aggravated, as women entrepreneurs often lack this skill (Kamberidou, 2020). Thus, developing digital skills would help women social entrepreneurs, especially in rural and semi-urban areas, not just survive and thrive in times of uncertainty. Furthermore, corporates as part of their corporate social responsibilities (CSR) can extend support in building capacity of women entrepreneurs and their staff from these areas and strengthen their skills in product designing, marketing and packaging with eco-friendly and attractive material.

Educational institutions also have a critical role to play in encouraging SE, including among women. Young students can be sensitised to the problems of society by integrating SE in the curriculum. These efforts can thus create a next generation of socially conscious entrepreneurs who can think beyond profit maximisation. Higher educational institutions (HEI) can also build with greater rigour a whole ecosystem—design courses, encourage research, create an incubation cell and formal and informal platforms, organise conferences, institute awards and grants, establish chair positions and invite speakers to encourage SE. Finally, HEIs could also design programmes to create a pool of future policy makers for social entrepreneurship.

**Acknowledgements** We thank Professor M H Bala Subrahmanya from the Department of Management Studies, Indian Institute of Science, Bangalore, for critical inputs and valuable discussions that helped improve the manuscript.

## References

Agarwal, S., Lenka, U., Singh, K., Agrawal, V., & Agrawal, A. M. (2020). A qualitative approach towards crucial factors for sustainable development of women social entrepreneurship: Indian cases. *Journal of Cleaner Production, 274*, 123135.

[7] https://www.rbi.org.in/Scripts/BS_ViewBulletin.aspx?Id=20021.

Alvord, S. H., Brown, L. D., & Letts, C. W. (2004). Social entrepreneurship and societal transformation: An exploratory study. *The Journal of Applied Behavioral Science, 40*(3), 260–282.

Anderson, A. R., & Jack, S. L. (2002). The articulation of social capital in entrepreneurial networks: A glue or a lubricant? *Entrepreneurship & Regional Development, 14*(3), 193–210.

Anderson, A. R., Younis, S., Hashim, H., & Air, C. (2019). Social enterprising informing our concept; exploring informal micro social enterprise. *Social Enterprise Journal, 15*(1), 94–110.

Asfiah, N., Anshori, M., & Mawardi, I. (2018). Analysis of women social entrepreneurship on micro and small enterprises. *Journal of Innovation in Business and Economics (JIBE), 2*(1), 1–12.

Austin, J., Stevenson, H., & Wei-Skillern, J. (2006). Social and commercial entrepreneurship: Same, different, or both? *Entrepreneurship Theory and Practice, 30*(1), 1–22.

Bastian, B. L., Metcalfe, B. D., & Zali, M. R. (2019). Gender inequality: Entrepreneurship development in the MENA region. *Sustainability, 11*(22), 6472.

Bastida, M., Pinto, L. H., Blanco, A. O., & Cancelo, M. (2020). Female entrepreneurship: Can cooperatives contribute to overcoming the gender gap? A Spanish first step to equality. *Sustainability, 12*, 2478.

Basu, S. (2012). Social capital and social entrepreneurship: Analysing links. *Interdisciplinary Journal of Contemporary Research in Business, 4*(3), 386–405.

Becattini, G. (1990). The Marshallian industrial district as a socio-economic notion. In F. Pyke, G. Becattini, & W. Sengenberger (Eds.), *Industrial districts and inter-firm co-operation in Italy*. IILS.

Bennett, R. J. (2014). *Entrepreneurship, small business and public policy: Evolution and revolution*. Routledge.

Bhatt, P., & Altinay, L. (2013). How social capital is leveraged in social innovations under resource constraints? *Management Decision, 51*(9), 1772–1792.

Boschee, J. (2001). Eight basic principles for nonprofit entrepreneurs. *Nonprofit World, 19*(4), 15–18.

Caldwell, P. K., & Akintunde, O. D. (2020). USA and Nigeria: SWOT analysis of social entrepreneurship. In *Social entrepreneurship and corporate social responsibility* (pp. 161–174). Springer.

Cardella, G. M., Hernández-Sánchez, B. R., Monteiro, A. A., & Sánchez-García, J. C. (2021). Social entrepreneurship research: Intellectual structures and future perspectives. *Sustainability, 13*(14), 7532.

Cherrier, H., Goswami, P., & Ray, S. (2018). Social entrepreneurship: Creating value in the context of institutional complexity. *Journal of Business Research, 86*, 245–258.

Chesbrough, H. (2010). Business model innovation: Opportunities and barriers. *Long Range Planning, 43*(2–3), 354–363.

Chipeta, E. M., Kruse, P., & Surujlal, J. (2020). Effects of gender on antecedents to social entrepreneurship among university students in South Africa. *International Journal of Business Management Studies, 12*, 18–33.

Chowdhury, I., & Santos, F. (2018). Gram Vikas 1, 2, 3. In *Case studies in social entrepreneurship and sustainability* (pp. 43–68). Routledge.

Coleman, J. S. (1994). *Foundations of social theory*. Harvard University Press.

Collier, P. (1998). *Social capital and poverty* (Social capital initiative working paper no. 4). The World Bank.

Creswell, J. W. (2007). *Qualitative inquiry & research design: Choosing among five approaches* (2nd ed.). Sage.

Dasgupta, P., & Serageldin, I. (Eds.). (2000). *Social capital: A multifaceted perspective*. World Bank Publications.

Datta, P. B., & Gailey, R. (2012). Empowering women through social entrepreneurship: Case study of a women's cooperative in India. *Entrepreneurship Theory and Practice, 36*(3), 569–587.

Dees, J. G. (2001). *The meanings of 'social entrepreneurship'* (Working paper). Stanford University.

Eisenhardt, K. M. (1989). Building theories from case study research. *Academy of Management Review, 14*(4), 532–550.

Elkington, J., & Hartigan, P. (2008). *The power of unreasonable people: How social entrepreneurs create markets that change the world.* Harvard Business Press.

Esposito, M., Kapoor, A., & Goyal, S. (2012). Enabling healthcare services for the rural and semi-urban segments in India: When shared value meets the bottom of the pyramid. *Corporate Governance, 12*(4), 514–533.

Estrin, S., Mickiewicz, T., & Stephan, U. (2013). Entrepreneurship, social capital, and institutions: Social and commercial entrepreneurship across nations. *Entrepreneurship Theory and Practice, 37*(3), 479–504.

Figurska, I. (2014). Sustainable entrepreneurship: Localization, acquiring and use of knowledge sources in competitive organization. *Entrepreneurship and Sustainability Issues, 1*(4), 210.

Fridhi, B. (2021). Social entrepreneurship and social enterprise phenomenon: Toward a collective approach to social innovation in Tunisia. *Journal of Innovation and Entrepreneurship, 10*(1), 1–21.

Gomez, G. M., & Helmsing, A. B. (2020). Social entrepreneurship: A convergence of NGOs and the market economy? In *NGO management* (pp. 391–402). Routledge.

Goyal, S., & Sergi, B. S. (2015). Social entrepreneurship and sustainability–Understanding the context and key characteristics. *Journal of Security and Sustainability Issues, 4*, 269–278.

Grootaert, C. (1998). Social capital: The missing link? In *Social capital and participation in everyday life* (pp. 2–29). Routledge.

Grootaert, C., & Van Bastelaer, T. (2001). *Understanding and measuring social capital: A synthesis of findings and recommendations from the social capital initiative* (Vol. 24). World Bank, Social Development Family, Environmentally and Socially Sustainable Development Network.

Guclu, A., Dees, J. G., & Anderson, B. B. (2002). The process of social entrepreneurship: Creating opportunities worthy of serious pursuit. *Center for the Advancement of Social Entrepreneurship, 1*, 1–15.

Guha, S., & Majumdar, S. (2021). *In search of business models in social entrepreneurship.* Springer.

Guo, C., & Bielefeld, W. (2014). *Social entrepreneurship: An evidence-based approach to creating social value.* Wiley.

Gupta, P., Chauhan, S., Paul, J., & Jaiswal, M. P. (2020). Social entrepreneurship research: A review and future research agenda. *Journal of Business Research, 113*, 209–229.

Hasan, S. (2005). Social capital and social entrepreneurship in Asia: Analysing the links. *Asia Pacific Journal of Public Administration, 27*(1), 1–17.

Haugh, H. M., & Talwar, A. (2016). Linking social entrepreneurship and social change: The mediating role of empowerment. *Journal of Business Ethics, 133*(4), 643–658.

Hoogendoorn, B. (2011). *Social entrepreneurship in the modern economy: Warm glow, cold feet* (No. EPS-2011-246-STR).

Hoogendoorn, B., Pennings, E., & Thurik, R. (2012). A conceptual overview of what we know about social entrepreneurship. *The community development reader* (pp. 117–124). Routledge.

House, S., Mahon, T., & Cavill, S. (2013). Menstrual hygiene matters: A resource for improving menstrual hygiene around the world. *Reproductive Health Matters, 21*(41), 257–259.

Humbert, A. L. (2012). *Women as social entrepreneurs* (Working paper). University of Birmingham.

Huybrechts, B., & Nicholls, A. (2012). Social entrepreneurship: Definitions, drivers and challenges. In *Social entrepreneurship and social business* (pp. 31–48). Gabler Verlag.

Huysentruyt, M. (2014). *Women's social entrepreneurship and innovation* (OECD Local Economic and Employment Development [LEED] Working Papers). OECD.

Isenberg, D. J. (2010). How to start an entrepreneurial revolution. *Harvard Business Review, 88*(6), 40–50.

Jeong, E., & Yoo, H. (2022). A systematic literature review of women in social entrepreneurship. *Service Business, 16*(4), 935–970.

Kamberidou, I. (2020). "Distinguished" women entrepreneurs in the digital economy and the multitasking whirlpool. *Journal of Innovation and Entrepreneurship, 9*(1), 1–26.

Kandaiya, M. (2020). Social enterprise and financial sustainability in South Asia: A grounded theory. *Third Sector Review, 26*(1), 35–65.

Lecoq, B. (2002). *Austrian time and Marshallian district-on process of location in an out of equilibrium economy.*

Lee, I. H. I., Kim, S. M., & Green, S. (2021). Social enterprises and market performance: The moderating roles of innovativeness, sectoral alignment, and geographic localization. *Journal of Business Research, 132*, 491–506.

Leyden, D. P. (2016). Public-sector entrepreneurship and the creation of a sustainable innovative economy. *Small Business Economics, 46*(4), 553–564.

Light, I., & Dana, L. P. (2013). Boundaries of social capital in entrepreneurship. *Entrepreneurship Theory and Practice, 37*(3), 603–624.

Locke, E. A., Noorderhaven, N. G., Cannon, J. P., Doney, P. M., & Mullen, M. R. (1999). Some reservations about social capital. *Academy of Management Review, 24*(1), 8–11.

Lortie, J., Castrogiovanni, G. J., & Cox, K. C. (2017). Gender, social salience, and social performance: How women pursue and perform in social ventures. *Entrepreneurship & Regional Development, 29*, 155–173.

Mair, J., & Marti, I. (2006). Social entrepreneurship research: A source of explanation, prediction, and delight. *Journal of World Business, 41*(1), 36–44.

Marshall, B., Cardon, P., Poddar, A., & Fontenot, R. (2013). Does sample size matter in qualitative research? A review of qualitative interviews in IS research. *Journal of Computer Information Systems, 54*(1), 11–22.

Mayoux, L. (1995). *From vicious to virtuous circles? Gender and micro-enterprise development* (No. 3). UNRISD Occasional Paper.

Mckay, S., Phillimore, J., & Teasdale, S. (2010, March). Exploring the 'gendered' nature of social entrepreneurship: Women's leadership, employment and participation in the third sector. In *60th political studies association annual conference* (Vol. 29).

Minniti, M. (2008). The role of government policy on entrepreneurial activity: Productive, unproductive, or destructive? *Entrepreneurship Theory and Practice, 32*(5), 779–790.

Morales, A., Calvo, S., Martínez, J. M. G., & Martín, J. M. M. (2021). Hybrid forms of business: Understanding the development of indigenous social entrepreneurship practices. *Journal of Business Research, 124*, 212–222.

Morris, M. H., Santos, S. C., & Kuratko, D. F. (2020). The great divides in social entrepreneurship and where they lead us. *Small Business Economics, 57*, 1089–1106.

Myers, P., & Nelson, T. (2010). Considering social capital in the context of social entrepreneurship. In A. Fayolle & H. Matlay (Eds.), *The handbook of research on social entrepreneurship* (pp. 271–285). Edward Elgar.

Naranjo-Valencia, J. C., Ocampo-Wilches, A. C., & Trujillo-Henao, L. F. (2020). From social entrepreneurship to social innovation: The role of social capital. Study case in colombian rural communities victim of armed conflict. *Journal of Social Entrepreneurship, 13*(2), 244–277.

Nawaz, F. (2019). *Microfinance and women's empowerment in Bangladesh: Unpacking the untold narratives*. Springer.

Neck, H. M., Meyer, G. D., Cohen, B., & Corbett, A. C. (2004). An entrepreneurial system view of new venture creation. *Journal of Small Business Management, 42*(2), 190–208.

Neumeyer, X., Santos, S. C., Caetano, A., & Kalbfleisch, P. (2019). Entrepreneurship ecosystems and women entrepreneurs: A social capital and network approach. *Small Business Economics, 53*(2), 475–489.

Nidumolu, R., Prahalad, C. K., & Rangaswamy, M. R. (2009). Why sustainability is now the key driver of innovation. *Harvard Business Review, 87*(9), 56–64.

Notais, A., & Tixier, J. (2017). Girlz'n the hood: Discovering the determinants of social entrepreneurial intention of women in deprived urban areas. *International Journal of Entrepreneurship and Small Business, 31*, 382–398.

OECD. (2010). *Social entrepreneurship and innovation, in SMEs, entrepreneurship and innovation*. OECD.

Osei, C. D., & Zhuang, J. (2020). Rural poverty alleviation strategies and social capital link: The mediation role of women entrepreneurship and social innovation. *SAGE Open, 10*(2), 2158244020925504.

Pillai, V., Pandey, M., & Bhatt, B. (2021). Social sustainability at the BOP Through building inclusive social capital: A case study of Drishtee. In *Sharing economy at the base of the pyramid* (pp. 301–318). Springer.

Prahalad, C. K., & Hart, S. L. (2002). Strategy+ business. *The Fortune at the Bottom of the Pyramid, 26*, 2–14.

Rosca, E., Agarwal, N., & Brem, A. (2020). Women entrepreneurs as agents of change: A comparative analysis of social entrepreneurship processes in emerging markets. *Technological Forecasting and Social Change, 157*, 120067.

Sahrakorpi, T., & Bandi, V. (2021). Empowerment or employment? Uncovering the paradoxes of social entrepreneurship for women via Husk Power Systems in rural North India. *Energy Research & Social Science, 79*, 102153.

Santos, F. M. (2012). A positive theory of social entrepreneurship. *Journal of Business Ethics, 111*(3), 335–351.

Sarin, A., & Chand, V. S. (2019). Supporting and sustaining state-initiated women's empowerment: Learning from a national programme in India. *Journal of International Development, 31*(5), 374–392.

Seelos, C., & Mair, J. (2005). Social entrepreneurship: Creating new business models to serve the poor. *Business Horizons, 48*(3), 241–246.

Sengupta, S., Sahay, A., & Croce, F. (2018). Conceptualizing social entrepreneurship in the context of emerging economies: An integrative review of past research from BRIICS. *International Entrepreneurship and Management Journal, 14*(4), 771–803.

Serageldin, I., & Grootaert, C. (2017). Defining social capital: An integrating view 1. In *Evaluation & development* (pp. 201–217). Routledge.

Setini, M., Yasa, N. N. K., Gede Supartha, I. W., Ketut Giantari, I., & Rajiani, I. (2020). The passway of women entrepreneurship: Starting from social capital with open innovation, through to knowledge sharing and innovative performance. *Journal of Open Innovation: Technology, Market, and Complexity, 6*(2), 25.

Singh, A., Patkar, S., Ramesh, R., & Babu, T. (2011). Social capital and MYRADA's pioneering approach: The power of women in community-based organisations in Southern India. *AI Practitioner, 13*(3), 16–23.

Spigel, B. (2017). The relational organization of entrepreneurial ecosystems. *Entrepreneurship Theory and Practice, 41*(1), 49–72.

Stam, W., Arzlanian, S., & Elfring, T. (2014). Social capital of entrepreneurs and small firm performance: A meta-analysis of contextual and methodological moderators. *Journal of Business Venturing, 29*(1), 152–173.

Surie, G. (2017). Creating the innovation ecosystem for renewable energy via social entrepreneurship: Insights from India. *Technological Forecasting and Social Change, 121*, 184–195.

Taylor, R. (2013). Case-study research in context. *Nurse Researcher, 20*, 4–5.

Weaver, R. L. (2020). The Impact of COVID-19 on the social enterprise sector. *Journal of Social Entrepreneurship, 14*, 177–185.

Yin, R. (1984). *Case study research.* Beverly Hills.

Yin, R. K. (1994). Designing single-and multiple-case. *Improving educational management: Through research and consultancy* (pp. 135–155). The Open University.

Yin, R.K. (2009). *Case study research: Design and methods* (4th ed.). Sage.

Zahra, S. A., Rawhouser, H. N., Bhawe, N., Neubaum, D. O., & Hayton, J. C. (2008). Globalization of social entrepreneurship opportunities. *Strategic Entrepreneurship Journal, 2*(2), 117–131.

Zhang, X. (2016). Institutional transition from welfare enterprise to social enterprise: The localization of legislation and policy in Chinese context. *Journal of Institutional Studies (журнал Институциональных Исследований), 8*(1), 121–131.

# Service Design Through Continual Engagement: Case Study of a Dementia Care Home in India

**Gauri Tillu and Pramod Khambete**

**Abstract** Dementia care is increasingly becoming a problem of scale in India. The scarcity of trained caregivers augments this complex issue. Normal medical care falls short of providing the quality of life that a Person Living with Dementia (henceforth mentioned as PLWD) deserves. Families of PLWDs (henceforth mentioned as FPLWD) lack the necessary knowledge and skills to cope with the conditions of dementia and may choose the option of a residential care home. This chapter presents a descriptive case study of Service Design Engagement in a Dementia Care Home setting. The objective of the engagement was to design solutions that could alleviate their anxiety, stress and make the experience smooth and reassuring during the journey. The study elucidates the processes and methods used, the solution concepts implemented and the evaluation of the concepts. It highlights the benefits of Service Design, Continual Engagement and Participatory Design in social organizations. We conclude by discussing the merits of the methods used along with the insights, possibilities and limitations of the paper.

**Keywords** Service Design · Value co-creation · Dementia Care · Dementia Care India · Service Ecosystem · Co-design · Participatory design · Continual engagement

## 1 Introduction

Dementia is the term used to describe a group of degenerative brain disorders that impact a person's memory, orientation (to time, place and people) and ability to think and communicate (Walsh, 2006). There is usually also a decline in other cognitive

G. Tillu (✉) · P. Khambete
Indian Institute of Technology Bombay, Powai, Maharashtra 400076, India
e-mail: gauritillu@gmail.com

P. Khambete
e-mail: pramod.khambete@gmail.com



E. M. Reji and S. Majumdar (eds.), *Social Enterprise Values and Processes*, India Studies in Business and Economics, https://doi.org/10.1007/978-981-97-3252-4_7

functions like judgement and thinking, planning, reasoning and processing of information. The degree of impairment ranges from mild to severe, where inability to undertake complicated tasks falls under mild while absolute absence of ideas falls under severe decline (Waite et al., 2009). There are around five million people in India who need Dementia Care and this is increasingly becoming a problem of scale (Kumar et al., 2020).

The societal challenges of Dementia care are rapidly increasing worldwide due to higher life expectancy, ageing population and lifestyle changes. Families of PLWD face tremendous issues from the get go. It is difficult to accurately identify mental health problems in the early stages as the symptoms look more or less like exaggerated idiosyncrasies of a person. For example, in the beginning a mild confusion with directions or getting confused with new names. There is little awareness regarding how to deal with mental health issues in elders. Once dementia is diagnosed, families do not have the knowledge and expertise to take care of the PLWD at home. Dementia often puts restrictions for family members on doing certain activities like going out for work or going on vacations. This often takes a toll on the mental and physical health of the family members. These factors together substantially increase the psychological, social and economic stress, often termed as "caregiver burden." The Quality of Life (QoL) of the family diminishes, in turn affecting the QoL of the PLWD.

Sometimes, the family members are not co-located, living in a different city or state or living abroad. That puts an additional stress on travelling due to medical emergencies. Such families have to look for someone trustworthy who can act like a proxy on their behalf in case of a requirement of quick decision-making during a medical emergency, which adds one more dimension to the challenges. In case, a family decides on admitting the PLWD in a care home, which usually happens in the fag end, they face societal pressure and guilt. Admitting an elderly family member in an external care home is considered by some societies as forsaking of responsibilities by the family members. All these factors contribute to the social aspects of the problems associated with Dementia.

## 2 Dementia Care: An Overview

Effective dementia care is a complex endeavour calling for appropriate knowledge and expertise. As a result, the demand for dementia care services is increasing (Bloom et al., 2010). The situation is no different in India. Figure 1 illustrates the common approaches to the care of a PLWD observed in India.

*A. Managing without external help*: Here, the family members (usually the spouse or the children) assume the responsibility of the everyday care of the PLWD. This would be feasible during the initial stages of dementia. However, as dementia is a progressive and degenerative condition, the challenges in caregiving exacerbate over time. At times the PLWDs are aggressive towards even the family members. Additionally, most families lack the necessary knowledge and skills to cope with the conditions of Dementia.

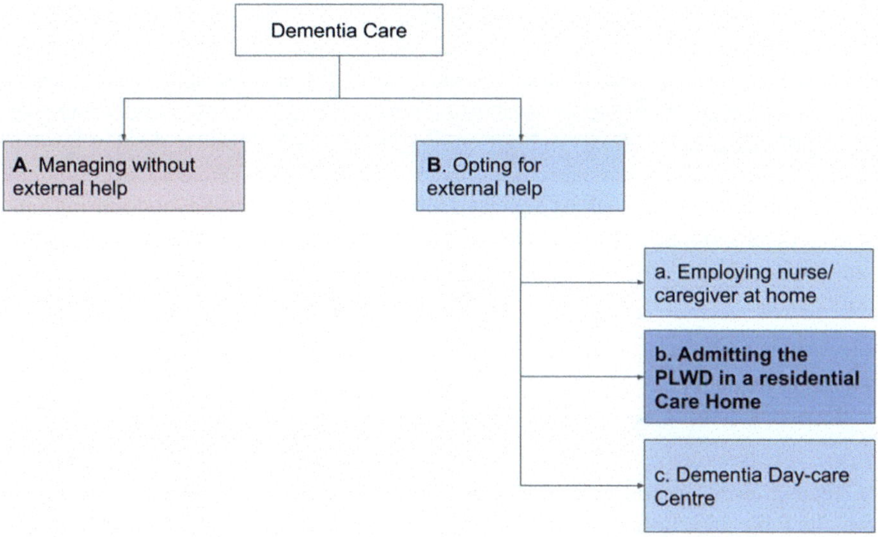


**Fig. 1** Common approaches towards dementia care

*B. Opting for external help*: There are two common approaches when it comes to opting for external help:

i. *Employing a nurse/caregiver at home*: A part-time or full-time nurse/caregiver is employed by the family to take care of the PLWD at their homes. These caregivers are usually equipped to address only the physical care needs of the PLWD, such as everyday hygiene, assistance in medication and physical wellness. Normal medical care, however competently it is done, always falls short of providing the quality of life that a PLWD deserves. This is because dementia care must include mental wellness care in addition to the normal physical wellness. Additionally, the PLWDs need to be cognitively stimulated and engaged in activities to delay further deterioration in the conditions.

ii. *Residential Care Home*: A family decides to admit the PLWD in a care home facility that is equipped to (it is hoped) provide holistic care. This choice is usually not the first one, and is often delayed as far as possible as the last resort due to the socio-cultural ethos in India. However, if admitted into the right residential facility, the Quality of Life of the PLWD can be maintained and even improved slowly over time. This often proves to be the best option for both the PLWD as well as their families.

iii. *Dementia Day-care centre*: Another common option to cope with dementia care is where the PLWD spends a certain amount of time of their day at the day-care centre. Day-care centres usually have activities and exercises to engage the PLWDs throughout the day. A day-care centre provides the facilities of a residential care centre but the daily change in the environment between the home and the day-care centre may become a source of stress to the PLWD.

There is an increasingly growing acceptance of Dementia Care Homes as a preferred option, although the number of such facilities are woefully insufficient as it is difficult to get well-trained multidisciplinary medical staff (psychiatrists, general doctors, psychologists, counsellors, nurses, caregivers, etc.) under one roof.

Considering the complexity of high-quality Dementia Care due to the requirement to address the needs (financial, emotional, social, etc.) of a range of stakeholders, a multidisciplinary field such as Service Design can make significant contributions. There is robust evidence of the benefits of Service Design in innovations and enhancements in healthcare outcomes, including Dementia care (Lee, 2011; Sangiorgi & Karine, 2010).

## 3 Tapas Elder Care—The Dementia Care Organization

The Tapas Elder Care, the Dementia Care Organization (henceforth called as Tapas) based in Pune is a home for around 40 PLWDs. It commenced the operation in 2015 and was only three years old when the authors' engagement started but grew rapidly due to its urban setting and as it serves a growing need. As a result of their organic growth and the scale of operations they were able to serve effectively with internalized, albeit unformalized processes and practices. As well, when the authors' engagement for the Service Design interventions with the organization commenced, there were no IT systems implemented. The full-time caregivers had a formal background in social work and psychology. There were in-house nurses, a dedicated panel of doctors, and other care professionals like physiotherapists to take care of the physical as well as mental well-being of the PLWDs. The technology readiness of the staff was limited to mobile apps, common social media platforms, and in some cases familiarity with Office Productivity suites. There is a well-informed and specialized board of advisors which consists of experts from the domain of geriatric care, psychological and psychiatric health, palliative care, etc. With these attributes we believe they can be considered representative of professionally run organizations of this kind in India.

One facilitating characteristic of Tapas was a highly motivated passionate team and leadership. The atmosphere at the organization was joyful and informal yet they maintained high professionalism and empathy. Additionally, there was a culture of mutual respect and active collaborative teamwork. Furthermore, there was eagerness to improve and innovate, combined with the willingness to explore contributions from other fields, particularly Service Design. All these factors made this organization a potent site for conceptualizing and implementing Service Design-led solutions and, in doing so, creating actionable knowledge that could be beneficial for similar organizations.

## 4 Benefits of Service Design in the Context of Dementia Care

Service design includes designing, refining and specifying user-facing touch points of an organization, and the supporting internal processes to improve customer experiences. Designing for service enrols many different people and objects in its projects and sees value as co-created in practice. Designing for service negotiates rationality, temporality and accountability (Kimbell & Park End Street, 2010). Service Design incorporates the following basic principles to address a complex problem area (Stickdorn & Schneider, 2010): (i) User-centred understanding through qualitative research, (ii) Participatory through the involvement of relevant stakeholders, (iii) Granularity, by partitioning a complex service into separate processes, (iv) Holistic, by considering touchpoints in the network of user interactions, (v) Co-creative, by involving relevant stakeholders in service execution.

It is now well-recognized that customer value is co-created with the active participation of the customers and other stakeholders. Services are value co-creation systems in which the Service Provider creates facilitating conditions and opportunities for resource integration for actualizing the value. This perspective provides granularity and a possibility of incremental improvement evolving into a holistic solution predicated on active collaboration with multiple stakeholders (Prahalad & Ramaswamy, 2004; Vargo et al., 2008). Conventionally, Healthcare providers did not adopt Service Design, but the situation has changed since some time now (Bate & Robert, 2006).

## 5 The Design Philosophy, Process and the Objectives

### *5.1 Design Philosophy*

Sangiorgi et al. (2015) emphasize that a good match between the client institution and the external, specialist designers is necessary for productive collaboration and avoiding friction. The factors that support include establishing trust, familiarisation and eventual use of professional languages and methods, activities to support implementation, and supporting the emergence of ad hoc innovation within client organizations. "Silent design" (Gorb & Dumas, 1987), i.e., design activity that is not formally called Design, is routinely undertaken by individuals who are not designated as "designers," without realizing it as design. Innovative people who are intent on improvements, embark on it to find solutions to the challenges they face. It was argued that forced adoption of "formal" design practices might inadvertently harm successful "silent design" practices. We found the organization indeed had a thriving culture of "Silent Design" and was mindful that it was leveraged rather than modified forcefully. In such situations, Participatory Design is ideal.

Co-design, i.e., Designing with Users, as against Designing for Users envisages the active engagement of the end users of products and services in the design process. Adapting service design and co-design approach provides benefits in a project like better ideas, better knowledge about customers' or users' needs, improved focus on customers or users, better cooperation between different people or organizations, and across disciplines, improving the service, better fit between service and customers' or users' needs, and better service experience, higher quality of service, continuous improvements and better relations between service provider and customers (Steen et al., 2011). However, the construct "Co-design" has varied interpretations in practice (Bradwell & Marr, 2017). They identified the common elements: (i) Participation: Collaboration, close working relationship, continuity, breadth of inputs and multiplicity of viewpoints, (ii) Development: Exchange of information and expertise on subject matter, and alignment of the process, (iii) Ownership and power: Maintaining the balance of rights and freedoms between participants, equality of the legitimacy and value in inputs from all and collective ownership, (iv) Outcomes and intent: Clarity of vision and direction, shared intent and outcome objectives, practical focus.

The groundwork for matching the above attribute was already in place in Tapas due to past relationships, and Co-Design was an excellent option. In our case, considering the organization's size, constraints and stakeholder availability, we found that Participatory Design, similar to Co-design in its ethos, was suitable. Specifically, we opted for Quasi-Participatory Service Design (Mahamuni et al., 2018).

Moore and Buchanan (2013) point out that often organizations striving for radical changes disrupt existing systems and practices and in healthcare, even small changes can have significant benefits for patients, staff and other stakeholders. Success in these efforts depends on considering various factors like context, content, processes and individual attitudes. These factors align well with User-Centered Design, particularly in the realm of Service Design.

Therefore, to retain the current quality of care maintained so far, a three-pronged strategy was adopted: (i) Conceptualizing new and radical service solutions, (ii) Implementing continuous incremental enhancements, (iii) Engaging with the people within the organizations as active partners in design on a continual basis. Considering this, the following approach was adopted: (i) Problem–solution co-evolution, (ii) Tacit knowledge triangulated with fresh data, (iii) Rapid, quasi-participatory design, (iv) Implementing concurrent micro-improvements, (v) Flexible design process, (vi) Enhanced Quality of Life for PLWD and Family, (vii) Human touch points with lightweight technology, (viii) Using available communication modes.

## 5.2 *The Service Design Process*

The research phase of the project followed the best practices in the design process and is described below.

### 5.2.1 Primary User Studies

Extensive user research through observational studies, semi-structured interviews with branching and laddering was conducted with multiple stakeholders—families of resident PLWDs, founder of the organization, counsellors, staff and doctors. The caregivers and counsellors at the organization were shadowed to closely observe and note their daily care routine. Through these studies, data was collected from various stakeholders and the insights were triangulated (Fig. 2).

Insights:

It was observed that the stages that a family goes through while admitting a PLWD in a care organization and thereafter are explained in Fig. 3.

Become Aware: Family becomes aware that they need external help.

Search and Evaluate: The family searches and evaluates the available options Engage for Admission: Assuming that they find the partner organization and decide to engage.

**Fig. 2** Observational studies of users (PLWD and families)

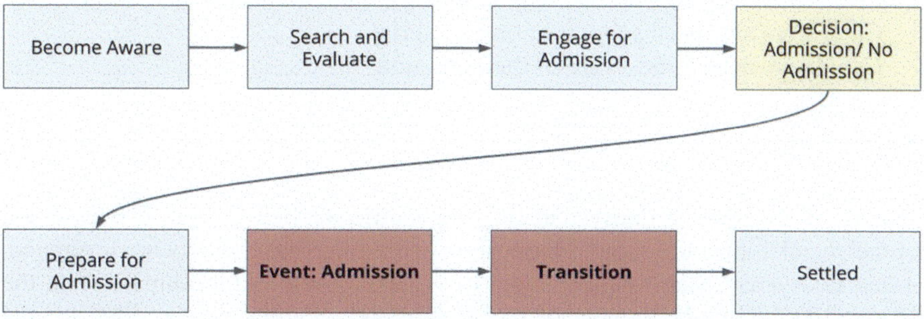


**Fig. 3** Process that a family goes through while admitting a PLWD

Decision—Admission/ No Admission: This may include consent from the PLWD, deliberation amongst the family members and close relatives and friends, etc.

Prepare for Admission: Assuming that the family decides to admit, they start preparing for the admission.

Event—Admission: This includes bringing the PLWD to the organization along with the belongings and formally admitting them into the organization.

Transition: The family goes through a change in their life with a family member away from home.

Settled: The family adapts to the change and eventually settles down.

Additional insights:

1. Families cannot identify the need for specialised care for dementia.
2. There is very little awareness about dementia and how to manage the symptoms.
3. The nurses from general bureaus are only capable of maintaining basic hygiene of the PLWD; they are not trained to manage conditions of dementia at home.
4. Family members get frustrated or helpless and do not always realize that the behaviour of the PLWD is caused because of the condition.
5. It is necessary to understand the background of the PLWD in order to make a better connection and help them better
6. It takes some time, effort and a lot of patience to understand what works and what does not with a particular PLWD
7. Knowing the background of PLWD helps in positioning the treatment on the spectrum.
8. The symptoms are just the top layer; the causes of the symptoms might be rooted deep. Doctors need to patiently find the cause of the trouble
9. If a family is looking after a PLWD for a long time, the primary caregiver develops tremendous stress and may show symptoms of mental disorders like depression
10. Family members interpret the symptoms of dementia very differently and the interpretation varies from person to person. Therefore, for proper diagnosis, medical reports are required. E.g., MRI Scan
11. Tremendous amount of empathy and patience is required
12. Caregivers need support and help to manage their stress and frustrations
13. Caregivers also need support in times of grief
14. Caregivers need to be aware of their emotions

### 5.2.2 Synthesis

Mapping of the Service Ecosystem: In user-centric Service Design, it is essential that the social connections and relationships with other stakeholders are leveraged. Service Ecosystem Map is a technique to visualize such relationships so that the opportunities for the betterment of the service and creating greater value for the intended service users are identified. The Service Ecosystem map is presented in Fig. 4.

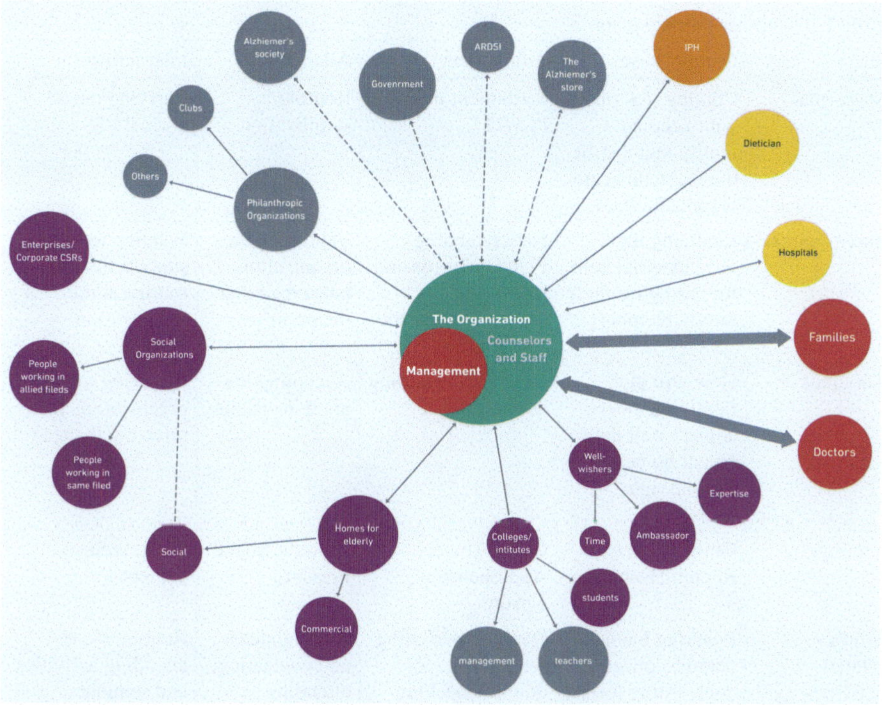


**Fig. 4** Ecosystem map

Mapping of the Customer Journey: Customer Journey Map (CJM) is a technique used to delve deeper to bring out the facets of their experience as Service Users go through the stages in availing of a Service. The CJM of the Service User (family of a PLWD in this case) during the admission and the transition phase was mapped with a focus on what the family members are thinking, feeling and doing at every stage of the journey (Table 1).

## *5.3 The Design Objectives*

Based on the insights from the primary research and synthesis it was evident that Family members and the caregivers are important stakeholders that need to be paid attention to in holistic care. These aspects are recognized in the field of Dementia care. For instance, Alzheimer's Association provides several high-level recommendations in this regard (Fazio et al., 2018). The synthesis also pointed to the potential opportunities.

The decision to admit and the initial days after admission into a residential care facility are stressful to the family members because of reasons like guilt, societal

**Table 1** Customer journey map

| Stage | Compromise | Adjustment | Adaptation | Internalization |
|---|---|---|---|---|
| Stage goal | Coming to terms with keeping a family member in the Dementia care organization | Settlement of PLWD | Routine stabilization | Carrying out a normal life |
| Stage context | Realizing they need external help for caring for their family member | Understanding PLWD's needs and role of the organization in the care routine | Validating the organization (start realizing the pros) | Wanting to help or support the care routine at the organization |
| Thoughts | How will my family members adjust? Will they feel at home? Is this the right decision? | How are they doing in my absence | Accepting the good decisions | Believing in the organization and referring it ahead |
| Feelings | Guilt, Anxiety, Regret, Hesitation | Guilt, Anxiety, Apprehension, Unsure | Secrecy, Social Pressure | Trust, security, content |
| Journey related activities | Planning financial details, collecting docs, filling forms, packing, plan and schedule, travel | Overcompensating for guilt, double-checking everything, observing PLWD settle, Visual confirmation, communication | Basic updates and contacting, attending activities and seminars | Routine visits, attending activities and seminars |
| Role of resources and enablers | Employees at the organization: providing info, updating, assigning the host Doctor- meeting, assessing | Initial meeting with doctor, daily communication | Counsellors and Doctors, Weekly reports | Friends and family of PLWD, help them get back to normal life |

stigma and anxiety of separation from a loved one. It takes time for them to cope with the emotional turmoil and settle down into a new life with the PLWD away from them. It is an equally crucial time for PLWDs to adjust to a new care routine at the care home which are unfamiliar surroundings. As part of settling in, it is often recommended that the family members do not visit the PLWD, a loved one, for a certain period. This exacerbates the anxiety and stress. The transition is therefore challenging for family members of new residents from several angles. This is often given inadequate attention and addressing this would help families of PLWDs ease their ordeal. The objective of the project was to design solutions that could alleviate their anxiety, stress and make the experience smooth and reassuring during the journey depicted in Table 1.

# 6 Services Concepts

## 6.1 Ideation

With the customer journey mapped, ideas were brainstormed to reduce the negative aspects of the experience and enhance the positive aspects at every stage of the journey as seen in Fig. 5. These stages were looked at from the point of view of different personas,[1] for example, an elderly spouse living away from the PLWD, a middle-aged daughter with her father as the PLWD, a young son with toddlers of his own having his mother admitted in the care organization, or a senior counsellor who has been with the organization for 2 or more years. Ideas to improve the experience of people belonging to these different personas were thought of which included ideas for better communication, smoother and more efficient processes and for addressing the emotional turmoil of the families. Progressively, the ideas having affinity were combined and converted into a concept with multiple touch points. A touch point is a point of interaction with a customer that a service provider can control.

## 6.2 Service Concept Design

### 6.2.1 Service Encounter Blueprints

Service Blueprints (Bitner et al., 2008) is a technique that identifies and visually depicts the Service Encounters (i.e., the goal seeking episodes of interactions with the Service providers) progresses. It helps in identifying the interconnections between the front-end Touch Points, the backstage and support processes, the dependencies and service failure possibilities. Detailed service encounter blueprints were created to assist the founder and the Caregivers of Tapas towards step-by-step execution of various new services introduced at the organization. Every step in the encounter (one interaction that has a clear beginning and end during the entire service execution) had details of the Touchpoint (a point and entity for interaction, which is controlled by the service provider) being used in it and the actions taken in the step. An example of two steps from the entire blueprint is provided in Table 2.

[1] Personas are a common technique used in User-Centred Design and Service Design. Personas are behavioural archetypes that are used as reference in the design process. We are unable to discuss in detail due to the paucity of space. Interested readers could refer to several excellent books on the topic.

**Fig. 5** Portion of the idea wall

### 6.2.2 Illustrative Service Concepts

Using the above process, the following interventions were conceptualized and implemented by the authors in collaboration with Tapas:

Micro-interventions

*Admission*: Multiple micro-interventions were introduced to smoothen the admission journey into the organization, reduce the anxiety of the family and help them be better prepared for the upcoming journey. This intervention included a redesign of the admission stage through increased communication, messages, check-lists for documents, medical tests, etc. An admission kit was designed to explain the admission process and make it smooth.

*Open When... letters*: This was a unique touchpoint designed to help build resilience towards the stress experienced by families during the transition period after admission. These letters would help the family members keep engaged in between the visits to the organization by specifying certain activities to do like creating a photo collage or creating a care package for a family member at the organization.

**Table 2** Service encounter blueprint for the steps

| Preparatory encounter | | |
|---|---|---|
| Step | Arrange the meeting | Wait till the Day of the Meeting |
| Step goal | Finalize the date, time, and venue (maybe virtual) | |
| User action | Converse and interact with touchpoint<br>Exchange information about availability<br>Finalize date, time, and venue<br>How much time will the meeting go on for?<br>Acknowledge queries about medical reports | Read material provided<br>See what relates to their PLWD<br>Prepare questions/doubts for the upcoming meeting<br>Start writing a journal—How did it start? How did they notice? etc.<br>Scan and send medical reports |
| *Line of interaction* | | |
| Touch point action | Touchpoint—The Organization Staff<br>Medium—Phone<br>Call the FPLWD<br>Converse and interact with FPLWD<br>Exchange information about availability<br>Finalize date, time, and venue<br>Immediately send an invite (Google invite/message)<br>Also, provide material to read if there is a gap between this phone call and meeting<br>Ask them to scan and send medical reports (e.g., over WhatsApp) | Touchpoint—The Organization Staff<br>Medium—Phone<br>Reminder/Confirmation of the meeting<br>(Depends on the duration of the gap)<br>Receive medical reports |
| *Line of visibility* | | |
| Backstage actions | Prepare the message to be sent with the invite, reading material, and reminder for medical reports | Prepare Admission Kit<br>Share reports with the doctors and gets their opinions and inputs |
| *Line of internal interactions* | | |
| Support activities, processes, and artefacts | Alternative dates<br>Note down preferred dates<br>System/records of calendar and appointment with people<br>Display board for upcoming meetings/ events + people assigned to organize the events<br>Public/The Organization Calendar<br>Notice boards<br>Reading material and brochure | Reading material<br>Brochure |

**Fig. 6** Servicescape redesign

## Servicescape Redesign

The staff had identified problems with visitor management causing stress and adversely affecting their care activities. As well, the unguided visitor movements caused disturbance to the PLWDs. The identification of root causes led to the self-regulation of visitors' entry through a redesign of the servicescape while considerably improving the privacy of the residents and the orderliness of visits. The area chosen for the family visits is close to the entrance of the organization, however, isolated enough so as to not disturb the residents. It is designed so as to provide shade for the family while they wait for the PLWD to arrive. The chairs in the family visit area are of a different colour than the chairs used by the residents as a visual cue for differentiation. A small centre table is placed with bottles of water for the visiting family. The area is also close to the doctor's clinic so that families can meet with the doctor in case of any questions regarding the health of the PLWD.

A large poster with a photo of the caregivers welcoming (posing in a "Namaste") is displayed in the visiting area adding to the visual cues differentiating the visiting area. The design strategy was to use "soft" cues, implicit constraints and nudges rather than regimentation of visits. These soft obstructions in the form of visual nudges (Thaler et al., 2013) have introduced a self-organizing flow to the visitor movements, while still giving them enough freedom to move around (Fig. 6).

Following a similar strategy, the entrance area in a sister facility was also developed by extending the same principles of visual nudges. By placing a board in the entrance, the entry into the area was diverted along the desired route. This soft obstruction also introduced a pause in the entrance where the visitors could enter their names in the visitors register near the security shed visible in the right part of the image in Fig. 7.

**Fig. 7** Entrance area developed at the sister facility

New Synergistic Service

Empathic host: This is a new service component that leverages the bonds of the organization with the residents' families. As the initial stages can be overwhelming for a new family admitting their PLWD in the care organization, a pair of empathic hosts, a counsellor from the organization and a family member of an older resident from the organization co-create support and help the family with their doubts, anxieties and emotional turmoil. A service blueprint was designed for a smooth and effective introduction of the empathic host with the new family.

# 7 Evaluation

## *7.1 Value Analysis*

Value is the net effect of benefits/costs (Table 3). There are intangible benefits like emotional, social and knowledge that also add value. Similarly, costs can be intangible in the form of time, efforts and psychic costs.

$$\text{Value} = \frac{\text{Benefits (Functional + Emotional + Social + Knowledge)}}{\text{Costs(Monetary + Time + Efforts + Physic)}}$$

**Table 3** Value analysis of the interventions

| Intervention/idea | Value for the family | Value for the organization |
|---|---|---|
| Admission | Increased Emotional Benefits ↑, Increased Knowledge Benefits ↑, Reduced Psychic Cost ↓ | Reduced Time Cost ↓, Reduced Effort Cost ↓ |
| "Open When…" Letters | Increased Emotional Benefits ↑, Reduced Psychic Cost ↓ | Reduced Time Cost ↓, Reduced Effort Cost ↓ |
| Servicescape redesign | Increased Emotional Benefits ↑, Increased Social Benefit ↑, Reduced Psychic Cost ↓ | Reduced Time Cost ↓, Reduced Effort Cost ↓ |
| Empathic host | Increased Emotional Benefits ↑, Reduced Psychic Cost ↓ | Reduced Time Cost ↓, Reduced Psychic Cost ↓ |

## 7.2 *Qualitative Feedback on the Service Concepts*

Feedback received over time from the staff and families has shown that these interventions have proved to be useful in reducing the anxiety of the families, refining administrative processes and streamlining the care routine.

### 7.2.1 Micro-interventions

Due to the additional touchpoints in the admission process like a checklist for the belongings of the patients, sending forms beforehand over the mail and introductory, reminders and confirmation messages it was observed that the time required for a new patient to get admitted reduced from approximately 2 h to around 30 min. Because the admission forms were sent to the family beforehand, the family filled them out at home and brought the ready forms to the organization for admission. This meant that the doubts and concerns related to the forms were addressed before the admission and the actual admission of the patient into the organization occurred smoothly and quickly. The checklist of belongings to be carried along attached in the mail makes the event of admission smoother, easier and efficient and is proving to be especially beneficial during the COVID pandemic times.

Another outcome of these added touchpoints means that the caregiver of the new resident is already introduced to the family and the caregiver is aware of the conditions of the resident or of any special requirements needed beforehand, making the actual admission smoother. WhatsApp messages containing instructions for admissions are converted into messages for updates post admission. Families get daily/weekly/monthly updates about their family members at the organization based on the severity of the symptoms and the time elapsed after admission. The updates include medical parameters like the blood pressure, sugar, pulse and oxygen level readings along with comments on the overall physical and mental health of the resident. The messages were later modified to also include the sleeping patterns, food intake and a couple of photos of the resident while performing their activities. This has led to the strengthening of the trust in the families about the caregivers of the organization in turn reducing their anxiety.

Development of a handbook, which is a more feasible form of "Open When... letters", is being developed at the organization with the help of physiatrists and physicians. This handbook will be provided to the family on the day of admission. It aims at creating awareness about the different types, stages and symptoms of dementia while providing more details into the processes and care routines carried out at the organization to assure the family about their PLWD's safety.

### 7.2.2 Servicescape Redesign

Without the family visiting area, the family members visiting their PLWDs would either wait in the entrance crowding it or directly barge in the area dedicated for the activities of the residents. This caused disturbance in the ongoing activities as well as other residents getting distracted from the activity. Sometimes, suddenly seeing a familiar face from the family, a PLWD would get very emotional causing more stress to other residents performing their activities. Having a dedicated family visiting area proved to be useful as a buffer zone to premeditate the arrival of a family member to the PLWD. It also meant that other residents were not disturbed while performing their activities. The family visit area gave the counsellors a dedicated area to discuss the health and the care routine of the respective PLWD without disturbing other processes in the organization.

### 7.2.3 Empathic Host

In this intervention, one dedicated counsellor is assigned to a new family who has recently decided to admit their PLWD into the organization. This counsellor remains as the primary point of contact to resolve any queries or doubts that the family may have. Along with that, an older family, preferably with a similar social and cultural background, that has gone through the initial stages of the journey and has now settled in, is assigned for additional emotional support. This new service has provided transparency and emotional assurance to the new families. It has also ensured continuity between the conversations between the family and the organization due to a dedicated point of contact who has a detailed history of all the conversations.

Another important outcome is that the founder of the organization has been able to delegate substantially to lead caregivers positively impacting their confidence and self-esteem—a corollary but crucial benefit.

## 7.3 *Impact of Service Design Interventions*

This section elucidates a few examples out of many at Tapas this service design engagement brought about on some PLWDs and their families. (Names changed)

### 7.3.1 Case 1: Mr. and Mrs. Kulkarni

This is an example of an elderly couple living in Mumbai. Mr. Kulkarni (81 years old) had been diagnosed with middle-stage dementia. His wife (76 years old) cared for him at home. Their only son lived abroad. But gradually as Mr. Kulkarni's dementia progressed, it was becoming difficult day by day for the elderly wife to manage the conditions on her own. So, she hired a nurse to take care of her husband. Due to the standard practice of working in shifts, she had to hire two nurses—one during the day and one during the night time. The nurses were trained in general medical nursing but did not have any experience in dementia care. Hence, they needed continuous instructions and close monitoring. Sometimes the nurses had clashes among themselves and also with Mrs. Kulkarni over additional pay and for raising their fees. The nurses took leaves and also discontinued working abruptly without informing beforehand. Mrs. Kulkarni had to then start searching for new nurses and go all over the process again to get them adjusted. It was a lot of hassle and was becoming extremely difficult for the elderly lady to manage the situation on her own.

The son who was abroad tried to look up care organizations near their home in Mumbai and nearby cities. The family came to know about Tapas Elder Care but were initially very hesitant. When they got in touch with Tapas, they were introduced to a family with a similar background, who had previous experience of admitting one of their family members in Tapas. They connected over a phone call, and discussed at length the challenges and doubts that Mrs. Kulkarni and her son had. That conversation gave them a lot of reassurance which was very much required at that stage. The family decided to move Mr. Kulkarni to Tapas and Mrs. Kulkarni also moved in with him. When they arrived at Tapas, they were given specific assistance and close support during the first couple of weeks to help them settle down into the new environment. This reassurance is crucial for any PLWD to adjust into a new place. There were attendants, nurses, counsellors and doctors on call to assess their physical and mental health on a continuous basis.

Mr. Kulkarni gradually adjusted to the new care routine and also started participating in the daily activities at Tapas. With dedicated and trained caregivers, his quality of life improved.

Just knowing that Mr. Kulkarni was doing well made Mrs. Kulkarni more relaxed. It was a big change for Mrs. Kulkarni who previously had to spend her entire day looking after her husband. Now she had a lot of time on her hands for pursuing her own activities and rekindled her passion for poetry and literature.

In this example, the intervention of Empathic host and smooth admission process with a focus on the transition period of the PLWD played a very important role in converting an exhausting and traumatic situation into a new positive journey of Mr and Mrs. Kulkarni at Tapas.

### 7.3.2 Case 2: Mrs. Sharma

Mrs. Sharma, a widow with 2 sons and a daughter lived with her younger sister (also a senior widowed person). All her children were married and lived with their respective families. They took turns to visit their mother and aunt several times a month. Mrs. Sharma loved her children and always wanted to see them. She used to request her sons and daughter to stay with her for a while. But having their own families and work responsibilities, they could not spend days together with her.

One day, Mrs. Sharma became very agitated as her son was leaving after his visit. Initially, he did not find this very odd and dismissed her loud tantrums as her regular resistance towards her children leaving for work. But this agitated and irrational behaviour kept on worsening until one day, Mrs. Sharma stepped out of the house, onto the road when she was alone with her sister and started screaming hysterically. Her eldest son who lived close by was called immediately. He got her to calm down but not before a lot of yelling on the road. It was soon thereafter that Mrs. Sharma was diagnosed with Dementia and her violent and erratic behaviour aggravated as days passed.

Since it was becoming difficult for Mrs. Sharma's sister to live with her in a constant fear of a violent attack, her close family came to the conclusion of admitting their mother to a care home.

After a lot of deliberation, they came across a general old age home and admitted her into it. But the organization being a generic elder care organization, the employees there could not handle Mrs. Sharma's violent behaviour. A week later, the organization called one night and asked the family to immediately take Mrs. Sharma away as they were not equipped to deal with her tantrums and agitation.

Extremely disheartened, they looked for other options and came across Tapas Elder Care for Dementia patients. Because of their previous experience, they did a thorough enquiry and spoke with multiple staff members as also with other families that had their PLWDs admitted in there.

They decided to get Mrs. Sharma admitted there. One of the counsellors was assigned to be in constant touch with the family and keep them updated. This counsellor was their empathic host. They followed the instructions of the counsellor and admitted Mrs. Sharma after a thorough medical and psychological evaluation. The family was then asked to let Mrs. Sharma settle down and visit only after 2 weeks.

At Tapas, Mrs. Sharma was included in all the day-to-day activities, exercises and prayers. She got to spend her time and energy on group activities with a lot of people of her age. A close eye was kept by the caregivers to see for any violent gestures or tantrums towards other residents. Mrs. Sharma was kept busy and engaged while being looked after well. During this period, her family was updated about her everyday activities, food intake, other medical parameters like blood pressure, oxygen levels and her sleeping time.

When her family came to visit her after 2 weeks, they were pleasantly surprised to see their mother, so well-settled in the care home, and actually enjoying herself. She met them all and behaved in a very jovial mood. The children were relieved to see such an improvement in the quality of life and have seen a positive change in their mother. They continued their regular visits which are now emotionally stress-free and feel relieved.

In this example, the family relied heavily on the empathic host to give them appropriate advice. The personal involvement of the empathic host from the very beginning built the trust of the family in the organization and its processes. The transition period acted as a cooling period for the PLWD to settle into the care home and get adjusted to the routine as well as for the family to relieve the accumulated stress over the past few months.

The regular updates to the family about their PLWD led to a reduction in the anxiety of the family.

### 7.3.3 Case 3: Mrs. Balan

Mrs. Balan's family consists of her son, her daughter-in-law and 2 young grandkids. Both the son and the daughter-in-law are employed and used to go for work leaving the elderly Mrs. Balan alone in the house. The problem started when Mrs. Balan displayed mild symptoms and was diagnosed with early-stage Dementia. Since there was no one around to take care of her throughout the day, they decided to try out a care home for a few weeks and see if Mrs. Balan was comfortable in such a facility.

The family came to know about and approached Tapas Elder Care. However, they had very specific constraints. Mrs. Balan did not eat the regular food served in the care home. She only ate food served in her hometown like rice, dosas (Indian bread made out of rice) or idlis (Indian rice-cakes). There was yet another barrier as Mrs. Balan could not speak or understand any language except Malayalam. None of the caregivers knew Malayalam. The family was very hesitant and doubtful if Tapas would be able to take care of this situation.

However, the counsellors at Tapas got together and worked out a plan for the care routine of Mrs. Balan. Initially, Mrs. Balan was very reserved and only communicated with gestures and refused to eat properly. The staff at Tapas made dosas for her as she would not touch any other food. Gradually though, she started bonding with her caregiver. The caregiver used to talk to her and communicated with her irrespective of the language barrier and soon their bond grew. They started communicating in their respective mother tongues, without completely understanding the meaning of the conversation. But Mrs. Balan started liking to chat with her empathetic caregiver. The caregiver also gradually started to introduce a variety in Mrs. Balan's meals. Overtime, she started to have a balanced diet regularly. The family was happy to see Mrs. Balan follow the diet and engage with the other residents, counsellors and caregivers.

In this example, the initial transition period was of the utmost importance for the PLWD to open up to the caregivers and settle into the new care home setting.

### 7.3.4 Case 4: Mr. Venkat

Mr. Venkat was admitted to Tapas Elder Care, at an early stage of his Dementia. His wife has been living alone for a few years now. She visits him often. So, the staff at Tapas includes her in the occasions and activities conducted at the organization. She likes to cook South-Indian dishes for different occasions and bring them to Tapas for everyone to eat.

The staff also helps her out with any medical emergencies she faces sometimes.

This example shows how the inclusion of family members of the PLWD willing to help in the care routine gives them satisfaction.

The above examples show the evolving and flexible nature of services. Service design helps incorporates and utilize these aspects to improve the processes of an organization and enhance the experience of the users.

## 8 Discussion

Although the case study presented in this paper is focusing on one organization, it can be used as an outline for iterative, continuous and incremental improvement in social organizations with similar background and context as it appears to be an effective approach towards enhancing services in social organizations. Also, using a service design approach in social enterprises serving in complex problem areas may prove to be beneficial due to the various attributes of service design like holistic, user-centred, granular and participatory.

This case study demonstrates the benefits of incremental improvements and participatory design. Incremental improvements let us quickly test and adapt. The ideas and concepts suggested in the paper can be easily contextualized to suit different organizations due to the flexibility and evolvability of the solutions. The methodologies used provide elastic guidelines rather than rigid standards so as to better suit different contexts and constraints.

Participatory design and continual engagement are long-term processes and allow room for internalizing and strengthening silent design based on the tacit knowledge of the domain experts or the stakeholders (Management and staff of the partner organization in this case). Participatory design also eliminates the power distance between the on-field workers and designers as designers do not play the role of consultants but enter into the field to study, ideate, prototype and test along with the on-field stakeholders. This internalization also empowers the stakeholders to improve and adapt continuously even without a designer or consultant. The staff at Tapas has developed sensitivity towards innovation in their day-to-day routine. The discussions during the design process triggered creative thinking in the staff and they have worked on the ideas and improved and adapted them to their context. Also, this change in attitude has been beneficial for the organization to cope with the sudden changes required in the processes and operations in the times of COVID-19. One such example is the modification of the visiting area during the pandemic, which followed the principles underlying the co-designed solution. The position of the welcome board is changed so as to indicate the family to arrive at the waiting area. Also, a soft barrier of a red ribbon is created to maintain safe distance between the visitors and the residents. These modifications have been tried and tested by the staff of the organization themselves having internalized the concepts of nudges.

The co-creative, participatory approach has also brought about a change in attitude of the families associated with the organization as well. During the times of the COVID-19 pandemic, families have been seen raising the morale of the caregivers and counsellors caring for their PLWDs through messages of appreciation. The families have also been compliant of all the new rules and regulations set at the organization to manage the safety of the residents (Fig. 8).

**Fig. 8** Modifications done to the visiting area done by the organization on their own

## 9 Directions for Future Work

A continual and participatory Service Design engagement leads to further ideas for value creation and service expansion. This is a significant outcome of the philosophy and approach. While working on this project, a need for a sister service of domiciliary residential care was identified for assisting the families in managing the early symptoms of dementia at home. The domiciliary residential care service, which leverages the tacit and explicit knowledge within the organisation, and reflects the empathic caring culture would allow the families to effectively take care of the PLWD at home during the initial stages of dementia with the help of professional care from the organization. The concept rests on the principles of co-creation of value and paying emphatic attention to the Quality of Life of the family members. It is aimed at empowering the families rather than rendering them exclusively dependent on professional support. This would also reduce the strain on the care facilities caused due to the scarcity of trained caregivers. A method and instrument for regularly assessing the Quality of Life (QoL) of the family members was developed as a corollary to the above service concept.[2] Both these were collateral outcomes of the project, which are to be taken forward. It is hoped they too would lead to knowledge outcomes like practices transferable for wider application to the benefit of the community.

The recent developments and changes in the processes and operations of a social organization during the times of COVID-19 may prove to be an interesting area of study. We may be able to understand how sustainable social organizations have come up with low-cost, low-overhead, but high-impact improvisations to cope with the changing situation. A dementia care centre would particularly be under high pressure during the pandemic due to the already vulnerable population that they care for. However, this organization has quickly adapted, developed and implemented new processes to maintain the safety and health of the PLWDs. It is planned to codify the knowledge for appropriate use even in normal times.

It is hoped that the experience and knowledge shared in the paper would benefit other organisations not only working in the same domain, but those interested in the field of Service Design as well.

**Acknowledgements** We would like to thank Mrs. Prajakta Wadhavkar, founder of Tapas Elder Care, Pune and entire staff and management of Tapas Elder Care, Pune for the continuous support and valuable feedback throughout the project; Mr. Kiran Sabnis, Gurumantra Academics, Pune for his support and guidance and Chandrima Biswas, a fellow designer who was a key contributor throughout the project.

[2] An early version was presented in 27th International Conference of Indian Association of Palliative Care, IAPCON 2020, Guwahati.

## References


Bate, P., & Robert, G. (2006). Experience-based design: From redesigning the system around the patient to co-designing services with the patient. *Quality & Safety in Health Care, 15*(5), 307–310. https://ncbi.nlm.nih.gov/pmc/articles/pmc2565809. Accessed 30 October 2019.

Bitner, M. J., Ostrom, A. L., & Morgan, F. N. (2008). Service blueprinting: A practical technique for service innovation. *California Management Review, 50*(3), 66–95.

Bloom, D. E., Canning, D., & Fink, G. (2010). Implications of population ageing for economic growth. *Oxford Review of Economic Policy, 26*(4), 583–612.

Bradwell, P., & Marr, S. (2017). Making the most of collaboration an international survey of public service co-design. *Annual Review of Policy Design, 5*(1), 1–27.

Fazio, S., Pace, D., Maslow, K., Zimmerman, S., & Kallmyer, B. (2018). Alzheimer's Association dementia care practice recommendations. *The Gerontologist, 58*(Suppl_1), S1–S9.

Gorb, P., & Dumas, A. (1987). Silent design. *Design Studies, 8*(3), 150–156.

Kimbell, L., & Park End Street. (2010). From user-centred design to designing for service. In *Design Management Conference* (Vol. 14, pp. 1–8).

Kumar, C. T. S., Shaji, K. S., Varghese, M., & Nair, M. K. C. (2020). *Dementia in India 2020.* Alzheimer's and Related Disorders Society of India (ARDSI).

Lee, S. (2011). Evaluating serviceability of healthcare servicescapes: Service design perspective. *International Journal of Design, 5*(2), 61–71.

Mahamuni, R., Sharma, S., Lobo, S., Hirom, U., & Khambete, P. (2018). Quasi-participatory service design in organizational context: A case study. In *Service Design Proof of Concept, Proceedings of the ServDes. 2018 Conference* (pp. 440–454). Linköping University Electronic Press.

Moore, C., & Buchanan, D. A. (2013). Sweat the small stuff: A case study of small-scale change processes and consequences in acute care. *Health Services Management Research, 26*(1), 9–17.

Prahalad, C. K., & Ramaswamy, V. (2004). Co-creating unique value with customers. *Strategy & Leadership, 32*(3), 4–9.

Sangiorgi, D., Prendiville, A., Jung, J., & Eun, Y. (2015). *Design for Service Innovation and Development (DeSID)—Final Report.* Arts & Humanities Research Council, UK.

Sangiorgi, D., & Karine, F. (2010). Service design and healthcare innovation: From consumption to co-production to co-creation. In *Service Design and Service Innovation conference.* Linköping Electronic Conference Proceedings (pp. 39–50).

Steen, M., Menno, M., & De Koning, N. (2011). Benefits of co-design in service design projects. *International Journal of Design, 5*(2), 53–60.

Stickdorn, M., & Schneider, J. (2010). *This is service design thinking: Basics, tools, cases.* BIS Publishers.

Thaler, R. H., Sunstein, C. R., & Balz, J. P. (2013). Choice architecture. In E. Shafir (Ed.), *The behavioral foundations of public policy* (pp. 428–439). Princeton University Press.

Vargo, S. L., Maglio, P. P., & Akaka, M. A. (2008). On value and value co-creation: A service systems and service logic perspective. *European Management Journal, 26*(3), 145–152.

Waite, J., Harwood, R., Morton, I., & Conelly, D. (2009). *Dementia care: A practical manual.* Oxford University Press.

Walsh, D. (2006). *Dementia care training manual for staff working in nursing and residential settings.* Jessica Kingsley Publishers.

# E-Commerce-Based Retailing and the Adoption of Information Technology by Small Shops to Manage Business Performance

**Vicky J. Nandgaye**

**Abstract** This chapter aims to analyze the influence of E-Commerce-based Retailing (ECR) on Small Retail Shops (SRS) and how SRS manages their business performance in light of the increasing use of ECR. Another major objective is to explore the adoption of Information Technology (IT) as a catalyst by SRS to enhance their businesses. The paper employs a qualitative research approach to achieve these objectives, utilizing in-depth interviews and an interview guide. It becomes evident that the transformation in the retailing sector has had varying effects on the business performance of different categories such as Apparel, Electronics, and Footwear. However, retailers with a solid understanding of market dynamics and technological proficiency have successfully embraced IT, thereby gaining a competitive edge. In contrast, food shops that leverage multiple electronic food service applications are experiencing strengthened business performance. This research sheds light on how ECR influences SRS businesses, emphasizing the pivotal role of IT adoption in shaping their competitiveness. The findings indicate that adaptability and technological literacy are key factors in navigating the changing landscape of retailing.

**Keywords** E-Commerce-based retailing · Adoption · Information technology and small shops

## 1 Introduction

The Indian retail industry is currently experiencing the most rapid growth globally. With the globalization of retailing, modern retail formats like Amazon, Flipkart, eBay, Snapdeal, Swiggy, Zomato, and others have made significant forays into the

V. J. Nandgaye (✉)
School of Management and Labour Studies, Tata Institute of Social Sciences, V N Purav Marg, Deonar P O, Mumbai, Maharashatra 400088, India
e-mail: vickynandgaye.mils@gmail.com



E. M. Reji and S. Majumdar (eds.), *Social Enterprise Values and Processes*, India Studies in Business and Economics, https://doi.org/10.1007/978-981-97-3252-4_8

Indian retail sector. Over the past decade, the retail landscape in India has undergone a profound transformation, driven by the entry of new players. Notably, the Indian retail sector contributes around 10% to the country's Gross Domestic Product (GDP), positioning India as the world's fifth-largest global retail destination. An A.T. Kearney (2021) study further underscores India's prominence, ranking it second in the Global Retail Development Index (GRDI) for 2021 with a score of 64.4. As of March 2021, India is ranked as the fifth-largest preferred retail destination globally, boasting the highest per capita retail store availability, as reported in the latest Indian Retail Industry report from India Brand Equity Foundation (IBEF). Projections indicate that the Indian market is poised to become the world's fastest-growing e-commerce market, driven by substantial investments and a rapid increase in the number of internet users. Within the e-commerce domain, E-Commerce-based Retailing (ECR) stands out as a significant segment, expected to account for 67% (USD 68.8 billion) of the total e-commerce market, according to KPMG (2016) findings.

E-commerce is a broad concept, but this study specifically focuses on 'e-commerce-based retailing (ECR),' often referred to as Business to Consumers (B2C). As per Vaithianathan's definition (2010: 84), ECR involves "a marketplace transaction in which customers learn about products differently through electronic publishing, buy them differently using electronic cash and secure payment systems, and have them delivered differently." E-commerce, in general, encompasses the use of the Internet, the World Wide Web (Web), mobile apps, and mobile device browsers for conducting business transactions (Laudon & Traver, 2013). The proliferation of lower-cost communication channels has significantly fueled e-commerce activities, while smartphones equipped with high-speed internet have streamlined online transactions (Gupta & Gupta, 2020). According to Choudhury and Jadhav (2020), the growth of e-commerce is influenced by factors such as internet and mobile penetration, along with affordable data rates (which are half those of China and one-third of the USA). Notably, their study revealed that mobile penetration alone does not necessarily lead to online shopping, but increased internet usage elevates the likelihood of e-shopping.

The E-commerce market in India has particularly captured the interest of the younger population (Singh, 2014; Singh & Ajmani, 2016). The attraction of home delivery, time-saving convenience, and 24/7 availability are the primary attractions for online buyers. However, security concerns and the complexities of policies pose significant deterrents. Research indicates that approximately three-fourths of buyers tend to visit online shopping platforms once or twice in six months (Singh & Ajmani, 2016). While the e-commerce industry has witnessed tremendous growth, especially in cosmopolitan and developed cities, in India, small retail shops (SRS) continue to dominate the retail landscape. This preference for SRS is rooted in the fact that a large portion of the population favors these traditional establishments. These family-run mom-and-pop stores have been a cornerstone of business for centuries. Nevertheless, the rapid expansion of ECR may have adverse effects on the business performance of SRS.

In the face of an increasingly competitive business landscape driven by the burgeoning ECR market, SRS finds themselves with limited survival options. Among these options, Information Technology (IT) emerges as a viable avenue for SRS to enhance its business performance, offering advantages such as increased operational speed and cost-saving benefits. IT also equips retailers with valuable market insights and enables them to effectively manage complex retail operations, granting them a competitive edge in the sector. The adoption of IT can empower small retailers to respond swiftly and adapt to the evolving marketplace, thus enhancing their agility and competitiveness. This research contends that IT serves as an enabler for small shops to navigate the challenges posed by the expanding ECR landscape. Consequently, SRS turn to IT as an alternative means to mitigate the negative influence of ECR. Therefore, this study endeavors to delve into how ECR influences the operations of small shops and how these businesses embrace IT to bolster their overall business performance.

## 2 Review of Literature

### *2.1 Small Retail Shops in India*

Small shops typically find their niche in neighborhood settings, offering convenience to the local population. According to Ramakrishnan (2010: 251), these establishments are characterized by their modest size, occupying less than 500 square feet of space, primarily situated in neighborhoods, and typically owner-managed with minimal hired assistance. They tend to carry a limited range of items in their stock. SRS have traditionally held a dominant position in India's retail industry, attracting customers through proximity, established goodwill, credit facilities, bargaining opportunities, and overall convenience (Joseph & Soundararajan, 2009). Factors such as the appeal of the location and the overall attractiveness of the street or city also contribute to the success of small shops (Coca-Stefaniak et al., 2010). Customers' preference for small shops is positively influenced by various factors, including the shop's location, helpful and trustworthy salespeople, home delivery services, cleanliness, promotional offers, and product quality. However, travel convenience can have a negative impact on these establishments (Goswami & Mishra, 2009). The collectivist nature of these shops and their orientation towards long-term relationships further enhance their appeal to consumers (Khare, 2013). Indian consumers are inclined to visit SRS due to the variety of products offered, personalized service, store amenities, and the relationships they develop with the shop owners (Khare, 2014).

Coca-Stefaniak et al. (2010) emphasize the significance of 'localization' as both a business practice and a marketing strategy for SRS. This approach involves understanding local socio-economic factors, cultivating customer loyalty through personalization (such as remembering customers' names), and relying on word-of-mouth promotion within the local community. Small stores often serve as central hubs for social interactions and advice within their proximity, playing a vital role for disadvantaged and socially excluded groups, including financially deprived, elderly, and disabled consumers. These shops contribute to enhancing consumer choice and creating value for their clientele. They serve as flexible pantries or larders, especially for geographically isolated communities (Clarke & Banga, 2010).

In India, a noteworthy retailing model prevails where small retailers typically procure goods in the morning and sell them in the afternoon. This model has proven successful, often overshadowing the dominance of large retail firms. Small retailers establish long-term relationships with their customers, and this continuity spans generations. India's substantial working-class population, many of whom are daily wage earners, frequently visit SRS to purchase groceries and other essential items in smaller quantities. According to Khare (2012), local retailers also play an active role in the social fabric of communities, enabling them to understand consumer needs better and enhancing the retailers' overall perception within these communities.

Nonetheless, the evolving preferences and choices of consumers are undergoing a shift, primarily due to the transformation in retail formats. The increased presence of industry giants in ECR, spanning from groceries to jewelry, is steadily capturing and dominating various retail market segments. Consequently, it is imperative to delve into how the entry of these corporate giants is impacting the established traditional shops, which will be elaborated upon in the following section.

## *2.2 Transformation in Retailing: Influence of ECR on SRS*

Retail markets are in a state of continual expansion and increasing complexity, primarily due to the exponential growth of the Internet and the rapid adoption of e-commerce by major industry players. This transformative wave in the retailing industry has given rise to a fiercely competitive environment for SRS (Doherty & Chadwick, 2010). The evolution of ECR has been a global phenomenon, with heightened internet utilization for business purposes notably prevalent in the US, UK, and Canada (Hawk, 2004). In Western countries, traditional offline players have transitioned to offer 'E' market services, including features such as e-search (24/7 availability), e-response to customer queries, e-payment facilities, e-assurance and trust-building mechanisms, and e-help functionalities like FAQs, all of which have positively impacted customers' online experiences (Singh, 2002).

In the post-ECR era, consumer expectations have shifted, with many now anticipating lower prices in online shopping as compared to traditional brick-and-mortar stores (Hardesty & Sutar, 2005). ECR is often perceived as a cost-saving option, but this shift has had adverse effects on small shops. Doherty and Chadwick (2010) have identified that ECR poses a significant threat to the high street market, primarily due to the diminishing role of intermediaries in the retail ecosystem.

However, demographic changes, shrinking markets, high real costs, and increasing price competition among retailers are emerging as threats to the Indian retail industry (Jhamb & Kiran, 2011). Even consumers are well updated than ever and they shop to greatly increased expectations for service (Shet, 2016) and price (Hardesty & Suter, 2005; Shet, 2016). Busy lifestyles, urban traffic congestion, and lack of time for offline shopping affect footfalls in SRS (Ruby, 2016). High growth in consumer expenditure, emerging brands, and fashion-conscious population are some other factors of modern retailing growth in India and convenient shopping experience at modern retail is negatively influencing SRS (Singh, 2014). Lower prices as compared to brick-and-mortar retail, reduced inventory, and real estate costs are the reasons behind the growth of ECR in India. Shopping is seen as a social and personal activity, where face-to-face contact with sellers is an important part of the shopping experience (Thomas & E. Carraher, 2014) in India. However, for the last three years, there has been a decline in the turnover and profit margin of retail shops (Saha, 2015). Perhaps increasing cross-channel free-riding (CCFR) behavior of customers (Chiu et al., 2010) influence badly on SRS, as live presentations given by small retailers about products, however, the same customers buy online. Hence, some of the retail shops are starting home delivery services to their products, trying to maintain a variety of stock and customer-oriented services (Chiu et al., 2010).

The evolution of retailing has been observed over a while where 'modernization of service' (Tumbe & Krishnakumar, 2018) can be a vital factor. Due to 'advanced service', consumers may be attracted to organized retailers. Thus, the very difference between the operations of SRS and ECR may be relied upon in the use of technology and service quality.[1] The service quality and technology can create a major difference between these two forms of retailing. Kalia's (2017) study shows that e-service quality is multidimensional. In every setting, it is of utmost importance to improve the service quality to gain in business. It is believed that the adoption of various technologies is functioning like modernization in services provided by retailers. Hence, advanced services and technology adoption by large business firms are attracting consumers towards ECR which leads to a reduction in footfalls of SRS. Moreover, for small retailers 'retail margin' (Shaikh & Gandhi, 2016) is a chief catalyst, however, due to the overwhelming expansion of ECR, the margin has been reduced to a minimal.

From the above intense discussion, it can be understood that outnumber studies have been conducted but limited aspects of e-commerce adoption are explained from the Indian perspective. Fewer writings from the lens of small retail shops and e-commerce-based retailing are identified. Limited research has been done on the obstacles small Indian shops face when using e-commerce. The question is pertinent to measures taken by and changes that occurred in the business process of small shops to manage the influence of e-commerce retail has not been addressed.

[1] Khare (2013) explains 'service quality' for Indian consumers are ambiance, layout, and service/relationship dimensions. For, Verma and Duggal (2015) salespeople, merchandise, convenience, prices, and customers are other dimensions of service quality.

## 2.3 Adoption of Information Technology in Retailing

Due to the usage of the internet and mobile penetration, big players introduced their business online. ECR are creating great competition before small retailers in terms of CCFR, reduction in footfall, brand attraction, deep discounts, increasing expectations of customers, and so on. SRS are losing its business gradually in the pretext of gaining market share of ECR. In this context, some changes in traditional forms of retailing need to be accepted. Here, IT is seen as an imperative factor that can save the business performance of SRS. IT is a much-required area in almost every business process. IT includes the management of complex data in the form of text, voice, image, audio, etc. It can also involve matters, which is related to the Internet. Due to the increasing usage of the internet, IT got a new meaning. IT enables shops to address these complex retail operations. Market knowledge and data obtaining are key advantages in a competitive retail sector (Saroja, 2012) and it is simply possible with IT adoption. The retail industry observes many challenges related to IT management. For instance, customer data, transparency and tracking, and global data synchronization.[2] IT is positively related to business performance. If the firms can integrate a product or process-oriented innovation strategy with investment in IT, then IT can enhance firms' relative performance in terms of profit and growth. There is a need to invest in IT and users must have the capacity to utilize IT to execute competitive business strategies (Dibrell et al., 2008).

IT improves the effectiveness of retail along with an emphasis on automation and customization of the offer. Success lies upon the capabilities of retailers and consumer attitudes towards innovative technologies (Kucharska, 2013). To compete with other retailing firms the need for IT installations in small business firms has been suggested by the researchers (Dibrell et al., 2008; Raymond et al., 2005; Riemenschneider et al., 2003). Raymond et al. (2005) view using technologies like websites, email, and telephones to communicate with customers, shops can provide better customer services and expand their customer base to reach out to a maximum number of consumers. Day-to-day challenges including dependency on consultants, vendors' unreliability of systems, and technical complexity are some of the major barriers to IT use (Harindranath et al., 2008).

Indian small shops are failing to attain their business potential due to the absence of strong foresight and short-sightedness further resulting in weak quality processes and products, late deliveries, weak inventory management, and the mismatch between demand and forecasts under uncertainty (Thakkar et al., 2009). Therefore, SRS fall into trouble in terms of sales, profit, and employment (Sivanesan & Green, 2019). In present retailing, an advanced retail information system needs to be installed to cope with all technical challenges involved under it. Schneider (2011: 13) stressed that "Increased competition and technological change require rapid adaptation. IT is in demand today because without it a business cannot react speedily to new information about competitors and its environment". Mixed responses on IT adoption by small

---

[2] Retrieved on 22nd July 2019 https://www.nirico.com/the-importance-of-information-technology-in-the-retail-sector/.

shops are found in the available literature. Studies from the context of developed countries identified largely. The limited literature on the theme is found in the Asian context. Many more aspects of IT adoption in retailing need to be explored.

## 3 Research Gaps

The transformation in the retailing industry has been creating a competitive environment for SRS (Doherty & Chadwick, 2010). Gradual expansion of ECR is gaining space due to economic factors like rising income, consumption levels, economic growth, and the large middle segment in India (Khare, 2013; Singh, 2014). High growth in consumer expenditure, emerging brands, and fashion-conscious population are some other factors of modern retailing growth in India and convenient shopping experience at modern retail is negatively influencing small shops (Singh, 2014). Consumers are well updated than ever and they shop to greatly increased expectations for service (Shet, 2016) and price (Hardesty & Suter, 2005; Shet, 2016). Endless inventory across all ECR channels, increasing smartphone-driven shopping, and the advent of browsing in stores but buying from cheaper ECR (Chiu et al., 2010) are pressurising factors for traditional retailers. Jain et al. (2017) found lower prices compared to brick-and-mortar retail, reduced inventory, and real estate costs are the reasons behind the growth of the ECR sector in India. Due to ECR price differentiation, changes in preference and tastes of consumers are increasing the scope of e-commerce retail in India. Even young urban Indian consumers are enhancing their perceived values of western brands and western retail formats (Mann et al., 2018).

In this context, some of the retail shops are starting home delivery services for their products, trying to maintain a variety of stock and customer-oriented services (Chiu et al., 2010). The neighbourhood shop owners perceived that their profit was negatively affected and operational costs were increased to meet the higher expectations of consumers regarding 'service quality'. It resulted in a sharp decline in turnover and profit margin of retail shops (Saha, 2015). A report (KPMG, 2016) on the impact of E-commerce on small businesses is generally presented thoroughly but it has not covered aspects of the retail sector. Retailers have been greatly affected in terms of turnover, profit margin, discount, variety of stocks, customer service, etc. dominating influences in ECR (Dahiya, 2017; Saha, 2015).

To face these emerging challenges due to the growth of ECR and other factors as mentioned above, SRS may adopt information technology to gain competitive advantages. Information Technology as an enabler speed up business processes and deliver cost-saving benefits to the shops. Literature shows that IT is positively related to business performance. Therefore, studies suggested that IT investment is imperative to execute competitive strategies (Dibrell et al., 2008). In modern retail shops, IT includes solutions like RFID, the mobile Shopping System, kiosk stores with touch screens, and Electronic Shelf labeling (Kucharska, 2013). IT improves the effectiveness of retail along with an emphasis on automation and customisation of the offer (Kucharska, 2013). To compete with other retailing firms the need for IT installations in small shops has been suggested by most of the researchers (Cragg & Mills, 2011; Dibrell et al., 2008; Qureshi et al., 2009; Raymond et al., 2005; Riemenschneider et al., 2003).

Studies on the adoption of IT were conducted in the context of developed countries (Cragg & Mills, 2011; Demoulin & Djelassi, 2016; Roy et al., 2018). The aspects of IT adoption by SRS as an enabler to manage the influence of the ECR environment have not been explained. Hence, the research seeks to study the adoption of information technology by small shop owners to face the challenges incurred due to e-commerce-based retailing. In this study, the researcher believes that the small shop outlets adopted IT in a way to counter the business of e-commerce players. The role of IT is an enabler for the business process. The usage of IT strengthens the business performance. Adoption may be advantageous to traditional players in order to manage the negative influence of ECR. Therefore, the present research interrogates IT adoption against the widening use of e-commerce. The present study contributed to the area of retailing in general and small retail shops in particular.

## 4 Methodology

This research adopts a qualitative research approach. This decision was based on the inherent nature of the objectives, which revolve around identifying the factors influencing traditional retail shops for the adoption of E-Commerce-based Retailing. Additionally, it aimed to investigate the adoption of information technology by Small Retail Shops and how it complements the adoption of E-commerce in enhancing their business operations. It's important to note that the academic literature has limited direct theoretical work on ECR, possibly due to its relatively new nature. ECR has mainly been explored from a marketing perspective, and attempts to develop theoretical and conceptual frameworks. As a result, the researcher has taken an inductive perspective on the relationship between theory and research, where theory can be generated through empirical research (Bryman, 2012). To uncover the factors influencing SRS for the adoption of ECR, the researcher relied on the narratives and perspectives of shop owners. Furthermore, in pursuit of the primary objective, the research delved into whether SRS have adopted information technology to complement their business operations and whether this adoption provides them with a competitive advantage. For this study, the researcher employed a multiple-case design, incorporating several cases. The use of multiple cases was essential to highlight both the distinctions and commonalities among them (Stake, 1995). This approach allows for a more comprehensive exploration of research questions and the development of theoretical insights (Eisenhardt & Graebner, 2007). Multiple-case sampling will enhance the reliability of research findings, enabling the researcher to develop a theoretical framework by examining various similar and contrasting cases. This approach also improves the precision and validity of research findings (Miles et al., 2014). Additionally, it adhered to a replication strategy, making the findings more robust by validating them in multiple settings (Yin, 2009).

## 4.1 Research Settings

The research was conducted in Mumbai city (Dadar) and its sub-urban parts (Chembur and Govandi). Mumbai is a commercial, industrial, and center of national-international financial transactions. The city gives number of opportunities for e-commerce businesses thus; it was interesting to look at the effects of ECR on traditional retail shops in a research setting. The different categories of SRS having the most selling online products were selected. Mumbai is a densely populated city; people have less time for shopping and it has the largest e-commerce market as a tier-I city. The variety of small shops was selected in a way to observe the impact and significance of ECR. The city is exposed to modern trends, which influence the lifestyle of residents in the city as compared to other Indian cities. The modern city comprises a diverse population having high demands of heterogeneous products in the market that gives an advantage to different shop owners to start their venture to mitigate the demands of the city. The metro city is growing in terms of infrastructure and employment opportunities increasingly witnessing pull migration to a great extent. However, the working-class masses invariably get deprived of leisure time, even for family. In this context, online shopping is majorly observed on a large scale. Thus, the study seeks to explore the effects of internet-based retail on the retail structure of Mumbai city.

## 4.2 Selection of Cases

In conducting this study, a multiple-case design was employed, necessitating the careful selection of several relevant cases aligned with the research's specific requirements. The primary research objective was to investigate the adoption of information technology by small retail shops and subsequently build a theoretical framework within the realm of retailing. In this context, each selected case was considered an experiment capable of either confirming or challenging emerging concepts and the relationships among these concepts (Eisenhardt, 1989; Eisenhardt & Graebner, 2007).

Although interviews were conducted with a total of 20 shop owners, only 12 shops were ultimately chosen as case studies. The selection process was guided by specific criteria, including (i) the shop had to be engaged in retailing activities, as defined in this study. (ii) the shop should have a workforce with a headcount ranging from 1 to 9 employees. (iii) the shop needed to be registered under the Maharashtra Shops and Establishment Act. (iv) tax compliance by the Central Goods and Services Tax Act of 2017. Once these criteria were met, the selected cases were further evaluated to determine their suitability for effectively addressing the research objectives. This rigorous selection process ensured that the chosen cases were most relevant to the study's objectives.

## 4.3 The Rationale for Selecting Sectors

Rising consumer expectations in shopping experiences, as well as innovation in novel technologies to provide adequate services to consumers, have resulted in a drastic transformation in the retailing sector over the period. With increasing mobile and internet penetration, India is regarded as the hottest destination for ECR. Products with the highest sales on online platforms were recognized to identify the sectors for the study. According to a survey report by Statista,[3] the most popular products ordered online are apparel (54%), consumer electronics and mobile (49%), footwear (47%), and food (24%). The list of sectors is matched with the markets in the universe (Mumbai and sub-urban Mumbai) where the sectors have been chosen based on the availability of shops.

## 4.4 Sampling

In this study, the selection of cases for data collection was driven by their relevance to the research objectives, rather than aiming to represent the entire population or universe. This approach aligns with the principles of theoretical sampling or replication logic within the context of case study research, as introduced by Eisenhardt (1989). "Theoretical sampling", as articulated by Eisenhardt and Graebner (2007: 27), involves the deliberate selection of cases because of their specific suitability in shedding light on and expanding upon relationships and logical constructs. Theoretical sampling logic entails the selection of cases that are anticipated to yield either similar outcomes (referred to as literal replication) or contrasting outcomes for well-grounded reasons (theoretical replication) (Yin, 2003). The chosen cases were primarily selected based on their theoretical relevance and capacity to provide rich, context-specific data (in line with Corbin & Strauss, 1990). The emphasis here lies on analytical generalization rather than statistical generalization (Yin, 2018). Ultimately, a total of 12 cases, representing diverse small retail shops, were selected within Mumbai city. These cases were categorized into four distinct types: Apparel, Footwear, Electronics and Mobile, and Food (restaurants), with three cases chosen from each category to ensure a balanced representation.

## 4.5 Data Collection

Before commencing the main data collection process, a pilot study was conducted to enhance the overall strategy for data collection. This practice is highly recommended whenever feasible, as it serves as a valuable preparatory step in refining the approach for gathering actual data. Conducting pilot research, especially before administering

---

[3] Products mostly bought online in India 2020 | Statista.

a semi-structured interview schedule to the targeted sample, is considered a best practice. Such pilot research plays a pivotal role in identifying potential issues and challenges that may arise during the full-scale data collection phase (Bryman, 2012).

The research focused on sectors that have experienced significant migration from traditional to online modes, notably apparel, footwear, mobile devices, and restaurants, where e-commerce has become integral. To collect data, observations were primarily conducted from a shopper's perspective, with communication of the research purpose to shop owners and prior appointments scheduled for their convenience, often during quieter noon hours to minimize disruptions. Detailed interviews were recorded, and comprehensive field notes were compiled based on these observations. During interactions, no leading questions were asked, and the primary emphasis was on evaluating technology adoption and readiness. The overarching objective was to discern the evolution of each shop's journey from its inception, focusing on differences between previous business practices and the contemporary landscape amidst increasing ECR. Interview questions centered on predetermined research themes and efforts were made to ensure minimal disruption to business operations when customers were present. Data collection tools included an interview guide for in-depth interviews, participant observation, and meticulous field note-taking. During the in-depth interviews, interviews were audio recorded and transcribed later. The interviews were conducted in a language (Marathi or Hindi) that comforted participants. Prior permission from research participants was obtained to use an audio recorder.

### *4.6 Data Analysis*

In this study, the qualitative data were analyzed by using techniques employed in the grounded theory (GT) approach. This approach is often described as iterative because it involves a continuous interplay between the collection and analysis of data. This means that the analysis begins after some data have been collected, and the insights gained from that analysis subsequently shape the next steps in the data collection process (Bryman, 2012). Grounded theory is not only used as a method of analysis but also as a strategy for data collection. GT employs several methods such as theoretical sampling, coding, theoretical saturation, and constant comparison for data collection and analysis. Theoretical sampling is already explained in detail in the sampling frame section. 'Coding' is the key process in Grounded Theory (GT) whereby data are broken down into parts, which are names. It starts soon after the data collection phase. Theoretical saturation is a process that is related to two phases in GT—the coding of data and the collection of data. Then, constant comparison refers to a process of maintaining a close connection between data and conceptualization, to balance correspondence between concepts and categories with their indicators (Bryman, 2012). Categorization of data was performed through manual coding as well as using the software Atlas.ti.

## 5 Results

This section delves into the impact of ECR on Small Retail Shops (SRS) across different sectors, including apparel, electronics, footwear, and food. As illustrated in the conceptual framework (Fig. 1), the diffusion of E-Commerce-based Retailing (ECR) is a phenomenon that transcends various sectors.

ECR practices are considered an innovation that has been diffused across the globe due to borderless transaction facilities. Extensive usage of ECR channels for shopping purposes may influence traditional retailing platforms because technology has become an integral part of young and educated generations. Besides competitive response of SRS to ECR players and complexities in adopting IT are incorporated in the study as illustrated in the framework (Fig. 1). A detailed explanation of each element in the framework is provided below.

### *5.1 Diffusion of Innovation: Influence of ECR on Traditional Retailing*

In this study technologies developed in retailing are considered as innovation (Rogers, 1983). These innovations in the forms of e-commerce platforms and omnichannel retailing technologies are diffusing among retailers and customers. Rogers (1983)

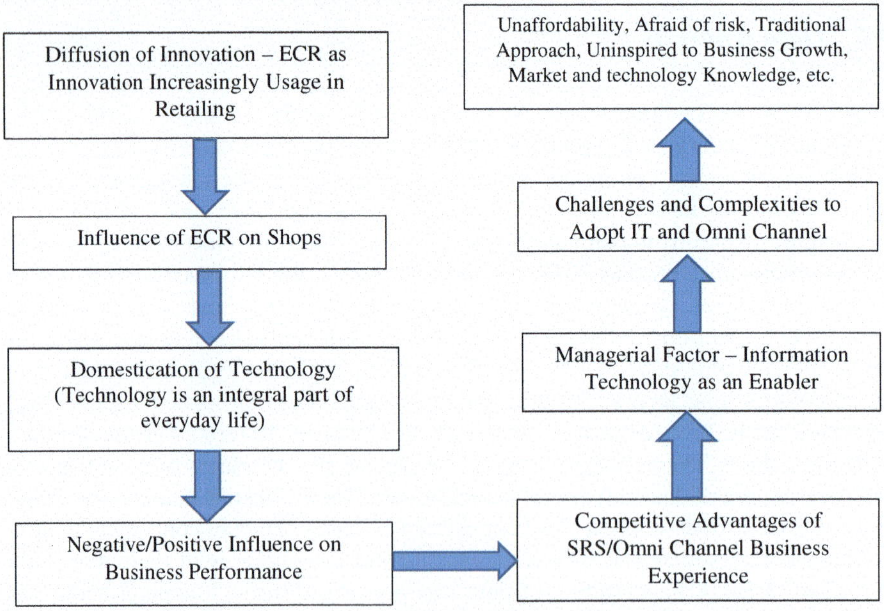


**Fig. 1** Adoption of information technology: competitive response of small retailers to ECR

defines diffusion as the gradual promotion and adoption of new technology among users within a specific social system, with the context of this study identifying retailing as the relevant social system. The enduring success of these technologies relies on achieving widespread acceptance within this context.

From the narratives of retailers, it has been found that small shop retailers know ECR however they are pursuing it slowly. ECR business needs retailers' readiness that is facilitated by a variety of products, warehouse facilities, market offers, strong supply chain integration, human resources, and market knowledge. Thus, in the second phase, most of the interviewees reduced its use although the usage of ECR provided an alternate marketplace to consumers that resulted in increasing footfall at SRS and business performance. However, except for ECR, other technology adoption has been studied in this research. Readiness includes financial stability and the availability of technology. The results are mixed across the sectors included in this study.

## 5.2 *Influence of ECR*

Shopping used to be a social activity, with people visiting physical stores. However, this dynamic has shifted towards a virtual mode of shopping. In the retail business, the impact and extent of Electronic Commerce on operations and profitability have been carefully assessed. In this section, we examine the influential factors that were prevalent in the traditional retail sphere, focusing on the perspective of retailers. We investigate whether the advantages that were once associated with traditional shopping still provide a competitive edge to the ECR model. Furthermore, we analyze the changes in the market environment that have occurred in the post-ECR.

A small shop retailer said that,

> There are no benefits of location now. Customers shop, wherever they find affordable. If there are, good relations with customers then can only beneficial for us. However, if customers get a good margin, then irrespective of relation they move to that place.

It shows retailers are expressing their concerns about the influence on the existing pattern of business. He continued that,

> The competition, which I have against other local shops is considerable since i.e. only a difference of 19-20. However, the difference between ECR and local shops is 80-20. For instance, in the case of mobile if, a retailer purchases 10 mobiles then the company gives a 1 per cent discount. Further, if you purchase 100 quantities then it gives 5 percent off. Again, if you go for 1000 handsets then you certainly get around a 40 per cent discount. Mine is only concerned if a company provides a 40 percent discount to big retailers, then why not to SRS. There is no growth of small retailers. We can see that online business is having great business as 100 local shops are equal to a big ECR. Online business players are much ahead of local shops. Then, where is the actual growth? Growth is for them.

Small retailers are facing significant frustration as their business performance takes a hit due to the influx of ECR. This downturn directly impacts their livelihoods, and they perceive the entry of ECR as a threat that has created a discriminatory marketplace. Business growth has become elusive, with ECR platforms dominating the scene. In recent times, it has become increasingly challenging to persuade customers. Customers often engage in debates with salespeople, requiring the latter to provide more extensive information. Unlike in the past, where salespeople didn't need to be as informative, today's SRS are compelled to offer in-depth product details due to advancements in technology. Salespersons must also allocate more attention to customers, catering to their specific needs and preferences.

During an interview with a customer, she said that,

> Deep discounts and varieties are major attractors of online shopping. During online shopping, a small box appears on the screen. For instance, if I go shopping at itokri.com, a small message box with 'May I help you' appears on the screen. A person can write patterns, designs, and range over there. Even a list of FAQs (Frequently Asked Questions) is available there. It benefits us comfortably to buy online. I find it very much convincing to shop online since in a locality where I live I do get some products at a nearby shop. So I have to place an order online.

The advent of ECR has empowered customers to shop at their convenience, offering a plethora of conveniences that traditional shops often miss. Virtual marketplaces excel in meeting customer demands, with the availability of a wide range of products, enticing discounts, and user-friendly websites and applications. Interestingly, our analysis of interviews has revealed a distinct pattern: while retailers acknowledge a decline in business performance following the rise of ECR, a separate group of customers continues to exist in both online and traditional shopping modes. As Sonawane, a retailer, notes, individuals who prefer local products may not opt for branded items, as brands often come with varying price ranges that may not be affordable for those who predominantly use local products. Online shoppers constitute a different demographic from offline shoppers, with minimal overlap between the two. Furthermore, some products available in online shops are not found in local stores.

However, an owner of a footwear shop highlights that the post-ECR landscape has intensified the challenges faced by traditional retailers due to the emergence of an alternative market for customers. Therefore, he suggests that different product offerings should be available through both channels to sustain the business of Small Retailers. In essence, the retail sector has undergone significant transformations with the advent of ECR, with technological developments serving as a vital catalyst in this evolution.

## *5.3 Domestication of Technology*

The rapid advancement of technology has seamlessly integrated into people's lives, providing convenience and becoming an integral part of daily routines. This section explores how individuals utilize technology for various purposes, such as placing online orders, comparing product prices through ECR channels, searching for offers, and managing banking transactions through mobile apps. The availability of low-cost data has made internet access widely accessible, and the proliferation of mobile applications has encouraged customers to shop from virtually anywhere. The abundant technological developments across various occupations have significantly enhanced ease and comfort for individuals.

Silverstone (2005) introduced the concept of 'domestication' to comprehend socio-technological changes and offer an analytical counterpoint to models of technological determinism. In this context, domestication of technology (DoT) can be seen as the process through which technology becomes familiar and seamlessly integrated into people's lives. It's akin to the "translation of new technologies into familiarity."

As outlined above, the diffusion of ECR has placed pressure on traditional forms of retailing. Similarly, the domestication of technology (DoT) represents how technology is becoming familiar and ingrained in people's lives, particularly in the context of various shopping modes. In this regard, we analyze the perspectives of retailers to shed light on the current retailing landscape.

Santosh was saying:

> Now customers are highly reliant on virtual retailers without seeing them. For instance, if a customer comes for a recharge it takes time to credit money but that person is not ready to wait until he has communicated with customer care. Customers hardly believe in us in the post-ECR phase.

From the perspective of customers, this concept is beneficial to understand how technology has become an integral part of individuals' lives. Technology adoption in retailing by both retailers and consumers has been observed. ECR is an output of technology development across the globe. 'Increasing reliability on ECR and decreasing credibility of SRS' is the biggest drawback for SRS.

A participant said that

> Technology is essential for development in the coming years. The future market will be only e-commerce retail. E-commerce can only save and finish all the businesses. In today's world, e-commerce has become a necessity. Before 10 years, mobile was not that much necessary. People were talking without phones. People are so active on social media. It has become part of everyday life.

To shield the business from the domination of ECR, SRS owners realize that they should install the technology. The Internet facilitates people to be informed about the newest technology developments and market trends. It familiarizes them with different techniques. As a result, ECR is creating a craze among shoppers. A retailer was expressing, "Today's era is of mobile phones, people spend their maximum time on devices. Customers come with a picture, asking for a product, shown on the internet." Increasing reliability over technology, accessibility in ECR platforms, penetration of mobile phones, online image attraction, and availability of a variety of products with lucrative offers in the age of associate marketing provide great scope for e-commerce players to expand their business. Thus, technology has become an integral part of everyday life which is replicated in the retail sector too where consumers are more clever and informed about different products.

## 5.4 *Positive Influence of ECR*

Social media platforms like Facebook, WhatsApp, and Instagram are the medium through which SRS can advertise and promote their business. In the case of the food business, Zomato, Food Panda, and Swiggy are popular platforms increasingly used by people to place their eating orders. These are the largest platforms for restaurants. A Chembur-based owner of a restaurant has created two pages in the name of Proud Mumbaikar and Proud Chemburkar on Facebook. There are 1000 followers on Facebook and 800 followers on Instagram. He has to upload an attractive picture of different dishes. People are attracted due to photos. These ECR companies in the food business provide huge discounts to consumers.

A customer was saying Zomato gives 50% off to customers who place orders for the first time. There is a cycle of marketing. For instance, Phone pay users get an offer through coupons. In a coupon, a customer gets 50% off on a food order on Zomato. In this process, a Banking app, a Phone Pay Company, a Zomato Company, and a restaurant are involved. A minimum of four parties are involved in this network. It is an associate business. There is a huge discount offer and schemes to make and attract customers on such ECR channels. A restaurant owner explains that 'now employees do not like to carry their lunch boxes as through these platforms they can get cheap food. They get good food at 100 rupees. There is ease in the supply chain due to ECR and cashless transactions increased post-demonetisation. Paytm, Phone Pay, Bhim App, and Google Pay are extensive with an audio machine that confirms a payment made by customers in traditional shops'.

A Restaurant owner said that,

> Due to the entry of Swiggy and Zomato people consider that there is less effort needed to run their business. As a result, people started food businesses. Most businesses are running through the kitchen only. They run their business with the help of Swiggy and Zomato, which automatically gets orders online. There is 30-40% growth in my business after business with these platforms.

It seems that ECR is largely beneficial for food businesses since with a kitchen facility they can run their business. However, other traditional shops like footwear, electronics, and apparel seem to be the least benefited due to ECR. In contrast, their business gets adversely affected.

Narratives of the retailers vary across businesses. Although policies of ECR in the food service business are favourable for customers and owners, SRS in other sectors do not motivate them to conduct business as an omnichannel. Thus, it may be inferred that food businesses are enjoying benefits out of ECR while other selected sectors are experiencing a negative influence on their business performances. The next section covers the aspects of the negative influence on traditional SRS.

## 5.5 *Negative Influence of ECR on the Business Performance of SRS*

Individuals accept technology for easiness and development purposes. As stated earlier DoT theory explains how it becomes an integral part of human life. In this theme, factors have been identified which are negatively influencing the business performance of SRS.

A Chembur based old retailer (Blue Star) said that

> We are experiencing footfall. Earlier it was affected because of mall culture. I am facing a loss in business because of this technology introduced by big retailers. Our sales have been decreased. It is a 20 percent reduction in business performance. For the last 5-6 years there has been a decline in business due to online business. So in the future, there will be difficulties for offline shops like us.

As one can observe, DoT is a factor primarily responsible for developing the interest of customers in new forms of retailing. DoT is useful for people since it bestows some facilities on them. But, from the perspective of retailers, it has a negative influence on the traditional retailing system. An Electronics shop owner confirms:

> To date, the main reason behind decreasing the footfall of customers is the online retailing. Online business players are big traders. Suppose we buy 1 mobile it costs us 8k but if a big online businessman buys 20 mobiles then he gets 250 rupees concession. Then he applies schemes and offers on it. Customers are attracted to offers and discounts. All businesses are turned there only, nothing remains with us. There is a huge margin in online retailing. Therefore, our business has dropped to around 50-60 percent. Not only business performance is reduced but local businesses closing up. Once, online retailing gets close then local shops can get some relief. Previously, we small traders used to be scared of malls, and now this online business. Hence, half of the business has collapsed due to malls and now online retailers are spoiling the remaining. If the online business will be sustained for the next 2-3 years then we are surely going to lock our stores. Nowhere, do we keep in mind that we have to save for shop rent, family, and business. On the other hand, customers are merely reiterating "online, online." Customers think that in online shopping there is a lesser price than traditional shopping has.

Similarly, other shop owners shared:

> Earlier there used to be fixed prices of products. If the price is, 10k then pay it and take it. Now customers cross-check with online retailers. Customers are going behind online to save 500/1000. We have been experiencing this for the last four years. It has been four years for online presence. Sometimes, they place their orders in front of us. I am placing my order since you are not giving me. Because they are providing me 10 percent discount.

ECR provide extra offers on cards. E.g. Axis, ICICI credit or debit cards get 10% instant discounts. '30 days' cashback/'90 days' cash back offered avail by ECR. It could not be afforded by SRS. Offers are around 1000/1500 rupees. Moreover, in ECR, companies give some products exclusively to online retailers. For instance, MI Company's mobile phone. People like to buy a new version of a mobile phone when it launches. A certain period is given for the launch of new handsets at the online forum. Due to this, SRS have to buy the same at a high cost from other retailers whenever customers demand. As a result, SRS have to charge more from customers. Even customers feel reluctant to buy from SRS. Companies give their products online first, and then they go to an offline sale. It badly affects offline stores. Many times, it does not reach to SRS. SRS seem helpless in the wake of increasing footfall that is negatively influencing on business performance of the former. This transformation in the retailing sector shows great domination of ECR which is equipped with different offers and even takes care of customers' preferences and tastes as per recent trends. Prices of products offered by ECR are varied. These are the prime causes behind the widening gap between traditional and modern retailing.

The drastic decline in the business performance of apparel, footwear, mobile and electronics, and food shops running with the traditional approach can be inferred from their narratives. Large-scale business operators can introduce fascinating discount offers and it makes customers habitual of online shopping. However, SRS are finding itself helpless to retain customers and strategize business to survive in a competitive marketplace. Some major changes one can observe in the entire retailing paradigm are online means money-saving, the influence of brands with discounts, ease of shopping, etc. CCFR practice is explicitly troubling existing retail chains where salespersons spend around 1–2 h with customers. However, after confirmation, they switch to online as they can save money on the same product. SRS gives their efforts but ECR takes advantage of it. Hence, footfall reduction, mega sales, or exclusive offers by ECR, price differentiation, rising practice of CCFR, attraction of brands, and so on are the major factors that often create challenges before SRS.

## *5.6 Competitive Advantages of SRS*

In the context of evolving ECR, traditional shops are facing challenges to retain old customers and attract new ones. They are noticing that attracting new customers is a much more difficult task. Hence, footfall is the biggest challenge for them. In this context, the existing competitive factors remain with retailers to manage their business performance studied.

Asha's owner revealed that,

> We should manage our stock according to the preferences of customers. If we go to wholesalers then we get confused because of the variety of clothes they have. Therefore, we should have a proper strategy for where and what to buy.

Here he explains a strategy to manage stock in the shop. Customers should be retained and old customers may show their loyalty towards the shop. Customers generally practice word of mouth in the previous retailing system. Therefore, SRS is generally used to depend upon the loyalty of old customers. But in the transformation of retailing, there is minimal scope for word of mouth. According to the owner, substantial knowledge of preference and taste is helpful to retain customers.

Chembur Electronics Shop owner shares:

> Those who do not understand how to order it online come to us. We have four shops in a lane then if a customer does not like the price he comes to the next shop. In today's business world, we have to focus on proper services and providing some complementary to customers. We were not providing after-sale services and complementary before. However, with post online business revolution we have introduced it to compete for online business.

In the Chembur market, different shops of footwear have been settled for years. But, after the introduction of ECR, there is a huge footfall in the shops. In a lane of the market, I observed there are 5–6 footwear shops. I interviewed a shop owner, he said there is no influence of ECR on his shop. But a neighbouring corner shop owner used different placards in his shop. The cards mainly target the online footwear market which is responsible for footfall reduction in retail chains. On posters, SRS highlighted discounts offered by them in the range of 20–40%. Even some of the cards show—Online se panga, rate me danga!! It may be interpreted as there is a contestation of SSR against ECR and therefore changes made by SSR to counter the ECR.

The owner of Blue Star Shop said that:

> Old customers have still come to our shop. Even they come along with people in their network. Bargaining is allowed in the shop. I get the advantage of it since after-sale 20 percent deduction on the total bill is done irrespective customers ask or not. It helps me to retain a long-term relationship with customers. It is a very old shop, so we have credibility in the market. However, there is a problem in making new customers. While the people who are using local clothes do not go for brand clothes. We are doing well as we have been working for a long time. We have continued our sale in a shop. I do not feel the necessity of advertising since the location of the shop is on the main road and beside the railway station.

So the owners' market knowledge, stock management strategy, the loyalty of old customers and staff, continuous sales, relationship, age of the shop, discount, and bargaining, the credibility of the owner, and location of the shop are some of the factors still benefiting to retain their business performance despite they agree on the negative influence of ECR on their business. In terms of service quality, the SRS is claiming to give the best service quality as compared to ECR. The narratives of almost all salespeople are similar regarding service quality given by them to their customers irrespective of their relations with them. According to SRS, it is highly lacking in ECR as they ask customers to go to the service center however, offline shops are looking after all the services if there is any damage to products even after the expiry date of the warranty period. Similarly, omnichannel business is also observed among some of the SRS as a competitive advantage at the verge of ECR.

## 5.7 *Omnichannel Business*

In the omnichannel business framework, a retailer can do business through both online and offline modes. Most of the single-brand outlets in India follow this business strategy. It manages customers' needs by serving facilities of ECR and the traditional way of retailing. This section includes the experiences of SRS during the omnichannel business.

A Chembur-based footwear shop sharing his experience via the ECR platform:

> I used to work with Snapdeal 3 years ago. In the beginning, what happened, policies were different, for instance, Amazon, Snapdeal, or Flipkart used to make a return in 7 days if the customer did not like it. When I was there, customers used to return products. I have to pay them. It is no issue if a customer does not like the item and returns it. However, during this process, I had to pay for all logistics charges. Even, though I had to give a discount on that product in the end, I had to bear a loss of return products. Therefore, I stopped it.

The retailer has earned a Master's in Business Management and has 10 years of working experience in the USA. So he is much more familiar with the present technologies and trends. He started his business online mode but according to him return policies, discounted rates and follow-up of the entire process are time-consuming. In a way to manage the business through both places, a team of qualified people is required. Therefore, he switched to traditional retailing. However, he is planning to launch a mobile app for footwear retailers. It will help customers to place an order.

In another case, a Dadar-based retailer said:

> Online retailers approach me often, but I never tried it. I have a concern suppose it will not sell online, then where I will keep such a huge stock. There is no proper place for sitting over here, so where to keep a stock. Suppose they order 500 pieces and I deliver them to them. But, if they return 300 pieces out of 500 then what will I do with that. There is a huge probability of return of products. In ECR, customers like a piece after seeing a pic, but they can return it once do not like the actual design. Ultimately, it is going to be a burden on my shoulders. They fix their price and do not give surety of selling of products. "*Wo to uske gale me nahi padega na woh to mere gale me ayega.*" (Un-sale stock create trouble for me, but it won't harm them).

A 58-year-old retailer does not have much experience with technology but he knows the basic facts regarding business through the ECR channel. He is afraid of return policies and unsold stock. He is a sole trader. Only one person is employed to manage the shop. Genuine concerns of traditional shop owners that online business players do not provide any surety of sale and preference to their stock over others. Hence, these common concerns of both small retailers make them unstable to work with ECR though its big platform conditions are unfavorable for small retailers.

## 5.8 Adoption of Information Technology

As discussed in the first section, diffusion of innovation in the form of ECR is mainly responsible for incurring losses for existing retail chains. ECR platform is the biggest threat to traditional retail shops, as they can hire big celebrities and promote these forums with no boundaries. However, local shops are confined to their localities at the mercy of the loyalty of old customers. In this context, adopting technologies to provide a competitive response to ECR business players may be possible. Technology is an enabler to strengthen the business process and manage business performance.

This section deals with themes relevant to technology acceptance strategies by the shops. Small apparel, footwear, and food shops are using social media accounts highly to promote their products, while mobile and accessories are advertised on big platforms by their respective companies. So they need the least advertisement and promotion. Former send new arrivals to customers. They create a database of customers. The owners save customers' contact numbers and send them new offers. Customers suggest to retailers about their liking and preference for clothes. It helps retailers to maintain stocks as per the taste and the preference of customers. These apparel are not brand clothes but they are designed in a way that provides the feel of branded clothes. SRS keep updated their customers. Thus, social media forums like Facebook, Instagram, and WhatsApp are immensely beneficial for small shops to manage their business in the high inclination of the new generation towards ECR.

About installing technologies in the shop, a retailer said, "We have a system where we save contact numbers of customers. We message them whenever new stuff arrives at our shop. We promote our shop through sending messages." Customers' database is advantageous to update them about new arrivals and offers during seasons and holidays. In the case of food shops, they have great scope to do omnichannel business provided shop owners have familiarity with technologies and knowledge to promote business on social media networks.

About business performance, a restaurant owner said, "Yes, there is around 30–35 percent growth in a restaurant. I got a good response from Swiggy-Zomato, which is beneficial to increase business performance". It gives a platform to new businesses. More interestingly, at a roadside, one can see five new restaurants due to ECR companies in the food sector. It could not be there before the arrival of these online platforms. Now there is no need to go for advertisement through an old medium, earlier SRS had to give a menu as small pamphlets with newspapers. These sorts of business styles have closed and outdated. It has been replaced by alternate media platforms like Instagram, Facebook, and WhatsApp. Therefore, there is the least requirement of advertisement through the traditional way. Some SRS are planning to go online. Few are going to launch their app. Customers can download it and order it online. However, it could not provide any offer to them. Some are going to start a website from where customers can see products available in the shop and even place their orders.

A restaurant owner said that,

> Now most people order from online apps like Swiggy and Zomato. People now think about why should go. They become lazy due to these apps. Earlier in my total business, 70 percent was dining and 30 percent was take away including 20 percent parcel. Percentwise, now we have 60 percent dining and 40 percent home delivery or online orders. Many changes have taken place.

The entire market is witnessing gigantic changes in the wake of ECR's entry into the retail market. Adoption of newer technology to retain old customers and fulfill the demands of the new generation as per their preferences and tastes is a prerequisite of the market.

## 5.9 Challenges in the Adoption of Technology

Most of the retail shops are three decades old. The owner of the shops is trained to follow the conventional method of advertising and marketing. Some of the shops are still dependent upon old techniques and technology is treated as a burden or unnecessary trouble.

Blue Star owner says:

> *Je chalat te chalu dya ajun paryant yavar kahi vichar kela nahi ahe. Jevha band hoil tevha baghata yeil. Atta tari chalalay vyavasthit. Jast headache nahi karun ghetal pahije Dhanda jasa chalu ahe tasach chalu rahila pahije.*
>
> (Still, I do not think of adopting any technology. When there is a collapse of business then I can see. It is going well now. There should not be any pressure on me. Business should be continued as it is.)

The 56-year-old man seems pessimistic about the future of his business. He said it is his retirement age so could not think much about business. He feels that if there is an expansion of the shop then family members' support is necessary. He has two daughters, one is an Engineer, and the other is an MBA graduate. But, he does not want to involve his daughter in this business line. The owner shows his wish to close it in the coming years. Therefore, he does not want to carry the unnecessary baggage of adopting technology as family support and his age does not allow him to expand shop. On a similar note, there are some common themes observed among shops which are described as follows:

*Affordability*

An old restaurant owner said if he opts for an online food services company, then they charge 20% of the food. It is very high for a small restaurant; it is not affordable for a restaurant as it does not have this much margin. Therefore, some SRS avoid starting a business with ECR. SRS are bothered about its capacity to start with new technology. A restaurant owner says ECR food companies are more concerned about delivery time and it would not be possible for him to deliver food on time. So, there are chances of poor reviews of their restaurant by customers and Swiggy-Zomato, or Food Panda. Reviews are decisive factors in running the business through ECR.[4] Swiggy company gives preference to such a restaurant that has lower rates, since customers prefer to go with reasonable rates. Thus, small retailers cannot afford to adopt technology in their shops.

*Knowledge of Technology*

Knowledge of technology changes and current trends of shoppers is much more vital in this sector. For technology adoption, retailers should be aware of technology in retailing and aspire to accept it. Awareness of Social media platforms is needed, which are helping to promote business with no budget. Most retailers do not know

[4] Accessed on 13 August 2021. https://www.wonderflow.ai/blog/how-is-e-commerce-influencing-traditional-retail.

about the growth in technology and they feel satisfied with their current business. They believe that customers will return to them as soon as the craze of ECR is over. Even most of the retailers think technology adoption is a burden and tension on them and they do not like to fall into such an unnecessary burden.

*Afraid of Risk*

Some of the retailers are scared to adopt any technology to run their business, as they know fraud and misguidance are at a high level. In India, technology is invariably considered a risk-bearing factor. Though they started a shop in the main market, they are afraid of banking apps. They still prefer cash transactions. Their orientation to the traditional way of business does not allow them to make a change in their existing set-up despite the negative influence on their business performance.

*Unawareness of Market Trends*

Some of the shop owners do not believe that there is a footfall due to ECR, as they believe it is a phase like inflation where once it goes away market will steadily work for them. Their educational level and rigidity of following old techniques of retailing do not compel them to make changes in their shop. Footfall is a challenging concern for them. However, they are least aware of market trends since they like to concentrate on their business with absolute reliability on old methods of business which is a major element of rejection of technology.

*Traditional Approach*

Overall, the shops that believe in the traditional approach of retailing do not agree to be involved in adopting IT, even some of the shops have yet to provide digital payment options. Post-demonetisation some of the small shops and vendors applied it through the adoption of banking apps. However, it is observed among people with no knowledge of technology. They still prefer transactions in cash. 'Word of mouth' and 'sale' in footwear and apparel shops are considered strengths of traditional retailers. Moreover, pamphlets are distributed for advertising purposes. According to them, shopping is a social activity, however, the emergence of ECR makes this activity virtual. Some of the retailers have strong religious faith and for them, the business performance lies on the wish of God. Their destiny decides their future. Thus, the traditional approach of retailers fails them to apply IT to improve business performance.

*Reluctant Attitude: Unaspiring for Business Growth*

Enormous fear and misconception are there among retailers who follow the conventional method. Here the age of retailers, educational level, and technology knowledge are major elements that reflect in their reluctant attitude. Besides old age and the absence of technology awareness among retailers found with the least aspiration to expand and survive in a competitive business environment. Some of the SRS are satisfied with business despite confirming business loss, the rigidity of conventional techniques, and orientation of old business skills do not aspire them towards installations of technology.

## 6 Discussion

It has been seen that technology brings ease and comfort to people. Technology has become an integral part of our daily life. The 'Domestication theory' (Silverstone & Haddon, 1996) which explains how technologies are integrated and adopted into everyday life can be elucidated from the empirical data. In the context of SRS, it has been seen that some of the SRS are accepting technology to improve their business performance in the wake of the increased competition from ECR. The adoption of technology by small shops is seen as a response to the competitive pressure of leading e-commerce-based companies. The small shops are also moving to accept information technology to some extent, for instance, placing an order on phones, home delivery, and card/online payments (Google Pay, Paytm, etc.). As we can see, e-commerce-based retailing is gradually becoming a part of a particular set of consumers' lives. From the perspective of the retailing process, changes with the aid of technology development consumers are attracted towards the online mode of the retail platform.

Domination of big ECR players over the market can be seen highly the study by Zaki Hussain and Parkhi Vats (2020) revealed big players engage in the merger and acquisition of small firms, they promote unethical practices, data mining, and exploiting markets with their dominant position, as found in the research ECR policies seem unfavorable for small retailers. As per the collected data, it has been found that some of the shop owners have experience of relative advantage, compatibility, and complexity of technology and are in favor of adopting technology. However, old-aged retailers lacking technical literacy seem afraid to adopt it. At the same time, new ventures with adequate knowledge and persuasion look positively towards accepting technology to run their shops. It was realized through the study as Rani and Ramachandra (2015) maintained that the SSRs should learn and upgrade their businesses as per technology adoption. Even the study found similarities with the previous work of Hardesty and Suter (2005) and Shet (2016) as in the modern retailing era consumers are well updated than earlier where their expectations are highly increasing for services and prices.

This is similar to the findings reported by Chiu et al. (2010) that increasing the 'cross-channel free-riding' behavior of customer influencing badly on SRS, as live presentation given by small retailers, however, it indirectly benefits ECR. Hence, as a counter to ECR, some of the retail shops are starting home delivery services for their products, trying to maintain a variety of stock and customer-oriented services. The study confirmed the findings of Rani and Ramachandra (2015) as to compete for ECR, small shops' value of money and variety of products are determinant factors in retaining customers and making new customers. Khare's work (2014) that collectivism and long-term orientation provide a competitive advantage to SRS. The only distinction in the present marketplace is that the value of money through attractive offers viz, deep discounts, brand attraction, increasing service quality, etc. are factors dominating over long-term relationships. To some extent, assortment, service quality, facilities, and relationship with owners help to retain consumers. However, as stated above cash back and deep discounts at the age of associate marketing reduction in footfall have been noticed explicitly in traditional shops. In India, the inclination of people towards ECR may consider that shopping as an activity is switching to virtual mode than previously face-to-face contact (Thomas & E. Carraher, 2014) where the retailer is hidden from the process. The study further confirmed the findings of (Saha, 2015) the decline in sales and profit margin of retail shops. Attraction towards western brands among Indian youth is observed highly post-transformation in retailing (Mann et al., 2018). The very emergence of ECR has made changes in price differentiation, influence on tastes and preferences of Indian consumers. In the contemporary retailing environment deep discount offers, a variety of stocks, and customer services are dominating factors in ECR (Dahiya, 2017).

## 7 Conclusion

This study analysed the influence of ECR on SRS in a cosmopolitan city like Mumbai where a high amount of businesses can be seen. Adoption of technology is feasible for owners having adequate knowledge, affordability, and attitude to take the risk and other technical understandings as per current market demands irrespective of years in a market. In the wake of ECR, the factors that are influencing both positive and negative were found in the study. It may be beneficial in the retailing and the e-commerce field. The level of the adoption process as per the theoretical framework was imperative to know through this research. The framework of 'domestication theory' and 'diffusion of innovation theory' was appropriate to apply in the present work to give analytical direction to research work. Small shops should upgrade their business as per the current technology and trends in the market. If they lag behind it despite affordability, market knowledge, and high experience of business then they might lose their business. Innovative and creative advertisement styles through social media and advertisement banners should be used to attract customers to their shops. Uniformity in prices and adequate service quality should be given to customers, therefore; an association of retailers should be formed and function.

The adoption of IT by SRS as an enabler helps to improve performance and counter ECR to a great extent. It may also be seen as a survival strategy of SRS. Some of the sectors are negatively influenced and some of them benefited due to the very adoption of IT and ECR channels. Here, electronics, footwear, and apparel shops have been worst affected. However, food businesses are experiencing adequate business performance. The shops have knowledge and awareness about modern e-commerce bases businesses are introducing different strategies to manage the influence of the latter. Small restaurants and kitchens are benefiting highly due to online food delivery apps they run their business as omnichannels. Thus, some of the young and informed retailers use both ways of business and even offline modes they upgrade their shop with the latest technologies. However, in the case of shop owners having unawareness and lack of knowledge pertinent to the usage of the technology do not find much difference. Type of industry, years of business, age of owner, aspirations of owners, support of family members, and educational qualification played a significant role in IT adoption in the retail industry. However, adequate knowledge of technology and ECR platforms are dominating factors for improving business performance irrespective of the age of the shop, location, and long-term relationship, since old shops in the prime location are aloof of 'technology and ECR' are suffering highly. Small shops running for more years and having different outlets in the city are managing to survive abreast of the competitive environment created by big e-commerce players. Shops run by the young and modern generation with the least prior experience in the business are successfully running their ventures due to knowledge of technology and usage of social media platforms as diffusion/adoption of e-commerce retail design is observed through the narratives of shop owners.

## References


Bryman, A. (2012). *Social research methods* (4th ed.). Oxford University Press.

Chiu, H., Hsieh, Y., Roan, J., Tseng, K., & Hsieh, J. (2010). The challenge for multichannel services: Cross-channel free-riding behavior. *Electronic Commerce Research and Applications, 10*(2), 268–277. https://doi.org/10.1016/j.elerap.2010.07.002

Choudhury, R. N., & Jadhav, P. (2020). Foreign investment in Indian e-commerce sector and its drivers. *E-commerce in India: Economic and legal perspectives* (p. 99). Sage.

Clarke, I., & Banga, S. (2010). The economic and social role of small stores: A review of UK evidence. *The International Review of Retail, Distribution and Consumer Research, 20*(2), 187–215. https://doi.org/10.1080/09593961003701783

Coca-Stefaniak, J. A., Parker, C., & Rees, P. (2010). Localisation as a marketing strategy for small retailers. *International Journal of Retail & Distribution Management, 38*(9), 677–697.

Corbin, J. M., & Strauss, A. (1990). Grounded theory research: Procedures, canons, and evaluative criteria. *Qualitative Sociology, 13*(1), 3–21.

Cragg, P., & Mills, A. (2011). IT support for business processes in SMEs. *Business Process Management Journal, 17*(5), 697–710. https://doi.org/10.1108/14637151111166141

Dahiya, M. (2017). Study on e-commerce and it's impacts on market and retailers in India. *Advances in Computational Sciences and Technology, 10*(5), 1495–1500.

Demoulin, N. T., & Djelassi, S. (2016). An integrated model of self-service technology (SST) usage in a retail context. *International Journal of Retail & Distribution Management, 44*(5), 540–559.

Dibrell, C., Davis, P. S., & Craig, J. (2008). Fueling innovation through information technology in SMEs. *Journal of Small Business Management, 46*(2), 203–218.

Doherty, N. F., & Chadwick, F. E. (2010). Internet retailing: The past, the present and the future. *International Journal of Retail & Distribution Management, 38*(11/12), 943–965. https://doi.org/10.1108/09590551011086000

Eisenhardt, K. M. (1989). Building theories from case study research. *Academy of Management Review, 14*(4), 532–550.

Eisenhardt, K. M., & Graebner, M. E. (2007). Theory building from cases: Opportunities and challenges. *Academy of Management Journal, 50*(1), 25–32.

Goswami, P., & Mishra, M. S. (2009). Would Indian consumers move from Kirana stores to organized retailers when shopping for groceries? *Asia Pacific Journal of Marketing and Logistics, 21*(1), 127–143. https://doi.org/10.1108/13555850910926281

Gupta, P., & Gupta, V. (2020). E-Commerce in India. *E-Commerce in India: Economic and legal perspectives* (p. 8). Sage.

Hardesty, D. M., & Suter, T. A. (2005). E-tail and retail reference price effects. *Journal of Product and Brand Management, 14*(2), 129–136. https://doi.org/10.1108/10610420510592626

Harindranath, G., Dyerson, R., & Barnes, D. (2008). ICT in small firms: Factors affecting the adoption and use of ICT in Southeast England SMEs. In *16th European Conference on Information Systems* (pp. 889–900).

Hawk, S. (2004). A comparison of B2C e-commerce in developing countries. *Electronic Commerce Research, 4*(3), 181–199. https://doi.org/10.1023/B:ELEC.0000027979.91972.36

Hussain, Z., & Vats, P. (2020). The e-platform economy. *E-Commerce in India: Economic and legal perspectives*, 61. https://doi.org/10.4135/9789354791390

Jain, N. K., Gajjar, H., Shah, B. J., & Sadh, A. (2017). E-fulfillment dimensions and its influence on customers in e-tailing: A critical review. *Asia Pacific Journal of Marketing and Logistics, 29*(2), 347–369.

Jhamb, D., & Kiran, R. (2011). Organized retail in India—Drivers facilitator and SWOT analysis. *Asian Journal of Management Research, 2*(1), 264–273.

Joseph, M., & Soundararajan, N. (2009). *Retail in India: A critical assessment*. Academic Foundation in Association with Indian Council for Research on International Economic Relations (p. 376). New Delhi.

Kalia, P. (2017). Webographics and perceived service quality: An Indian e-retail context. *International Journal of Services, Economics and Management, 8*(3), 152–168.

Kearney, A. T. (2021). *Leapfrogging into the future of retail*. https://www.kearney.com/global-retail-development-index. Accessed on 2 March 2022.

Khare, A. (2012). Moderating effect of age and gender on consumer style inventory in predicting Indian consumers ' local retailer loyalty. *The International Review of Retail, Distribution and Consumer Research, 22*(2), 223–239. https://doi.org/10.1080/09593969.2011.652644

Khare, A. (2013). Culture, small retail stores, and Indian consumer preferences : A moderating role of demographics. *The International Review of Retail, Distribution and Consumer Research, 23*(1), 87–109. https://doi.org/10.1080/09593969.2012.734256

Khare, A. (2014). Consumer-small retailer relationships in Indian retail. *Facilities, 32*(9/10), 533–553. https://doi.org/10.1108/F-06-2012-0044

KPMG. (2016). *Impact of e-commerce on employment in India*. https://assets.kpmg.com/content/dam/kpmg/in/pdf/2016/12/impact-of-ecommerce-on-employment-in-india.pdf. Accessed on 5 July 2021.

Kucharska, B. (2013). Information technology in retail trade. *Studia Ekonomiczne, 150*, 109–119.

Laudon, K. C., & Traver, C. G. (2013). *E-commerce*. Pearson.

Mann, M., Kwon, W., & Byun, S. (2018). Shifting value perceptions among young urban Indian consumers : The role of need for distinctiveness and western acculturation. *Journal of Retailing and Consumer Services, 44*(November 2017), 127–133. https://doi.org/10.1016/j.jretconser.2018.06.006

Miles, M. B., Huberman, A. M., & Saldana, J. (2014). *Qualitative data analysis: A methods sourcebook*. Sage.

Qureshi, S. S., Kamal, M., & Wolcott, P. (2009). Information technology interventions for growth and competitiveness in micro-enterprises. *International Journal of E-Business Research, 1*(5), 117–140.

Ramakrishnan, K. (2010). The competitive response of small, independent retailers to organized retail: Study in an emerging economy. *Journal of Retailing and Consumer Services, 17*(4), 251–258. https://doi.org/10.1016/j.jretconser.2010.02.002

Rani, N. M., & Ramachandra, K. (2015). Growth in grocery retailing in India-competitive landscape of modern vis-à-vis traditional grocers. *SDMIMD Journal of Management, 6*(2), 9–18. https://doi.org/10.18311/sdmimd/2015/2655

Raymond, L., Bergeron, F., & Blili, S. (2005). The assimilation of E-business in manufacturing SMEs: Determinants and effects on growth and internationalization. *Electronic Markets, 15*(2), 106–118.

Riemenschneider, C. K., Harrison, D. A., & Mykytyn Jr, P. P. (2003). Understanding IT adoption decisions in small business: Integrating current theories. *Information & Management, 40*(4), 269–285.

Rogers, E. M. (1983). *Diffusion of innovations* (3rd ed.), p. 11.

Roy, S. K., Balaji, M. S., Quazi, A., & Quaddus, M. (2018). Predictors of customer acceptance of and resistance to smart technologies in the retail sector. *Journal of Retailing and Consumer Services, 42*, 147–160. https://doi.org/10.1016/j.jretconser.2018.02.005

Ruby, M. (2016). E-tailing in India-growth, challenges and opportunities. *Journal of Marketing and HR, 2*(1), 102–112.

Saha, A. (2015). A study on "The impact of online shopping upon retail trade business." *IOSR Journal of Business and Management, 2*, 74–78.

Saroja, S. (2012). Information technology–Key success factor in retail. *Gian Jyoti Journal, 2*(1), 221–233.

Schneider, G. P. (2011). *Electronic commerce* (9th ed.). Cengage Learning.

Shaikh, A., & Gandhi, A. (2016). Small retailer's new product acceptance in emerging market: A grounded theory approach. *Asia Pacific Journal of Marketing and Logistics, 28*(3), 547–564. https://doi.org/10.1108/APJML-06-2015-0087

Shet, A. R. (2016). Information technology in retail sector. *International Journal of Scientific Engineering and Research, 4*(5), 43–46.

Silverstone, R. (Ed.). (2005). *Media, technology and everyday life in Europe*. Ashgate.

Silverstone, R., & Haddon, L. (1996). Design and the domestication of ICTs: Technical change and everyday life. In R. Silverstone & R. Mansell (Eds.), *Communication by design: The politics of information and communication technologies*. Oxford University Press.

Singh, A. K., & Ajmani, A. (2016). Future of B2C e-commerce (Buyers perspective) in India: An empirical analysis. *Asia-Pacific Journal of Management Research and Innovation, 12*(3–4), 203–216.

Singh, K. (2014). Retail sector in India: Present scenario, emerging opportunities and challenges. *Journal of Business and Management, 16*(4), 72–81.

Singh, M. (2002). Perspectives e-services and their role in B2C. *Managing Service Quality: An International Journal, 12*(6), 434–446. https://doi.org/10.1108/09604520210451911

Sivanesan, R., & Green, G. J. (2019). Impact of organized retail on unorganized retail sector. *Asian Journal of Managerial Science, 8*(1), 28–34.

Stake, R. E. (1995). *The art of case study research*. Sage.

Thakkar, J., Kanda, A., & Deshmukh, S. (2009). Supply chain management for SMEs: A research introduction. *Management Research News, 32*(10), 970–993. https://doi.org/10.1108/01409170910994178

Thomas, T., & E. Carraher, C. (2014). A retail perspective on the shopping behavior, cultures and personalities for China, United Arab Emirates, Belgium, India, Germany and America. *Journal of Technology Management in China, 9*(3), 289–296.

Tumbe, C., & Krishnakumar, S. (2018). From bazaar to big bazaar environmental influences and service. *Journal of Historical Research in Marketing, 10*(3), 312–330. https://doi.org/10.1108/JHRM-12-2017-0078

Vaithianathan, S. (2010). A review of e-commerce literature on India and research agenda for the future. *Electronic Commerce Research, 10*(1), 83–97.

Verma, H., & Duggal, E. (2015). Retail service quality in India: Construct exploration and measure development. *South Asian Journal of Global Business Research, 4*(1), 129–148. https://doi.org/10.1108/SAJGBR-10-2013-0075

Yin, R. K. (2003). Designing case studies. *Qualitative Research Methods, 5*(14), 359–386.

Yin, R. K. (2009). *Case study research: Design and methods* (Vol. 5). Sage.

Yin, R. K. (2018). *Case study research and applications: Design and methods*. Sage.

# Perspective and Directions for Future Research

# Social Enterprise as Means to Solving Social and Environmental Problems: The Case of Four Indian Ecopreneurs

**Niraj U. Joshi**

**Abstract** Using a phenomenological approach and case study methodology, this chapter sought to understand how the processes and outcomes of ecopreneurship are distinct from those of commercial entrepreneurship especially how ecopreneurs create, deliver and capture "blended value" in their enterprise. Ecopreneurship, (acronym for ecological entrepreneurship) refers to a special breed of social entrepreneurship that aims at ecological preservation, restoration and sustainable use of resources. Four Indian ecopreneurial ventures from the small and medium manufacturing sector were selected based on an a priori assessment of eco-friendliness from a larger pool of ecopreneurial ventures. The findings suggest that, a diverse range of disruptive strategies and business models are deployed by ecopreneurs in their pursuit of blended value creation, several of which distinguish these ecopreneurs from traditional entrepreneurs. A set of specific propositions have emerged as new contributions from this empirical research which will serve as pointers for future research.

**Keywords** Ecopreneurship · Social enterprise · Business model · Innovation · Blended value · Triple bottom line · Sustainable development

## 1 Introduction

India has had a rich tradition of recycling and reusing materials especially in light of the Indian society's value system of frugal living. However, with modernisation and rapid industrialisation over the last few decades the issue of environmental externalities generated by western models of development (adopted by India) has become a matter of serious concern. Pioneering work by environmentalists such as Anil Agarwal and Sunita Narain who have been publishing the periodical "Down to Earth" for over 25 years, the Chipko movement for protecting trees in the Garhwal

N. U. Joshi (✉)
Global Economic Dynamics and the Biosphere Program, Royal Swedish Academy of Sciences, Stockholm, Sweden
e-mail: niraj.joshi@alum.cept.ac.in

 
E. M. Reji and S. Majumdar (eds.), *Social Enterprise Values and Processes*, India Studies in Business and Economics, https://doi.org/10.1007/978-981-97-3252-4_9

Himalayas, the movement for vermicompost making among the farming community among others have made people realise the need for alternative [sustainable] models of development.

Creating an inclusive society is also imperative because if a person is struggling for survival, one cannot expect him/her to exercise choices in favour of environment. Commercial entrepreneurs typically are motivated to meet a social and economic need. Barring a few exceptions (such as the Tata group of companies in India), most commercial enterprises have taken a transactional approach wherein they believe that profits are the rewards for a service offered to society. As profits become the bottom line, they may either ignore negative environmental externalities or consider these as a necessary evil. At most they may try to minimise these but would not think of giving up their business purely on environmental considerations.

Ecopreneurs, on the other hand are motivated to meet the triple bottom line of planet, people and profit (Elkington & Burke, 1989) or the three Ps where profits serve as a means to the larger goals of environmental conservation and social wellbeing. They therefore hold promise in contributing towards building an ecologically sustainable future for humankind. This is a major point of difference between traditional entrepreneurs and ecopreneurs.

Ecopreneurs can be defined as individuals who are motivated to solve a larger environmental problem of society through the entrepreneurial route. Involving people affected by environmental externalities and marginalised people by creating sustainable livelihood is seen as part of the solution by many ecopreneurs. Pastakia (2002) in a review of key drivers of ecopreneurship in India, found three external forces strong enough to bring about change—namely,

> The power of judicial activism, enabling policies and the power of regulatory agencies.

He points out that basic religious and cultural values too are favourable for the conservation of nature. However, the dominance of the competitive and economic advantages of making profit in the short run proves to be an obstacle for business to go green. Hence, it has taken time for ecological values to express themselves in the business arena. According to Pastakia (2002)

> At the grass-roots level, where economic stakes are not very high, expression of such values seem to be less inhibited and the same is applicable to the upper end of industry, where large industrial houses and multinationals have to meet international standards to remain competitive.

However, this trend is fortunately changing and India is witnessing the rise of ecopreneurs who want to bring change in the way micro and small business operates.

## 2 Review of Literature

Recent literature on hybrid organisations especially social enterprises (Battilana & Dorado, 2010; Battilana et al., 2012, 2015; Hockerts, 2015; Jay, 2013; Majumdar & Guha, 2021; Singh, 2016; Smith et al., 2013), has focused on these organisational forms and their role in addressing social problems. It has been pointed out that values and motivations of entrepreneurs who initiate social enterprises are quite distinct from purely commercial enterprises (Grimes et al., 2013; Miller et al., 2012). For instance, hybrid enterprises are driven by compassion in addition to making profit (Battilana & Lee, 2014; Besharov & Smith, 2014; Haigh & Hoffman, 2012; Smith et al., 2013).

While the extant literature on hybrid enterprises throws light on how entrepreneurs address social issues, it is largely silent on how hybrid organisations address environmental sustainability (Haigh & Hoffman, 2012; York et al., 2016).

**Role of Entrepreneurship in Sustainable Development**

In a substantive review of literature on sustainable development and entrepreneurship (Hall et al., 2010) conclude that

> Sustainable development has emerged as an influential, albeit controversial concept for business and policy, and there is growing recognition that a fundamental transformation is needed to reduce detrimental environmental and societal impacts created by unsustainable business practices. Within this context, entrepreneurship is increasingly being recognized as a significant conduit for bringing about a transformation to sustainable products and processes, with numerous high-profile thinkers advocating entrepreneurship as a panacea for many social and environmental concerns.

The authors argue that though entrepreneurship holds promise to contribute towards sustainable development, it is more in the realm of the potential and its role remains as yet uncertain. Part of the reason may be attributed to the lack of empirical research on social enterprises. The academic discourse within the mainstream entrepreneurship literature on how enterprises can support sustainable development has been scant. At the same time, some scholars have pointed out the significance of disruptive shifts in organisational as well as economic structures to address climate change (Ansari et al., 2013; Hiatt et al., 2015; Howard-Grenville et al., 2014; IPCC, 2014). However, the role of entrepreneurs in such change has received little investigation. While the concept of ecopreneurs has been theoretically discussed (Dean & McMullen, 2007; Lenox & York, 2012), there is very little empirical research literature available on such ventures. Indeed, a recent review of sustainable entrepreneurship found only 25% studies to be empirical in nature while 60% were conceptual and the rest were reviews (Hall et al., 2010).

**Defining Ecopreneurship**

Ecopreneurs are considered as change agents, due to their unique vision and modus of operations (Anderson, 1998; Azzone & Noci, 1998; Keogh & Polonsky, 1998; Pastakia, 1998). Anderson (1998) even argues that "with their uncommon confluence of environmental concern and business savvy, ecopreneurs are in the unique position to do what most other businesses cannot—incorporate and consolidate the value perceptions of the individual into the inner workings of an eco-friendly business". Melay and Kraus (2012) reviewed ten different definitions of ecopreneurship and observed a strong focus on innovation (Allen & Malin, 2008; Pastakia, 1998; Schaltegger, 2002; Schick et al., 2002). Furthermore, another scholar (Pastakia, 1998) who studied grassroots ecopreneurs in the Indian context presented the following broad definition of ecopreneurship which is adopted by this research:

> Ecopreneurship refers to individuals/ institutions that attempt to popularise eco-friendly ideas and innovations either through market or non-market routes.

Ecopreneurs are increasingly being seen as crucial change agents, or champions, driving the collective learning process that society needs to engage in (Anderson, 1998; Isaak, 1998).

**Social Entrepreneurial Process**

While the mainstream entrepreneurship has been studied extensively and is replete with process models, the same cannot be said in the case of ecopreneurship. Although some theoretical studies focusing on the triple bottom line were located, they did not throw much light on the empirical process of value creation. For instance, one author (Santos, 2012) argues that a central difference between commercial entrepreneurship and social entrepreneurship is that social entrepreneurs are driven primarily by a motivation to create value for society, not to capture value. In a significant departure from the predominant social entrepreneurship literature focused on non-profits the same author (Santos, 2012) points out the following:

> What is distinctive about social entrepreneurs is that they are economic agents who, due to their motivation to create value without concern for the amount they capture, will enter areas of activity where the more severe market and government failures occur. These are usually areas with neglected positive externalities affecting disadvantaged populations. In order to explain the distinctive role and approach of social entrepreneurship, I start by defending a holistic conception of value and proposing that the trade-off between value creation and value capture is a central choice for organizations.

An important distinction between value creation and capture and its implications for strategy by the entrepreneur is made thus (Santos, 2012). This distinction between value creation and value capture is becoming a key concept for the field of strategy as pointed by another scholar (Lavie, 2007). Both these authors propose that value creation is a necessary condition for sustainable value capture. It is also however made clear that some level of value capture is important to ensure the growth and sustainability of the enterprises whose activities create value.

Social entrepreneurs are skilled individuals, who provide innovative and sustainable solutions to social and environmental problems. Their primary goal is always social value creation, though they can create economic value as well. They create social enterprises to achieve their social mission. Social entrepreneurs have thus created models for efficiently catering to basic human needs that existing markets and institutions have failed to satisfy (Seelos & Mair, 2005).

> The business model of social enterprises is characterized by unique strategies based on the competencies of the entrepreneurs, and is not aimed primarily at the maximization of profits, but rather at carrying out goals for the benefit of society. (Szegedi et al., 2016)

Recognising the potential of networking and partnership in social value creation, another author (Singh, 2016) proposes in her theoretical framework that social entrepreneurs, using their abilities, creativity and entrepreneurial skills identify social problems as opportunities, mobilise resources to create social value (including environmental value). The framework however is silent on the actual process of environmental value creation as well as outcomes and scaling up of the enterprises. Several other theoretical frameworks in the literature on entrepreneurial process were reviewed including the following:

- People Context Deal and Opportunity (PCDO) framework (Sahlman et al., 1996)
- Process model of Commercial Entrepreneurship (Bhave, 1994; Choi & Gray, 2008)
- Commercial and Social Entrepreneurship (Austin et al., 2006)
- Value creation Framework (Santos, 2012)
- Interface between Corporate Social Responsibility and Social Enterprise (Singh, 2016)
- Belz and Binder (2015)
- Identity theory, Environmental Entrepreneurship (York et al., 2016) and
- Ecological Sustainable Entrepreneurship (Gast et al., 2017).

The above frameworks either captured social or commercial value creation but failed to capture environmental value creation for which a new framework was needed. The generalised models presented by scholars while holding good for ecopreneurs begged the following question: if motives and values of eco-entrepreneurs are different from mainstream entrepreneurs, would the process and outcomes too not be distinct? and that is something that needed to be explored. Furthermore, in order to make impacts, ecopreneurs need effective strategies for scaling up their solutions. This should also be an important part of the framework.

**Broad Framework for Exploring the Process of Ecopreneurship**

In order to overcome the lacuna (mentioned in sections above) of understanding the process of ecopreneurship, an exercise to identify the main aspects of ecopreneurship which were different from mainstream commercial entrepreneurship was carried out as part of this research. The general process of value creation by a business enterprise was then assessed with a view to modify it to accommodate the perspectives and actions of ecopreneurs. This led to the development of a modified framework (Fig. 1) which was found useful in assessing the process of ecopreneurship. The broad framework includes three main components viz. genesis of the enterprise, functioning of the enterprise and scaling up for impact, as shown in Fig. 1.

Though all three phases are crucial in understanding the role of values and processes in ecopreneurship, this paper focused upon the second phase namely the phase of creating and delivering blended value through the interplay of variables such as strategies, technological, social as well as business model innovations, types of stakeholders and their involvement in the value creation process.

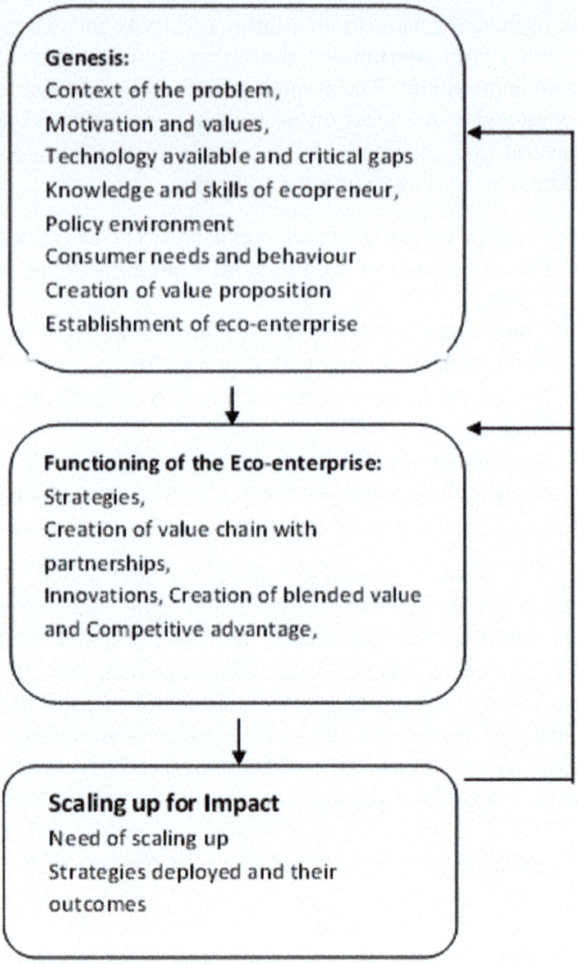


**Fig. 1** Framework for assessing process of ecopreneurship. *Source* Self developed

## 3 Rationale and Research Questions

During the literature review on ecopreneurship, it became clear that the field is still relatively young and under-researched. Most of the research has been focused on ecopreneurship in the developed countries. Furthermore, the research is characterised by relatively few empirical studies on ecopreneurial companies and even fewer studies in developing country contexts especially India (Schaper, 2002). The purpose of this research is therefore to explore the phenomenon of ecopreneurship as it unfolds in India. Further, it is important to frame ecopreneurship in terms of eco-friendliness and inclusivity and to explore how those concepts manifest in emerging companies especially start-ups across different geographies in India. This is in order to establish a base of understanding of the ecopreneurship field, especially to explore how ecopreneurship can be described in terms of value creation, value delivery and value capture by ecopreneurs in practice. In addition, the theoretical advancements in this field would have high external validity and would also be of use to ecopreneurs in other parts of the globe particularly in the developing country context. The research questions that this study therefore addresses are the following:

How and what process is followed by ecopreneurs to meet the triple bottom line of planet, people and profit? What strategies do ecopreneurs deploy to create value on the three domains of planet, people and profit?

## 4 Methodology

This study falls under the broad standpoint of Phenomenology—the science of the study of phenomena, things as they are perceived as opposed to the study of being, it is an approach which is also part of interpretivism. Ontologically this research falls under subjectivism. Subjectivism (also referred to as constructionism or interpretivism) perceives that social phenomenon is created from perceptions and consequent actions of those social actors concerned with their existence. Formally, constructionism can be defined as an "ontological position which asserts that social phenomena and their meanings are continually being accomplished by social actors" (Oliver, 2010).

**Development of Questionnaire/Checklist for the Interviews**

The unit of analysis for the study is the eco-enterprise. The key informants are the (co-) founders, who have been engaged with the entrepreneurial journey from the genesis to market entry. A framework of assessment was developed which served as a guide to the development of the checklist of questions used for the interviews with ecopreneurs. A semi-structured indicative list of questions was prepared for one-to-one interviews with the ecopreneurs as well as various stakeholders (consumers, Primary producers, suppliers, NGO representatives, employees, retailers etc.) which was based on the framework (see Fig. 1).

**Conducting the Interviews**

An iterative process of collecting information was followed by visiting each location, following up to fill gaps and sharing the draft with the ecopreneurs for possible corrections. Personal face-to-face interviews with founders as well as various stakeholders (consumers, Primary producers, suppliers, NGO representatives, employees, retailers etc.) were conducted. All interviews were recorded, and the respondents were notified of the recording before beginning the interviews. The recorded interviews were then transcribed to facilitate analysis and discussions as well as to increase the accuracy of information collected. Furthermore, field visits and inspection of production units too were carried out for triangulation of the information provided in interviews.

The questions focused on activities, events and outcomes to reduce the potential for retrospective bias. The interviews were conducted during the years 2013–2016 at various locations in India. All were digitally recorded, transcribed and documented.

**Other Sources of Information**
Secondary data on the enterprise including Newspaper and periodicals' articles, websites, printed material of the company as well as archival material, financial statements and internal reports, websites, blogs, media reports, publicity material, etc. were referred for triangulation (Santos & Eisenhardt, 2009). The co-founders were then asked to review drafts of their case study reports (Yin, 2009).

**Data Analysis**
Time-ordered and concept-ordered displays were analysed to capture the process of creating blended value through the business enterprise (Miles & Huberman, 1994).

**Criteria and Process Adopted for Selecting Ecopreneurs for the Study**
Cases were identified and shortlisted based on reports and advertisements in the media, research articles, websites of venture funds and business associations such as the Confederation of Indian Industry (CII—Godrej Green Business Centre) as well as personal communication with individuals. An a priori assessment of prospective cases was carried out using the following criteria:

1. A Priori assessment of eco-friendliness of the enterprise:
   (a) *Addressing an environmental problem, challenge or opportunity through an eco-friendly solution. For example, does the enterprise address an important ecological problem or try to take advantage of an opportunity to improve the quality of natural environment or augment the existing base of natural resources that would support the planet?*
   (b) *Emphasis on creating "blended value" which emphasizes Planet, People and Profits where profits serve as a means to the larger end of protecting the environment and affected people.*
   (c) *Absence of any major environmental externality in the life-cycle (cradle to grave) of the product.*
2. Only start-up enterprises with a proven track record of five years were selected for the study. These belong to the micro, small and medium category [MSME].
3. Manufacturing sector was the focus rather than the service sector. This is because manufacturing sector is likely to have greater negative environmental externalities than the service sector on account of production processes.

The above assessment led to the identification of potential case studies for the study. Given the limitations of time it was decided to restrict the sample to four cases. The final selection was made based on the following considerations:

i. Willingness of the ecopreneur to share information freely, including financial performance data

**Table 1** Location and size profile of eco-enterprise

| Eco-enterprise name | Size | Scale of operations (Annual turnover in INR) | Location | Age |
|---|---|---|---|---|
| Tamul plates marketing private limited | Small; Employees 40 | 18 million | Barpeta, Assam, North east India | 7 years |
| Daily Dump (PBK waste solutions private limited) | Small; employees 15 | 23 million | Bengaluru, South India | 5 years |
| Claro Energy private limited | Medium; Employees 105 | 237 million | New Delhi, North India | 5 years |
| NEEV herbal handmade soaps | Small; employees 10 | 5.2 million | Jamshedpur, East India | 10 years |

*Source* Self developed

ii. Geographical and contextual diversity
iii. Diversity of sub-sectors and nature of environmental problem being addressed

**Profile of the Sample**
Table 1 profiles the sample cases on the basis of size, scale of operations, location and age. The four enterprises represented different geographical locations in India. One was from the Northeast, one from east, one from south and one from North of India.

The diversity of sub-sectors and value propositions of the four enterprises is exhibited in Annexure 1. The eco-enterprises selected in the final sample were from different geographical parts of India, representing diverse sub-sectors of the economy.

# 5 Results

## *5.1 Strategies Deployed*

All four enterprises have customised their strategies to meet the triple bottom line of planet people and profit and create blended value in the process. Among the prominent strategies identified were the following:

**Creation of Value Chain Through Strategic Partnerships**
Value delivery by all four eco-enterprises has involved successful partnering with a range of stakeholders both in the supply chain and marketing of products. The range of partners along the value chain includes formal and informal; private and

public; and primary producers and NGOs; essentially retooling the supply chain and creating a new value chain where partners share a common mission and value system. These partnerships may be considered strategic in as much as each one is selected on the basis of its ability to contribute something unique which gives the company a strategic advantage over its competitors and makes it possible for the chain as a whole to create blended value within a price that the consumer is willing to pay.

**Leveraging Government Policy**

Some of the ecopreneurs were fortunate to have a favourable government policy and could leverage that to their advantage, for instance Claro and Neev. The government's solar energy promotion policy made it easier for Claro to make quick revenue even with a high capital cost product such as solar powered pumps. The high level of state and central government subsidy polices coupled with loans made it easier to sell more pumps and spread across more geographical locations by getting empanelled on the suppliers list.

**Inclusive Sourcing and/or Production**

Tamul and Daily Dump have used inclusive sourcing as a key part of their business model benefitting primary producers and marginalised communities by making them an integral part of their supply chain while Claro and Neev have done it partially. Tamul has been able to run the enterprise in spite of being located in an insurgency area principally because of this strategy. However, dependence on a single raw material and single source of supply has made it vulnerable and affected profitability. In a move to stabilise its economic performance it has taken steps to expand the base to other regions as well, although dependence on a single raw material continues. It managed to empower and improve livelihoods of more than 2000 households and created a lot of goodwill but profitability suffered making it vulnerable.

**Developing Multiple Delivery Channels**

Claro has used diverse scaling up strategies and has managed to grow rapidly in the last three years by developing diverse delivery channels to cater to different clients. It is also adept at using technology and innovating in its business model. Some examples include innovative product financing, promoting its product as a service model, partnering with government and NGOs for promotion and providing after sales service to remote locations within 48 h as its unique selling proposition. It has taken the growth by competition route by decisively focusing on developing its competitive advantage. In a sector of growing competitors, by quickly innovating it has carved out a niche for itself.

**Establishing Entry Barriers to Ward Off Competition**

Like conventional business entities, ecopreneurs too feel the need to develop some kind of entry barriers when dealing with competition in the marketplace. Among the sample ecopreneurs, all except Daily Dump have developed some entry barriers to address the competition. Daily Dump has focused largely on collaboration with other agencies due to the nature of the problem that it is addressing as well as the missionary orientation of its founder. The competitive advantage developed by each over time, (discussed in the following section) by default, serves as entry barriers to other players at least in the short run. None of the ecopreneurs have formally pursued intellectual protection even when they have developed innovative solutions/recipes/designs. Claro, Neev and Tamul have used a closed or partially closed business model while Daily Dump opted for an *open business model*. Closed business models generally offer greater control but require more resources from their owner. These are adopted when wanting to increase profits; protect intellectual property or brand, certain proprietary technology; or maintain a high level of quality control for the business success. Open models like that of Daily Dump on the other hand are normally adopted by highly mission-driven entrepreneurs and when the technology used is relatively simple (Zuerkar et al., 2016).

**Awareness and Education Campaign**
Communication and education have been used by all ecopreneurs as a key strategy to raise awareness about their products. While Claro has proactively participated in more than twenty agricultural fairs across Bihar and other states to promote their pumps, it has also set up the first of its kind demonstration pilot at its own expense in Vaishali district of Bihar where 35 defunct government tube-wells were rejuvenated by connecting them to solar pumps. This has contributed to making the government and others aware about the advantages of this technology and dispel myths about the costs of maintenance, performance issues, etc.

Daily Dump has among all four enterprises used this strategy extensively to promote waste management as a larger issue of behaviour change rather than just its products. One focus area has been to develop its website as an educational resource; secondly it has promoted a series of free, downloadable, applicable do-it-yourself (DIY) educational and communication products such as books, posters, films on issues of waste segregation, recycling and management. It also has an active program of engaging with schools and children through exposure visits to its office as well.

Tamul has done its campaigns largely through Dhriiti its incubating partner while Neev has leveraged its internship program and trade fairs as well as its informative website to do the same. Indeed except for Claro the rest have found a smart way of doing promotion by using NGO partners to do the same. This strategy is important in changing attitude and behaviour of consumers who should also see themselves as responsible global citizens.

## 5.2 *Outcomes*

The strategies implemented through the value chains created by ecopreneurs seem to have generated two kinds of outcomes. The first is the creation of blended value which is what the ecopreneur had in mind while starting the enterprise. The other is the competitive advantage created which would enable it to face competition from other players in the sub-sector.

**Blended Value Created**
All four eco-enterprises have succeeded in creating blended value encompassing the three domains of sustainability namely ecological(planet), society(people) and economic(profit). Annexures 2, 3, and 4 show the environmental, social and economic value created over the last three years by the four eco-enterprises. Furthermore, three of them have achieved this while building their competitive edge in their respective sectors. The fourth, Daily Dump has taken a different approach-that of collaboration as opposed to competition as the founder has a missionary approach and the problem being addressed too is of a widespread nature.

Ecopreneurs use a wide variety of strategies for creating value along the three domains of planet, people and profit. In general, the background and context of the ecopreneurs influences their strategies to a significant extent. Though ecopreneurs customise their strategies to meet the triple bottom line of planet people and profit and create blended value, there appear to be some common characteristics. Ecopreneurs leverage favourable government policy at an early stage of their growth and deploy inclusive sourcing of their supply chain by involving marginalised communities. Furthermore, they also involve vulnerable communities by incentivizing them along the value chain. Ecopreneurs also tend to develop innovative technological solutions specially to create environmental value. Further, they develop multiple channels for marketing their products and services and cater to a wide variety of market segments including local, regional, national and institutional as well as export markets. Last but not the least ecopreneurs develop competitive advantage through control over technology, raw materials, accreditation and their unique business models. While the enterprise captures some economic value in terms of profits, much of the value created is passed on to various stakeholders. For instance, consumers, marginalised communities who become part of the value chain among others also capture some of the socio-economic value and/or ecological benefits in terms of better quality of life, but much of the ecological benefit is captured by the natural environment itself. Hence both present and future generations get benefitted.

## *5.3 Business Models*

Business model refers to the blue-print of strategy. Interest in the business model concept has grown rapidly among academicians and practitioners since the turn of this century both from the operational and strategic perspectives. In this research, the strategic aspect of the business model has been adopted as that is the objective. The individual business models deployed by all four eco-enterprise cases are described below followed by a brief cross case comparison of these.

### 5.3.1 Claro Energy Private Limited

Claro Energy Private Limited is an enterprise that provides solar powered water pumping solutions (as of year 2017). The water pumping solutions are geared to meet irrigation and drinking water needs in off-grid rural areas as well as to offset the negative externalities generated by existing diesel and electric pump sets. As shown on the right-hand side in the Fig. 2 in numbered boxes, Claro has diversified into more than four major verticals to access solar powered pumping markets across the country. The first vertical/revenue stream catered to direct institutional sales to corporates such as Sula Vineyards in Nasik, Maharashtra and others. The second vertical focused on providing irrigation as a service. This vertical/customer channel/revenue stream was an innovation that Claro piloted with grant funding from the "Powering agriculture-an energy grand challenge for development" launched worldwide by the United States agency for international development (USAID).

Claro was awarded a grant of USD 500,000 to pilot irrigation as a service to small and marginal farmers who could not afford to invest upfront in solar pumps. As part of this project, Claro mounted a solar pump on a tractor trolley and promoted irrigation as a service. This was done through local entrepreneurs in the eastern states of Bihar and others where farmers especially small and marginal ones have scattered land holdings. The third revenue stream was by incentivising existing customers (farmers) and interested individuals with a "strong rural network access" to act as

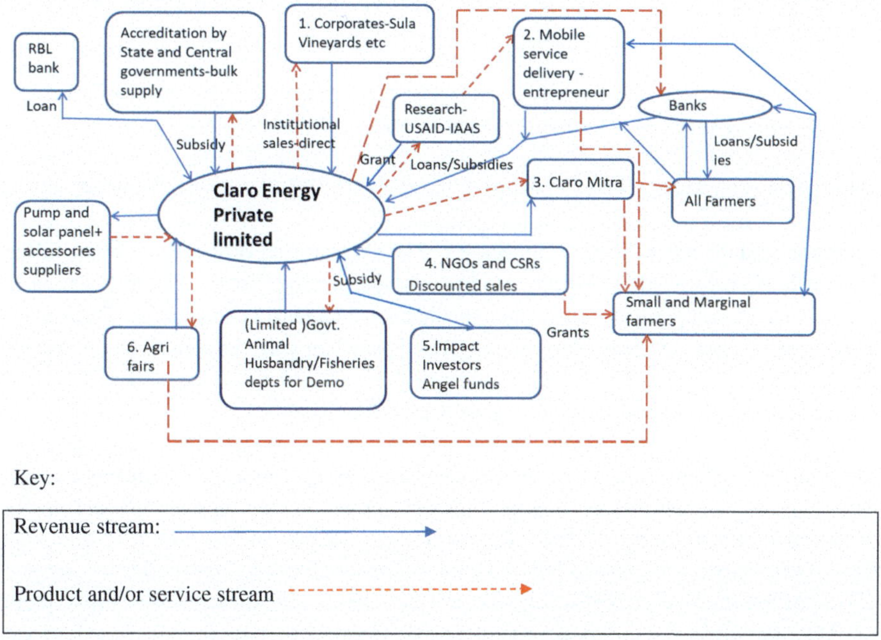


**Fig. 2** Schematic business model of Claro energy. *Source* Self drawn

Claro Ambassadors called Claro Mitras (more than 100 of these Claro mitras existed as of year 2016). The Claro Mitra is selected through a rigorous formal process and is paid an incentive for every customer that they bring to Claro as per Claro's written policy in this regard. Finally, for its fourth vertical/revenue stream, Claro partners with NGOs and CSRs to source small and marginal farmers who are beneficiaries of NGOs to make solar pumps accessible to them. In addition to the above, some new activities mentioned below indicate emerging revenue streams that could become important in the coming years.

Claro has partnered with state governments to directly bid for bulk orders in Rajasthan, Maharashtra and MP where these state governments took up a target-driven approach to promote solar powered pumps. Claro also uses agricultural fairs (as of year 2016) organised by state governments from time to time to promote and demonstrate this technology and make direct sales on the spot.

Thus, Claro uses a multiple range of formal partners such as Banks, state government departments, informal partners such as Claro mitras (local farmers), local entrepreneurs for irrigation as a service (IAAS) and non-profits to reach out to a larger customer base as well as benefit the poorer sections of the population. It also sponsors drawing and elocution competitions in schools to raise awareness on the benefits of solar technology and its diverse applications. In yet another significant departure from other players in this sector Claro has a dedicated team of service provider units of its own at the regional and local levels which get into operation as soon as the complaints are registered on Claro's unique remote monitoring system (Global Positioning System enabled) of any problem in pump operation or maintenance at the village/farm level.

### 5.3.2 Tamul Plates Marketing Private Limited (TPMPL)

Tamul plates marketing Private limited (henceforth TPMPL) was founded in the year 2009. It received initial mentoring support from the NGO (Non-governmental organisation) Dhriiti. TPMPL manufactures biodegradable dinnerware from fallen arecanut leaf sheaths. In addition to a centralised production facility at Barpeta in Assam, TPMPL supports decentralised production by local communities. The decentralised units help provide employment to rural youth in lean seasons. The enterprise also provides employment to local community members who collect the fallen leaf sheaths both for the centralised and decentralised units.

TPMPL has therefore established a value chain for manufacturing biodegradable dinnerware providing employment and capacity-building opportunities to rural youth who would otherwise remain under-employed or unemployed (see Fig. 3). As shown in the figure, TPMPL was incubated by Dhriiti, an NGO, from years 2004–2009. Dhriiti's role included carrying out research especially in identifying and piloting of the innovative technology to produce disposable dinnerware. Subsequent to TPMPL becoming an independent enterprise, Dhriiti has remained its close partner. As Dhriiti's headquarters are in New Delhi, it is well placed to support TPMPL's grant raising and forward linkages such as marketing and building relationships etc.

As shown on the left-hand side of the Fig. 3, TPMPL developed a host of partnerships to scale up production of arecanut dinnerware across other parts of the North-eastern Indian region without TPMPL's own investment. For instance, one of these was with a firm called Sandhya Engineering Concern (SEC). SEC makes plate production machines based on designs provided by TPMPL. TPMPL entered into an agreement with SEC initially for the supply of these. Further, TPMPL also sold these machines to the decentralised village level production units throughout the north-eastern region. TPMPL earned 30% commission for each machine sold.

The partnership between SEC and TPMPL went beyond pure technical and financial agreements. TPMPL by giving feedback from machine usage helped SEC improve its technology and SEC kept up its machine supply to TPMPL even when TPMPL faced a fund shortage and delayed part payments.

Furthermore, raw material harvesters, agents who aggregate and sell the raw material (leaf sheaths of Areca-nut Palm) and the village level production units are critical components of TPMPL's supply chain (all shown on the left side of the Fig. 3). The harvesters and agents are typically from landless or small and marginal farming community who earlier used to migrate to earn their livelihood. Similarly, the village level production units too belong to small and medium land owners who benefit from the plate-making activity, 70% of whom are women.

To enhance production as well as improve employment opportunities among the larger north-eastern region TPMPL took up building capacity and awareness by joining hands with Axum Agri. Axum Agri (NGO) manages trainings in disposable dinnerware in areas where TPMPL does not reach directly. TPMPL further partnered with the Assam State Government's Prime Minister's Employment Guarantee Program (PMEGP). As part of this the Commissioner of Industry and Commerce tasked TPMPL with training rural youth in plate making and also placed orders for supplying machines to self-help groups via TPMPL.

The village level producers also sell disposable dinnerware locally to rural customers as well as to TPMPL. Thus, local communities are not only producers but also suppliers and consumers in the value chain. TPMPL on the other hand has a largely urban clientele across urban centres in the country and even exports to western countries such as UK.

### 5.3.3 Daily Dump—PBK Waste Solutions Private Limited

PBK Waste Solutions Private Limited (popularly known as Daily Dump) was incubated by the NGO Play-n-Speak from 2006–2012. Daily Dump (DD henceforth) is a brand created for designing products for composting of household waste at source itself. DD designs its own products, trains potters in making them and then sources its largest selling product the Khamba (as of 2016) from local potters. As shown in Fig. 4, DD's major revenue streams in numbered boxes, are as follows: (1) by selling its products directly through its website (2) by its office in Bengaluru and (3) through more than 90 wholesalers and retailers. Furthermore, it has pursued a unique scaling up model which is its revenue stream number (4) wherein it encourages the

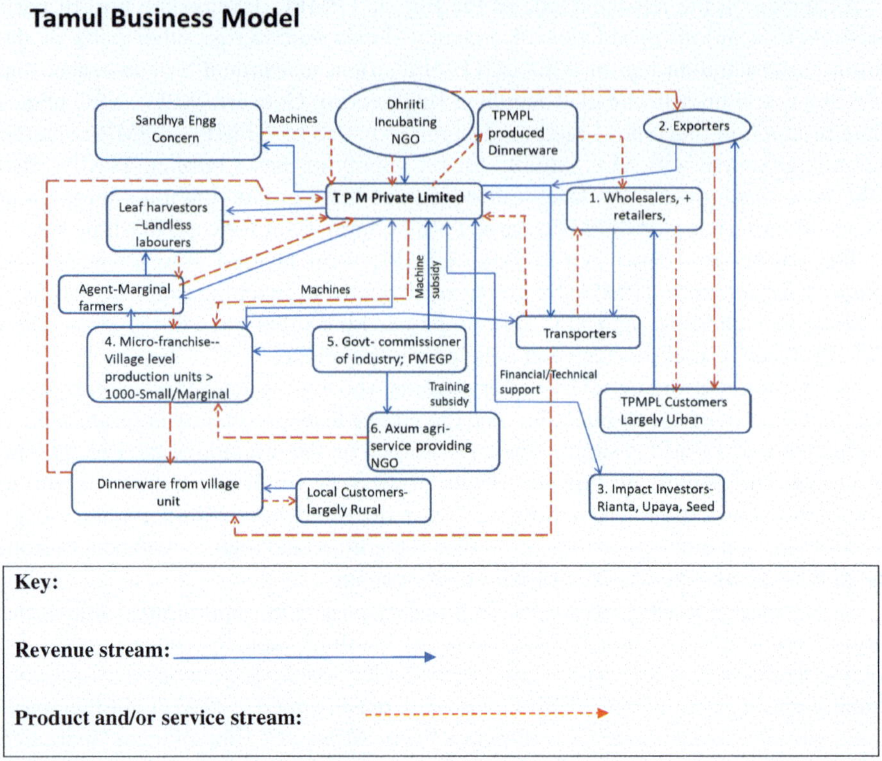


**Fig. 3** Schematic business model of TMPML. *Source* Self drawn

proliferation of clones with which it shares its product design for a small fee and then allows these clones to develop, innovate and sell the Khambhas in their respective catchment markets. DD also encourages clones to source the product from their own local potter artisans. This is in keeping with its professed goal of addressing disposal and recycling of waste as a larger environmental and social challenge across urban India.

More recently DD has also received investments from impact investors such as Ankur capital who have bought stake in the company which makes it a fifth revenue stream. Furthermore, in keeping with its core design competence DD has recently designed large composters that can cater to composting urban waste at large office complex levels or large residential colonies level in addition to already existing household level composters (Khambhas). As shown in the Fig. 4, the large composter manufacturers make “Aaga” (product name) composters based on designs provided by DD, supply these composters to DD which then directly transports these across the country or through its clones to customers. Thus, DD has continuously endeavoured to evolve its product offerings in its efforts to tackle the waste challenge at various consumer levels.

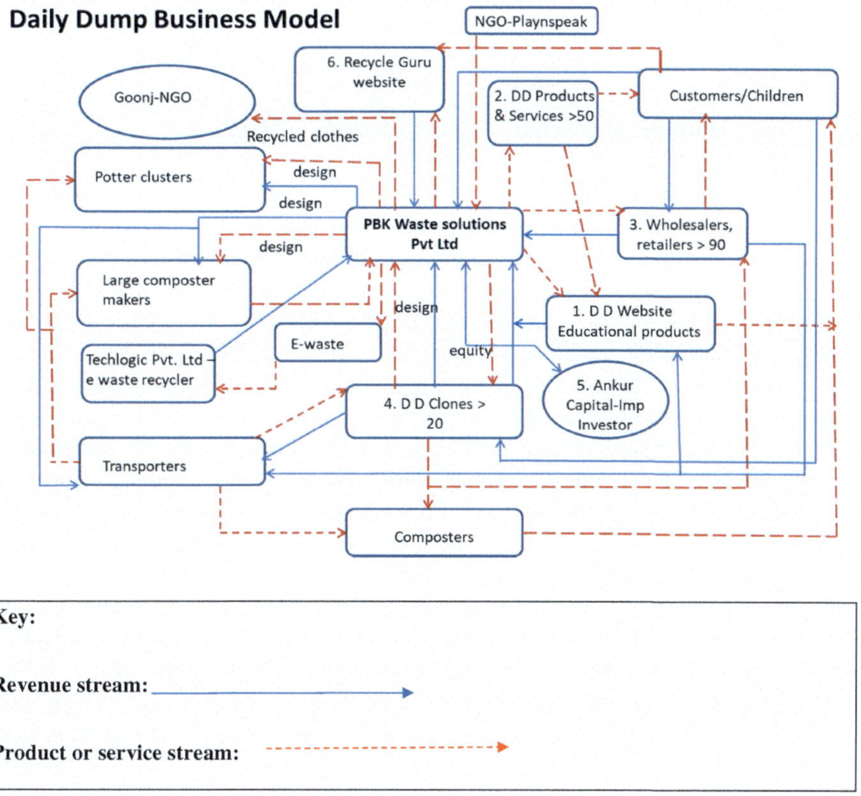


**Fig. 4** Schematic business model PBK waste solutions private limited. *Source* Self drawn

DD as part of this larger goal also partners with schools and electronic (E-waste) waste recyclers (Techlogic for example) and the informal urban waste recyclers such as *kabadiwallahs (waste collectors)* through a website called recycle guru (*as shown in boxes on top and on the left-hand side of the* Fig. 4). Thus, DD not only sends its own e-waste to Techlogic but also spreads awareness about E-waste disposal on its website and encourages its clientele and school children etc. to send their e-waste to certified e-waste recyclers such as Techlogic for appropriate recycling and responsible disposal.

Recycle guru is a website established by DD to connect informal recyclers with the urban households to streamline recycle their used newspapers, plastic and metal items. In addition to having created a very resourceful/educative website, DD has designed and published a variety of (DIY) Do-it–Yourself downloadable Kits, text-books, posters, etc., for raising awareness on waste disposal, composting household waste, segregating, recycling and reusing various commonly used materials. It also functions as a collection centre for used recyclable/reusable discarded clothes that are then sent to Goonj-an NGO that collects and distributes such clothes among the needy across the country.

### 5.3.4 Neev Handmade Herbals Private Limited (NHHPL)

NHHPL manufactures a variety of premium quality, handmade and all natural skin care products. NHHPL was incubated by Neev charitable trust in the initial years when the Neev public school was established simultaneously with the Neev handmade herbal soap making enterprise. Neev partnered with essential oil suppliers and base oil manufacturers who are its main suppliers. Other raw materials are procured from its own herbal garden (refer the left-hand side of the Fig. 5). Canara bank too supported NHHPL with initial working capital loans, while Khadi and Village industries commission (KVIC) provided accreditation and an initial subsidy to invest in the manufacturing plant. NHHPL has employed only women from the marginalised communities residing in Hurlung village who make soap and allied skin care products from all natural ingredients. Neev Public school serves as a centre of learning (as of 2016) for the children of the women who earn their livelihood from the Neev soap enterprise along with children from other disadvantaged families.

These children are exposed to the natural soap making enterprise at NHHPL as part of their education on environment friendly production and consumption processes. The Neev School is supported by surplus funds from the Neev enterprise.

Further, as shown by the revenue streams (see numbered boxes) on the right-hand side of Fig. 5, NHHPL has multiple revenue streams shown by numbers in the revenue streams on the right-hand side of Fig. 5. Direct selling through its website is NHHPL's main revenue stream. In addition to this, it has partnered with more than 180 retailers and e-tailers which is its second revenue stream. Further, it has successfully leveraged the trade fairs (as a minor revenue stream) both domestic and international that are promoted by the government and private agencies to promote Ayurveda and natural products. It has partnered with Craft mark an international certification standards organisation to gain international recognition for its products and leverage the same for the export market (yet another revenue stream) in addition to the niche upper end domestic market. This has helped NHHPL get national and international acceptance in the competitive and fast-growing herbal skin care market. NHHPL has smartly partnered with academic institutions through its ongoing internship hosting program which has helped it to develop not only its internal quality control such as process and procurement procedures, safety measures but also its marketing strategy at a fraction of the market cost.

### 5.3.5 Cross Comparison of Business Models

Some common characteristics of the business models of sample eco-enterprises can be listed as follows:

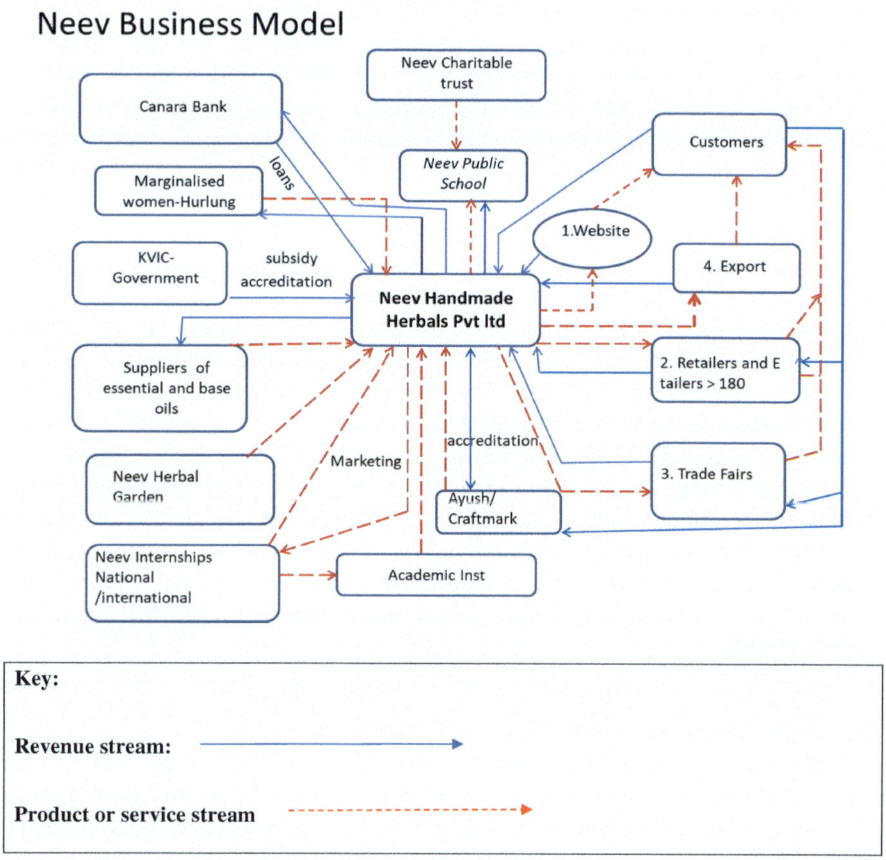


**Fig. 5** Schematic business model-NHHPL. *Source* Self drawn

## Nurturing Multiple Partnerships

All four ecopreneurs have forged and nurtured multiple partnerships between a range of formal and informal stakeholders including banks, NGOs, local community members, research agencies, academic institutions and government agencies. They have also involved NGOs in various capacities:

1. *As Incubators* (3 cases): Dhriiti incubated Tamul in its early phase of technology development, community mobilisation and capacity development of marginalised communities in the north-east region. Play-n-Speak incubated the initial technology designing, material experimentation and community mobilisation and skill building parts of Daily Dump with local artisans such as potters and others. Neev Charitable trust initially supported the soap making process technology and community mobilisation process through self-help group formation and capacity building of marginalised women.

2. *Education of Customers and Extension* (all): Play-n-Speak organises waste trails, office visits, classroom sessions and textbooks, games for school going children on the issue of waste reduction and recycling. Dhriiti, Tamul and Axum Agri together educate the community on areca leaf sheath waste recycling while Neev charitable Trust through its public-school endeavours to foster a more environmentally conscious generation of children and future citizens. Claro has organised multiple competitions in schools to make children aware of the solar energy applications from an early age.
3. *Marketing*: Dhriiti in case of Tamul engages in outreach with customers in urban areas outside the Northeast which are major markets for disposable dinnerware. It also sources export markets and helps Tamul in certification as for instance Tamul has the SGS certification. SGS stands for Société Générale de Surveillance—a Geneva-based certifying company that certifies food and agriculture commodities that are safe for consumption and use. SGS is one of the world's leading inspection, verification, testing and certification company recognised as the global benchmark for quality and integrity. Their certification services demonstrate that certified products, processes, systems or services are compliant with national and international regulations and standards. Claro has leveraged its partnerships with NGOs and CSR organisations to reach out to small and marginal farmers at a lesser cost as NGOs already have their own identified catchment beneficiaries.

**Innovations to Create Inclusive Supply Chains**

All four enterprises have also ensured the involvement of local communities as suppliers, producers, consumers making the value chain inclusive and more sustainable. Some of the key innovations developed by the four ecopreneurial cases can be listed as follows.

As shown in Table 2, providing irrigation as a service through mounting solar pumps on trolley and thus reaching out to farmers who cannot afford to invest in high cost of product is an innovation piloted by Claro energy. Similarly, training of micro-franchisees in decentralised production has been carried out by TPMPL. Focusing on the marginal producer providing the product as is done by TPMPL, Daily Dump and Neev. All three have supported the landless labourers, marginal farmers and potters by sourcing raw material and/or involving them in production processes. In Tamul's case the village units are not only producers but also consumers of machines and suppliers of disposable dinnerware. Further, the basic concepts of traditional franchising have been leveraged by Tamul, specifically focusing on creating opportunities for the poor to own and manage their own businesses in an innovative micro-franchising model.

Thus, all four have innovated in their business models not only in creating environmental value through technology and research but also to incentivise the disadvantaged local communities to engage in the value chain as producers, suppliers and consumers.

**Table 2** Types of inclusive business models promoted by the sample Ecopreneurs

| Inclusive business models → Eco-enterprises ↓ | Product as a service | Inclusive sourcing | Micro franchising |
|---|---|---|---|
| Claro energy | √ | | |
| Tamul plates | | √ | √ |
| Daily dump | | √ | |
| Neev | | √ | |

*Source* Self drawn

**Differences**

The cross-comparison of all four business models also reveals some significant differences in strategies deployed by these enterprises. While Claro energy was found to be the only one which did not go through an incubator, the rest had an incubation phase where an NGO had played that role for several years before market entry. Thus, some initial costs were taken over by the NGO during the incubation phase for the three socially oriented ecopreneurs. Claro on the other hand had to invest its own funds (the initial pilot in Vaishali, Bihar) and leveraged an international grant directly to pilot one of its verticals. Thus, Claro strategically innovated in its service delivery process. Indeed, while the incubated enterprises are all involved in manufacturing their own products, Claro is more of an integrator/service provider as opposed to being a manufacturer/producer. Claro has had the fastest revenue growth among all four eco-enterprises partly due to a favourable policy environment and partly due to its versatile strategies of reaching out to different market segments in a short span of time.

On the other hand, the other eco-enterprises namely Tamul, DD and Neev have had a slower growth as they had to invest in the social part of their value chains and have not diversified as much in reaching wider customer segments. Thus, Claro energy has exhibited characteristics of a more market-oriented business model while Tamul, DD and Neev exhibit a more socially oriented business strategy and model. This is also borne out by the relative openness of their business replication models especially the competitiveness and scaling up strategies. If one were to visualise a spectrum of business models ranging from closed to most open business models then one would place Claro at the closed end of the spectrum and Daily dump at the open end of the spectrum while Tamul and Neev can be placed somewhere in between the former two eco-enterprises i.e., at relatively closed and relatively open end of the spectrum respectively as shown in Fig. 6.

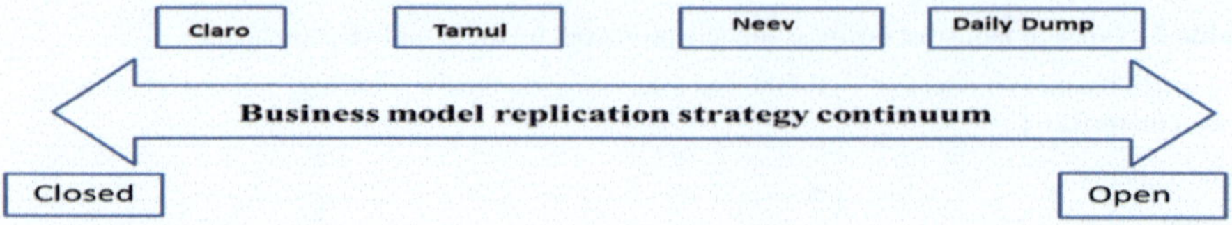


**Fig. 6** Typology of business models of the sample ecopreneurial cases based on their replication strategies. *Source* Self drawn

# 6 Discussion

## *6.1 Importance of Inclusiveness in Solving Environmental Problems*

Since all ecopreneurs in this study tried to involve excluded/affected stakeholders as part of the solution delivery process, the question arose whether it is an integral part of ecopreneurship? At a conceptual level it is possible to think of an enterprise which is focused on eco-friendly solutions without worrying about excluded/marginalised/affected people. Pastakia (2014) proposed a typology for socially responsible business using a matrix formed by the two variables of inclusiveness and eco-friendliness (Fig. 7).

Starting from the left, the first cell includes enterprises that are both socially inclusive and eco-friendly. The second cell refers to enterprises that are socially inclusive only, while the third cell refers to enterprises that are eco-friendly only.

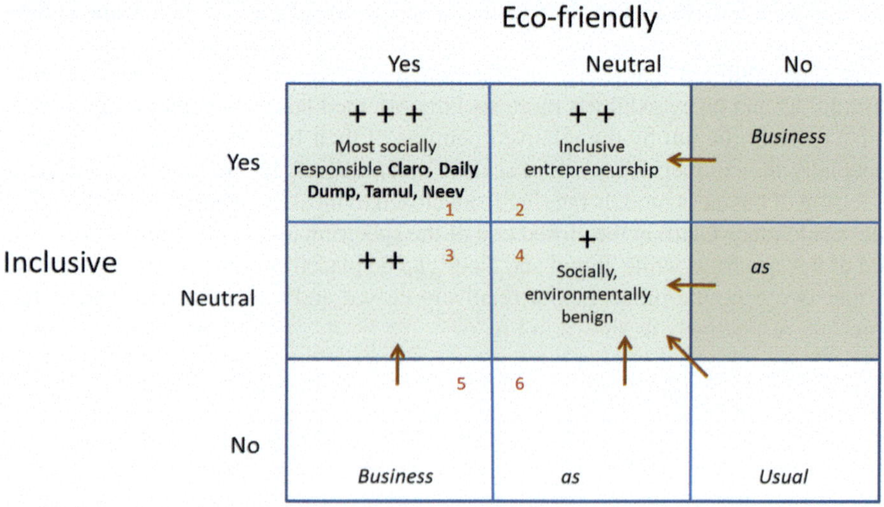


**Fig. 7** Typology of socially responsible business. *Source* Pastakia (2014)

The fourth cell includes enterprises that are both socially and environmentally neutral (Pastakia, 2014; Pastakia & Joshi, 2013). In the context of entire industries being eco-unfriendly, a business that is non-polluting while providing valuable services to society may also be perceived as being eco-friendly as it displaces eco-unfriendly business from the market place.

For example, there are eco-enterprises that may currently fall in the quadrant 3 where eco-enterprises may be socially neutral and quadrant 5 below quadrant 3 where inclusiveness may be negative but still, they create environmental value by their products and services.

From the above discussion it is clear that not only conceptually but also practically ecopreneurship can take place without addressing the social dimension of inclusiveness. However, more often than not, people working on social issues end up looking for sustainable livelihoods of their affected communities leading to an eco-enterprise. Three cases in the sample were of this type. Even those entrepreneurs who start with an environmental concern as a business opportunity are also sensitive to create sustainable societies. It is therefore not surprising that majority of ecopreneurs encountered in real life are also people who promote sustainable business/enterprise. Another word for it is socially responsible enterprise.

Involving all key stakeholders and creating inclusive society is an integral part of ecopreneurship as only such enterprises can hope to be sustainable. In their review of environmental entrepreneurship literature, Lenox and York (2012) discuss the rationale behind the engagement of multiple stakeholders in the environmental entrepreneur's new venture quoting Schlange (2009) and Shane (2000) among others. They suggest that based on research by Freeman (1984), it would be important to look at the process of building new stakeholder groups in the entrepreneurial process in general, to better understand the process of how environmental entrepreneurs create selective incentives.

In an extensive review of sustainable development and entrepreneurship, Hall et al. (2010) question the extent to which entrepreneurs have the potential for creating sustainable economies. They also ask what are the conditions where entrepreneurship simultaneously creates economic growth, while advancing environmental objectives and improving social conditions. Their review assumes that:

> Social pressures, especially those within impoverished communities, are a major hindrance to environmental improvement, yet few studies have empirically explored this relationship. (Hall et al., 2010)

However, this research finds that contrary to the above perception, ecopreneurship actually is able to create both environmental and social value within impoverished communities.

## 6.2 Seeking Business Opportunity in Environmental Problems

Cohen and Winn (2007) argue that environmental and social problems are created as a result of market failure and provide entrepreneurial opportunities. Dean and McMullen (2007) too basing their assertions from environmental economics theory suggest that pollution and other negative environmental externalities are primarily a result of market failure and present possible entrepreneurial opportunities. Addressing such market failures as "environmentally relevant" market failures they argue that environmental entrepreneurship or ecopreneurship as this research suggests is defined to be:

> The process of discovering, evaluating, and exploiting economic opportunities that are present in environmentally relevant market failures.

## 6.3 Business Model Innovation

According to Schaltegger et al. (2015);

> While a consensus appears to have evolved among many sustainability researchers and practitioners that sustainable development at the societal level is not very likely without the sustainable development of organizations, the business model as a key initiating component of corporate and entrepreneurial sustainability has only recently received attention in sustainability management research…
>
> ….The business model perspective is particularly important in the context of sustainability as it highlights the value creation logic of an enterprise and its effects and potentially allows for new governance forms such as ecopreneurial ventures thus helping transcend narrow traditional for-profit forms.

Boons and Lüdeke-Freund (2013) based on an extensive literature review proposed the following normative requirements for each of the constituting elements of business models (emphasis added):

> The *value proposition* must provide *both ecological or social* and economic value through offering products and services, the *business infrastructure* must be rooted in principles of sustainable supply chain management, the *customer interface* must enable close relationships with customers and other stakeholders to be able to take responsibility for production *and* consumption systems (instead of simply "selling stuff"), and the *financial model* should distribute economic costs and benefits equitably among actors involved.

Schaltegger et al. (2015) also proposed that sustainable value cannot be created for customers without creating value to a broader range of stakeholders. This research too finds that sample ecopreneurial ventures began with a blended value proposition that provided for ecological along with social and economic value. Further, as part of the value creation, delivery and capture process these ecopreneurs also made sure to engage with a multitude of formal and informal stakeholders to capture environmental value for a broader group of stakeholders by reducing negative externalities of conventional products and services.

In this context it is worth asking the question: how important is competitive advantage for ecopreneurs? The competitive advantage developed by ecopreneurs over time, serve as entry barriers to other players at least in the short run. However, none of the ecopreneurs in the sample have invested in intellectual property protection for the innovative solutions/recipes/designs developed by them. In fact, ecopreneurs with non-commercial background prefer to make their technology open access so as to trigger a movement that would be needed to tackle the problem on a wide scale. Hence competitive ecopreneurs used a closed or partially closed business model and collaborative ones used an open business model.

## 7 Conclusions

Though ecopreneurship is a form of social entrepreneurship, ecopreneurs distinguish themselves and their approach from traditional entrepreneurship in several ways. They seek to solve larger problems of negative environmental externalities also in the process addressing related social challenges and making profits. They thus seek to create blended value benefitting planet, people and economy. Ecopreneurs have shown the way to disrupt the value chain by shifting incentives, making it more inclusive and sometimes creating altogether new value chains through their innovative partnerships and networks including civil society and academic organisations and overall frugal approach. Significantly, ecopreneurs have even demonstrated collaborative business models to address widespread and larger ecological problems. Two distinct forms of ecopreneurship based on their background and orientation could be identified in the sample studied namely the market oriented or competitive ecopreneur and the socially oriented or the collaborative ecopreneur. Thus, the strategies used and approach adopted for blended value creation by these two ecopreneur types too were significantly different.

The following are a set of propositions for future research based on the learning emerging from this research:

P1. *Ecopreneurs come up with blended value propositions that address the three domains of sustainable development viz. ecology (planet), society (people) and economic (profit).*

P2. *Ecopreneurs display exceptional skills in building partnerships across formal and informal, organised and unorganised stakeholders when it is of strategic interest.*

P3. *Ecopreneurs with a strong market orientation approach the problem from a commercial angle building partnership with social change agencies in order to reach target segments.*

P4. *Ecopreneurs with a social orientation adopt strategies from the social development angle first and later add commercial/competitive strategies.*

P5. *Market oriented or competitive oriented ecopreneurs create strong entry barriers, while the socially oriented ecopreneurs create low or no entry barriers as they believe in collaboration as opposed to competition.*
P6. *Market oriented ecopreneurs follow conventional competitive closed business model scaling up strategies while socially oriented ecopreneurs adopt a collaborative scaling up strategy using replication by design approaches.*
P7(a). *Ecopreneurs use a variety of communication and education techniques as a key strategy to raise consumer awareness about eco-friendly products and services.*
P7(b). *In cases where ecopreneurs address environmental problems that are intertwined with social problems, marginalised communities are part of the solution in their quest for creation and delivery of blended value.*

The above set of seven propositions emerging from this research can very well serve as testable hypotheses for future research on ecopreneurship. As the efforts to move towards a green economy grow, it is increasingly being realised worldwide that it must also be a "pro poor" approach. In that context this research has provided empirical evidence of how value is created to meet social inclusion/pro poor and ecological objectives by ecopreneurs.

**Acknowledgements** The author is very thankful to all co-founders of the eco-enterprises for giving generously of their time and knowledge for this research. The field research was funded by the WWF's Prince Bernhard Doctoral Research Scholarship and the Case centre Scholarship from Cranfield University awarded to the author which is gratefully acknowledged. Guidance and mentorship provided by Prof. Astad R Pastakia and an anonymous reviewer's comments helped immensely in improving this paper and is acknowledged with gratitude.

## Annexure 1: Profile of Selected Case Studies in Terms of Value Proposition and Diversity of Sub-Sectors Represented

| Eco-enterprise name | Industry sector | Eco-enterprise value proposition | Incubation period | Market entry |
|---|---|---|---|---|
| Tamul plates marketing private limited | Biodegradable Disposable Dinnerware | All natural arecanut palm leaf sheath dinnerware through employing local youth in insurgency prone region. Safe product | 6 years—2004–2009 by Dhriiti | 2010 |
| Daily Dump (PBK waste solutions private limited) | Urban Solid Waste Management | All natural and recyclable composting products and services for urban solid waste recycling | 6 years—2006–2011 by Play-n-speak | 2012 |

(continued)

(continued)

| Eco-enterprise name | Industry sector | Eco-enterprise value proposition | Incubation period | Market entry |
|---|---|---|---|---|
| Claro Energy private limited | Solar power/ Energy use in agriculture and rural areas | Solar powered pumping solutions for irrigation, drinking water and fisheries | Nil | 2012 |
| NEEV herbal handmade soaps | Natural Herbal Skin Care products | All natural cold pressed pollution free, safe hygienic skin care products | One year—2006 by Neev Charitable Trust | 2007 |

## Annexure 2: Environmental Value Created

| Enterprise | Assessment | Environmental value created |
|---|---|---|
| Claro | High-very high | • Replaced polluting diesel and fossil fuel-based electric pumps by off-setting 3073 tons of carbon dioxide annually. Cumulative over last three years estimated at 9219 tons of carbon dioxide emission offset/prevented @3073 tons/year<br>• 2584 Kilowatts of clean energy produced as on May 2017 |
| Daily dump | High | • Reduced burden of urban waste. At least three truckloads or roughly 35 tons of organic waste recycled daily as on 2017. Cumulative over last three years—38325 tons of waste recycled @ 35 tons /day<br>• Load on landfill, fuel costs and labour costs saved by corporation/ civic bodies<br>• 34 tons of GHG emissions prevented just in one city per day at no extra cost. (May 2017). Cumulative over last three years—37230 tons GHG emission prevented in one city |
| Tamul plates | High | • Prevented 60 tons of GHG emissions every year<br>• 180 tons of GHG emissions prevented in last 3 yrs<br>• Replaced 5 million plastic and Styrofoam plates in 3 yrs |
| Neev | Medium | • Natural safe biodegradable product<br>• No GHG emissions and safe disposal due to natural biodegradable ingredients<br>• Prevented 1650 kg GHG emissions per every kg of soap produced |

## Annexure 3: Social Value Created

| Enterprise | Assessment | Social Value created |
|---|---|---|
| Claro | High | • 11,969 acres brought under irrigation<br>• Agriculture income augmented of 105,000 farmers |
| Daily dump | High | • 34 potter clusters with approximately four to five potter families in each cluster benefitted through being part of value chain exchange. Rs. 1.2 million earned in first two years by two potter clusters. Each potter cluster would roughly earn Rs. 1.8 million over three years @Rs. 0.6 million per year<br>• Informal recyclers—approximately 100 families—benefitted |
| Tamul | High | • Annual income per family of Rs. 10,000/yr. Total 2000 families benefitted till 2017 |
| Neev | Medium | • 35 marginalised women and their children benefitted from income and education. Rs.120,000/- earned per family per annum<br>• Children of 35 families getting educated with eco-values ingrained at a tender age:<br>• Awareness creation regarding the need for sustainable life-styles (sustainable production and consumption) |

## Annexure 4: Economic Value Created

| Enterprise | Assessment | Economic Value created |
|---|---|---|
| Claro | High | • Net worth of company in 2016—Rs.649,99,377<br>• Reserves and Surplus as on 2016—Rs. 60 million [five years]<br>• CAGR—105% in four years' time since inception<br>• ROE—29%<br>• ROA—8%<br>• Debt/Equity—2.7 as on 2016 |
| Daily dump | High | • Profits earned in 2016—Rs. 2 million<br>• Net worth of company—Rs. 3 million [2016]<br>• Reserves and Surplus as on 2016. Rs. 2.6 million [five years]<br>• CAGR—36% [2012–2016]<br>• ROA—21%<br>• ROE—56% |
| Tamul | Medium | • Low—medium<br>• ROA—−7.9%<br>• ROE—−43% and Debt/Equity Ratio—4.4<br>• As on year 2015<br>• Reserves and Surplus Rs. 2,727,020 |
| Neev | Medium | • Low—medium ROA—11%<br>• ROE—17.5% and Debt/Equity Ratio—0.39<br>• As on year 2015. Reserves and Surplus Rs. 2,528,883 |

## References


Allen, J. C., & Malin, S. (2008). Green entrepreneurship: A method for managing natural resources? *Society & Natural Resources, 21*(9), 828–844. https://doi.org/10.1080/08941920701612917

Anderson, A. R. (1998). Cultivating the garden of Eden: Environmental entrepreneuring. *Journal of Organisational Change Management, 11*(2), 135–144.

Ansari, S., Wijen, F., & Gray, B. (2013). Constructing a climate change logic: An institutional perspective. *Organization Science, 24*, 1014–1040.

Austin, J., Stevenson, H., & Wei-Skillern, J. (2006). Social and commercial entrepreneurship: Same, different or both? *Entrepreneurship Theory and Practice, 30*, 1–22.

Azzone, G., & Noci, G. (1998). Seeing ecology and "green" innovations as a source of change. *Journal of Organizational Change Management, 11*, 94–111.

Battilana, J., & Dorado, S. (2010). Building sustainable hybrid organizations: The case of commercial microfinance organizations. *Academy of Management Journal, 53*, 1419–1440.

Battilana, J., & Lee, M. (2014). Advancing research on hybrid organizing—Insights from the study of social enterprises. *Academy of Management Annals, 8*, 397–441.

Battilana, J., Lee, M., Walker, J., & Dorsey, C. (2012). In search of the hybrid ideal. *Stanford Social Innovation Review, 10*, 50–55.

Battilana, J., Sengul, M., Pache, A. C., & Model, J. (2015). Harnessing productive tensions in hybrid organizations: The case of work integration social enterprises. *Academy of Management Journal, 58*, 1658–1685.

Belz, F. M., & Binder, J. K. (2015). Sustainable entrepreneurship: A convergent process model. *Business Strategy and the Environment*, 1–17. https://doi.org/10.1002/bse.1887

Besharov, M., & Smith, W. (2014). Multiple logics in organizations: Explaining their varied nature and implications. *Academy of Management Review, 39*, 364–381.

Bhave, M. P. (1994). A process model of entrepreneurial venture creation. *Journal of Business, 9*, 223–242.

Choi, D. Y., & Gray, E. R. (2008). The venture development processes of "sustainable" entrepreneurs. *Management Research News, 31*, 558–569.

Cohen, B., & Winn, M. I. (2007). Market imperfections, opportunity and sustainable entrepreneurship. *Journal of Business Venturing, 22*, 29–49.

Dean, T. J., & McMullen, J. S. (2007). Toward a theory of sustainable entrepreneurship: Reducing environmental degradation through entrepreneurial action. *Journal of Business Venturing, 22*(1), 50–76.

Elkington, J., & Burke, T. (1989). *The green capitalists.* Victor Gollancz.

Frank, B., & Lüdeke-Freund, F. (2013). Business models for sustainable innovation: State-of-the-art and steps towards a research agenda. *Journal of Cleaner Production, 45*, 9–19.

Freeman, E. R. (1984). *Strategic management: A stakeholder approach.* Pitman.

Gast, J., Gundolph, K., & Cesinger, B. (2017). Doing business in a green way: A systematic review of the ecological sustainability entrepreneurship literature and future research directions. *Journal of Cleaner Production, 147*, 44–56.

Grimes, M. G., McMullen, J. S., Vogus, T. J., & Miller, T. L. (2013). Studying the origins of social entrepreneurship: Compassion and the role of embedded agency. *Academy of Management Review, 38*, 460–463.

Haigh, N., & Hoffman, A. J. (2012). 'Hybrid organizations'. The next chapter of sustainable business. *Organizational Dynamics, 41*, 126–134.

Hall, J. K., Daneke, G. A., & Lenox, M. J. (2010). Sustainable development and entrepreneurship: Past contributions and future directions. *Journal of Business Venturing, 25*, 439–448.

Hiatt, S. R., Grandy, J. B., & Lee, B. H. (2015). Organizational responses to public and private politics: An analysis of climate change activists and U.S. oil and gas firms'. *Organization Science, 26*, 1769–1786.

Hockerts, K. (2015). How hybrid organizations turn antagonistic assets into complementarities'. *California Management Review, 57*, 83–106.

Howard-Grenville, J., Buckle, S. J., Hoskins, B. J., & George, G. (2014). Climate change and management. *Academy of Management Journal, 57*, 615–623.
IPCC. (2014). *Climate change 2014: Impacts, adaptation and vulnerability.* IPCC Working Group II (Ed.).
Isaak, R. (1998). *Green logic: Ecopreneurship, theory and ethics.* Greenleaf Publishing.
Jay, J. (2013). Navigating paradox as a mechanism of change and innovation in hybrid organizations. *Academy of Management Journal, 56*, 137–159.
Keogh, P. D., & Polonsky, M. J. (1998). Environmental commitment: A basis for environmental entrepreneurship? *Journal of Organisational Change Management, 11*(1), 38–49.
Lavie, D. (2007). Alliance portfolios and firm performance: A study of value creation and appropriation in the US software industry. *Strategic Management Journal, 28*, 1187–1212.
Lenox, M., & York, J. G. (2012). Environmental entrepreneurship. In P. A. Bansal (Ed.), *The Oxford handbook of business and the natural environment* (pp. 70–82). Oxford University Press.
Majumdar, S., & Guha, S. (2021). Introduction: In search of business models in social entrepreneurship—Concepts and cases. In S. Guha & S. Majumdar (Eds.), *In search of business models in social entrepreneurship.* Springer. https://doi.org/10.1007/978-981-16-0390-7_1
Melay, I. (2012). *Green strategic entrepreneurship in small and medium enterprises: A configuration approach* (Unpublished Master's Dissertation in Entrepreneurship). Graduate School, University of Liechtenstein, Liechtenstein.
Melay, I., & Kraus, S. (2012). Green entrepreneurship: Definitions of related concepts. *International Journal of Strategic Management, 12*(2), 1–12.
Miles, M. B., & Huberman, A. M. (1994). *Qualitative data analysis.* Sage.
Miller, T., Grimes, M., McMullen, J., & Vogus, T. (2012). Venturing for others with heart and head: How compassion encourages social entrepreneurship. *Academy of Management Review, 38*, 460–463.
Oliver, P. (2010). *Understanding the research process.* Sage Publications limited.
Osterwalder, A., Pigneur, Y., & Tucci, C. I. (2005). Clarifying business models: Origins, present, and future of the concept. *Communications of AIS, 15*, 1–44.
Pastakia, A. (1998). Grassroots ecopreneurs: Change agents for a sustainable society. *Journal of Organizational Change Management, 11*(2), 157–173.
Pastakia, A. (2002). Assessing ecopreneurship in the context of a developing country: The case of India. *Green Management International, 38*, 93–108.
Pastakia, A. (2014). *Socially responsible business in India and the Asia-Pacific: Meeting the challenges of inclusive sustainable development* (Working Paper). Entrepreneurship Development Institute of India.
Pastakia, A., & Joshi, N. (2013). Heuristics of ecopreneurship: An Indian perspective. In *Proceedings of the 10th international biennial conference on entrepreneurship.* Entrepreneurship Development Institute of India.
Sahlman, W. A. (1996). Some thoughts on business plans. In H. S. W. A. Sahlman (Ed.), *The entrepreneurial venture* (pp. 138–176). Harvard Business School Press.
Santos, F., & Eisenhardt, K. (2009). Constructing markets and organizing boundaries: Entrepreneurial power in nascent fields. *Academy of Management Journal, 52*(4), 643.
Santos, F. M. (2012). A positive theory of social entrepreneurship. *Journal of Business Ethics, 111*, 335–351.
Schaltegger, S. (2002). A framework for ecopreneurship: Leading bioneers and environmental managers to ecopreneurship. *Greener Management International, 38*, 45–58.
Schaltegger, S., Hansen, E., & Ludeke-Freund, F. (2015). Business models for sustainability: Origins, present research, and future avenues. *Organization & Environment, 29*(1), 3–10.
Schaper, M. (2002). The challenge of environmental responsibility and sustainable development: Implications for SME and entrepreneurship academics. In H. J. U. Fuglistaller (Ed.), *Radical changes in the world—Will SMEs soar or crash?* (pp. 541–553). University of St Gallen KMU-HSG.

Schick, H. M. S. (2002). Sustainability issues for start-up entrepreneurs. *Green Management International, 38*, 59–70.
Schlange, L. E. (2009). Stakeholder identification in sustainability entrepreneurship. *Greener Management International, 55*, 13–32.
Seelos, C., & Mair, J. (2005). Social entrepreneurship: Creating new business models to serve the poor. *Business Horizons, 48*, 241–246.
Shane, S. (2000). Prior knowledge and the discovery of entrepreneurial opportunities. *Organization Science, 11*(4), 448–469.
Singh, A. (2016). *The process of social value creation: A multiple case study on social entrepreneurship in India*. Springer.
Smith, W. K., Gonin, M., & Besharov, M. L. (2013). Managing social-business tensions: A review and research agenda for social enterprise. *Business Ethics Quarterly, 23*, 407–442.
Szegedi, K., Fülöp, G., & Bereczk, A. (2016). Relationships between social entrepreneurship, CSR and social innovation: In theory and practice. *International Journal of Social, Behavioral, Educational, Economic, Business and Industrial Engineering, 10*(5), 1504–1509.
Yin, R. K. (2009). *Case study research: Design and methods*. Sage.
York, J. G., O'Neil, I., & Sarasvathy, S. D. (2016). Exploring environmental entrepreneurship: Identity coupling, venture goals, and stakeholder incentives. *Journal of Management Studies, 53*(5), 695–737.
Zuerkar, M., Meyer, C., Frank, L., & Dumkow, J. (2016). *Collaboration for impact: Building the ecosystem for replication support services*. SEED.

# Process of Talent Acquisition in Startups—Conceptualization and Implications on Future Research

**Leena Barshikar and Satyajit Majumdar**

**Abstract** Entrepreneurs and their Startups play an important role in the growth of the developing economies. Also important is the knowledge on capability that they acquire through talent acquisition at different phases of the enterprise. Talent acquisition is a process that involves actors, factors (causes and needs), activities or event, outcomes, patterns and the sequences. While entrepreneur remain the central actor in this process, Theory of Causation explains the causal factors leading to the desired results of events of talent acquisition. Reference is made to the historical events as proposed by the Path Dependence Theory so as to explain the presence and/or rationale of the absence of patterns in the process. This provides to set the agenda for future research on talent acquisition in Startups including the research methodologies.

**Keywords** Entrepreneur · Startup · Talent · Talent acquisition · Talent acquisition process

## 1 Background

Entrepreneurs and their Startups are critical for growth in developing economies (Baumol, 2004). The process of enterprise creation or setting up Startup has been one of the major themes of research (Katz & Gartner, 1998; Reynolds, 2010). The incidents like Startups going for Initial Public Offering (IPO) in India also added new avenues for scholarly research (Balsmeier et al., 2021) with added interest on related aspects such as job creation, innovation and growth (ibid.). The success of Unicorns

L. Barshikar (✉) · S. Majumdar
School of Management and Labour Studies, Tata Institute of Social Sciences, VN Purav Marg, Deonar PO, Mumbai 400088, Maharashtra, India
e-mail: bleena@gmail.com

S. Majumdar
e-mail: satyajit@tiss.edu

 
E. M. Reji and S. Majumdar (eds.), *Social Enterprise Values and Processes*, India Studies in Business and Economics, https://doi.org/10.1007/978-981-97-3252-4_10

and Soonicorns[1] with serial entrepreneurial acts or small manageable team, venture capitalist investment, sharper focus on products and markets and rapid innovation has been the other areas of research interests (De Massis et al., 2016). Lehmann et al. (2019) in a comparative study on Unicorns and Mainstreet or Hidden Champions[2] reported talent as the major reason for success, in addition to access to the financial capital. In an earlier research Gibbons and Waldman (2004) posited that technical and task-specific talent influences investment and hence high growth enterprises.

Startups also create jobs and deal with the issues of unemployment (Reynolds et al., 1994), policy supports by the governments play an important role. According to Global Entrepreneurship Monitor Report (GEM) (2018), Startups create 20% of the 50% jobs created in the developing countries (who participated in the Study) and this number is expected to grow further. The process of job creation by Startups and hence talent acquisition is a new area of scholarly inquiry, with entrepreneurs as the principal actor.

Scholar has been keen to research on various aspects of entrepreneurship and startups. Popular themes of research have been entrepreneurial motive, motivation, opportunity identification and resource mobilisation. Aspects of financial capital are also researched especially in the light investment while talents despite being at the core of successes or failures of new ventures is yet to be studied in depth (Lehmann et al., 2019).

In early scholarly research on the failure of startups (Vesper, 1990) were majorly attributed to financial problems, lack of business knowledge, problems of team management; commonly referred as 'Startup problems' (Núñez, 2007; Salamzadeh & Kawamorita Kesim, 2015) but scholarly studies are not available on selection and management of people. Phenomenon like Unicorns or Hidden Champions (Audretsch et al., 2018) or Industry 4.0 offers a wide spectrum of Startup creation and opportunity for such studies (Lehmann et al., 2019) to know about the process of talent acquisition. While startups clusters at specific locations with the advantage of eco-system and available talent (Ellison et al., 2010) is an important area of research; arrival of investors is also attributed to location specificity (Balsmeier et al., 2021) which enhances the possibility of attracting talents. Though we have some understanding on these themes in countries like Germany, USA, Japan, Austria and Switzerland considering the higher number of Hidden Champs, studies on growth of startup attributed to talent acquisition remain a knowledge gaps. Further, we also need an understanding on economic growth attributed to innovative products, processes and business models with high calibre talent.

We submit again, human resource-related issues and outcomes in startups are as one of the major reasons of success or failure; absence of entrepreneurs' ability to manage human resource adds up to problems in startups (Baron, 2004). Hence, talent

[1] Unicorns are Startupsthat are valued at One Billion Dollar or more (De Massis et al., 2016) while Soonicornshave the potential to become Unicorns.

[2] Mainstreet or Hidden Champions are companies other than from high-tech or ICT Sector which are market leaders in their respective industry and niches in their own continent or worldwide on account of specialised products and/or services designed by highly talented people (Lehmann et al., 2019).

acquisition is critical for the survival and growth of startups (Buller & Napier, 1993; Coad & Timmermans, 2016; Salamzadeh & Kawamorita Kesim, 2015). Guided by Katz and Gartner (1998), we raise research questions—how do entrepreneurs enhance the process of talent acquisition, and, do entrepreneurs do anything different for talent acquisition to take locations specific advantages? Our article is guided by the knowledge gaps and research questions on talent acquisition in startups referred above.

## 2 Conceptualising Talent and Talent Acquisition

Talent is defined as competence, commitment and contribution (Beechler & Woodward, 2009). Schiemann (2013) explained it as, "the collective knowledge, skills, abilities, experience, values, habits and behaviours of all labour that is brought to bear on the organization's mission". Talent acquisition as a process relates to identification, attracting and acquiring people with the right skills who can fulfil the needs while fitting in the culture of the organisations (Bhatnagar & Srivastava, 2008).

Acquiring talent is an indicator of growth of startups (Reynolds, 2003). This is an inseparable and important organisational activity since the formation of startup (Brush et al., 2008; Gartner, 1985) with several economic, social and cultural complexities. In startups the first talent acquisition corresponds to a 'growth milestone event' because with this 'event' startups progress from being driven by solo entrepreneur 'to doubling the workforce' (Coad & Timmermans, 2016).

We restate that talent acquisition as a "process is so critical to succeed and if the founder lacks enough knowledge of the field; and the startup might fail due to human resource management issues" (Salamzadeh & Kawamorita Kesim, 2015). The other important managerial aspect important for talent management relates to salary with the job roles of the current and potential employees during the formative years and startups face resource limitations in this account. Further, absence of process of finding the right talent results in gaps in 'right fit' between the employees which in turn pose challenges at subsequent phases of growth (Barrett & Mayson, 2008). Entrepreneurs being a solo actor fully engaged in routing operations mostly ignore this responsibility (Nagda et al., 1999). Our idea of this Article resides on the need for systematic study on talent acquisition at the early stage of Startup life cycle (Nyström, 2019).

The processes of talent acquisition are well defined in the large organisations and scholarly literature has also evolved accordingly (Williamson, 2000). We are aware that talent acquisition as a process in large organisations is different from that of small and emerging organisations (Williamson et al., 2002) and hence calls for focused studies. On the other hand we are also aware, that ours is not the first study on the process in this area. Multiple perspectives were used by the scholars to study this process while listing various elements. Talent acquired in the form of entrepreneurial team (founding team) was explained by Forbes et al. (2006) using Grounded Theory and Resource Dependence Theory while the acquisition process of top management team members was established by Beckman and Burton (2008) using Path Dependence Theory. Edelson et al. (2011) highlighted the Person-Organization fit with the Signalling Theory to explain the Organisational Personality and the process of talent acquisition from the Job Seekers' perspective. Krenzi (2020)studied the Swiss Markets proposed a Seven-Step Process framework of talent acquisition; the steps proposed are the identification of talent acquisition need, preparing drafts of job description for advertising, publishing advertisement, screening the applications received, interviewing candidates, selecting the candidate and making job-offer and onboarding and retaining. In a study on Iranian Startups, Boudlaie and Kenarroodi (2020) used the concept of Gamification.

The literature on talent acquisition in startups is at the initial stage wherein scholars have been using different theoretical lenses and attempting to report the unique features. We observe the entrepreneur as the central actor engaged in the process of talent acquisition influences the process of talent acquisition. In this article, we attempt to advance the scholarly discussion considering entrepreneur as the actors who not only feels and establishes the need for talent acquisition but also designs and initiates the process (Coad & Timmermans, 2016; Forbes et al., 2006; Greer et al., 2016; Moser et al., 2017; Nyström, 2019; Zhao, 2013). We propose to unfold the subject while presenting deeper meaning on various aspects of the process which might support in opening avenues for future research. Considering this we have taken views of the actors, factors, actions, sequences and consequences in defining the process of talent acquisition (Van de Ven, 1992) with interlinkages thereof, if any.

## 3 Talent Acquisition in Startups

We have drawn inspirations from the Mintzberg's Role Theory (1973, 1978), Theory of Causation and Explanation?, and the Path Dependence Theory to build our arguments. While the Theory on Causation provides the opportunity to consider 'purposefulness' in talent acquisition, Path Dependence supports to understand the non-linearity in enterprise creation (------). Enterprise creation is not limited to a mega-process, rather it constitutes several sub-processes and their alignments in achieving the entrepreneurial aspiration (Majumdar, 2008). In the entrepreneurial process framework of Timmons (---) 'Team' has been considered as one of the major aspects of enterprise creation and growth. Acquisition of talent leads to mobilisation of the desired team, to implement the enterprise processes.

### 3.1 *Talent Acquisition as a 'Process'*

Van de Ven (1992) referred 'process' in three ways namely, (a) a logic used to explain a causal relationship in a variance theory; (b) category of concepts that refer to the activities of individuals or organisations; and (c) a sequence of events that describe how things change over time. The dimensions of talent acquisition include—Actors, Activities, Outcomes, Contexts and Phases (Barber, 1998) and the process is 'a combination' of actors, factors or causes, events, outcomes and patterns and sequences.

As referred earlier, the actor 'Entrepreneur' plays a central role in the acquisition of talent and the subsequent allocation of work to them (Dunphy & Meyer, 2002; Mintzberg's Role Theory, 1973); 'Causes and Need' explain this process of talent acquisition. Causes answer 'whys' (Aristotle). Efficient explanation of causes bring about 'the change', to be viewed as the effect(s). Aristotle explained the importance of 'causal factors' for initiating the process. Hempel and Oppenheim (1948) referred with the Theory of Causation argued that specific causal factors lead to 'an Event' and 'Event' includes the identification of sources, and attracting and assessing the necessary talent. The 'Outcomes' was referred by Hempel and Oppenheim (1948) with the Theory of Explanation. Path Dependence, as theory, was popularised by Economist Arthur (1994) which explains "what has happened at an earlier point in time will affect the possible outcomes of a sequence of events occurring at later points of time" (Mahoney, 2000). Path Dependence provides ways to analysing the causality of the processes that take place in the earlier stages of a historical sequence (Mahoney, 2000) thereby seeking explanations on the Organisational Evolution (Nooteboom, 1997).

"Theory of Effectuation" propounded by Sarasvathy (2001) provides a different perspective to explain the entrepreneurial decision-making. The Theory considers goal setting as a result of reviewing the means, with affordable loss. Exploitation of contingencies and dealing with the nature of unknown form the basis to control the future with the least interest by the entrepreneurs to predict it. However, in later literature critiquing this argument for and against almost settles to propose that a combination of both causation and effectuation is critical for the success of enterprise.

In this article, therefore, we further explore the process of talent acquisition with the help of actors, factors (causes and needs), activities or events, outcomes, patterns and their sequences and interrelationships.

### 3.2 Dimensions of Process of Talent Acquisition

a. Entrepreneur-the Actor:

Talent acquisition process is influenced by the entrepreneur's vision, competencies, convenience etc. (Majumdar, 2008). Entrepreneur inducts 'Entrepreneurial Team Members' (Forbes et al., 2006) including the top management team (Beckman & Burton, 2008) to take various roles. They deeply involve in acquiring the talents (Mathias & Williams, 2017). Despite desiring to select 'the best talent', factors like capital restriction, inexperience, business risks and uncertainties pose challenge to attract qualified and skilled talents. Resource constraint limits entrepreneur's ability to invest in talent acquisition process (Coad & Timmermans, 2016). As a result at the initial stage entrepreneurs rely more on social and business networks to source talents, however at growth phase they gain the necessary competencies to refine the process (Leung et al., 2006).

b. Causes and Need-the Factors:

Attracting, selecting and training talents are the major activities of talent acquisition process (Bendickson et al., 2017; Crowne, 2002). Also important is to consider the roles and responsibilities the acquired talents take up in startups. Talent is critical for product or service to solve the customer problems (Moogk, 2012). On similar note, Katz and Gartner (1998) submitted that activities—identifying specific customers, selling and managing sales channels, as important behaviours for the survival and success of startups affecting their growth. Other functional responsibilities considered to be important for new talents are accounting (Ries, 2011; Soto, 2015), Quality Assurance (Shikta et al., 2021), New Product Development, R&D, Marketing and Human Resource Management. Human resource management issues related to talent, inexperience of the entrepreneurs and lack of team-coordination factors are responsible for failure of startups (ibid.).

c. Events:

Sources of talent–Most business startups do not begin with outside talents (Aldrich & Langton, 1997); rather they start with family members as the first employees. In general, the potential source of first talent for startups are family members, friends and known networks (Aldrich & Langton, 1997). Interns are another preferred choice (Zhao, 2013). The other potential source of talent is co-workers from the earlier jobs of the entrepreneurs (Chen, 2013). Top management team also influence the resource mobilisation in general and talent acquisition in specific (Hellman & Puri, 2002).

Attracting—Organisational attractiveness is important for innovativeness, founders' vision and legitimacy (Nyström, 2019). Talent attraction in startup is attributed to the pay offered, degree of independence and intellectually stimulating work content (Sauermann, 2018), work environment and new opportunities (Gjerløv-Juel & Guenther, 2018). Favourable work profile includes team, flexibility, responsibility and work environment (Tumasjan et al., 2011). Stimulating work profile is one of the major reasons for new talents to join startups (Shane, 2009). Shane (2009) also reported a lack of desired salary as a reason for the lack of attractiveness by the potential employees while Burton et al. (2016) contradicted this view.

Assessing—Entrepreneurs desiring to acquire talents in alignment with their business concept, values and philosophy (Vallaster, 2005) remain careful in assessing and selecting new talents (Rode & Vallaster, 2005). Searching fit or match between entrepreneur and the potential employee (Nyström, 2019) is also reported to be critical. Generally, entrepreneurs tend to develop or adopt Organisational Models to operate and organise activities which forms the basis of the assessment of new employees (Phillips, 2002). As reported earlier, entrepreneurs rely more on social networks more during the early phase while at the growth phase they look towards the business networks to search the potential talents (Leung et al., 2006). This provides them the advantage of finding people from known settings and provides ease in assessment due to familial or close business ties. Assessing previous co-workers as potential employees is reported to be easy due to prior acquaintance (Chen, 2013).

Interview is the most popular method of assessment for formal selection process. Entrepreneurs engage in Behavioural Interview, if they want to know about candidates' competency based on the behaviour which might have a bearing on the future performance (Rode & Vallaster, 2005). Selection of new talent at an early stage of startup is also a process discovery of suitable talent capable to meet the job requirements (Florea & Duica, 2016). Entrepreneurial-minded job seekers stand better chances of selection in startups (Kristof-Brown et al., 2005). The other sought-after characteristics in the prospective employees are innovativeness, proactive behaviour and risk-taking ability (De Jong et al., 2015).

d. Outcome—for the Organisation:

Theory of Causation explains the Cause, Need and Event which lead to Outcome. The acquired talents are expected to know about how to utilise and orchestrate the available resources efficiently and productively and thus converting them into firm-specific resources i.e. technologies, processes, networks and services (Berglund & Wennberg, 2016; Gruber et al., 2010; Penrose, 1959). Entrepreneurs manage talents for Organisational Performance especially the financial performance (Hiltrop, 1996) and to gain competitive advantage (Katz et al., 2000). Building organisational functions with the help of talents help in building different dimensions of capabilities of Startups; they include New Product Development, identification of customers, acquiring and managing talent, maintaining accounts for credibility and transparency and for attracting new investments and ensuring Quality Assurance for maintaining the Product standards.

We summarise the dimensions discussed above in Table 1.

However, sequence and consequence form an integral part of a process. Hence, the links between these sequence and consequence need to be explored.

**Table 1** Dimensions of process of talent acquisition

| Dimensions of the talent acquisition process | Factor(s)related to the dimension | Theoretical underpinnings | Brief description |
|---|---|---|---|
| Actor | Entrepreneur | Mintzberg's Role Theory (1973), and Dunphy and Meyer (2002) | Influenced by the entrepreneur (Majumdar, 2008);<br>Inducts Entrepreneurial Team Members (Forbes et al., 2006) and Top Management Team (TMT) (Beckman & Burton, 2008);<br>Initiates and involves deeply in talent acquisition (Mathias & Williams, 2017);<br>Resource limitations restrict investment in formal process (Coad & Timmermans, 2016); dependent on social and business networks during initial phase but gain necessary competency during the growth phase (Leung et al., 2006) |
| Causes and need | Functions, skill or roles | Causes are important to answer the why (Aristotle); Causal factors lead to the 'Events' (Theory of Causation, Hempel & Oppenheim, 1948) | For New Software Product Development (Crowne, 2002);<br>Introducing new product or service to solve customer problems (Moogk, 2012);<br>Functional Activities (Shikta et al., 2021; Soto, 2015) |

(continued)

**Table 1** (continued)

| Dimensions of the talent acquisition process | Factor(s)related to the dimension | Theoretical underpinnings | Brief description |
|---|---|---|---|
| Events | Identifying sources of talent; Attracting; and Assessing | Causal factors lead to outcomes (Theory of Causation, Hempel & Oppenheim, 1948) | Potential sources of initial talents for Startups are family, friends and known networks (Aldrich & Langton, 1997); interns (Zhao, 2013); co-workers from earlier jobs (Chen, 2013) and Top Management Team (Hellman & Puri, 2002)<br>Attributes to attract talents are pay offered, degree of independence and intellectually stimulating work content (Sauermann, 2018), work environment and new opportunities (Gjerløv-Juel & Guenther, 2018)<br>Desire to acquire talent in alignment with business concept, values and philosophy (Vallaster, 2005), evident is fit or match between entrepreneur and employee (Nyström, 2019); familiarity coming from family, friends, networks or from previous organisation (Chen, 2013);<br>Behavioural interview and formal assessment (Rode & Vallaster, 2005) |
| Outcomes | Organization as an integrated entity | Actor, cause and needs and events culminates into the Outcomes (Theory of Explanation, Hempel & Oppenheim, 1948) | Talent acquired utilises and orchestrates available resources and convert them into firm-specific resources such as technologies, processes, networks services (Berglund & Wennberg, 2016; Gruber et al., 2010; Penrose, 1959);<br>Impacts organisational performance (Hiltrop, 1996); gain competitive advantage (Katz et al., 2000) |

*Source* Compiled by the Authors

## 4 Discussion–Setting Agenda for Research

We restate, the process of talent acquisition alters the developmental stages of Startups (Nyström, 2019). In the absence of talent acquisition process it would be difficult to know—how individuals fit into the subsequent phases of Startup growth (Barrett & Mayson, 2008). The first cycle is critical (Coad & Timmermans, 2016); the first talent constitutes the biggest growth event while it also corresponds to overcoming the mindset from being a solo entrepreneur to doubling the workforce. Subsequent cycles of talent acquisition are about transition from being entrepreneur-centric to business-centric organisation, and more formalised. In sum, the processes from first talent acquisition to the subsequent cycles, till the Startup becomes fully business-driven and formal, are less explored area in scholarly research. It would be valuable to know about the variations and commonalities in approaches pursued by entrepreneurs in designing and implementing the process of talent acquisition starting from the first cycle. We must know, what are the specific functions of talent acquisition and the outcomes thereof at the end of each cycle, and how are the transitions managed to become entrepreneur-driven to the business driven. It would be interesting to get insights on behaviour and act in the talent acquisition process. Entrepreneurs use different decision logic in stable and uncertain business environments, this could also form the basis of research question for the future research (Morris et al., 2002). Future research should let us know about new learnings out of the previous experience of the entrepreneurs since entrepreneurial acts are non-linear and reasonably unpredictable due to context specificity (Barad, 2010). The related research question could be, are the subsequent events of talent acquisition resulting in better outcome (Lichtenstein, 2016)? Also, influence of co-founders, investors, etc. as moderating agents or actors can be studied in detail.

In order to set the context of the probable research question for the future research we have conducted a dipstick study at six Mumbai (India) based Startups, two each non-technology and technology-based business startups and social enterprises. Our Study reported mix patterns with variations. We found that the founder-entrepreneurs play a critical role in the talent acquisition process (Mathias & Williams, 2017), and the first acquisition is based on the Founder- Entrepreneur's plan on how he/she wants to manage the business (Majumdar, 2008). We also found that the first acquisition is mostly sourced from the family or professional networks of the entrepreneur (Aldrich & Langton, 1997; Hoang & Antoncic, 2003). For this entrepreneurs rely on multiple sources and networks. Entrepreneurial learning from the previous cycles in refining the actions in subsequent cycles was also reported. The future decisions are guided by the need of the functional areas or enhancement of the current functions or proposed new areas of business and the complimentary skills of the entrepreneurs. They all provide inputs to the next cycles of talent acquisition and variations observed are in the form of better alignment with the business objectives (Nyström, 2019).

We propose, the first major objective for future study should be the development of a broad framework to explain the 'process of talent acquisition', to initiate studies on this subject which is currently not available. We also need to challenge the existing or available research mostly guided by the established literature on large business organisations. Every dimension, right from the entrepreneur, causes and needs in the form of functions and talents, identification of sources, attracting potential candidates, assessment of candidates, outcomes and impact of talent acquisition process on Startup, to the formalisation of the processes, offer avenues for research.

Secondly, we need to question whether talent acquisition process rests in the context (Granovetter, 1973; Sarasvathy, 2001; Senge, 1990). The context-related factors can be the location, competitive business environment posing (specific) talent shortage or high demand of talent. The related research question is—do the entrepreneur consider such situation relevant; if yes, how do the entrepreneurs deal with them? In parallel, do context-related situation trigger any acts of innovation in talent acquisition? If yes, what are they—resource constraint situations (Witt, 2004) or new opportunities or specific technical skills required (Davidsson et al., 2020)? Further, whether and how do entrepreneurs compete for talent acquisition (McEvily & Zaheer, 1999)? There is also the possibility of large data-based studies to develop the robust theoretical view.

Thirdly, in recent times in India, Startups have experienced phenomenal growth while going for public listing (popularly known as IPO-Initial Public Offering), and also becoming Unicorns and Soonicorns. Though distribution of investments is skewed (Lehmann et al., 2019), they seem to have achieved breakthrough, thereby posing competition to the established business organisations (De Massis et al., 2016). While this is sometimes attributed to entrepreneurs being a serial entrepreneurs, enterprise team size, rapid innovation, financing by venture capitalists (De Massis et al., 2016), organisational cultures also need to be studied, to know the reasons for sustaining growth of the Startups. Specific research questions are—how do the Startups acquire talent in such high growth conditions?

Lastly, research on talent acquisition by Startups has wide implications on the subjects like economic growth, labour market, job creation, innovation and location-specific growth. This can also be a subject of interest by the scholars of labour economics.

Methodological considerations are important for future research. For this, we refer back to the explanation of Van de Ven (1992) on the 'process'. We agree with Pettigrew (1997) that the social processes are embedded in the contexts hence case studies provide meaningful data to construct deeper meanings. Yin (2003) posits case study to answer the 'how' and 'why' related questions. Since, research is at a nascent stage and the 'process' of talent acquisition in scholarly literature is yet not reported adequately, we first need to establish 'the constructs' and the related research agenda. Hence at this stage qualitative research methodology in general and case study method in specific would be appropriate. In the early stage of research questions like 'what, how and why' are to be answered first in the contexts beyond researcher's control (Yin, 2003). We also draw strength from the literature (Leung et al., 2006) to argue that case study method would be appropriate to study talent acquisition at different stages of entrepreneurial firms and 8–10 cases would be a good starting point (Mukul & Saini, 2021; Pettigrew, 1997). As we progress, sector-specific, location-specific and growth-oriented (such as Unicorns and Soonicorns) would provide the needed basis for developing robust research constructs. To develop sound theoretical insights, scholars may critically analyse patterns and variations as appropriate. This can follow studies based on larger groups or large pool of data using quantitative methods for generalisation.

Here, we also raise an epistemological question. For future research scholars may consider managerial function discharged by entrepreneurs in the new venture creation process overlapping with entrepreneurial thinking for the realisation of a mission (Majumdar, 2008). On the other hand managerial approach for talent acquisition can be questioned purely from entrepreneurial resource mobilisation view.

## 5 Conclusion

Success of Startups not only benefits the entrepreneurs and the employees but also brings positive changes in the economy with rapid innovation and growth. Due to limited scholarly literature on the process of talent acquisition by the startups or entrepreneurial ventures (Greer et al., 2016) vast scope for research available (Greer et al., 2016; Nyström, 2019).

In this article we argued talent acquisition as critical organisational need right from the startup phase (Brush et al., 2008; Gartner, 1985). Aspects of human resource management are felt essential immediately after the first talent is acquired; any gap to deal with such issues may lead to failure of Startups (Baron, 2004). Hence, this article has been an attempt to present a basic literature for reference to develop a framework for developing critical insights on the 'process of talent acquisition in startups'. We attempted to provide an agenda or a way forward to open avenues for future research with an argument that the process of talent acquisition involves entrepreneur as actor; and cause and need as factors, events and organisational outcomes. We also explained the interrelationships thereof.

We presented broad areas of research which can act as guide rails to develop research constructs for future research. This opens up the avenues for research to explore related elements too. Our research will not only provide important insights to the research scholars and academicians, but will also guide entrepreneurs in establishing and managing Startups. Potential entrepreneurs, potential job seekers in Startups would equally benefit from this article.

## References

Aldrich, H., & Langton, N. (1997). Human resource management practices and organizational life cycles. In P. D. Reynolds, W. D. Bygrave, N. M. Carter, P. Davidsson, W. B. Gartner, C. M. Mason, & P. P. McDougall (Eds.), *Frontiers of entrepreneurship research* (pp. 349–357). Babson College Center for Entrepreneurship.

Aristotle's work https://plato.stanford.edu/entries/aristotle-causality/#Bib

Aristotle's work https://managingresearchlibrary.org/glossary/aristotle-causality

Arthur, W. B. (1994). *Increasing returns and path dependency in the Economy*. University of Michigan Press.
Audretsch, D. B., Lehmann, E. E., & Schenkenhofer, J. (2018). Internationalization strategies of hidden champions: Lessons from Germany. *Multinational Business Review, 26*(1), 2–24.
Balsmeier, B., Fleming, L., Marx, M., & Shinf, S. R. (2021). Startups, unicorns, and the local supply of inventors.
Barad, M. M. (2010). *A study of liquidity management of Indian steel industry* [Doctoral dissertation, Saurashtra University].
Barber, A. (1998). *Recruiting employees* (1st ed.). SAGE Publications. https://www.perlego.com/book/1004211/recruiting-employees-pdf (Original work published 1998).
Baron, R. A. (2004). The cognitive perspective: A valuable tool for answering entrepreneurship's basic "why" questions. *Journal of Business Venturing, 19*(2), 221–239.
Barrett, R., & Mayson, S. (2008). Introduction: At the intersection of entrepreneurship and human resource management. In R. Barrett & S. Mayson (Eds.), *International handbook of entrepreneurship and HRM* (pp. 1–17). Edward Elgar.
Baumol, W. J. (2004). Entrepreneurial enterprises, large established firms and other components of the free-market growth machine. *Small Business Economics, 23*(1), 9–21.
Beckman, C. M., & Burton, M. D. (2008). Founding the future: Path dependence in the evolution of top management teams from Founding to IPO. *Organization Science, 19*(1), 3–24. https://doi.org/10.1287/orsc.1070.0311
Beechler, S., & Woodward, I. C. (2009). The global "war for talent." *Journal of International Management, 15*(3), 274.
Bendickson, J. S., Muldoon, J., Liguori, E. W., & Midgett, C. (2017). High performance work systems: A necessity for startups. *Journal of Small Business Strategy, 27*(2), 1–12.
Berglund, H., & Wennberg, K. (2016). Pragmatic entrepreneurs and institutionalized scholars? On the path-dependent nature of entrepreneurship scholarship. In H. Landstrom, A. Parhankangas, A. Fayolle, & P. Riot (Eds.), *Challenging entrepreneurship research* (pp. 37–52). Routledge.
Bhatnagar, J., & Srivastava, P. (2008). Strategy for staffing: Employer branding and person-organisation fit. *Indian Journal of Industrial Relations, 44*(3), 35–48.
Boudlaie, H., & Kenarroodi, M. (2020). A qualitative study of gamification based recruitment process in startups. *Journal of Management Studies in Development & Evolution, 29*(96), 121–148.
Brush, C. G., Manolova, T. S., & Edelman, T. F. (2008). Properties of emerging organizations: An empirical test. *Journal of Business Venturing, 23*, 547–566.
Buller, P. F., & Napier, N. K. (1993). Strategy and human resource management integration in fast growth versus other mid-sized firms. *British Journal of Management, 4*, 77–90.
Burton, M. D., Sørensen, J. B., & Dobrev, S. D. (2016). A careers perspective on entrepreneurship. *Entrepreneurship: Theory and Practice, 40*(2), 237–247.
Chen, J. (2013, June 17–19). *Firm characteristics and employee entrepreneurs? Choice of cofounders and early employees*. Presented at 35th DRUID Celebration Conference 2013.
Coad, A., & Timmermans, B. (2016). My first employee: An empirical investigation. *Small Business Economics*. Retrieved August 26, 2018, from https://doi.org/10.1007/s11187-016-9748-3
Crowne, M. (2002, August). Why software product startups fail and what to do about it. Evolution of software product development in startup companies. In *IEEE International Engineering Management Conference* (Vol. 1, pp. 338–343). IEEE.
Davidsson, P., Recker, J., & von Briel, F. (2020). External enablement of new venture creation: A framework. *Academy of Management Perspectives, 34*(3), 311–332.
De Jong, J. P. J., Parker, S. K., Wennekers, S., & Wu, C.-H. (2015). Entrepreneurial behavior in organizations: Does job design matter? *Entrepreneurship Theory and Practice, 39*(4), 981–995. https://doi.org/10.1111/etap.12084
De Massis, A., Frattini, F., & Quillico, F. (2016). What big companies can learn from the success of the unicorns. *Harvard Business Review*, 1–5.

Dunphy, S. M., & Meyer, D. (2002). Entrepreneur or manager? A discriminant analysis based on Mintzberg's managerial roles'. *Journal of Business and Entrepreneurship, 14*(2), 17–37. https://search.proquest.com/scholarly-journals/entrepreneur-manager-discriminant-analysis-based/docview/214229833/se-2?accountid=130296.

Edelson, S. A., Haynie, J. M., & McKelvie, A. (2011). Working for a startup? Investigating the role of "venture personality" in the recruitment of human capital. *Frontiers of Entrepreneurship Research, 31*(9), 322–337.

Ellison, G., Glaeser, E. L., & Kerr, W. R. (2010). What causes industry agglomeration? Evidence from coagglomeration patterns. *American Economic Review, 100*(3), 1195–1213.

Florea, N. V., & Duica, A. (2016). Selection interview—A necessary tool in discovering the best candidates. *Valahian Journal of Economic Studies, 7*(3), 105.

Forbes, D. P., Borchert, P. S., Zellmer-Bruhn, M., & Sapiencza, H. J. (2006). Entrepreneurial team formation: An exploration of new member addition. *Entrepreneurship Theory and Practice, 30*(2), 225–248. Retrieved January 31, 2021, from https://doi.org/10.1111/j.1540-6520.2006.00119.x

Gartner, W. B. (1985). A conceptual framework for describing the phenomenon of new venture creation. *The Academy of Management Review, 10*(4), 696–706.

Gibbons, R., & Waldman, M. (2004). Task-specific human capital. *American Economic Review, 94*(2), 203–207.

Gjerløv-Juel, P., & Guenther, C. (2018). Early employment expansion and long-run survival; examining employee turnover as a context factor. *Journal of Business Venturing*. Retrieved July 13, 2018, from https://doi.org/10.1016/j.jbusvent.2018.05.005

Global Entrepreneurship Monitor. (2018). *GEM 2017/2018 global report.* Retrieved from September 10, 2018, from https://www.gemconsortium.org/report/50012

Granovetter, M. S. (1973). The strength of weak ties. *American Journal of Sociology, 78*(6), 1360–1380.

Greer, C. R., Carr, J. C., & Hipp, L. (2016). Strategic staffing and small-firm performance. *Human Resource Management, 55*(4), 741–764.

Gruber, M., Heinemann, F., Brettel, M., & Hungeling, S. (2010). Configurations of resources and capabilities and their performance implications: An exploratory study on technology ventures. *Strategic Management Journal, 31*(12), 1337–1356.

Hellman, T., & Puri, M. (2002). Venture capital and the professionalization of start-up firms: Empirical evidence. *The Journal of Finance, 57*(2), 169–197.

Hempel, C. G., & Oppenheim, P. (1948). Studies in the logic of explanation. In Brody (pp. 8–38).

Hiltrop, J. M. (1996). The impact of human resource management on organizational performance: Theory and research. *European Management Journal, 14*(6), 628–637.

Hoang, H., & Antoncic, B. (2003). Network-based research in entrepreneurship: A critical review. *Journal of Business Venturing, 18*(2), 165–187.

Katz, J. A., Aldrich, H. E., Welbourne, T. M., & Williams, P. M. (2000). Special issue on Human resource management and the SME: Toward a new synthesis. *Entrepreneurship: Theory and Practice, 25*(1), 7–11.

Katz, J., & Gartner, W. B. (1998). Properties of emerging organizations. *Academy of Management Review, 13*(3), 429–441.

Krenzi, L. (2020). How to optimize the Talent Acquisition Strategy and Recruitment Process in Swiss Startups and young ventures to build a winning team? (Bachelor of Science) *Haute école de gestion de Genève*. Retrieved from December 12, 2020, from https://doc.rero.ch/

Kristof-Brown, A. L., Zimmerman, A. D., & Johnson, E. C. (2005). Consequences of individuals' fit at work: A metaanalysis of person-job, person-organization, person-group, and person-supervisor fit. *Personnel Psychology, 58*, 281–342.

Lehmann, E. E., Schenkenhofer, J., & Wirsching, K. (2019). Hidden champions and unicorns: A question of the context of human capital investment. *Small Business Economics, 52*(2), 359–374.

Leung, A., Zhang, J., Wong, P. K., & Foo, M. D. (2006). The use of networks in human resource acquisition for entrepreneurial firms: Multiple "fit" considerations. *Journal of Business Venturing, 21*, 664–686.

Lichtenstein, B. B. (2016). Emergence and emergents in entrepreneurship: Complexity science insights into new venture creation. *Entrepreneurship Research Journal, 6*(1), 43–52.

Mahoney, J. (2000). Path dependence in historical sociology. *Theory and Society, 29*(4), 507–548. https://www.jstor.org/stable/3108585

Majumdar, S. (2008). Modelling growth strategy in small entrepreneurial business organisations. *The Journal of Entrepreneurship, 17*(2), 157–168.

Mathias, B. D., & Williams, D. W. (2017). The impact of role identities on entrepreneurs' evaluation and selection of opportunities. *Journal of Management, 43*(3), 892–918.

McEvily, B., & Zaheer, A. (1999). Bridging ties: A source of firm heterogeneity in competitive capabilities. *Strategic Management Journal*, 133–1156.

Mintzberg, H. (1973). *The nature of a managerial work*. Harper and Row.

Mintzberg, H. (1978). Patterns in strategy formation. *Management Science, 24*(9), 934–948.

Moogk, D. R. (2012). Minimum viable product and the importance of experimentation in technology startups. *Technology Innovation Management Review, 2*(3), 23–26.

Morris, M. H., Schindehutte, M., & LaForge, R. W. (2002). Entrepreneurial marketing: A construct for integrating emerging entrepreneurship and marketing perspectives. *Journal of Marketing Theory and Practice, 10*(4), 1–19.

Moser, K. J., Tumasjan, A., & Welpe, I. M. (2017). Small but attractive: Dimensions of new venture employer attractiveness and the moderating role of applicant's entrepreneurial behaviors. *Journal of Business Venturing, 32*(5), 588–610.

Mukul, K., & Saini, G. K. (2021). Talent acquisition in startups in India: The role of social capital. *Journal of Entrepreneurship in Emerging Economies, 13*(5), 1235–1261. https://doi.org/10.1108/JEEE-04-2020-0086

Nagda, B., Harding, S., & Holley, L. (1999). Social work and multicultural organization development: Toward empowerment and empowered organizations. In W. Shera & L. Wells (Eds.), *Empowerment practice in social work: Developing richer conceptual foundations* (pp. 278–306). Canadian Scholars' Press.

Nooteboom, B. (1997). Path dependence of knowledge: Implications for the theory of the firm. In L. Magnusson & J. Ottosson (Eds.), *Evolutionary economics and path dependence* (pp. 57–78). Elgar.

Núñez, L. G. (2007). The process and problems of business Start-Ups. Pensamientoygestión: revista de la División de Ciencias Administrativas de la Universidad del Norte, (22), 232–255.

Nyström, K. (2019). Working for an entrepreneur: Heaven or hell? *Small Business Economics, 56*, 919–931.

Penrose, E. T. (1959). *The theory of the growth of the firm*. John Wiley.

Pettigrew, A. M. (1997). What is a Processual analysis? *Scandinavian Journal of Management, 13*(4), 337–348.

Phillips, D. J. (2002). A genealogical approach to organizational life chances: The parent-progeny transfer and Silicon Valley law firms, 1946–1996. *Administrative Science Quarterly, 47*(3), 474–506.

Reynolds, P. (2003). *Entrepreneurship over time: Measures of activity and recent changes in the US: 1993–2002*. Papers on Entrepreneurship, Growth and Public Policy, No. 4404, Max Planck Institute for Research into Economic Systems, Jena. Retrieved February 12, 2021, from http://hdl.handle.net/10419/19989

Reynolds, P. (2010). *New firm creation in the United Sates: A PSED I overview in Foundation & Trends in Theoretical Computer Science*. Retrieved January 1, 2021, from https://doi.org/10.1561/0300000010

Reynolds, P., Storey, D. J., & Westhead, P. (1994). Cross-national comparisons of the variation in new firm formation rates. *Regional Studies, 28*(4), 443–456.

Ries, E. (2011). *The lean startup: How today's entrepreneurs use continuous innovation to create radically successful businesses.* Crown Business.

Rode, V., & Vallaster, C. (2005). Corporate branding for start-ups: The crucial role of entrepreneurs. *Corporate Reputation Review, 8*(2), 121–135.

Salamzadeh, A., & Kawamorita Kesim, H. (2015). Startup companies: Life cycle and challenges. In *Proceedings of the 4th International Conference on Employment, Education and Entrepreneurship (EEE).*

Sarasvathy, S. D. (2001). Causation and effectuation: Toward a theoretical shift from economic inevitability to entrepreneurial contingency. *Academy of Management Review, 26*(2), 243–263.

Sauermann, H. (2018). Fire in the belly? Employee motives and innovative performance in start-ups versus established firms. *Strategic Entrepreneurship Journal, 12*(4), 423–454.

Schiemann, W. A. (2013). From talent management to talent optimization. *Journal of World Business.* https://doi.org/10.1016/j.jwb.2013.11.012

Senge, P. M. (1990). *The fifth discipline: The art and practice of the learning organization.* Doubleday.

Shane, S. (2009). Why encouraging more people to become entrepreneurs is bad public policy. *Small Business Economics, 33*(2), 141–149.

Shikta, S., Mahir Shahriyar, H. M., Das, S. K., Mahal, S. N., Al Jannat, K. B., & Alam, S. (2021). Quality assurance guidelines for successful startups. In *2021 IEEE/ACIS 19th International Conference on Software Engineering Research, Management and Applications (SERA)* (pp. 81–85). https://doi.org/10.1109/SERA51205.2021.9509046

Soto, E. (2015). *Innovation accounting methods to assure validated learning: The case of Finnish startups.*

Tumasjan, A., Strobel, M., & Welpe, I. M. (2011). Employer brand building for start-ups: Which job attributes do employees value most? *ZeitschriftfürBetriebswirtschaft, 81*, 111–136.

UNDP Goals from https://www.undp.org/sustainable-development-goals

Vallaster, C. (2005, February). *Markenbildungnachinnen und Personalauswahl: Der Versuchein-erstrukturationstheoretischen Integration.* Paper submitted to conference on 'Bewertung und Management von Intangible Asset', Innsbruck (Austria).

Van de Ven, A. H. (1992). Suggestions for studying strategy process: A research note. *Strategic Management Journal, 13*(S1), 169–188.

Vesper, K. H., & New Venture Strategies. (1990). University of Illinois at Urbana-Champaign's Academy for Entrepreneurial Leadership Historical Research Reference in Entrepreneurship. Available at SSRN: https://ssrn.com/abstract=1496217

Williamson, I. O. (2000). Employer legitimacy and recruitment success in small businesses. *Entrepreneurship Theory and Practice, 25*(1), 27–42.

Williamson, I. O., Cable, D. M., & Aldrich, H. E. (2002). Smaller But not necessarily weaker: How small businesses can overcome barriers to recruitment. In *Managing people in entrepreneurial organizations* (Vol. 5, pp. 83–106). Elsevier Science Limited. ISBN: 0-7623-0877-X

Witt, P. (2004). Entrepreneurs' networks and the success of start-ups. *Entrepreneurship & Regional Development, 16*(5), 391–412.

Yin, K. R. (2003). *Case study research: Design and methods* (3rd ed.). Sage.

Zhao, H. (2013). Turning small business interns into applicants: The mediating role of perceived justice. *Journal of Business Venturing, 28*, 443–457.

# Framework for Assessing the Value of Healthcare Innovations in India for Universal Health Coverage

**Kanchan Mukherjee and Satyajit Majumdar**

**Abstract** Health is an important contributor to economic and social wellbeing, and has been the focus of many social enterprises. Healthcare, whose primary purpose is to preserve or promote health, is a multi-billion-dollar industry that is growing very rapidly given the push of innovations for value addition. However, there is very limited literature on how to assess the value of a healthcare innovation. Hence, in this paper, we propose a framework to assess the value of healthcare innovations using an ecosystems approach within the context of Universal Health Coverage (UHC). The proposed framework has four dimensions, with measurable and analyzable attributes within each dimension. The four value dimensions are relevance, effectiveness, frugality and equity. A case study on digital health innovations has been used to discuss this framework to provide a nuanced understanding of the value of digital health innovations in India for social enterprises and policymakers. This proposed framework is a work in progress for discussion among scholars in this field as well as further empirical testing and refinement in different country contexts.

**Keywords** Innovation · Healthcare · Ecosystems · Responsible innovation in health (RIH) · Health technology assessment (HTA) · Social enterprise

## 1 Introduction

Social enterprises exist with the primary purpose of common good, and as business model are located between charity and for-profit business ventures (Global Forum on Innovation in Health Professional Education, 2015). They also innovate to address social needs in the areas of healthcare while serving the individuals and communities

K. Mukherjee (✉)
Centre for Health Policy, Planning and Management, School of Health Systems Studies, Tata Institute of Social Sciences, Mumbai, India
e-mail: kanch@tiss.edu

S. Majumdar
School of Management and Labour Studies, Tata Institute of Social Sciences, Mumbai, India
e-mail: satyajit@tiss.edu

 
E. M. Reji and S. Majumdar (eds.), *Social Enterprise Values and Processes*, India Studies in Business and Economics, https://doi.org/10.1007/978-981-97-3252-4_11

while generating revenue (Calo et al., 2019). During the ongoing novel coronavirus disease (COVID-19) pandemic, innovation has become a central discourse in policy and healthcare. While there has been extensive literature on enterprises using innovative solutions to address health needs, typologies of innovation and theories on innovation adoption and diffusion; there is limited literature available on frameworks or methods to assess the value of innovation in healthcare. Assessment of innovation is important not only for the enterprise responsible for innovation but also for the policymakers to prioritize decisions on funding, regulations, approvals, etc., through an evidence-based approach.

This chapter attempts to address this gap by creating a conceptual and operational framework for the assessment of value of healthcare innovations. This chapter is structured in four sections. Section 1 introduces the goals and objectives of healthcare system and Universal Health Coverage (UHC) followed by the concept of innovation and healthcare innovation. Section 2 discusses the systems approach to healthcare innovation and provides a conceptual ecosystems framework for assessing the value of healthcare innovations while Sect. 3 explains the operational framework which is then applied in Sect. 4 to a case study on digital health innovations. The article concludes with key messages for future research and also for the policymakers and social enterprises.

## 2 Healthcare, UHC and Healthcare Innovation

### *2.1 Health and Healthcare System*

"The promotion and protection of health is of value to all, and essential to peace and security and dependent on the fullest cooperation of individuals and states; unequal promotion of health in different countries is a common danger", statement released by WHO two years into the COVID-19 pandemic reflects the importance of values and processes in healthcare. Valuing healthcare is not only an important goal of the healthcare sector but also has wider ramifications for the Sustainable Development Goals (SDG). The maintenance and improvement of health are at the core of the healthcare system; organizations, institutions and people have to demonstrate through their actions (WHO, 2000). In addition, WHO in its World Health Report, 2000, identified two other objectives of healthcare systems: financing and responsiveness.

These objectives above capture effectiveness outcomes (improved health), equity (financial risk protection from costs of ill health across all strata of society) and quality processes (responsive to client autonomy, choice, respect and dignity). To achieve them, the healthcare system functions broadly at three levels, namely primary, secondary and tertiary. Primary healthcare is the first point of contact of individuals or families with the healthcare system for basic healthcare issues. Secondary healthcare refers to the second tier of the health system, and can also serve as the first referral level for health issues, which cannot be addressed by primary healthcare. Tertiary healthcare refers to the third level of the health system where specialized consultative care is provided, and also acts as a referral from primary and secondary healthcare centres. In Indian context, the primary healthcare is provided through a network of primary health centres, sub-centres, health and wellness centres (in rural areas) and urban health posts and family welfare centres (in urban areas). Rural hospitals, sub-district/divisional hospitals, women's hospitals and community health centres at the block level have been created to provide secondary healthcare, while district hospitals and medical college hospitals across different districts and cities in India are designated as tertiary care centres (MOHFW, 2011). Private healthcare sector also provides this range of services through primary care physicians in urban and rural areas and multispecialty hospitals in urbanized cities and towns.

Globally, primary healthcare has been the focal point of health policy and health systems-related initiatives after the Alma Ata Declaration (1978), which targets to achieve health for all (12 targets and 19 indicators) by 2000 (WHO, 1978). While the developed countries progressed towards this goal, the developing countries (including India) lagged behind. This resulted in the creation of Millennium Development goals (MDG) with time-bound targets (18 targets and 48 indicators) to achieve by 2015 (WHO, 2018). Despite improvements several gaps remained and a more holistic approach was proposed by the United Nations (UN) through its Sustainable Development Goals (SDG) (UN, 2015) with time-bound targets (169 targets with 230 individual indicators) for 2030 (IAEG-SDG, 2016). India, being a signatory to all the declarations, is policy-bound to plan, prioritize and take necessary actions to meet these targets. Among the 17 SDG, health is the focus of SDG 3 (good health and wellbeing), and the concept of UHC is included within SDG 3 (Fig. 1).

The dimensions of UHC include availability and access to trained health workers, safe and effective treatment and medicines, affordable quality healthcare and evidence-informed decisions. The Astana Declaration (The Lancet, 2018) re-commits to the importance of primary healthcare in UHC. The concept of UHC brings a systems approach to healthcare to address the issues of physical accessibility,

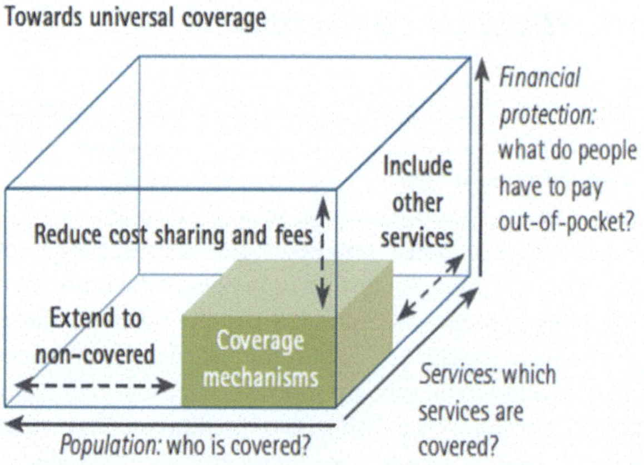


**Fig. 1** The UHC cube (*Source* WHO Report, 2010)

financial affordability and quality, by improving health, financial risk protection and responsiveness of the healthcare system.

Currently, healthcare is one of the largest and fastest-growing sectors (Compounded Annual Growth Rate 22.9%) in India both in terms of revenue and employment (fourth-largest employer), and has reached a value of $372 billiion by 2022 (India Brand Equity Foundation (IBEF), 2024). Growth is mainly attributed to the private healthcare sector with innovation as the major driver, favoured by a strong policy push. Healthcare innovations are complex and develop in a milieu called 'an ecosystem'. In the next section, the concept of healthcare innovation and ecosystem is explored through a literature review.

## 2.2 Innovation

The term 'innovation' originates from the Latin word '*innovare*', which means to make something new (Lin, 2006) and dates back to the early man innovating to survive. Gradually, the focus of innovation shifted from survival to value creation in society. Several terms such as *change, development, evolution, mutation, creation, growth, modernization, reform, revolution, progress, discovery, imitation, invention, insight, cognition, idea or imagination* have been used to describe the concept of innovation (Moldaschl, 2010). Hence, missing is a uniform description and explanation of the term 'innovation'. Researchers and practitioners have used their own subjective assessment and interpretation to define this term. As a result, theories on innovation have also spanned from multiple disciplines—sociology, psychology (Tarde, 1897), economics (Smith, 1776; Schumpeter, 1912), management (Drucker, 1985), communication science (Rogers, 1983), entrepreneurship and business research (Christensen et al., 2015).

## 2.3 Healthcare Innovation

Länsisalmi et al. (2006) in their review of healthcare innovations, identified three characteristics of innovations: (a) novelty, (b) an application component and (c) an intended benefit. These have been reflected in the definition of innovation given by West (1990), "the intentional introduction and application within a role, group, or organization, of ideas, processes, products or procedures, new to the relevant unit of adoption, designed to significantly benefit the individual, the group, or wider society". The consideration of 'intended benefit' leads to the role of stakeholders (patients, physicians, caregivers, insurers, organizations, innovator companies, regulatory agencies) in the healthcare innovation process (Omachonu & Einspruch, 2010). The factors also affect the diffusion of healthcare innovation which is a social process and requires collaboration, communication and knowledge exchange between different stakeholders within and outside the system (Hemphälä & Magnusson, 2012). Adaption and implementation of innovation, and scalability are dependent upon the social, political, policy, economic, institutional and cultural contexts of a particular system. Innovation can make healthcare better and cheaper by either changing the ways *consumers* buy or use or/and through the usage of *technology* to develop new products and treatments to improve care or/and generating new *business models* (Herzlinger, 2006). The factors that affect acceptability, adaptability and diffusion of healthcare innovation include actor interfaces (stakeholders and their interests), financial interface (funding and cost), innovation ecosystem (policies, government regulations, competition, accountability) and user interface (consumer views and opinions) (Hemphälä & Magnusson, 2012; Herzlinger, 2006).

On the other hand the WHO definition of healthcare innovation highlights on development and delivery of new or improved health policies, systems, products and technologies and the related services and delivery methods, to improve efficiency, effectiveness, quality, sustainability, safety and affordability of healthcare (WHO, n.d.). These definitions above cover a wide range of aspects of innovations (macro policies to micro-level implementation), includes processes and products, and provides ways to optimize or improve performance of healthcare systems and the overarching goals of healthcare innovation. This also aligns with the goals and objectives of UHC (Mukherjee, 2021a, 2021b).

Healthcare innovation is thus a complex phenomenon involving a multi-level, multi-dimensional and multidisciplinary web of interactions and sustainable healthcare innovation would demand behavioural change in the health systems and the actors (including end-users or patients) (Plamping et al., 2009; McNichol, 2012). We conclude, holistic systems approach to innovation is the key to generating, adapting, diffusing and sustaining healthcare innovations since innovation is embedded in both policy and institutional contexts and different innovation outcomes emerge as a result of the interactions between those with a techno-centric focus, and the traditional habits and practices of the actors towards innovation. Hence, a systems approach would help us to understand the adoption and diffusion of innovation in healthcare sector.

## 3 Healthcare Innovation and Ecosystems

### *3.1 Systems Approach to Healthcare Innovation*

An innovation system can be defined as a network of institutions, organizations and individuals from university, industry, government, civil society ('quadruple helix') that focuses on bringing new products, processes and forms of organization into social and economic use, together with institutions, policies and other factors that affect their behaviour and performance (Etzkowitz & Leydesdorff, 2000; Leydesdorff, 2012).

Health innovation system extends beyond healthcare provision to encompass agencies namely, regulatory, science and technology, health technology assessment (HTA) and production, in dynamic interaction with healthcare professionals, hospitals and the national healthcare system (Thune, 2013). We are also witnessing emergence and strengthening of a global health innovation system (Mahoney & Morel, 2006) in filling the gaps in science, market and public health in poor countries, through industrial development networks and partnerships that extend beyond national borders. At the policy level, the 'innovation system' concept, while acknowledging research and technology commercialization, also recognizes it as an interactive process involving individuals and different organizations within social, political, policy, economic and institutional context (Baldwin & Von Hippel, 2009; Burlon et al., 2008). Empirical studies concluded that a systems approach to innovation is strongly correlated with the capacity to innovate and its adoption in society (Nelson, 1993).

The notion of 'ecosystem' includes a dynamic collaborative network of individuals and organizations with an innovative objective (Smorodinskaya et al., 2017). In the era of digital and non-linear change, innovations are no longer limited to business networks and extend to communities engaged in for innovation (Smorodinskaya et al., 2017). Ecosystems have expanded from inter-organizational networks or innovative-supportive milieu (Wessner, 2005) to self-organizing properties of natural ecosystems (European Commission, 2007) to co-creation of value through collaboration (Ranjan & Read, 2016). Innovation ecosystems can take forms like collaborative innovation networks, innovation clusters, global value chains and platforms. In the recent times the concept of innovation ecosystem has been around the phenomenon of actors, activities and artefacts with institutions and relations for new levels of performance (Granstrand & Holgersson, 2020). Global innovation ecosystem in action was seen in innovative COVID-19 diagnostics and vaccines. The Access to COVID-19 Tools Accelerator (ACT-A), COVID-19 Technology Access Pool (C-TAP) and COVID-19 Vaccine Global Access Facility (COVAX) have facilitated global collaborations among the health expert to ensure the availability of affordable and high-quality COVID-19 rapid tests, treatments and vaccines. This clearly demonstrates the importance of working collaboratively with the stakeholders to make healthcare innovations available and accessible. Equity issues emerging from access, affordability and availability of the innovations emphasizes on governing the innovation for common good (WHO, 2021).

With the increasing number of technological innovations also arise complex policy challenges with regard to socio-cultural-political dimensions of innovation adoption (Silva et al., 2018). These challenges have been established through studies in the areas of sociology, anthropology, cultural studies, political studies and history. From the perspectives of scholarly research, what is considered 'healthy' is being increasingly defined through the newly deployed biotechnologies. One influential perspective in this regard is the Actor-Network Theory (ANT), which considers non-human actors (devices, equipments, etc.) as allies of human actors for knowledge production. In this, medical technology is not viewed as a passive object invested in social meaning by human actors, but as an actor in its own right (without intentionality) shaping social relations (Latour, 1992). This can be observed in the instances wherein certain sections of society are more likely to use technology not based on scientific evidence, but on social prestige. An important aspect of medicine as 'a social and cultural product' is to know how scientific technologies are developed, adopted and translated into everyday use by the people. Technologies have a major role to play in healthcare delivery and are integral to the experiences of those practising scientific medicine and those receiving care (Lupton, 2012). The social construction of technology theory argues that technology does not determine human action, but human action shapes technology. Technology is not rendered as an artefact in the structuration theory but examines how people, as they interact with technology in their ongoing practices, enact structures that shape their emergent and situated use of that technology. Critical theories question the moral and political values, and power relationships in determining a technological configuration and their usage (Geuss, 1981).

The COVID-19 pandemic has brought many of these dimensions of technology innovations to the forefront. For example, the emergence of the innovative COVID-19 vaccines within a year of the pandemic highlighted the importance of collaborative engagements for a common cause though its pricing created issues for its adoption and diffusion. Vaccine also exposed the systemic voids of accessibility, affordability and quality of healthcare in society. These voids in turn affect the efficiency, equity and responsiveness of the healthcare systems. Given the complex interactions between healthcare innovations, policy and society, and the need for sustainable solutions for the future, there is an urgent need for assessing the value of healthcare innovations responsibly by policymakers and social enterprises. The next section explains a framework (for researchers) to generate evidence on the value of healthcare innovations for UHC. This would be useful for policymakers and social enterprises in decisions regarding the emergence, adoption and diffusion of healthcare innovations towards UHC.

### *3.2 Framework for Assessing the Value of Healthcare Innovations for UHC*

An extensive review of literature was conducted on this subject to propose the framework presented below. The literature consisted of systems approach for assessing the values of healthcare innovations—HTA and Responsible Innovation in Health (RIH). The concept of HTA has evolved, beginning with the office of technology assessment (Banta & Jonsson, 2009) in USA to the HTA core model (Kristensen et al., 2017) by the European Union network of HTA (EUnetHTA). Countries like United Kingdom (UK) and Thailand use it as a national approach for decision-making to achieve efficiency and equity, while its use currently being limited is gradually increasing among the low-and low-middle-income countries (LMICs) (Babigumira et al., 2016). HTA is described as "a multidisciplinary process that uses explicit methods to determine the value of a health technology at different points in its lifecycle with the purpose to inform decision-making to promote an equitable, efficient, and high-quality health system" (O'Rourke et al., 2020). This explicitly provides a systems approach for determining the value of health technologies. Health technology includes preventive, diagnostic, clinical or health system interventions (Mukherjee, 2020).

Advancing the systems perspective, more recently, a holistic concept of responsible innovation (RI) (Stilgoe et al., 2013) and 'responsible research in innovation' (RRI) (Burget et al., 2016) was introduced in innovation literature by the developed countries, which is based on the dimensions of anticipation, reflexivity, inclusion, responsiveness, sustainability and care (Mukherjee & Walley, 2022). The concept of RI resonates with the concept of 'appropriate technology', which is also one of the elements of primary healthcare postulated in the Alma Ata Declaration of 1978 (WHO, 1978). RRI has grown rapidly over the past decade and has significantly influenced the European research policy landscape, and has been suggested as a new lens to consider and govern the innovation process (Demers-Payette et al., 2016). These concepts were developed further and applied to health systems literature in Canada, to develop the concept of RIH. RIH is a relatively new concept and described as a "collaborative endeavour wherein stakeholders are committed to clarify and meet a set of ethical, economic, social and environmental principles, values and requirements when they design, finance, produce, distribute, use or discard socio-technical solutions to address the needs and challenges of health systems sustainably" (Lehoux et al., 2018). This posits that RIH encompasses social and sustainable innovation aiming at social change to benefit health and wellbeing.

However, application of HTA and RIH is heavily dependent on the availability of resources, data, capacities of researchers and political institutionalization. While HTA is well established in the high, middle and upper-middle-income countries, its use and application have been limited in low- and low-middle-income countries. The RIH framework has been empirically tested only in Brazil and Canada among 16 healthcare innovations and needs further revisions based on the country contexts. In this article, we adapt the guidance from RIH and HTA both, to offer conceptually integrated ecosystems framework, for assessing the value domains and attributes of healthcare innovations for UHC (Fig. 2).

The innovation ecosystem is conceptualized as a dynamic and evolving interaction of actors (stakeholders-public, private, community, etc.), institutions (public healthcare system, private healthcare system, academia, media, etc.), activities (collaboration, competition) and artefacts (innovative processes, products, services, etc.). Their interactions create the context of the innovation ecosystem, which is also dynamic and evolving with time. It is within this ecosystem context that healthcare innovations emerge and need to be assessed for their value towards the UHC goals.

We propose four value domains for operational assessment of healthcare innovations:

1. Relevance
2. Effectiveness
3. Frugality
4. Health Equity

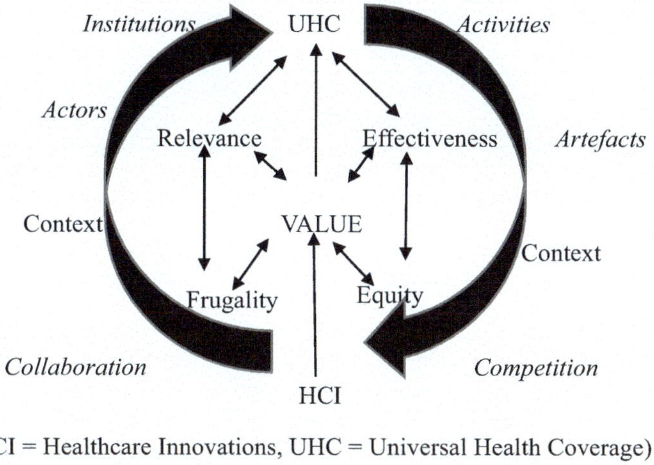


**Fig. 2** Integrated ecosystems framework for value assessment of healthcare innovation

For each value domain, we identify key attributes for measurement, the corresponding research questions and the methodologies and methods required to answer these research questions. Table 1 summarizes this operational framework for assessing the value of healthcare innovations in the innovation ecosystem for UHC. This is proposed as a work in progress to stimulate further discussion on the value domains, attributes and methodologies. We suggest empirical testing of this framework by interdisciplinary teams of scholars for refinement and adaptation considering the local contexts. In the next section, we discuss this operational framework in detail.

# 4 Operational Framework for Assessing the Value of Healthcare Innovation

## *4.1 Relevance*

The value of relevance assesses the innovation's response to population health and health system challenges. The proposed research question is—Does the innovation address a public health concern? To answer this question, existing epidemiological data on population disease burden (incidence, prevalence studies, etc.), and economic data on the cost of the disease being addressed by the healthcare innovation need to be assessed to verify its relevance to the health of populations.

For understanding the relevance of the innovation to the health system, we propose the application of WHO model for health systems functions (WHO, 2000). With the Model, four key challenges have been identified—service delivery, human resources, financing and governance. The aim of innovation needs to be analyzed to assess

**Table 1** Operational framework for valuing healthcare innovations for UHC

| Value domains | Attributes | Research questions | Methodology/Method |
|---|---|---|---|
| Relevance | Population health<br>Health Systems | Does the innovation address a public health concern?<br>Is the innovation responding to a healthcare system challenge? | Analysis of epidemiological and economic data, global burden of disease studies, epidemiological and economic models<br>Analysis of innovation's main objective/outcome through primary and secondary data, expert elicitations, stakeholder analysis |
| Effectiveness | Actual effectiveness<br>Relative effectiveness | Does the innovation effectiveness/benefit outweigh the risks?<br>Does the innovation give better outcomes than currently existing comparable interventions? | Analysis of data from RCTs and SRs<br>Analysis of RCTs and SRs comparing similar interventions with the innovation |
| Frugality | Affordability, Availability<br>Acceptability | Does the innovation provide value for money AND value for many? | Analysis of innovation pricing, economic evaluation techniques; stakeholder analysis, Mixed methods, user reviews, star ratings, focus group discussions |
| Health Equity | Disparities in health | Is the innovation putting populations who are already socially disadvantaged (e.g. poor, female, tribal, rural population etc.) at a further disadvantage? | Analysis of data on innovation use, acceptability and health outcomes across different social strata<br>Application of HEMF, DHEF, ECHTA to local context |

RCT = Randomized Clinical Trial; SR = Systematic Review; HEMF = Health Equity; Measurement Framework; DHEF = Digital Health Equity Framework; ECHTA = Equity checklist health technology assessment.

whether it targets any or some or all of the health system challenges. This would require analysis of documents on innovation purpose/aims, analysis of innovations outcomes using primary and secondary data, expert elicitation and stakeholder analysis. Healthcare innovations addressing these attributes need prioritization by the policymakers and social enterprises for the achievement of UHC.

## 4.2 Effectiveness

The value of 'effectiveness' is integral to healthcare innovation because it deals with matters of life and death. Effectiveness can be assessed with bioefficacy, bioequivalence, effectiveness and safety studies. However, it is important to acknowledge that almost all therapeutic interventions, medical, surgical, etc., have some side effects on the patients. Hence, from a pragmatic clinical and public health point of view, the assessment should ask the question—Does the innovation effectiveness/benefit outweigh the risks? The gold standard for assessing effectiveness are Randomized Clinical Trials (RCTs) and Systematic Reviews (SRs) (if available). Using these high grade quality of evidence, researchers can answer questions related to the actual effectiveness of the innovation and provide the evidence to policymakers and the social enterprises. Healthcare innovation that does more harm than good either at the individual or community level raises serious social and ethical concerns. Hence, policymakers and social enterprises should ensure that such innovations should not move to the subsequent stages of innovation adoption and diffusion.

The second proposed attribute is 'relative effectiveness'. If the innovation is found to be safe and effective, the next research question for valuing the innovation is, whether the innovation gives better outcomes than currently existing interventions? The answer would also emerge from the analysis of results from RCTs and SR with a comparative assessment. The results would provide evidence on the relative relevance of healthcare innovation and also a comparative perspective for prioritization among competing healthcare innovations. This would constitute the evidence for the value addition of innovation for policymakers to decide on regulatory approvals, funding, etc., and for social enterprises to decide on the strategies for the adoption and diffusion.

## 4.3 Frugality

'Frugal innovations' can be considered a new source of innovation to meet the needs of low-income customers and make them more inclusive. Hossain et al. (2016) defined frugal innovation as "a product, service or a solution that emerges despite financial, human, technological and other resource constraints, and where the final outcome is less pricey than competitive offerings (if available) and which meets the needs of those customers who otherwise remain un-served". It overlaps with many other concepts including good enough, the base of the pyramid, inclusive, grassroots, disruptive, 'jugaad' and reverse innovations (Hossain, 2017). A multi-method study from innovation management literature identified substantial cost-reduction, concentration on core functionalities and optimized performance as three criteria for frugal innovation, irrespective of target market or specific attributes (Weyrauch &

Herstatt, 2017). Though frugal innovation has been described and classified differently by different authors, the elements relevant to the Indian context are, need-based, bottom-up approach, which is adaptable and simple.

Financial risk protection during ill health is an explicit goal of UHC and the affordability attribute is critical in countries like India, where households pay very high out-of-pocket (OOP) expenditure on healthcare, estimated to be 49.82% of current health expenditure (World Bank, 2024). This can be catastrophic and push households below the poverty line resulting in medical poverty trap. In India, about 50–60 million are pushed below the poverty line due to the high cost of healthcare (Selvaraj et al., 2018). Hence, addressing affordability is of important value to consider while assessing healthcare innovations. Also, even if available, health insurance card is of no use without the availability of a doctors, nursing staff and medicine, at the nearest healthcare facility (Mukherjee, 2019). Both affordability and availability affect the 'accessibility' of healthcare services and acceptability of innovation affects its use and diffusion. Acceptability explains and predicts important outcomes of interest of the innovation like user engagement, effectiveness and adoption (Perski & Short, 2021). It is also one of the fundamental prerequisites for successful outcomes of internet and mobile-based interventions (Philippi et al., 2021). In sum, to assess frugality dimension, we provide three attributes of innovation—affordability, availability and acceptability and propose the research question—Does the innovation provide *value for money* AND *value for many*? Economic evaluation techniques like cost-effectiveness analysis, cost–benefit analysis and cost-utility analysis for assessing 'value for money' which compares cost/price of innovation and with the outcomes, are well established. However, important variables such as ease of use, convenience, sociocultural factors, etc., affect innovation acceptability, but are not captured through the quantitative economic evaluation techniques (Mukherjee, 2020). Hence, it is desirable to combine these techniques with stakeholder analysis, qualitative interviews of end-users (mixed methods design) across different gender and income groups, geographical settings and stakeholder perspectives to capture information on convenience, ease of use, barriers, facilitators, barriers to use, etc., for assessing the value of innovation. User reviews, star ratings and focus group discussions have also been reported in literature as useful methods to qualitatively assess the acceptability of healthcare innovations. This would provide a better understanding and a holistic perspective on innovation which might be useful for policymakers and social enterprises.

## 4.4 Health Equity

'Health inequities' have been described as differences in health that are unnecessary, avoidable, unfair and unjust. The Health Equity Measurement Framework (HEMF) (Dover & Belon, 2019) has developed as a comprehensive equity framework to assess social inequalities in health. Based on the HEMF, Crawford and Serhal (2020) created the Digital Health Equity Framework (DHEF) and Benkhalti et al. (2021)

developed a checklist for guiding equity considerations in HTA-Equity Checklist for Health Technology Assessment (ECHTA). The frameworks provide useful guidance to generate evidence on equity dimensions. The concept of health equity has become even more important to achieve given the COVID-19 pandemic, and the need for innovation as a common good is essential to address inequity (WHO, 2021).

Equity in health is a normative concept, ethically valued and in congruence with human rights principles. To assess the health equity value of innovations, we propose to use the operational definition of health equity as 'the absence of health disparities (and in its key social determinants) that are systematically associated with social advantage/disadvantage' (Braveman & Gruskin, 2003). Hence, we propose the research question—Is the innovation taking population who are already socially disadvantaged (e.g. poor, female, tribal, rural population, etc.) at a further disadvantage? Comparative analysis of data on usage of innovation, acceptability and related health outcomes across the strata of society and use of equity frameworks (mentioned above) would provide insights to answering this question.

In the next section, we apply the above operational framework to digital innovations in healthcare in India, as a case study. This can also be considered as an illustration to demonstrate the usability of the framework.

## 5 Case Study on Digital Innovations in Healthcare

Digital technologies are redefining the healthcare delivery system and are projected to be the future of healthcare. They are also considered as an outcome of fourth Industrial Revolution known as Industry 4.0. In the healthcare sector, it refers to the amalgamation of modern technologies like the internet of things, cloud computing, block chain, artificial intelligence, etc., with healthcare data (Kickbusch, 2009). Digital technologies have been used for pharmaceuticals (e-pharmacies), creating digital platforms and apps for healthcare services, telemedicine, healthcare financing, etc. While the private sector has been the leader in digital initiatives, Government of India (GoI) through its recently launched National Digital Health Mission (NDHM) is working on the interoperability of digital healthcare data in India. Also, social enterprises are using digital health innovations and telemedicine to provide healthcare. Given the high-level policy focus on digitalization, its application for the transformation of business model by social enterprises and potential for the future, we apply the operational framework described above, to assess the value of this innovation.

*Relevance to Population Health and Health System Challenge*: Digital platforms can cater to a range of health problems, from primary care to tertiary specialized care and surgeries, as well as to provide teleconsultation and medicines at doorsteps. E-healthcare platforms provide convenience, information and a tool for comparing ratings, prices, facilities, etc., useful for patients and the caregivers to make informed choice for fulfilling their healthcare needs. They address relevant health issues and are responsive to the healthcare system challenge of shortfalls in service delivery and human resources.

*Effectiveness*: Digital healthcare is safe and effective if applied with care and caution. The use of mobile apps for scheduling doctor appointment, and ordering medicines through e-prescriptions provide convenience and saves time of patients and caregivers. During the COVID-19 pandemic, several digital health innovations were devised and applied to provide effective healthcare while minimizing risk of infection. However, the effectiveness in real terms depends on doctor-patient interactions, barriers and facilitation. A systematic review identified ease of usage, cost saving, patient training and internet and phone availability as the common facilitators for telemedicine-based online consultation. The barriers to adoption include internet speed, access, video and audio quality and resistance to technology (Almathami et al., 2020).

Evidence from an SR on relative effectiveness shows that teleconsultations and videoconferences were as effective as face-to-face in-person consultations in improving clinical outcomes in primary care services and for consultation on adult mental health conditions (Carillo de Alboronoz et al., 2021). However, the review also identified high discontinuation rates and hence recommended appropriate training to healthcare professionals, and management of technical issues.

*Frugality*: Evidence on the cost-effectiveness of digital health interventions is limited and the evidence on the behaviour change due to digital platforms or mobile apps is insufficient (Hazel et al., 2021). However, digital health interventions have been found to be cost-effective for acute myocardial infarction recovery in the USA (Bharadwaj et al., 2021), neurosurgical emergency management in Italy (Kadel et al., 2018), general practitioner-patient communication during COVID-19 in Poland (Kludacz-Alessandri et al., 2021) and in simulated experimental patients (Tates et al., 2017). A systematic review of digital health interventions (DHI) in the management of cardiovascular diseases (CVDs) has also reported DHI to be cost-effective (Jiang et al., 2019). In the Indian context, mobile-based health technologies (mHealth) intervention developed by community health workers were reported to be saving cost, from societal perspective in the state of Uttar Pradesh (Prinja et al., 2018).

Acceptability is at the core in digital health (Perski & Short, 2021). Evidence on the acceptability of digital health innovations though slowly emerging, is highly contextual due to sociocultural factors. Meta-synthesis of qualitative and mixed methods study on expectations and pre-existing beliefs about DHI's impacting patient experience and engagement concludes on the need to be personalized to improve uptake, retention and health outcomes (Patel et al., 2020). Using the Unified Theory of Acceptance and Use of Technology (UTAUT), performance expectancy, effort expectancy and social influence were found to be the key predictors of acceptance of internet and mobile-based interventions (Philippi et al., 2021).

*Health Equity*: Although digital health innovations have been reported to be effective with the potential to address the healthcare challenges, they may also have unintended consequences in health equity (Crawford & Serhal, 2020). Some existing social inequities may cause disparities in access and usage of digital health innovations, for example, poverty, poor digital literacy, poor engagement with communities, and lack of availability of internet may result in digital health innovations not leading to effective health outcomes in illiterate, rural, tribal and economically poor populations. The VOCAL study (Greenhalgh et al., 2016), which is also the first major study using qualitative data and analysis from a socio-material perspective, highlight apprehensions regarding clinical risks, patient acceptability, technical, logistic and regulatory challenges in virtual consultation processes.

In India, the Digital Health Mission—a government initiative, is on a mammoth project to create unique digital health ID for the citizens as part of a technology-centric overhaul of public healthcare, primarily focusing on the Ayushman Bharat Scheme (Dalal, 2021). However, clear regulatory framework is yet to be established. This techno-centric focus on UHC makes certain assumptions about the availability of internet and smartphones which do not hold when facts were examined. For example, only 502.2 million adult own smartphones; with the elderly, disabled and poor—those with likely in health needs, have the least access (Silver et al., 2019). Internet access in rural India is limited to one in three persons (Kawoosa, 2020), with significant gender disparity (Bhuyan, 2020). The mobile network connectivity remains poor in many regions of India, and people from remote and/or rural areas are not updated explicitly with current technology platforms. This might hinder effective communication during video consultations, which is essential to prescribe List A drug teleconsultation. Even the healthcare personnels' skills are limited in utilizing the available technology solutions. The guidelines laid down by the authorities mention that unique online education course would be formulated, and registered medical practitioners (RMPs) would be directed to undergo such courses within the next three years. This might enhance digital literacy of RMPs and translate to the effective application of telemedicine. On the other hand, text and audio consultations are feasible across the country despite limitations. RMPs need to send prescriptions online while availability of internet services is essential at both ends. When the patient receives such prescriptions, drugs for mental illness like psychotropics are seldom available in remote areas which limits the benefit of teleconsultation. Drugs, that can be misused, are not permitted for a prescription through e-consultation (Dinakaran et al., 2021). Hence, access to medicines and doctors remains dependent on factors not within the purview of the guidelines. Also, there is no check on whether patient data is being sold or shared with pharmaceutical or insurance companies by the online platforms without the consent of the data principal (patient or caregiver). Conflict of interest issues between doctors, pharmaceutical companies and insurance companies remain undisclosed to the data principal which affect the ethics and transparency of digital healthcare.

## 6 Conclusions

In this article, we presented an ecosystems framework (Fig. 1) to conceptualize the value assessment of healthcare innovation for UHC. Using existing literature on systems approach to valuing health technologies and innovations, we then created an operational framework to assess these values and the related identified attributes with research questions, methodologies and methods for assessment. We applied this framework to assess the value of digital health innovations as a case study using available data in the secondary sources. The Case Study though generic in nature and limited by secondary data, provides insight into the healthcare scenario of digitalized healthcare in India, and also gaps and challenges for policymakers and social enterprises, to address in future. We report, in India the digital innovations progressed faster than the policies; policies are unable to keep pace with the changing technologies. We also add that digital technology has significantly evolved to include Artificial Intelligence (AI) and Machine Learning (ML) tools and algorithms for machine-based diagnosis. Hence, data usage and privacy issues are becoming more complex and data can be misused in the absence of a standardized regulatory framework.

We conclude and submit, social enterprises have been providing primary healthcare in low resource settings through digital health interventions (Lokman & Chahine, 2021). Applying the value framework discussed above would help these enterprises align their business model with the requirements of UHC and also benchmark their performances. However, majority of the local healthcare enterprises have limited data literacy and analytical capabilities which prevent them from leveraging the gains of readily available data while at the same time posing privacy risks. In the absence of demonstrated public health or clinical utility, process and algorithmic transparency will be essential for the success of digital healthcare innovations in India (Sarbadhikari & Pradhan, 2020). The NDHM is attempting to integrate the IT Act, the draft PDP bill and various judiciary judgements on data privacy and security, to set up a data policy framework. However, it is important to note, currently in India, digitalization of healthcare services is a technological innovation without accompanying infrastructural and social support that is creating a digital divide by favouring urban society. This needs to be addressed urgently by policy interventions and technology innovation by the social enterprises and to establish social cohesion.

This assessment framework might be considered as a 'work in progress' to subject it open for discussion among the scholars, as well as also for empirical testing across healthcare innovations in different contexts. Through this article, we propose to focus on UHC with a systems approach for assessing healthcare innovations. We also believe, application of this framework would help researchers generate the necessary evidences for policymaking for evidence-informed approval, regulatory and funding decisions for healthcare innovations. It would provide information to innovate by the social enterprises working in the healthcare-related areas while evaluating value of their innovations, and to plan for the future plans.

## References

Almathami, H. K., Win, K. T., & Vlahu-Gjorgievska, E. (2020). Barriers and facilitators that influence telemedicine real-time online consultation at patient's home: A systematic literature review. *Journal of Medical Internet Research, 22*(2), e16407.

Baldwin, C. Y., & Von Hippel, E. (2009). Modeling a paradigm shift: From producer innovation to user and open collaborative innovation. (MIT Sloan School of Management Working Paper # 4764-09). Viewed April 12, 2022, http://web.mit.edu/people/evhippel/papers/Carliss%20Eric%20Paradigm%20shift%20model%20WP%20Nov%2021%2009.pdf

Babigumira, J. B., Jenny, A. M., Bartlein, R., Stergachis, A., & Garrison, L. P. (2016). Health technology assessment in low- and middle-income countries: A landscape assessment. *Journal of Pharmaceutical Health Services Research, 7*(1), 37–42.

Banta, D., & Jonsson, E. (2009). History of HTA: Introduction. *International Journal of Technology Assessment in Health Care, 25*(1), 1–6.

Benkhalti, M., Espinoza, M., Cookson, R., Welch, V., Tugwell, P., & Dagenais, P. (2021). Development of a checklist to guide equity considerations in health technology assessment. *International Journal of Technology Assessment in Health Care, 37*(1), e17.

Bharadwaj, V., Spaulding, E. M., Marvel, F. A., LaFave, S., Yu, J., Mota, D., Lorigiano, T. J., Huynh, P. P., Shan, R., Yesantharao, P. S., Lee, M. A., & Padula, W. V. (2021). Cost-effectiveness of a digital health intervention for acute myocardial infarction recovery. *Medical Care, 59*(11), 1023–1030.

Bhuyan, A. (2020, December 17). 4 in 5 Bihar women have never used the internet. *Indiaspend.* Viewed April 25, 2022, https://www.indiaspend.com/gendercheck/4-in-5-bihar-women-have-never-used-the-internet-702855

Braveman, P., & Gruskin, S. (2003). Defining equity in health. *Journal of Epidemiology & Community Health, 57*(4), 254–258.

Burget, M., Bardone, E., & Pedaste, M. (2016). Definitions and conceptual dimensions of responsible research and innovation: A literature review. *Science and Engineering Ethics, 23*(1), 1–19.

Burlone, N., Andrew, C., Chaisson, G., & Harvey, J. (2008). Horizontalit´e et gouvernance d´ecentralis´ee: Les conditions de collaboration dans le contexte de l'action communautaire. *Canadian Public Administration, 51*(1), 127–142.

Caló, F., Roy, M. J., Donaldson, C., Teasdale, S., & Baglioni, S. (2019). Exploring the contribution of social enterprise to health and social care: A realist evaluation. *Social Science & Medicine, 222*, 154–161.

Carrillo de Albornoz, S., Sia, K.-L., & Harris, A. (2021). The effectiveness of teleconsultations in primary care: Systematic review. *Family Practice, 39*(1), 168–182.

Christensen, C., Raynor, M., & Mcdonald, R. (2015). *What is disruptive innovation?* Harvard Business Review. Viewed April 10, 2022, https://hciforstartups.org/wp-content/uploads/2021/10/What-Is-Disruptive-Innovation.pdf

Crawford, A., & Serhal, E. (2020). Digital health equity and COVID-19: The innovation curve cannot reinforce the social gradient of health. *Journal of Medical Internet Research, 22*(6), e19361.

Dalal, M. (2021). Why telemedicine needs an urgent fix. *Mint.* August 27, 2020, Viewed April 25, 2022. https://www.livemint.com/news/india/why-telemedicine-needs-an-urgent-fix-11598448423482.html

Dinakaran, D., Manjunatha, N., Kumar, C. N., & Math, S. B. (2021). Telemedicine practice guidelines of India, 2020: Implications and challenges. *Indian Journal of Psychiatry, 63*(1), 97–101.

Dover, D. C., & Belon, A. P. (2019). The health equity measurement framework: A comprehensive model to measure social inequities in health. *International Journal for Equity in Health, 18*(36).

Drucker, P. F. (1985). *Innovation and entrepreneurship: Practice and principles.* Heinemann.

Etzkowitz, H., & Leydesdorff, L. (2000). The dynamics of innovation: From national systems and 'Mode 2' to a triple helix of university–industry–government relations. *Research Policy, 29*(2), 109–123.

European Commission, Director General for the Information Society and Media. (2007). *Digital business ecosystems.* Publications office, Viewed April 25, 2022, https://op.europa.eu/en/publication-detail/-/publication/53e45e55-4bd2-42a4-ad25-27b339b051e0

Geuss, R. (1981). *The idea of a critical theory: Habermas and the Frankfurt School*. Cambridge University Press.

Global Forum on Innovation in Health Professional Education, Forum on Public-Private Partnerships for Global Health and Safety, Board on Global Health, Institute of Medicine (2015). *Empowering women and strengthening health systems and services through investing in nursing and midwifery enterprise: Lessons from lower-income countries—Workshop summary*. National Academies Press.

Granstrand, O., & Holgersson, M. (2020). Innovation ecosystems: A conceptual review and a new definition. *Technovation, 90–91*, e102098.

Greenhalgh, T., Vijayaraghavan, S., Wherton, J., Shaw, S., Byrne, E., Campbell-Richards, D., Bhattacharya, S., Hanson, P., Ramoutar, S., Gutteridge, C., Hodkinson, I., Collard, A., & Morris, J. (2016). Virtual online consultations: Advantages and limitations (VOCAL) study. *British Medical Journal Open, 6*(1), e009388.

Hazel, C. A., Bull, S., Greenwell, E., Bunik, M., Puma, J., & Perraillon, M. (2021). Systematic review of cost-effectiveness analysis of behavior change communication apps: Assessment of key methods. *Digital Health, 7*, 1–13.

Hemphälä, J., & Magnusson, M. (2012). Networks for innovation—But what networks and what innovation? *Creativity and Innovation Management, 21*(3), 3–16.

Herzlinger, R. E. (2006). *Why innovation in health care is so hard*. Harvard Business Review. Viewed April 20, 2022. https://hbr.org/2006/05/why-innovation-in-health-care-is-so-hard

Hossain, M., Simula, H., & Halme, M. (2016). Can frugal go global? Diffusion patterns of frugal innovations. *Technology in Society, 46*, 132–139.

Hossain, M. (2017). Mapping the frugal innovation phenomenon. *Technology in Society, 51*, 199–208.

IAEG-SDG. (2016). Report of the Inter-Agency and Expert Group on Sustainable Development Goal Indicators. Final list of proposed Sustainable Development Goal indicators. Viewed April 15, 2022, https://sustainabledevelopment.un.org/content/documents/11803Official-List-of-Proposed-SDG-Indicators.pdf

India Brand Equity Foundation (IBEF). (2024). *Healthcare industry in India, Indian healthcare sector, services*. Viewed June 15, 2024. https://www.ibef.org/industry/healthcare-india

Jiang, X., Ming, W. K., & You, J. H. (2019). The cost-effectiveness of digital health interventions on the management of cardiovascular diseases: Systematic review. *Journal of Medical Internet Research, 21*(6), e13166.

Kadel, R., Evans-Lacko, S., Tramarin, A., & Stopazzolo, G. (2018). Cost-effectiveness of tele-video-consultation for the neuro-surgical emergency management at the general hospitals in Italy. *Frontiers in Neuroscience, 12*(908).

Kawoosa, V. M. (2020, August 14), Connectivity gets better but parts of India still logged out. *Hindustan Times*. Viewed April 25, 2022, https://www.hindustantimes.com/india-news/connectivity-gets-better-but-parts-of-india-still-logged-out/story-VSqXriMdGUudWb7eBcWzjN.html

Kickbusch, I. (2009). *Policy innovation for health*. Springer.

Kludacz-Alessandri, M., Hawrysz, L., Korneta, P., Gierszewska, G., Pomaranik, W., & Walczak, R. (2021). The impact of medical teleconsultations on general practitioner-patient communication during COVID-19: A case study from Poland. *PLoS ONE, 16*(7), e0254960.

Kristensen, F. B., Lampe, K., Wild, C., Cerbo, M., Goettsch, W., & Becla, L. (2017). The HTA Core Model ®—10 years of developing an international framework to share multidimensional value assessment. *Value in Health, 20*(2), 244–250.

Länsisalmi, H., Kivimäki, M., & Aalto, P. (2006). Innovation in healthcare: A systematic review of recent research. *Nursing Science Quarterly, 19*(1), 66–72.

Latour, B. (1992). Where are the missing masses? The sociology of a few mundane artifacts. In W. Bijker & J. Law (Eds.), *Shaping technology/building society*. MIT Press.

Lehoux, P., Silva, P., Sabio, R. P., & Roncarlo, F. (2018). The unexplored contribution of responsible innovation in health to sustainable development goals. *Sustainability, 10*(11), e 4015.

Leydesdorff, L. (2012). The triple helix, quadruple helix..., and an N-tuple of helices: Explanatory models for analyzing the knowledge-based economy? *Journal of the Knowledge Economy, 3*(1), 25–35.

Lin, C. (2006). A study on the organizational innovations in Taiwan's logistics industry. *The Business Review, 5*(1), 270–275.

Lokman, L., & Chahine, T. (2021). Business models for primary health care delivery in low-and middle-income countries: A scoping study of nine social entrepreneurs. *BMC Health Services Research, 21*(1), e211.

Lupton, D. (2012). Theoretical perspectives on medicine and society. In *Medicine as culture: Illness, disease and the body*. SAGE.

Mahoney, R. T., & Morel, C. M. (2006). A global health innovation system (GHIS). *Innovation Strategy Today, 2*, 1–12.

McNichol, E. (2012). Patient-led innovation in healthcare: The value of the 'user' perspective. *International Journal of Healthcare Management, 5*(4), 216–222.

Ministry of Health and Family Welfare (MoHFW), Government of India. (2011). *Human resources for health. National Rural Health Mission*. Viewed April 25, 2022. uhc-india.org/reports/hleg_report_chapter_4.pdf

Moldaschl, M. (2010). *Why innovation theories make no sense* (Papers and Preprints of the Department of Innovation Research and Sustainable Resource Management (BWL IX), Chemnitz University of Technology. No. 9/2010).

Mukherjee, K. (2019). Selective universalism: A paradoxical strategy to achieve UHC in India. *Journal of Health Management, 21*(1), 154–159.

Mukherjee, K. (2020). A SMART framework for HTA capability development: Lessons from India. *Health Policy and Technology, 9*(1), 42–44.

Mukherjee, K. (2021a). Integrating technology, innovation and policy: COVID-19 and HTA. *Health Policy and Technology, 10*(1), 16–20.

Mukherjee, K. (2021b). Relevance of the newly defined health technology assessment: COVID-19 and beyond. *International Journal of Technology Assessment in Healthcare, 37*(e44), 1–2.

Mukherjee, K., & Walley, T. (2022). Assessing the value of healthcare innovations: A proposal for an integrated health technology assessment–responsible innovation in health approach in the 'new normal'. *International Journal of Technology Assessment in Health Care, 38*(1):e47. https://doi.org/10.1017/S0266462322000319

Nelson, R. R. (1993). *National innovation systems: A comparative analysis*. University of Illinois at Urbana-Champaign's Academy for Entrepreneurial Leadership. Historical Research Reference in Entrepreneurship.

Demers-Payette, O., Lehoux, P., & Daudelin, G. (2016). Responsible research and innovation: A productive model for the future of medical innovation. *Journal of Responsible Innovation, 3*(3), 188–208.

Omachonu, V., & Einspruch, N. (2010). Innovation in healthcare delivery systems: A conceptual framework. *Innov J, 15*(1), 1–20.

O'Rourke, B., Oortwijn, W., Schuller, T., & The International Joint Task Group. (2020). The new definition of health technology assessment: A milestone in international collaboration. *International Journal of Technology Assessment in Health Care, 36*(3), 187–190.

Patel, S., Akhtar, A., Malins, S., Wright, N., Rowley, E., Young, E., Sampson, S., & Morriss, R. (2020). The acceptability and usability of digital health interventions for adults with depression, anxiety, and somatoform disorders: Qualitative systematic review and meta-synthesis. *Journal of Medical Internet Research, 22*(7), e16228.

Perski, O., & Short, P. E. (2021). Acceptability of digital health interventions: Embracing the complexity. *TBM, 11*, 1473–1480.

Philippi, P., Baumeister, H., Apolin´ario-Hagen, J., Ebert, D. D., Hennemann, S., Kott, L., Lin, J., Messner, E. M., & Terhorst, Y. (2021). Acceptance towards digital health interventions—Model validation and further development of the unified theory of acceptance and use of technology. *Internet Interventions, 26*, 100459.

Plamping, D., Gordon, P., & Pratt, J. (2009). Innovation and public services: Insights from evolution centre for innovation. In *Health Management*. University of Leeds.
Prinja, S., Bahuguna, P., Gupta, A., Nimesh, R., Gupta, M., & Thakur, J. S. (2018). Cost effectiveness of mHealth intervention by community health workers for reducing maternal and newborn mortality in rural Uttar Pradesh, India. *Cost Effectiveness and Resource Allocation, 16*(25), 1–9.
Ranjan, K. R., & Read, S. (2016). Value co-creation: Concept and measurement. *Journal of the Academy of Marketing Science, 44*(3), 290–315.
Rogers, E. (1983). *Diffusion of innovations.* Free press.
Sarbadhikari, S. N., & Pradhan, K. B. (2020). The need for developing technology-enabled, safe, and ethical workforce for healthcare delivery. *Safety and Health at Work, 11*(4), 533–536.
Schumpeter, J. A. (1987). *Theorie der wirtschaftlichen Entwicklung* (7th ed.). (Orig 1912).
Selvaraj, S., Farooqui, H. H., & Karan, A. (2018). Quantifying the financial burden of household's out-of-pocket payments on medicines in India: A repeated cross-sectional analysis of National Sample Survey data 1994–2014. *British Medical Journal Open, 8*(5), e018020.
Silva, H. P., Lehoux, P., Miller, F. A., & Denis, J. L. (2018). Introducing responsible innovation in health: A policy-oriented framework. *Health Research Policy and Systems, 16*(1), e90.
Silver, L., Smith, A., & Johnson, C. (2019). *Mobile connectivity in emerging economies.* Pew Research Centre. Viewed April 30, 2022. https://www.pewresearch.org/internet/2019/03/07/mobile-connectivity-in-emerging-economies/
Smith, A. (1997). *Der Wohlstand der Nationen. Eine Untersuchung seiner Natur und seiner Ursachen.* dtv (Orig. 1776).
Smorodinskaya, N., Russell, M. G., Katukov, D., & Still, K. (2017). Innovation ecosystems vs. innovation systems in terms of collaboration and co-creation of value. *Proceedings of the 50th Hawaii International Conference on System Sciences* (pp. 5245–5254).
Stilgoe, J., Owen, R., & Macnaghten, P. (2013). Developing a framework for responsible innovation. *Research Policy, 42*(9), 1568–1580.
Tarde, G. (1999). *'L'opposition universelle. Essai d'une théorie des contraires.* Institut Synthélabo (Orig. 1897).
Tates, K., Antheunis, M. L., Kanters, S., Nieboer, T. E., & Gerritse, M. B. (2017). The effect of screen-to-screen versus face-to-face consultation on doctor-patient communication: An experimental study with simulated patients. *Journal of Medical Internet Research, 19*(12), e421.
Thune, T. (2013). *Medical innovation: Radical breakthroughs and evolutionary system.* Center for Technology, University of Oslo.
The Lancet. (2018). The Astana Declaration: The future of primary health care? *Lancet, 392*(10156), 1369.
United Nations (UN). (2015). *Sustainable development goals.* Viewed April 10, 2022, https://www.un.org/ga/search/view_doc.asp?symbol=A/RES/70/1&Lang=E
Wessner, C. W. (2005). Entrepreneurship and the innovation ecosystem policy lessons from the United States. in D. B. Audretsch, H. Grimm, & C. W. Wessner (Eds.), *Local heroes in the global village: Globalization and the new entrepreneurship policies.* Springer.
West, M. A. (1990). The social psychology of innovation in groups. In M. A. West & J. L. Farr (Eds.), *Innovation and creativity at work: Psychological and organizational strategies* (pp. 309–334). Wiley.
Weyraucht, T., & Herstatt, C. (2017). What is frugal innovation? Three defining criteria. *Journal of Frugal Innovation*, 2(1), 1–7.
World Bank. (2024). *World Bank data.* Viewed June 16, 2024, https://data.worldbank.org/indicator/SH.XPD.OOPC.CH.ZS?locations=IN
World Health Organization (WHO). (n.d.-a). *Constitution of the WHO.* Viewed April 25, 2022. https://www.who.int/about/governance/constitution
World Health Organization (WHO). (n.d.-b). *WHO Health Innovation Group.* Viewed April 12, 2022. https://www.who.int/life-course/about/who-health-innovation-group/en/

World Health Organization (WHO). (1978). *Primary health care: Report of the International Conference on Primary Health Care Alma Ata, USSR.*

World Health Organization (WHO). (2000). The world health report 2000. Health systems: Improving performance. Viewed 10 April 2022, https://www.who.int/whr/2000/en/

World Health Organization (WHO). (2010). *The world health report 2010. Health systems financing: The path to universal coverage*. World Health Organization.

World Health Organization (WHO). (2018). *Millennium development goals*. Viewed April 10, 2022, http://www.who.int/topics/millennium_development_goals/about/en/

World Health Organization (WHO). (2021). Governing health innovation for the common good. The WHO council on the economics for health for all, 2021, Council Brief No. 1.

SPRINGER NATURE

# GPSR Compliance

*The European Union's (EU) General Product Safety Regulation (GPSR) is a set of rules that requires consumer products to be safe and our obligations to ensure this.*

*If you have any concerns about our products, you can contact us on ProductSafety@springernature.com*

In case Publisher is established outside the EU, the EU authorized representative is:

Springer Nature Customer Service Center GmbH
Europaplatz 3
69115 Heidelberg, Germany

The manufacturer's authorised representative in the EU is Springer Nature Customer Service Centre GmbH, Europaplatz 3, 69115 Heidelberg, Germany. If you have any concerns regarding our products, please contact ProductSafety@springernature.com

Printed and bound by CPI Group (UK) Ltd, Croydon, CR0 4YY
01/10/2026
02225926-0009